Bob Woodward

___

THE COMMANDERS

SIMON & SCHUSTER

NEW YORK   LONDON   TORONTO   SYDNEY   TOKYO   SINGAPORE

Paperback edition
first published in Great Britain by
Simon & Schuster Ltd in 1992
A Paramount Communications Company

Simon & Schuster Ltd
West Garden Place
Kendal Street
London W2 2AQ

Simon & Schuster of Australia Pty Ltd
Sydney

A CIP catalogue record for this book is
available from the British Library
ISBN 0-671-71168-7

Printed and bound in Great Britain by
Butler & Tanner Ltd, Frome and London

AUTHOR'S NOTE

Two colleagues have helped me in every step of researching and writing this book:

WILLIAM F. POWERS, JR., a former aide to Senator John H. Chafee, Republican of Rhode Island, supplied much of the brainpower and editing skills. A remarkable man of grace and high purpose, Bill provided a truly independent evaluation of every step and idea. He made this book possible. No author ever had a better collaborator or friend.

MARC E. SOLOMON, a 1989 Yale graduate, joined us in this enterprise for the last 15 months. No one could have offered more intelligence, tact and resourcefulness. He chased down information, edited drafts, transcribed endless tapes and brought a sense of fairness and balance to each task. Without Marc's maturity, energy and spirit, we never would have finished.

To Ben Bradlee and Dick Snyder,
THE BEST FRIENDS A WRITER COULD HAVE

CONTENTS

PRESIDENT

(adviser)

SECRETARY OF DEFENSE

(adviser)

CHAIRMAN, JOINT CHIEFS OF STAFF

CINC of:

Atlantic Command
Central Command
European Command
Forces Command
Pacific Command
Southern Command
Space Command
Special Operations Command
Strategic Air Command
Transportation Command

COMMANDERS-IN-CHIEF (CINCs) OF THE 10 UNIFIED & SPECIFIED COMMANDS

(communications and oversight)

VICE CHAIRMAN

CHAIN OF COMMAND

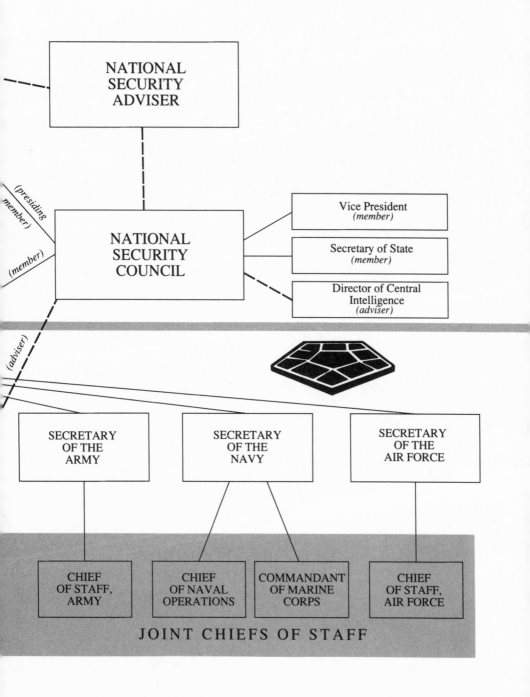

NATIONAL
SECURITY
ADVISER

(presiding member)

(member)

NATIONAL
SECURITY
COUNCIL

Vice President
(member)

Secretary of State
(member)

Director of Central
Intelligence
(adviser)

(adviser)

SECRETARY
OF THE
ARMY

SECRETARY
OF THE
NAVY

SECRETARY
OF THE
AIR FORCE

CHIEF
OF STAFF,
ARMY

CHIEF
OF NAVAL
OPERATIONS

COMMANDANT
OF MARINE
CORPS

CHIEF
OF STAFF,
AIR FORCE

JOINT CHIEFS OF STAFF

= *chain of command*

2

Dick Cheney and Colin Powell aboard a military airplane on a trip to the Gulf.

3

Panamanian leader General Manuel Noriega on October 4, 1989, the day after he suppressed a coup attempt against his regime.

4

Lieutenant General Carl W. Stiner, warfighting commander of the 1989 Panama invasion.

Admiral William J. Crowe, Jr., Chairman of the Joint Chiefs of Staff from October 1, 1985, to October 1, 1989.

BELOW—General Maxwell R. Thurman, Commander-in-Chief of the U.S. Southern Command, on December 22, 1989, two days into the Panamanian operation.

7

Secretary of State James A. Baker III voting at the United Nations November 29, 1990, for the resolution authorizing the use of force to eject Iraqi occupiers from Kuwait.

BELOW—Prince Bandar bin Sultan, Saudi Arabian ambassador to the United States, with Secretary of Defense Cheney in Cheney's Pentagon office.

8

Iraqi President
Saddam Hussein.

BELOW—President Bush meets in
the Oval Office with the Emir of
Kuwait, on September 28, 1990.

10

August 4, 1990, meeting at Camp David to review military options two days after the Iraqi invasion of Kuwait. From left, Paul Wolfowitz, Dick Cheney, President Bush, Vice President Quayle, John Sununu, William Webster, Marlin Fitzwater, Richard Haass, James Baker, General Colin Powell, Brent Scowcroft, General Norman Schwarzkopf.

President Bush meets with his inner circle at Camp David.

On Sunday, August 5, 1990, President
Bush, speaking on the White House
lawn about the Iraqi invasion, asserts,
"This will not stand."

General Powell addresses the troops in September
1990 on the battleship USS *Wisconsin* in the Persian
Gulf.

14

Dick Cheney at his desk in the Secretary's third-floor Pentagon office.

General Schwarzkopf and Saudi Arabian King Fahd reviewing coalition ground troops before the air war began.

16

17

18

19

BELOW–The War Room in the National Military Command Center of the Pentagon.

22

Pentagon spokesman
Pete Williams.

Lieutenant General Thomas W.
Kelly, Director of Operations for
the Joint Chiefs of Staff.

23   Oval Office meeting in December 1990. From left, Robert Gates, Cheney, President Bush, Powell, Sununu, Scowcroft.

The Big Eight meet in the Oval Office on January 15, 1991, to review the National Security Directive ordering the offensive operation to liberate Kuwait. From left, Gates, Sununu, Cheney, Quayle, President
24   Bush, Baker, Scowcroft, Powell.

The Joint Chiefs of Staff, May 4, 1990. Left to right: General Alfred M. Gray, Marine Corps Commandant; General Carl E. Vuono, Army chief of staff; Admiral Carlisle A. H. Trost, Chief of Naval Operations; General Larry D. Welch, Air Force chief of staff; General Colin L. Powell, Chairman of the Joint Chiefs of Staff; Admiral David E. Jeremiah, Vice Chairman of the Joint Chiefs of Staff.

25

Powell, Cheney, and Schwarzkopf meeting in Saudi Arabia.

26

27

28

A Note to the Reader

This is an account of U.S. military decision making during the 800 days from November 8, 1988, when George Bush was elected President, through January 16, 1991, the beginning of the Persian Gulf War.

I initially planned to focus on the military and civilian leadership of the Pentagon, headquarters for one of the world's largest enterprises, the modern American defense establishment. I had worked in the Pentagon for a year in 1969–70 as a 26-year-old Navy lieutenant. Few can serve in that unique, five-sided structure with its 23,000 employees, its maze of floors, corridors, rings and offices—or even visit as a tourist—and not wonder how it all fits together.

Eighteen years later, I was still curious.

My initial research emphasized the Pentagon under Bush, but I also did extensive interviewing with former secretaries of Defense and other former senior officials going back as far as the Kennedy administration. The fast-approaching end of the Cold War suggested it could be a quiet time for the military, an opportunity for me to try to understand the Defense Department's subtle intricacies.

The December 1989 Panama invasion, and more importantly the 1990 Gulf crisis, changed all that. The military was not going to play a smaller role in the new world, as some had expected. It was moving to center stage. These two operations allowed me to study post-Vietnam, post–Cold War military decision making in action. After the brief Panama operation, I spent months piecing together the meetings and decision points leading up to it. From the time of the Iraqi invasion of Kuwait in August 1990, I concentrated on the evolution of the Persian Gulf crisis and the decision to go to war against Saddam Hussein.

Nearly all of the information comes from interviews with people directly involved in the decisions. More than 400 people were interviewed over the course of 27 months. The key sources were administration and Pentagon officials, both civilian and military. President Bush was not interviewed. Many key participants were interviewed repeatedly, some on a regular basis as events unfolded. Several were interviewed two to three dozen times. I interviewed one important source 40 times, sometimes in a rushed four-minute phone call during a crisis, at other times in freewheeling one-hour conversations. Several important sources allowed me to tape our conversations, so their stories and recollections could be retold more fully than if I had been relying on my notes alone. A number of sources provided access to documents, memos, contemporaneous handwritten notes, schedules and chronologies.

Direct quotations from meetings or conversations come from at least one participant who specifically recalled or took notes on what was said. Quotation marks are not used when the sources were unsure about the exact wording.

Thoughts, beliefs and conclusions attributed to a participant come from that individual or from a source who gained knowledge of them directly from that person. Participants' written notes were also used on occasion to describe personal attitudes about events.

I've tried wherever possible to preserve the language the participants themselves used to describe meetings, attitudes and emotions.

Often I spoke to participants within hours or days of events in which they played a role. In some cases, I talked to sources right after an event and then several weeks or months later, only to find that in retrospect they had partially, and at times conveniently, altered their original version. I have generally found that accounts given soon after an event are the most reliable.

It is impossible to reconstruct conversations and meetings perfectly. I have made every effort to present statements in the order in which participants said they were made, and to re-create as closely as possible the way the discussion flowed. Many of the sources for this book have decades of experience participating in important policy discussions and are trained to recall the details. Nonetheless, the sources' accounts were carefully checked and rechecked against each other.

The sources are not identified in the text. Nearly all the interviews were conducted under journalistic ground rules of "deep background," meaning the sources provided the information with the understanding that they would not be identified by name or title.

This book falls somewhere between newspaper journalism and history. The daily newspaper tells *what* happened, but rarely gives the full *why* and *how* that are traditionally the specialty of historians. While the book seeks to provide a fuller explanation than daily journalism can, it does not have history's distance from events. It aspires to be a closely focused snapshot of contemporary events.

The more I learned about the military through this project, the more it was apparent to me that the Pentagon is not always the center of military decision making. The building's top civilian and military officials, most notably the Secretary of Defense and the Chairman of the Joint Chiefs of Staff, can have a great, at times even dominant, role in the process when the attention of the White House is turned elsewhere. This was largely the case in the months prior to the Panama operation, though the President, as commander-in-chief, ultimately made the decision to invade.

The Persian Gulf crisis was different. President Bush and his White House staff devoted great attention to it from the outset, managing the crisis from Pennsylvania Avenue. When the President and his advisers are engaged, they run the show.

So this is not a book about the Pentagon, although the building and the military play central roles. This book is not about most of the things the military does. It is not about weapons procurement, defense budget fights, recruiting, training or military field exercises. With a few brief exceptions, it does not touch on the way the military has actually fought the wars of the last few years. It will not take you into the helicopters descending on Panama City, or to the desert tank battles in Iraq and Kuwait.

It is above all a book about how the United States decides to fight its wars before shots are fired. The main setting is Washington, and the main action is the tug-and-pull among the players in the military decision-making process, both inside and outside the Pentagon.

Decision making at the highest levels of national government is a complex human interaction. The inside story of government involves conversations, arguments, meetings, phone calls, personal attitudes, backgrounds and relationships. This human story is the core.

There is always some historical mystery about events such as the Panama operation or the Gulf War. Government officials are by nature protective of information, and are often less than fully candid. As I write these words, the Persian Gulf War is winding to a conclusion. I am aware there is much I don't know. Over the first two years of his administration, President Bush and his close advisers made a series of important, at times momentous, choices about the military. The choices and the process deserve scrupulous examination, even at this early date.

The decision to go to war is one that defines a nation, both to the world and, perhaps more importantly, to itself. There is no more serious business for a national government, no more accurate measure of national leadership.

Bob Woodward, March 14, 1991

PROLOGUE

THE RETIRED CHAIRMAN OF THE JOINT CHIEFS OF STAFF, Admiral William J. Crowe, Jr., hurried through security at the Pentagon's River Entrance in the early afternoon of Tuesday, November 27, 1990. He was late for a private 1 p.m. lunch with his successor, Army General Colin L. Powell. As soon as he entered the building, Crowe, who was 65, felt the Pentagon's familiar, oppressive atmosphere—the colonels, bursting with self-importance, rushing around the E-Ring, the outermost corridor. It was a building dedicated to appearing busy, he thought.

Wheeling to the right, he slipped into the first doorway, Room 2E878, the office of the Chairman. He passed through a reception area and entered the room where he'd worked for four years, until Powell had taken over from him 14 months earlier.

At 53, Powell was the youngest Chairman in history and the first black to hold the post. He usually conveyed a sense of energy and stamina, but today he looked tired.

The general had redecorated. New windows offered a magnificent view across the Potomac River to the national monuments. There was a rich, dark blue carpet, and a comfortable couch and matching chair upholstered in a delicately patterned maroon fabric.

As they sat down at a small antique table set for lunch, Powell joked that he wished he'd never accepted the job. Why didn't you warn me? he asked.

Crowe knew he didn't mean it for a minute. It was the classic, transparent lament of a man who loves being at the top.

A steward from the Chairman's mess in a bright yellow jacket took their orders. Both chose light lunches.

In the previous four months, Powell had overseen the largest American military deployment since Vietnam. Some 230,000 U.S. military men and women had already been sent to the Persian Gulf as part of Operation Desert Shield, following Iraq's invasion and takeover of Kuwait. Three weeks earlier, President Bush had announced his decision to nearly double the troop strength, to give himself the option of using offensive force to expel Iraq from Kuwait. The decision had set off a fierce debate, and the national consensus that had been supporting Bush now seemed to be unraveling.

"I hear you're going to testify," Powell had said when he had called Crowe the previous week to invite him to lunch. Crowe had agreed to give public testimony on the Gulf crisis before the Senate Armed Services Committee, chaired by Sam Nunn, the Georgia Democrat.

Although he had supported Bush's initial deployment of forces to defend Saudi Arabia from Iraq, Nunn had publicly criticized the decision to create an offensive military capability. He was demanding to know how Bush had determined that it was in the vital interest of the United States to liberate Kuwait. What was the hurry? Why not give the unprecedented United Nations economic sanctions that had shut down trade between Iraq and most of the world time to work?

Crowe now recounted how he had been traveling around the country giving speeches, and had heard serious doubts raised about whether the liberation of Kuwait was worth a war. There was great concern in the country about the prospect, duration, objectives and necessity of war.

Yeah, I have detected the same thing, Powell confided.

Crowe's guard went up. Over the years, he'd watched Powell operate up close, especially in 1988 when Powell was Reagan's national security adviser. Powell had a tendency to read people and then tell them in a very general and circumspect way what he thought they wanted to hear, Crowe thought.

Despite the President's statements that he did not want war, Crowe felt that Bush was too anxious to throw hundreds of thousands of troops into combat. One was Crowe's son Blake, a Marine captain commanding a company of 200 in the Saudi Arabian desert.

"Not everyone is going to like what I'm going to say," Crowe said. He didn't want to give a full dress rehearsal of his testimony, so he resisted telling Powell the specifics.

Powell sensed the reserve.

Crowe said he wondered about the apparent rush to go to war. "Everyone is so *impatient.*" Some seemed to think the U.S. military had trained its soldiers for combat and hostile fire, but not to be patient and wait.

Patience had paid off handsomely in the Cold War. Waiting out the Soviet Union for 40 years would be marked as one of the great victories of all time. Why can't we think in the long term? he asked. A war in the Middle East—killing thousands of Arabs for whatever noble purpose—would set back the United States in the region for a long time. And that was to say nothing of the Americans who might die. War is messy and uncertain, he said.

Powell neither agreed nor disagreed. He listened, nodded, and seemed to encourage Crowe to go on.

As Crowe spoke, he sensed that Powell was trying to dope him out, to learn something that would give Powell an edge.

Crowe wanted to ask some of his own questions. Where is Cheney on this? he asked. Secretary of Defense Dick Cheney was Powell's immediate boss.

"Beats me," Powell replied.

What does that mean? Crowe asked, lowering his voice.

"He holds his cards pretty close, as you know," Powell replied.

Crowe knew that, indeed. His last six months as Chairman had coincided with Cheney's first six as Secretary. He'd seen how unrevealing Cheney usually was.

Cheney comes back from the White House and tells nothing, Powell said. As a member of the cabinet, Cheney had meetings with Bush apart from the formal National Security Council meetings that Powell attended.

Imagine, Crowe reflected to himself, the Chairman of the Joint Chiefs of Staff not knowing where the Secretary of Defense stands on the most important military–foreign-policy decision of the day, perhaps the last several decades.

Where are you on the Gulf deployment? Crowe inquired.

"I've been for a containment strategy," Powell replied, "but it hasn't been selling around here or over there." He pointed out the window, north across the river.

Crowe knew that gesture well. The orders and the political decisions that guided the life of the Chairman came from there. "Across the river" meant the White House.

To a military man like Crowe, "containment" had a definite meaning—standing firm to resist further advances by an opponent. In this case, it would mean keeping the economic sanctions and the diplomatic pressure on Iraqi President Saddam Hussein, without attacking him, with the hope of eventually forcing him to withdraw from Kuwait. It was something very different from President Bush's decision to double the forces to provide an offensive option.

Powell said he had been trying to keep the administration tamped down, attempting to dampen any enthusiasm for war.

Crowe grasped the problem. He didn't have the nerve to ask whether Powell had made these arguments explicitly to the President. The Bush administration was presenting itself publicly as one happy team marching in unison. If Powell was being honest, he disagreed with Bush to some degree, and might have a genuine moral dilemma on his hands. The law designated the Chairman as the "principal military adviser" to the President, Secretary of Defense and National Security Council. It directed that when he advised them, the Chairman, "as he considers appropriate," give "the range of military advice and opinion with respect to that matter."

As Crowe interpreted the law, the Chairman had an obligation, at least on the major questions, to honestly and fully give the President his views. Had Powell told Bush what he thought about containment? Would Bush tolerate a chairman who had a fundamental disagreement with administration policy? From his nine months in the Bush administration, Crowe knew its obsession with consensus, and with loyalty to the President and his positions. What was Powell's concept of his duty and job as Chairman?

Crowe believed that the Chairman had to give more than just military advice. For a presidential adviser—even the principal military adviser—to talk only about the military at White House meetings was a sterile exercise. Those who disagreed with him would tell the President: that's just military advice, but when you factor in the political, diplomatic and economic recommendations, here's what you ought to do.

No, Powell had to give his overall policy advice. If it was rejected, he could choose to resign, or stay on and accept the decision. There was no way around giving advice direct and undiluted.

In White House meetings during the Reagan and Bush administrations, Crowe had observed a common gimmick that some cabinet officers used as a halfway measure. They would say that a certain option ought to be discussed and examined, in the interest of a full debate. It was a way of putting an idea on the table without getting in trouble. In Crowe's view, that was a cop-out. A presidential adviser had to be willing to place his personal prestige on the line and say, here's my overall conclusion. Advice without a bottom line meant little. It was a lot to ask, but that's what they were paid for, Crowe believed.

He had no notion what Powell had done, and he felt it was neither his place nor the moment to ask him. But God, he wanted to believe that Powell had presented his thoughts fully. He had never felt more empathy for Powell, or put so much hope in him.

"I've been thinking," Crowe said, "it takes two things to be a great president and I ought to tell you because you may be President some day."

"No, no," Powell said insistently, dismissing the reference to his political prospects—a subject of endless forecasting in the media.

"Yes, you may and I want to tell you," Crowe said. "First, to be a great president you have to have a war. All the great presidents have had their wars."

Laughing, Powell acknowledged the truth of the statement.

"Two, you have to find a war where you are attacked."

Powell nodded in agreement.

Crowe could see Powell understood him.

When they finished their meal, Crowe thanked Powell for lunch and left. He realized that Powell had not even attempted to persuade him that the current policy of developing an offensive military option was correct. He hadn't defended the administration position.

Afterwards, Crowe brooded about Powell's possible dilemma. He recalled that he himself had been Chairman for a year before he had unraveled the secret of the job. When he was convinced he was right, the Chairman had to stand up to the President. Crowe's chance had come after the 1986 Reagan–Gorbachev summit in Reykjavik, Iceland, when Reagan had proposed the elimination of all ballistic missiles. Crowe had been under intense pressure to endorse the plan, but he had gone to a National Security Council meeting and said that he could not go along because the Reagan proposal "would pose high risks to the security of the nation." Afterwards, the Reagan inner circle had listened to him more. He'd won respect.

The simple truth was that the Chairman could not be a player unless he disagreed at times and fought the White House. It was risky, but sometimes the best choices were the most dangerous. In 1987 he had made an alliance with his Soviet counterpart, Marshal Sergei Akhromeyev, the chief of the Soviet General Staff. Although they were the leaders of the world's two great military adversaries, Crowe and Akhromeyev had hit it off personally. Both believed it was too easy for politicians to let a misunderstanding throw the superpowers over the brink to nuclear war. That would be suicide, they agreed, and they had to do everything they could to avoid it. They had set up a secret, private communications channel, with the understanding that each was to contact the other if he saw any hostile, dangerous or confusing action by the other side that might lead to war.

Crowe knew it was a dicey move for the Chairman of the Joint Chiefs to enter into such an agreement without clearing it through the administration. But it had been worth the risk. Two years later the two militaries had signed an agreement that effectively legitimized military communications to avoid war.

· · ·

After the lunch, Powell concluded that the Bush administration was probably in for a mild blast from Crowe's testimony the next day. He generally found Crowe's musings thoughtful, but often somewhat abstract. Crowe had taken an intellectual's approach to the chairmanship. He had bequeathed Powell a Joint Staff that operated as a think tank—hesitant, inclined to debate and to churning out papers endlessly. Powell had remade it in his own image, transforming it into an action staff that got things done.

As far as the Gulf operation was concerned, Powell had given up pushing the containment strategy. He had his orders. He wasn't giving the slightest thought to containment now. The President had decided, unequivocally, to build the offensive option. The Chairman had thrown himself into preparing as effective an offensive force as possible.

Powell recalled vividly the efforts he had made to present all the options in the Persian Gulf—including containment of Iraq—to the President, to make sure the full range of possibilities had been considered. It had been hard.

The previous month, he had written down some notes for himself that laid out the arguments for containment. Several times he had used the term "strangulation," a more active word than "containment." It referred to the tight U.N.-mandated blockade of Iraq and all the other allied measures that were putting the squeeze on Saddam. He'd taken these notes and the argument to Cheney— twice. Then to the national security adviser, Brent Scowcroft, and to Secretary of State James A. Baker III.

One Friday afternoon in early October, Cheney finally had said to Powell, "Why don't you come over with me and we'll see what the man thinks about your idea." Cheney had a private Oval Office meeting scheduled that day with the President. This was time reserved for the key cabinet members—"the big guys," as Powell called them. Normally he was not included.

Cheney and Powell had gone to the Oval Office to see Bush and Scowcroft. The sun was streaming in. For some reason the atmosphere wasn't right. There were interruptions; it was the President's office, the wrong place for this kind of discussion, Powell felt. He preferred the formality of the Situation Room, where Bush could stay focused. The mood in the Oval Office was too relaxed, too convivial—the boys sitting around shooting the shit before the weekend.

It was a general problem with these kinds of meetings, Powell felt. Often they had no beginning, middle or end. They would kick the ball around. Feet would be up on the table, cowboy boots gleaming. Powell was being given his chance, but he felt his presentation was not going as well as it had in his individual talks with Cheney, Baker and Scowcroft. Still, he plunged ahead.

To achieve the policy of forcing Saddam out of Kuwait, Powell told the President, there are two courses of action. One, build up the forces for an offensive option. Two, containment, which would take longer. But either way, the policy success could be achieved.

"There is a case here for the containment or strangulation policy," he told the President. "If you do not want to make more military investment, here is the alternative." The force level associated with containment, the Chairman said, was what they would reach by December 1, about 230,000 troops. Saddam would be fully boxed in. Containment would grind him down.

"This is an option that has merit," he said. "It will work some day. It may take a year, it may take two years, but it will work some day." He tried to speak as an advocate, adopt the tone of an advocate, support it with his body language. He sat on the edge of his seat, his hands were in the air emphasizing his points, he spoke with conviction. But he did not go so far as to say to the President that containment was his personal recommendation.

In military terms, Powell said he could live with either containment or an offensive option.

The others, Cheney and Scowcroft, had a few questions. No one, including the President, embraced containment. If only one of them had, Powell was prepared to say that he favored it. But no one tried to pin him down. No one asked him for his overall opinion. Not faced with the question, Powell was not sure what his answer would have been if he had to give it without support from one of the others.

"Where do you want to go, Mr. President?" Powell finally asked. "As each week goes by, I am doing more. There are more and more troops going in."

"I don't think there's time politically for that strategy," Bush said, referring to containment.

Powell took this to mean that the President hadn't made up his mind completely. He felt that the President had not yet fully shot down containment.

Afterwards, Powell said his conscience was clear. He had presented the military implications of each choice. There was only so much he could do.

PART ONE

1

WEDNESDAY, NOVEMBER 9, 1988. Powell, then a three-star general and the national security adviser to President Reagan, stepped briskly along one of the narrow, carpeted hallways in the West Wing of the White House. He was heading toward his spacious corner office, perhaps the second-most prestigious in the White House, and a nerve center formerly inhabited by the likes of Henry Kissinger.

It was about 4 p.m. Vice President George Bush was in the hall outside his own small West Wing office. The day before, Bush had been elected President. A Rose Garden ceremony welcoming him back to the White House as President-elect had just ended and he was in the corridors saying hello and shaking hands, all jittery enthusiasm. He spotted Powell.

"Come on in here," Bush said. "I want to talk. Let's talk."

Powell said Bush must be busy.

"Tell me what's going on," Bush insisted, drawing Powell into the vice presidential office. By both title and temperament, Powell was information central on world events, often the first within the upper ranks of the White House to know the latest, whether it was a developing crisis or the freshest high-grade foreign affairs gossip.

Congratulating Bush, Powell flashed a broad, confident smile.

The Bush administration-to-be was already taking shape. That morning in Houston, Bush had announced his first cabinet appointment, naming his campaign manager and old Texas friend Jim Baker Secretary of State. Baker was seen as the Bush insider to watch.

Bush asked about Powell. What were his plans? Where might he fit?

"Mr. Vice President," Powell said, "you have got a lot more on your hands and on your mind than me."

Bush had three specific suggestions. Would Powell like to stay on as national security adviser for, say, six months, while he figured out what he wanted to do next? Or would he like a different, permanent position in the Bush administration? Bush suggested Director of the Central Intelligence Agency, an assignment he himself had had at about Powell's age. Or how about becoming Baker's number two at the State Department, a key post in foreign affairs? Either of those jobs could be his. Exciting and important times are coming, Bush said.

Powell noted that the Army was his chosen career and that he had the opportunity to stay in. Also, he was considering some offers to leave government to make some money. He was flattered by Bush's offers and would consider them along with everything else. As Bush would understand, he was at an important crossroads. His service as national security adviser gave him many options.

Bush, who had changed jobs more than most, indicated he understood completely.

There was a lot to consider, Powell said, and he would get back to him. Congratulations again.

· · ·

One thing was clear to Powell. The offer to stay on in his current post for a few months was merely a courtesy. It meant: I don't want you to be my permanent national security adviser.

Realizing he had to make a serious analysis of his prospects, Powell later took out a piece of paper and listed the reasons to stay in government and the reasons to get out.

The only argument favoring departure from public service was money. Money didn't interest him particularly, and the résumés he had been quietly circulating in the business world had drawn only a mild response in any case.

The offers to head the CIA and to be number two at State had to be weighed. It would be a demotion to go from the security adviser's post, coordinating all foreign and defense policy issues, to the number-two slot at State, responsible for managing the bureaucracy. And in most respects, the security adviser was more powerful than the CIA director.

Powell had another problem. He felt uneasy about the man who was about to become President.

Unlike Powell himself, who had been the consummate administration insider, Bush was a stepchild in the Reagan White House. Though more in the loop than most vice presidents, he was nevertheless not a player. Bush and Powell had built no bond of loyalty, and as Powell knew, personal alliances were everything with Bush.

Powell was also troubled by the way the Bush presidential campaign had been run. The race-baiting Willie Horton television commercial especially bothered him. Horton, a black first-degree murderer, had been given a weekend pass from a Massachusetts prison when Bush's Democratic opponent, Michael Dukakis, was governor. While on the furlough, Horton stabbed a white man and raped a white woman in Maryland. Did the people around Bush believe that stuff belonged in the campaign?

Powell sought out his good friend Richard L. Armitage, the outgoing assistant secretary of defense for international security affairs. Armitage, a burly, intense 1967 Naval Academy graduate, was known for the aggressive way he did his job as the head of the Pentagon's own little state department.

From 1983 to 1986, Armitage and Powell, who was then military assistant to Secretary of Defense Caspar Weinberger, had managed much of the department's business.

Armitage knew that Powell's charm and offhandedness hid his competitiveness and ambition. He agreed that the half-offer to stay on in the national security post was about politeness. Don't go to the State Department as number two, Armitage advised. You should be the Secretary. The CIA is not your image, he also told Powell. It is demoralized and rundown.

Let things shake out, Armitage recommended.

Powell had taken care to ensure that he could return to the Army. Before the election, he'd gone to see his friend General Carl Vuono, the Army chief of staff. Vuono, who controlled Army promotions and assignments, was a 1957 West Point graduate who had entered the Army just a year before Powell. A meaty, happy-go-lucky officer with dark Mediterranean eyes, Vuono had known Powell since they'd worked together as junior officers in the Pentagon 17 years earlier. Powell considered Vuono one of his mentors.

Although he wanted Powell back in the Army, Vuono urged him to do what would make him and his wife, Alma, happy. If Powell wanted to come back, there would be a place for him. Vuono intentionally had kept a slot open: promotion to a fourth star to head the Forces Command. This was the nation's strategic reserve of some 1 million land forces—most in the National Guard and Reserves.

While it was not a glamorous assignment, it would make Powell one of the ten commanders-in-chief—CINCs, pronounced "sinks"—of U.S. military forces and warfighting units worldwide. It was an important ticket to punch, and it would put him in line to succeed Vuono as Army chief.

"Carl," Powell said, "if I decide to come, I'll do what you want."

Powell considered himself a soldier first. Beginning in 1958, he had spent his first 14 years as a garden-variety infantry officer, without a West Point ring or any other reason to think he was on a fast track. As a young officer, he wasn't particularly dedicated to the Army. His plan was to stick it out for 20 years so he could retire with a 50 percent pension.

His introduction to the upper reaches of government came in 1972. That year, Lieutenant Colonel Powell was chosen for the prestigious White House Fellows program, which gives young businessmen, lawyers, military officers and other professionals a taste of the federal executive branch for one year. In 1977 he went to the Pentagon as military assistant to the Deputy Secretary of Defense.

His four years in that job, and then the three with Weinberger, were a chance to see the top military leadership up close. He had a notion that a new, more worldly brand of senior officer could be more useful to the Secretary and the President. The Joint Chiefs of Staff, the top uniformed echelon, were too insulated from the outside world, not sufficiently able or inclined to assess the political aspects of defense decisions. They also tended to be inept at public relations. Yet politics and public relations were the arenas in which the Secretary lived, where he flourished or failed.

Powell decided he had better stay in the Army. It was home, and the prospect of four stars held a certain mystique.

"I couldn't be happier," Vuono said when he heard the news. "We'll send you to Forces Command."

Powell knew he was in for a different kind of life down in Atlanta, where Forces Command had its headquarters. As security adviser, he'd felt a constant sense of risk. Risk in every word, every recommendation, every choice, every action. President Reagan had delegated an enormous part of his responsibility to his staff. Powell found that if he told Reagan he didn't have to worry about something, the President would soon be happily gazing out the window into the Rose Garden. It was in Powell's hands. Although Powell was on two medications for high blood pressure, he had enjoyed that risky, stressful existence.

He shared his decision with Reagan's chief of staff, Kenneth Duberstein, a street-smart pol from Brooklyn. Powell said he was going to be a soldier again. It was his life. "Some day I'd like to be Chairman of the Joint Chiefs of Staff," he confided. There was also a chance he could become Army chief, he said, but his political and policy experience in Weinberger's office and the White House probably made him more qualified to be Chairman.

Duberstein made sure the fourth-star promotion, necessary before Powell could take over Forces Command, went through without delay.

Powell went to see Bush, thanked him for the offers, and said he wanted to move on. "Out with the old and in with the new," Powell said. He knew the rules. The new President picked his own team.

The President-elect accepted his decision without argument.

Powell also told Reagan that he planned to become commander-in-chief of Forces Command.

"That is a promotion, isn't it?" Reagan asked.

"Yes, sir."

"Well, okay."

. . .

Retired Air Force Lieutenant General Brent Scowcroft received a call on November 23, 1988, the day before Thanksgiving, from his close friend R. James Woolsey, Jr., a lawyer and former Undersecretary of the Navy. Woolsey had seen a recent editorial in *The New York Times* suggesting that Bush select Scowcroft for Secretary of Defense.

"It isn't going to happen," Scowcroft said.

Within an hour, Woolsey heard on the radio that Bush had just made the surprise announcement that Scowcroft would be his national security adviser, replacing Powell.

Woolsey laughed to himself. Scowcroft was certainly discreet, perhaps to a fault. Although they had worked together over the years on top-secret government studies, in addition to numerous articles and proposals on arms control and defense policy, Scowcroft wasn't even going to hint to Woolsey a secret the President-elect wanted kept.

A model of the trustworthy, self-effacing staffer, Brent Scowcroft had been a low-profile presence in top national security circles for two decades. He'd started as Henry Kissinger's deputy national security adviser, moved up to the security adviser's post under President Ford (when Bush was CIA director) and then worked on various presidential commissions and as a highly paid international consultant at Kissinger Associates. He tended to stay in the background, as a mirror and implementor of the President's views.

A head shorter than Bush, balding and slight, the 63-year-old Scowcroft was a Mormon who avoided the Washington social scene, and had a priestlike dedication to his work. It was his one interest. Scowcroft's idea of recreation was attending a seminar on arms control, a subject he loved in all its obscure detail. He had once spent an hour and a half refereeing a debate over a single phrase proposed for a blue-ribbon commission report on strategic missiles. It was at such times, arguing policy issues he cared about —his voice rising almost to a screech and his arms waving—that he showed there was a passion beneath the pale exterior.

Scowcroft's confidants knew that in recent years there was one subject that had made him emotional. Although he'd had many close ties to the Reagan administration, in private he'd been a scathing critic of its foreign and military policy. He thought that under Reagan the United States had first taken a naive and foolish hard-line approach to the Soviet Union, and then had turned around and rushed blindly into Mikhail Gorbachev's arms.

He'd seen no coherent administration policy on nuclear deterrence, and had called Reagan's 1986 Reykjavik proposal to eliminate all ballistic missiles "insane." To Scowcroft, the administration's vision of a shield in space to protect the United States against nuclear missile attack, the Strategic Defense Initiative, was a wild fantasy. He believed the Reagan national security team had failed to compensate for their boss's inadequacy and romanticism in the realm of foreign affairs.

Since Scowcroft's differences with the Reagan line were well known, his return to the White House as national security adviser was a clear signal that Bush intended to cut a new path in defense and foreign policy.

2

ON THE MORNING OF DECEMBER 7, 1988, at the United Nations in New York City, Mikhail Gorbachev announced that the Soviet Union would make unilateral military cuts of 500,000 troops and 10,000 tanks. The announcement was a departure, in both tone and substance, from the traditional Soviet way of doing business. Previously, Soviet leaders would not have considered giving up any of their military might without a reciprocal cut by the United States. But now, faced with serious internal economic pressure at home as he sought to reform the Soviet Union, Gorbachev was willing to make this grand gesture to reinforce his image as a statesman and peacemaker.

Gorbachev's staff people had pushed hard for a meeting with President Reagan after the speech, and Colin Powell, finishing out his last few months as Reagan's national security adviser, personally handled the request. Powell told the Soviets the United States had thought it was finished meeting with Gorbachev for the year. There were to be no tricks or surprises, Powell warned. The Soviets promised they were not playing games nor looking for trouble. After coordinating with the White House East Wing (meaning Nancy Reagan), and with Bush's people, Powell told the Soviets that the meeting had been approved. But he reminded them that it was a meeting with President Reagan and *Vice President* Bush. The Vice President would stay in the background. The two sides decided on an informal lunch at Governor's Island in New York Harbor.

As Reagan was greeting Gorbachev, Bush walked out of the 27-room Georgian mansion where the leaders were going to eat and strolled uneasily over to them. When Gorbachev spotted the President-elect, he brightened visibly and took Bush's right hand in both of his.

Bush's advisers had warned him to act skeptical, tough, even remote with the Soviet leader. Gorbachev, they said, might try to pick his pocket. High-level negotiations with the Soviets required preparation, and caution.

Before the lunch meeting began, Reagan and Gorbachev went into a small room to pose for press photos. Powell was standing with some of his Soviet counterparts when Alexander "Sasha" Bessmertnykh, the Soviet first deputy foreign minister and an expert on the United States, came up to him.

"Colin, how are you?" he asked. "Congratulations on your promotion."

Powell's elevation to four stars had come through that day.

"Sasha, that's very kind of you. I'm surprised you learned about it so quickly. Yuri [Yuri Dubinin, the Soviet ambassador to the U.S.] must be reporting more quickly than he usually does, or maybe you're using the new fax machine you guys put in."

"No," Bessmertnykh said, laughing, "I saw it on CNN."

"Come on," Powell replied, "you only had CNN during the [Moscow] summit in May. . . . You had it in all the hotels."

"No, we have it there permanently. I have it in my office and I watch it all day long."

Powell said he did too, joking that the two countries could save a lot on communications and intelligence just by relying on CNN.

Every Friday, Bessmertnykh continued, a week's worth of *The Washington Post* and *The New York Times* was delivered to his office. "I take them all home and I read them all weekend, because reports that we get from our intelligence services simply don't give me enough insight into America and into what Americans are about and what moves your country. So I have to use things like CNN and reading your newspapers."

As Powell and Bessmertnykh chatted, Anatoly Dobrynin, the

recently replaced, longtime Soviet ambassador to the United States, walked up and listened closely. He joked that he wanted to know how to get CNN in Moscow.

. . .

At the lunch meeting, the United States was represented by six men—Reagan, Bush, Secretary of State George Shultz, Powell, Ken Duberstein and Secretary of Defense Frank Carlucci. From his side of the table, where six Soviets sat, Gorbachev opened with a ten-minute monologue about the problems he was having with his radical programs of economic restructuring and political open-ness—the famous *perestroika* and *glasnost*. The Soviet bureau-cracy was fighting him at every turn, he said.

Reagan responded that bureaucracies were the same throughout the world. He was sympathetic to Gorbachev's complaint.

Gorbachev remarked that there were those in the United States who were fearful of his reform movement.

Reagan replied that a recent White House poll had showed that 85 percent in the United States supported the new, positive U.S.-Soviet relationship.

"I'm pleased to hear that," said Gorbachev. The relationship could not sustain itself in an atmosphere of suspicion. "The name of the game is continuity," he said, reaching out for some assur-ance from Bush. The Vice President appeared unmoved.

Gorbachev brought up horses, a subject that always engaged Reagan, and they had a lively conversation.

Bush finally chimed in. "What assurance can you give me that I can pass to American businessmen who want to invest in the Soviet Union that *perestroika* and *glasnost* will succeed?"

Gorbachev's eyes grew steely as he listened to the translation. "Not even Jesus Christ knows the answer to that question!" he replied.

Duberstein was astonished at the brush-off. Gorbachev had seemed to dismiss not only the President-elect's question but Bush himself.

Powell thought Bush's question was curious, and in a way naive. It was as if Bush was asking for Gorbachev's assurance that the Soviet Union was safe for American capitalism, or the busi-nesses of large Republican campaign contributors.

Bush was mostly silent for the rest of the long lunch, assuming a remote, you're-not-going-to-pick-my-pocket stance. Everyone was aware that the Gorbachev–Bush relationship was the most important one in the room, and it seemed to be going nowhere.

Finally, Gorbachev turned to Bush. "Let me take this opportunity to tell you something," the Soviet leader said. "Your staff may have told you that what I'm doing is all a trick. It's not. I'm playing real politics. I have a revolution going that I announced in 1986. Now, in 1988, the Soviet people don't like it. Don't misread me, Mr. Vice President, I have to play real politics."

Powell took note. He often told his staff not to hyperventilate at every Soviet statement or speech coming out of Moscow. But this one had the ring of truth. Gorbachev and the Soviet system had no choice—the reality of their revolution was that there were no alternatives. The statement was so unguarded. Powell had heard similar expressions from the Soviet leader before, but never one given with such conviction, such finality. It struck him as sincere and enormously accurate. After so many years, the Cold War was foundering on real politics.

After two and a half hours, Reagan lifted a glass of Chardonnay and said to Gorbachev, "I'd like to raise a toast to what we have accomplished, what we together have accomplished and what you and the Vice President after January twentieth will accomplish together."

Gorbachev stood, raised his glass, lowered it, turned to Bush and said, "This is our first agreement."

3

IN A PRESS CONFERENCE ON THE MORNING OF DECEMBER 16, Bush announced his selection of John Tower, the former Texas senator, as his nominee to be Secretary of Defense.

Craig Fuller, Bush's vice presidential chief of staff, watched in dismay. Along with Treasury Secretary Nicholas Brady, a long-time Bush friend, and Bush pollster Robert Teeter, he had run an unsuccessful behind-the-scenes campaign to derail the Tower nomination. Fuller and Teeter were worried about Tower's reputation as a heavy drinker and womanizer. Brady disliked Tower personally.

Despite regular secret strategy breakfasts at the Treasury Department Building, and meetings they had set up for Bush with other possible candidates, the three had failed to come up with a consensus alternative.

During one discussion with Fuller about possible candidates, Bush had said that Tower had been there "in good times and bad times." He had helped Bush in his losing 1964 and 1970 Senate races. He had come to Houston in 1968 when Congressman Bush was in reelection trouble because of a vote for fair-housing legislation, and had defended Bush to important conservatives. Tower had been one of the first senior Republicans to come out for Bush's 1988 presidential bid, and had been a tireless campaign soldier, making appearances, giving speeches, advising on defense.

Fuller knew loyalty was a core value for Bush, and there was no budging him.

A preliminary FBI investigation had discounted many of the allegations swirling around Tower. Though the investigation was not complete, Bush told Fuller, "I know there are some problems, but I can get him confirmed."

Fuller wasn't surprised when Bush, often given to impulsive decisions, jumped out on Tower before all the information was in. Bush's management style frustrated Fuller. As Vice President, Bush had been secretive, never sharing everything with one person, not even his chief of staff. Like an intelligence agent, Bush would "compartment" information, dividing it into pieces so that only he himself knew the whole. Sometimes he tested the system. He would act on some matter without telling his chief of staff, then wait to see how long it took to reach Fuller. "I'm glad that got to you," Bush would say when Fuller finally found out, sometimes more than six hours after the fact. Fuller often wondered what developments he might have missed entirely.

By early February 1989, just a few weeks into the Bush administration, the Tower nomination was in serious trouble. Rumors and allegations about Tower's drinking habits and personal life were popping up everywhere. A former Tower aide who was now a congressman, Representative Larry Combest, recently had come forward to Senator Sam Nunn's Armed Services Committee, which was preparing to vote on the nominee in two weeks, with stories about alcohol abuse by Tower during his Senate years.

On Tuesday, February 7, C. Boyden Gray, Bush's White House legal counsel, ran into the President's personnel chief, Chase Untermeyer, in a White House men's room. Gray, who had been monitoring the troubled nomination for Bush, had just learned of a new allegation linking Tower to defense contracting corruption. "Remember you heard it here first," Gray told Untermeyer. "Start looking for a new defense secretary. He can't bleed for another two weeks."

At about 11 p.m. that night, Tower called Gray at home. "I

don't think the President should have to put up with this for two weeks," Tower said. "I think I'm going to withdraw."

"Don't do anything more until you hear from someone," Gray said.

Tower promised to wait until Bush had considered his offer.

Early the next morning Gray went to see Bush to report what Tower had said.

"You look relaxed about this and dapper," Bush said.

Gray said he had in fact not slept very well. His recommendation, he said, was that Bush ought to consider pulling the plug on the nomination.

The President did not respond.

About an hour later Gray saw Tower in the White House. Tower had just come from breakfast with Baker and Scowcroft, who both advised him to stick in there.

"Are you still of the same mind?" Gray asked.

"No," Tower replied. "I slept on it and the President wants me to hang in."

That same morning, Nunn went to the Senate TV gallery to answer reporters' questions about the nomination. The most influential senator on Pentagon issues, Nunn had not yet announced his position. Asked about the alcohol issue, Nunn said, "It's a matter of a person in the chain of command that has control over the arsenal of the United States of America, and it's a very serious position as Secretary of Defense. The Secretary of Defense has to, in my view, have clarity of thought at all times. There's no such thing as an eight-hour day in that job. The young men and young women who defend our nation have to have people all the way up the chain of command that have entirely clear thought at all times."

On the evening of Thursday, February 23, Nunn's committee voted 11 to 9, along straight party lines, to recommend that the Senate reject the Tower nomination.

Across town at his official residence high up on Observatory Hill, Bush's Vice President, Dan Quayle, a former U.S. senator from Indiana, had two visitors that night—his friends and fellow Republican conservatives Ken Adelman and Dick Cheney. Adelman, a cocky 42-year-old Shakespeare scholar, had headed the Arms Control and Disarmament Agency under Reagan, and now wrote a nationally syndicated newspaper column. In a recent column, he'd criticized Tower's lack of discretion in his private life and argued that "private behavior is fair game for judging a public servant."

Dick Cheney had been President Ford's White House chief of staff, and was now Wyoming's sole member of the House of Representatives. Soft-spoken and serious, Cheney had an impeccably conservative voting record. He had risen from freshman congressman to House Republican Whip, the second-ranking party leader, in only ten years.

Quayle blamed conservatives for abandoning the good fight on Tower. "Goddamn, we have got to get this man confirmed," the Vice President said.

"Don't put me on the team to do it," Adelman said. "It's not my job."

"Tower's down the tubes," Cheney said flatly. "You've got to get someone to work with Congress."

Quayle blamed Nunn. It was a partisan power play by a very ambitious man.

Cheney disagreed. Nunn was being pretty straight, he said. Cheney spoke admiringly of Nunn's handling of the nomination so far, and of his ability to win a no-vote in a committee that Tower himself had once chaired. "Don't blame Nunn."

On Thursday, March 9, the Senate rejected the Tower nomination, 53 to 47.

Bush called Tower to say he thought his friend had fought the good fight and had demonstrated courage in the battle. His treatment had been unfair, the President said. Barbara Bush came on the line, echoing her husband. It was a warm, buck-him-up call. In his formal statement, Bush said: "The Senate made its determination. I respect its role in doing so, but I disagree with the outcome. . . . Now, however, we owe it to the American people to come together and move forward."

4

THE AFTERNOON THE TOWER NOMINATION was voted down by the Senate, Dick Cheney received a call from White House Chief of Staff John Sununu, the 50-year-old former New Hampshire governor whom Bush had chosen over Craig Fuller to be his principal aide. Could Cheney come to the White House at 4 p.m.? Sununu wanted to talk about what to do now that Tower was going down in flames. Cheney said he could be there at five.

Based on his own experience 14 years earlier as White House chief of staff, Cheney knew it was unlikely that the current chief of staff would be merely soliciting the opinion of the second-ranking House Republican in the heat of a nomination decision controlled by Senate Democrats. Something was up.

Cheney, like all of political Washington, had been paying close attention to the Tower battle. The first dust-up of the new administration might be an indicator of how the next four years would unfold. He thought that the President had to bounce back fast; he should come up with a new candidate within 48 hours and then select a new topic "A" for Washington. Cheney was convinced that the attention span of the nation's capital was about five minutes, and if Bush got out front on drugs or some foreign-policy initiative, the political and media world would quickly follow.

As the newly elected number-two House Republican leader, Cheney worked in the shadow of Republican leader Representative Bob Michel of Illinois, who had adopted Cheney as a political son and heir apparent. Though Cheney was only 48, his eyeglasses, thinning hair, and calm and reasonable demeanor gave him an older, wiser look.

With the party balance in the House so lopsided in favor of the Democrats, Republican leadership posts were frustrating. In previous years in the leadership, Cheney had learned that even senior administration Republicans couldn't always be counted on to help. At times, he'd wanted Vice President Bush to carry some water for the House Republicans, but Bush wouldn't do it if there was any chance it might jeopardize his own relationship with Reagan. Bush's reticence had bothered Cheney, and he often complained privately about it.

.   .   .

At 5 p.m. Cheney arrived at his old, corner White House chief of staff's office, now John Sununu's. Scowcroft was also there. The three talked about Tower's defeat, and about what should be done next.

"If the President offered you the Secretary of Defense post, would you consider it?" Sununu asked.

Cheney said he would.

Scowcroft asked Cheney about his health.

Although he was still in his forties, Cheney had had three heart attacks. The previous August, he had undergone a quadruple coronary bypass operation, a procedure in which four new passages for the flow of blood are grafted onto the heart to compensate for blocked arteries. Cheney said that he had elected to have the operation not because it was medically necessary but because he wanted to be able to continue backpacking and downhill skiing. His Washington doctor had given him a clean bill of health—his cholesterol level was way down and the medication he was taking had no side effects. He said his physician would supply records and a statement.

They all agreed that Cheney should have a night to sleep on this. He needed to consult with his family.

Scowcroft had been Gerald Ford's national security adviser when Cheney was chief of staff. Running the daily obstacle course of White House business together, they had become close. Now Scowcroft was pushing hard for Cheney for Defense. He wanted a known commodity in the Pentagon.

Jim Baker had already given his support to Cheney. He and Cheney had weathered the 1976 Ford campaign together, with Cheney supervising from the White House end as Baker managed the campaign itself. At the time, both had been new to national politics. Their friendship had survived Ford's defeat.

After the meeting, Sununu quietly asked White House counsel Gray to have the FBI do a quick background check on another prospective nominee for Secretary of Defense: John F. Lehman, Reagan's aggressive and highly controversial Secretary of the Navy.

Gray was dubious. The outspoken, 46-year-old Lehman had been in and out of government during his career, and might have a revolving-door problem. Worse, one of Lehman's former Navy Department assistants was a key figure in the Justice Department's "Ill Wind" investigation of fraud and corruption in the Pentagon procurement process. Nonetheless, Gray requested a check on Lehman.

. . .

Back at his House office, Room 104 of the old Cannon House office building, Cheney ran into his press secretary, Pete Williams. Williams, 37, a tall, outgoing former Wyoming television reporter, asked how it had gone at the White House. He did not know the purpose of the meeting.

Okay, Cheney said. They were concerned about the Tower replacement.

Cheney's administrative assistant Patricia Howe later stuck her head in Cheney's office. "Anything we should know about?"

No.

Cheney and his wife, Lynne, a Ph.D. in English literature who was chairman of the National Endowment for the Humanities, went out for dinner that evening with friends from Wyoming to La Colline, a French restaurant four blocks north of the Capitol. Cheney felt he could not bring up the subject at dinner. Walking in the door of their McLean, Virginia, house after dinner, the

Cheneys were greeted by their 19-year-old daughter, Mary, home from college on spring break, who said that Jim Baker had called.

Cheney called Baker at once, and they had a long conversation. Baker said he was 100 percent behind the idea of Cheney as Defense Secretary, and urged him to take the job. After hanging up, Cheney sat down with Lynne, who had caught the drift of the call, and they talked it over.

Cheney liked the House of Representatives. After the White House staff years, when his job and future had depended entirely on someone else's political success, he enjoyed being his own man. He had been home only one full day during the last six months of the 1976 Ford campaign. Cheney also loved the personality of the House, its rough-and-tumble atmosphere and its history and traditions. In 1983, he and Lynne had co-authored an affectionate 226-page book about House Speakers from Henry Clay to Sam Rayburn, entitled *Kings of the Hill*.

In his mind he ran through the advantages of the Defense job. He had decided previously that he would not go back to the executive branch unless one of two or three slots opened up. This was one. The Secretary of Defense mattered.

The idea of working with Baker and Scowcroft carried great weight. In the Ford years, Cheney had seen how the national security process could get mired down in useless infighting and power plays. Here was a chance to work with people he knew, and possibly to get it right.

He boiled the decision down to the short term. How did he want to spend his next four years? Did he want to work in the double shadow of the House job—with Bob Michel above him and the frustration of the Republicans' minority status? Or did he want to be number one at Defense, in an executive branch run by his own party?

Cheney realized that in the final analysis it wasn't really a close call. He decided if the job was offered, he would accept.

The next morning, after speaking to a group of newspaper editors over breakfast at the Willard Hotel, Cheney went up to his office on the Hill. He called in the staff to discuss the usual array of subjects important to Wyoming's sole congressman—irrigation, weeds, pests, and the fires in Yellowstone National Park that summer. The American public had been left with the impression that the park had burned down, and Cheney was worried that tourism would die. He did not share with his staff the question that dominated his thoughts.

A call came in from Sununu. The staff left the room so he could talk in private.

Cheney told the chief of staff he wanted to go to the next step.

Sununu said come to the White House about noon.

When it came time to leave for the White House, he had the driver of his official Whip's car go to the East Wing—the social and First Lady's entrance—so he would not be noticed by the media people on alert for a new Defense play by the President.

. . .

Meanwhile, Gray had reported to Sununu that John Lehman would be a problem. Though there was no direct incriminating evidence against the former Navy Secretary, the Ill Wind investigation would poison the nomination.

Sununu said Gray should have the FBI quietly check out Cheney.

Cheney entered an office the President had set up in the second-floor residence. There was a large desk off to one side. On one wall was a painting of Lincoln meeting with Generals Grant and Sherman toward the end of the Civil War, entitled *The Peacemakers*. Bush sometimes referred to it in speeches.

The two men talked about Defense, and the reforms that Bush thought were needed.

After half an hour Sununu joined them.

"If the President asked you to be Secretary of Defense," Sununu asked, "would you accept?" This conditional offer protected the President from a turn-down.

"Yes sir, I would," Cheney replied.

The three talked some more. The job was not formally offered.

When Cheney arrived back at his office, the FBI had already been there, asking Kathie Embody, his executive assistant of 15 years, for names of people to contact for their background investigation. He had been there no more than a few minutes when Bush called.

Let's do it, Bush said.

Okay, Mr. President.

Bush said he wanted to announce it right away.

At 4 p.m. Bush and Cheney appeared before reporters. It seemed to Cheney that Bush took great delight in springing his unexpected nominee on the press.

. . .

Pete Williams had been at a briefing on acid rain, a big issue in Wyoming. Since it was a nice Friday afternoon, he hoped to sneak out of work early. Arriving back at his office, however, he was amazed to find a large stack of phone messages, almost a full pad of them. Odd, he thought. What could be happening? The other staffers had to tell him three times before it sank in. He glanced up at his television set, which was tuned in to CNN. There was Bush with Cheney, the new Secretary of Defense–designate.

About 5:30, Cheney returned to the office. Congratulations were barely out when FBI agents entered a few paces behind. Cheney took them into his office and closed the door.

Williams finally got hold of Cheney, and the two of them sat down in a quiet corner.

"Why have you done this?" Williams asked, his voice full of bafflement, perhaps tinged with mild resentment for being cut out. But Williams knew it was classic Cheney—he had been told not to mention it to anyone, so he hadn't.

"When the President of the United States looks at you . . ." Cheney began to answer.

Williams thought to himself: oh come on, don't give me this crap.

Cheney continued on about the power of a presidential request, the honor of presidential service.

Williams thought: the White House can't razzle-dazzle you. You have been there as chief of staff, as a Republican leader. You can't possibly hear the chorus of angels singing.

Cheney said he wanted the administration to succeed and he was looking forward to working again with Scowcroft and Baker, who had said, "We need you."

Williams realized it was those two, the old ties, that had been decisive, much more than Bush.

People would react to Cheney in two stages, Williams knew. Observing and listening to him, they first would say: here's this nice, charming, fair player who seems to be moderate and doesn't burst into flames over anything. Then they would look at his conservative voting record and his tendency to hang out with the rabid right-wing Republicans—the people Williams liked to call "the flesh-eating zombies"—and they would wonder. But Cheney was not conservative on many social issues. Overall, Williams thought his boss was a pragmatist, who weighed the evidence on each question, and usually came out conservative.

The general feeling among Cheney's staff was: What is he getting us into? What is he doing to our careers in order to promote his own? What has he decided about our futures?

There were two staffers who were contemporaries of Cheney's and who, like Williams, wanted an explanation. One was Alan Kranowitz, who'd been at Yale with Cheney, both in the class of 1963, when Cheney left because of poor grades.

The other was David Gribbin. Gribbin, Cheney and both their wives had gone to Natrona County High School in Casper together. Gribbin had dedicated his own career to furthering Cheney's. He was virtually in a state of shock.

Why? Gribbin asked.

"The President asked," Cheney said. "How do you say no?" Apparently detecting the distress etched on the faces of his aides, Cheney added, "I thought about the decision. There is no looking back. Let's go forward."

Cheney said that in light of the Tower fiasco he did not want the White House to handle his Senate confirmation. Turning to Kranowitz, he asked, "Alan, will you handle my confirmation hearings?"

Kranowitz agreed.

. . .

Even to his closest aides, Cheney was something of an enigma. If they asked him something specific, he generally would give an answer, but he was not one to relax and unburden himself to others. Talking about himself and his feelings did not come naturally. Pete Williams even had a name for the loose, unofficial group of people like himself who tried to better understand the inscrutable Cheney by following and closely analyzing his movements: "Cheney-watchers."

One of the subjects Cheney didn't talk much about was his time at Yale. Kranowitz recalled that at some point during the first or second year Cheney took six months off to be a manual laborer and power-line worker back in Wyoming. He returned to New Haven, but by the end of sophomore year he was gone for good. Cheney would joke with staff about his academic problems, but he had never shared the full story about his lackluster academic career at Yale.

He had received a bachelor's degree in 1965 from the University of Wyoming, followed the next year by a master's in political science. He and Lynne, whom he'd married in 1964, were both Ph.D. candidates at the University of Wisconsin in 1968 when Cheney won a one-year fellowship that brought him to Washington to work as a Capitol Hill staffer. While on the Hill, he was noticed by Donald Rumsfeld, director of Nixon's Office of Economic Opportunity (OEO), who had given him a job. When Ford named Rumsfeld his chief of staff in 1974, he brought Cheney to the White House as deputy, and Cheney's career took off.

· · ·

Kranowitz, who was going to pilot the nomination through the Senate, had to be sure he knew as much as he could about Cheney. A longtime Cheney-watcher, he knew all about his boss's conservative record in Congress, and was familiar with Congressman Cheney's pet issues. One was aid to the Nicaraguan contras, a cause Cheney cared deeply and emotionally about; he believed Nicaragua was another Cuba in the making, and that the Sandinista regime had to be dislodged from the hemisphere. Another passion was Soviet submarines, which he'd studied intensely as a member of the House Intelligence Committee.

Cheney's past was comparatively easy. There was no revolving-door problem, few financial assets. He had lived in the same house for years and had been married only once. But after a large staff meeting on Saturday, March 11, Cheney privately told Kranowitz that he should know there were some "youthful indiscretions" that might come up. He had been arrested twice, he said, for drunk driving—both times more than 25 years ago, when he was in his early 20s. And he had been caught fishing out of season once and been fined.

"The twenty-five-dollar fine was not the worst part," Cheney said. "They took my fucking fish."

5

COMING INTO THE BUSH ADMINISTRATION SO LATE, Cheney knew that he was months behind the curve. He needed to play some quick catch-up. So the next day, Sunday, March 12, he drove over to Frank Carlucci's McLean home. It was Carlucci who, as Rumsfeld's assistant at OEO, had hired Cheney for his first executive branch job in 1969. If Cheney were confirmed, he would for practical purposes be succeeding Carlucci, who had been notified that he had to leave his office by January 20, when Bush ordered all Reagan holdovers out. Carlucci was still annoyed.

Carlucci said that Cheney should stay close to Bill Crowe, that Crowe would not steer him wrong.

The next day Cheney went to the Pentagon to see Crowe.

Right after they had sat down, Cheney said, "I understand you're going to stay on." Crowe's second two-year term as Chairman of the Joint Chiefs was going to expire at the end of September, and Bush had asked him to remain for another term.

"I haven't decided yet," Crowe replied. There were personal considerations.

Crowe wasn't definite, but Cheney got the impression he wanted out.

After nearly two months without a confirmed Secretary of Defense in the new administration, Crowe said he was looking forward to Cheney's arrival. The department desperately needed a political leader.

Crowe recommended that Cheney go ahead and begin to move into the Secretary's office on the third floor. Confirmation looked assured.

Rear Admiral William A. Owens, the military assistant to the Secretary, ought to be kept on, Crowe added. Owens, a nuclear submariner, was the best man Crowe had ever seen in that job. He knew how to stay in the background and he realized he was not Deputy Secretary.

The quality of the military as a ready, well-equipped fighting organization was very high, Crowe said. And happily there was no immediate problem that Cheney had to concern himself with, no pressing crisis on the horizon. There were sensitive operations, war plans, contingency plans and procedures that he would want to be briefed on as soon as possible, but for the moment he could focus on getting confirmed and then on the upcoming budget battle with Congress, where his status as a former member would be really helpful.

The next afternoon at 2 p.m., Cheney, wearing cowboy boots and a business suit, walked across a light green carpet to take his seat in a small, packed Senate hearing room before Nunn's Armed Services Committee.

"I, as you all know, am not here because I sought the position of secretary of defense," Cheney told the senators. It was well known that Tower had actively pursued the job. "I am here because the President has asked me to undertake a very difficult assignment."

Senator John Warner of Virginia, the ranking committee Republican, asked Cheney about his military deferments during the Vietnam War.

"Senator, I have never served in the military in uniform," Cheney began. He explained that when he was in college he'd gotten a 2-S student draft deferment, and after his first daughter was born in 1966, a 3-A deferment that was granted to parents. "I basically always complied with the Selective Service System, did not serve, and would have obviously been happy to serve had I been called."

In three hours of questioning, Cheney referred frequently to his past work on intelligence and defense issues, but also admitted that he had to get up to speed in many areas.

The next day Nunn and Warner reviewed the summary memo on the FBI's background investigation of Cheney and then briefed the committee in closed executive session.

"He got fined for fishing out of season," Nunn reported. The two charges of driving while intoxicated were ancient. Nunn and Warner did not see them as impediments to confirmation. All the members agreed.

Cheney joined the committee during the closed session. He said he thought it would be best to make public the old driving-while-intoxicated charges, but the committee said there was no need.

At 9:30 the next morning, Nunn called the full committee of 20 to order in public session. The committee's conclusion was that there was nothing in Cheney's background that "would render him unfit to serve," Nunn said. The remarks of the few senators who spoke were brief and enthusiastic. The sense of relief was palpable. The vote to confirm was 20 to 0.

At 10:50 a.m. March 17, St. Patrick's Day, Nunn took to the Senate floor. He said the committee had approved Cheney unanimously, "after careful and thorough consideration." Nunn spoke quickly and matter-of-factly, dismissing any suggestion that he or the Armed Services Committee was rushing to judgment. Without even hinting that he was talking about the driving-while-intoxicated charges, which still remained confidential, Nunn said that he and Warner had found "a couple of items" in the FBI reports that had no bearing on the committee's final positive decision, but which they had felt obligated to share in closed session with the other committee members.

As senators filed in to pass judgment on Cheney, they saw a sign at each end of the long table in the Senate well that said LAST VOTE TODAY in red capital letters.

The final tally was 92 to 0 to confirm.

Within minutes Cheney received a call in his Republican Whip's office. The caller identified himself as Rear Admiral Owens, the military assistant to the Secretary of Defense. Cheney thought to himself, "Admiral—I don't need this now." But Cheney knew that his new life was starting, and that he had to listen. Addressing

Cheney as "sir," Owens said he wanted to come right up to the Hill with Doc Cooke—David O. Cooke, the Pentagon's director of administration and management—to swear Cheney into office. Cooke, 68, was known as the mayor of the Pentagon to the staff of more than 23,000, military and civilian, who worked there. A fixture of the defense bureaucracy, he oversaw the daily housekeeping of the Pentagon, from parking spaces to office space, and had sworn in the last seven secretaries.

Cheney had wanted to be sworn in by the House Sergeant-at-Arms, as a final gesture to the institution he was leaving. But Cooke and Owens pressed him to continue the tradition.

Cheney shrugged his shoulders and went along. He resigned his House seat, and with aides and his family crowded around, he took the oath.

Cheney had asked his press secretary, Pete Williams, to be the new Pentagon spokesman, and Williams had accepted. After the swearing in, Cheney was going over to the Pentagon, and Williams intended to drive there separately. But David S. Addington, a Cheney aide and former CIA attorney who was now going to be Cheney's special assistant in the Pentagon, told Williams to make sure he arrived at the Pentagon in the Cheney motorcade. You've got to be seen—this is important in Washington, Addington told Williams.

"Be seen by whom?" Williams inquired.

The people who work there, Addington said. It's tremendously important that they see you as one of the people who are arriving with the new man. It will help you immeasurably in your job.

So Williams, Addington, Dave Gribbin and Kathie Embody all piled into the Secretary's limousine with the red light on top. Uniformed staff people as well as civilians and all kinds of hangers-on were waiting at the Pentagon door to observe and take note of the little entering parade.

Up on the third floor, where the Secretary's suite is located, a nameplate emblazoned *Richard B. Cheney* was already on the door. Williams thought, now there's one thing we're going to have to change. He's not a "Richard B." kind of guy. It would have to be "Dick," he thought, and made a mental note to have it changed.

Inside the office, photos were taken, and Cheney looked pleased.

Cheney had given some thought to reorganizing the Pentagon.

Its multilayered, bureaucratic complexity was a conservative Republican's nightmare of waste. But he soon decided that even if it were possible to rearrange the organizational boxes, to cut and streamline the place, it might not be worth the trouble.

On Tuesday afternoon, March 21, thousands of civilians and military men and women streamed into the Pentagon's internal courtyard for Cheney's formal swearing in as the 17th Secretary of Defense. President Bush spoke first, delivering a stock speech about peace through strength, reform, teamwork and opportunity. Vague on the world situation Cheney's Pentagon would face, the speech reflected the uncertainty of national security policy in the new administration.

Cheney was then sworn in again, this time by federal appeals Judge Laurence H. Silberman.

"It is a humbling experience to assume office," Cheney began, reading from a prepared text, his voice bouncing off the building's five inner walls.

"To the men and women of America's armed forces: I am honored to serve with you in the defense of freedom," he said. Then, departing from the text, he added, "You, our uniformed men and women, are my number-one priority."

Afterwards, Williams told Cheney his emphasis on people had played well.

Later that day, Cheney went to the White House to see Sununu and the personnel chief, Chase Untermeyer. Sununu—in public a strong opponent of racial and gender quotas—told Cheney the White House wanted 30 percent of the remaining top 42 jobs in the Defense Department to be filled by women or minorities.

6

CHENEY WENT TO WORK filling the key posts. He had already decided to keep one Tower holdover, Don Atwood, as Deputy Secretary. A competent, undynamic former General Motors executive, Atwood would be responsible for some of the nuts-and-bolts management of the Pentagon Building and budget.

To run the talent hunt for the other jobs, Cheney brought in Steve Herbits, a 47-year-old Republican political operator who had served as special assistant to Secretary of Defense Rumsfeld.

Toward the end of the first week Cheney was in office, Herbits came in and presented a one-page diagnosis of each of the services and the kinds of civilians Cheney should appoint to run them.

The Army, he'd written, was in deep trouble. It was going to take the biggest budget cuts over the next eight years, when perhaps four of its 16 divisions would be eliminated. For Secretary of the Army, Cheney should choose someone who could plan the cuts logically and then beat the shit out of the generals to implement them.

Herbits said the Navy was run by tradition-bound admirals who were defiant of civilian authority and spoke a language outsiders didn't understand. They had to find a secretary who understood the tradition and the language, but would not be captured by the admirals.

The Air Force is totally out of control, Herbits's diagnosis said. The chief of staff, General Larry Welch, was disdainful of civilians, and the whole service was cliquish.

There was only one way to beat them: brains. They had to find a civilian secretary who knew the Air Force culture, weapon systems and habits. An inexperienced secretary would soon be coopted, giving the Air Force a representative in Cheney's civilian circle, rather than Cheney a representative in the Air Force's inner circle.

Cheney already knew enough to be wary of the Air Force. The officers were a smooth lot, who made a great show of being helpful and responsive. Make a request and lots of colonels and generals would appear and talk to you until you had briefings and viewgraphs and neatly tabbed studies coming out your ears. Lots of motion, lots of paper flying around, lots of men in light blue uniforms and crisp shirts to answer any question. The Air Force seemed craftier than the other services, more familiar with Washington's ways, more adept at throwing up a smoke screen. Like almost everyone in the Pentagon, they were selling, but Air Force salesmanship was more consistent and better packaged, as if the service spoke with one persuasive voice. You had to look hard to see exactly what was up. The senior Air Force officer corps was so unified and impenetrable, it was often called the "Blue Curtain." Herbits and Cheney agreed it would be necessary not only to understand the Air Force, but to learn how to get around it, if necessary.

· · ·

Air Force Chief Larry Welch had a chilly reputation not just inside the Pentagon, but all around Washington. He seemed to emerge with reluctance from the absolute order of his fourth-floor E-Ring office, where papers, pens, folders and documents were arranged in perfect stacks and rows. On the inside of his attaché case was a neatly aligned collection of a dozen black binder clips, at the ready to organize any unruly stack of papers that might come his way.

From the moment Welch arrived at congressional hearings, his manner left no doubt about his low view of the messy legislative-media arena. But Welch realized he had to accept the congressional role in military issues. One such issue that he thought it was time to resolve was the decade-long debate over how to upgrade the Air Force's land-based intercontinental ballistic missiles (ICBMs).

The Bush White House had put off a decision for the time being, but in Congress a debate had been raging over whether the Air Force should go with the small missile known as the Midgetman or the larger one called the MX. Welch had spent time on the Hill talking to members about the options, and he knew the lay of the land.

Before Cheney's confirmation, Welch had gone to acting Secretary William Howard Taft IV, seeking permission to participate in the Hill debate. The Air Force couldn't be silent on this, he told Taft. Congressmen were asking for the Air Force's position, yet there was no clear administration policy for the service to push.

Shall we fall off the wagon? Welch had asked Taft. It would be unwise to leave a vacuum. There was no telling what decision the Congress might reach without Air Force input. He would like to talk to the key members in the House and Senate.

Taft told Welch he was right, and that he should go do it.

Welch also had visited Scowcroft at the White House. Although the administration hadn't decided what mix of MX and Midgetman it wanted, he told Scowcroft, the Air Force couldn't let the issue lie in limbo. He needed to take the congressional pulse and lay out some options.

Scowcroft said he didn't have any trouble with some discussion and information sharing, but that ultimately it would be up to the White House, not the Air Force, to make a recommendation to Congress.

Welch began visiting Hill offices.

George Wilson, the Pentagon correspondent for The Washington Post, was familiar with the way the White House and the Pentagon often shopped ideas around in Congress before making decisions. He was told by some lawmakers that Welch was making the rounds with a compromise ICBM proposal.

The night of March 23, Wilson called Welch, who confirmed he had been "pulsing the system."

A front-page story in the next morning's Post, headlined "Air Force Acts to End ICBM Deadlock," reported that Welch had suggested a compromise plan. Next to the story was a photo of Welch.

Cheney read the story. It was his eighth day in office. He had heard several days earlier from the ranking Republican on the House Armed Services Committee, William L. Dickinson of Alabama, that Welch had been over trying to make a deal with Chairman Les Aspin.

Since his time as White House chief of staff, Cheney had believed that strategic missiles were the President's turf. It wasn't so much the Secretary's business that Welch was trying to do, it was the President's business.

Cheney was scheduled that day to give his maiden press conference as Secretary. Dan Howard, the holdover Pentagon spokesman, slated to be replaced by Pete Williams as soon as Williams was confirmed, came in to go over potential questions. Howard said that Cheney was sure to get a question on the *Post* story about General Welch's pulsing mission on the Hill.

"You've got two choices," Howard said. "You can slide off it or come out swinging."

"My instinct is to cut him off at the knees," Cheney responded.

Howard said that normally he would not agree, but this situation called for strong action. The word from Taft's office was that he had authorized Welch to seek information from the Congress, but not to negotiate. Welch will be pissed off, Howard said, but the damage can be repaired later.

Cheney understood the symbolic importance of first impressions. In the earliest days of his presidency in the summer of 1974, Gerald Ford had been photographed toasting his own English muffin for breakfast. Widely publicized, the photo had set a tone of nonimperial simplicity that endured and boosted Ford's popularity. Now Cheney knew he would be setting his own tone, not just publicly but in the suites and corridors of the Pentagon itself. Washington was watching his early moves. Just after his nomination, Evans and Novak had written in their column, "Cheney cannot soon seize control of the building."

.   .   .

At noon, like thousands of others in the Pentagon, Welch settled down to watch the first public performance by the new Secretary, a press conference televised live over the Pentagon's closed-circuit television system.

The first question to Cheney was about talk of an ICBM compromise.

"To say that a compromise is near, I think, would be premature," Cheney replied.

The second question was specifically about Welch.

"Mr. Secretary," a reporter asked, "General Welch, the Chief of Staff of the Air Force, apparently has been up on the Hill working this program himself. Is that a change of policy for the Defense Department to have a service chief negotiate his own strategic system?"

"General Welch was freelancing," Cheney said. "He was not speaking for the department. He was obviously up there on his own hook, so to speak."

Cheney was asked if he accepted that sort of action.

"No, I'm not happy with it, frankly," Cheney added, his voice steady.

"I think it's inappropriate for a uniformed officer to be in a position where he's in fact negotiating an arrangement. I have not had an opportunity yet to talk to him about it. I've been over at the White House all morning. I will have the opportunity to discuss it with him. I'll make known to him my displeasure. Everybody's entitled to one mistake."

Wilson, the *Post* reporter who had written the story, said now to Cheney that Welch had "made very clear he was not preempting you or the President."

"Good," Cheney replied. "Well, I'm sure he'll make that clear when he talks to me about it." There was laughter in the press room.

Welch was stunned. One of the first rules they taught in any beginning military leadership course was that you praised subordinates in public and rebuked them in private. Nothing could be more humiliating or demoralizing than a public scolding. This reprimand had been broadcast to the entire world.

The general took several minutes to compose himself, then walked out of his office and down one flight of stairs to the Secretary's suite.

"I am not a freelancer," Welch said, standing before Cheney. "I have never been a freelancer. I support the administration's position and have worked harder than anybody in this town to make it come out the way the administration wants it to."

Cheney said the issue was closed.

Welch saw that he was not going to get an apology. Cheney seemed to want to smooth the issue over. Maybe, Welch thought, Cheney could not afford to backtrack. Welch did not mention the explicit permission he had received from both Taft and Scowcroft. After all, it had been his own idea to go to Congress; and he was senior enough to take responsibility for his actions, no matter who had approved them.

Welch tried to convince Cheney that he could count on the military. The greatest support he would get in the building would come from the military leadership.

Cheney did not want to discuss it further.

. . .

Downstairs in the Chairman's office, Crowe was almost beside himself. He had had no advance warning that the new Secretary was going to dress down one of the chiefs publicly. Cheney had not discussed it with him.

Crowe knew this was going to hurt. He had been trying to get the chiefs to be more open, more a part of the defense debate. Now this public lashing would drive them even further away from dealing with the Congress and the press.

Pitiful, Crowe said to himself. In his first week in office, a new Secretary who has never served in the military, never served on any of the armed services committees, publicly chastises a senior officer? Crowe had never heard anything like it. Clearly, Cheney felt a need to establish his machismo, to lay down a marker that he was the number-one guy around the building. Cheney also was pandering to the media, where the rebuke would surely be given big play.

Late that afternoon, Crowe and Cheney had their daily private meeting.

"I hope that blast didn't cause you a problem," Cheney said. He added that Welch had not denied going to the Congress.

Crowe had decided it would be best to speak frankly. "I just plain disagree with you, Mr. Secretary," he began. "It's not right." Crowe explained the seriousness of the matter. Cheney effectively had accused Welch of willful disobedience of an order, which was a violation of a military officer's oath. "You picked the wrong guy. If you want a chief to slap down, I can give you plenty." Welch, Crowe explained, was the most quiet, buttoned-down and inhibited service chief. In the Tank, the second-floor Pentagon conference room where the Joint Chiefs of Staff hold their regular meetings, he was a listener. And of all the chiefs he was the most flexible and "purple," Crowe said, using the Pentagon term for officers open to points of view outside that of their own service— "purple" referring to a combination of all the service uniform colors.

Crowe went further. For Cheney to get in a public spat with one of the chiefs was below his dignity as Secretary. By trying to demonstrate his authority in such a public fashion, Cheney had suggested that he himself was uncertain of it.

Cheney seemed a little chastened, Crowe thought, but very calm as he listened to his Chairman rake him over the coals.

As Crowe expected, the story made a splash in the media. Most major newspapers carried it on page one, with headlines reporting Cheney "assails," "rebukes" and "scolds" the Air Force chief.

Within the military, it was soon known as the shot heard round the world. Officers traded analyses of what it foreshadowed for the military's fortunes under Cheney, as well as for the Air Force and for Welch himself. Welch was considered one of the leading contenders to succeed Crowe.

Welch went deep into his shadow. He said nothing publicly, but he felt it necessary to speak to the active-duty four-star Air Force generals. A veteran of 137 combat missions in Vietnam, he told one of the generals, "I've been shot at by professionals and I'm still here. So being shot at by an amateur is not likely to cause me any pain."

The rebuke also reverberated among retired Air Force generals, a tight-knit group that kept tabs on Pentagon politics. Two retired four-stars told Welch they were going to make a big stink. They planned to go to Congress and get some of the Air Force's friends there to demand a public apology from Cheney. Both had access to influential congressmen and the media.

Welch told them not to do it. A feud between the Air Force and the Secretary of Defense would be bad for everyone. Suppose they succeeded in making a big deal of it—how could that be to the advantage of the Air Force? By reducing the effectiveness of the Secretary of Defense? They had to be kidding, Welch thought. If Cheney needed this kind of small victory to be effective, let him have it.

Welch said that he would resign his office at once if the two retirees did anything privately or publicly. They never did.

Within several days of the rebuke, two former secretaries of Defense suggested to Cheney that he had taken the wrong course. Harold Brown, Secretary during the Carter administration, told Cheney that saving face was important in the service cultures, and that he should take care not to alienate the military.

James Schlesinger, who had run the Pentagon under Nixon and Ford, told Cheney that he was in no danger of a military coup, and that the senior military officers would be his crucial supporters when he tried to get his programs and budgets approved. They knew how the system worked, and could implement or sabotage the Secretary's agenda. Overall, Schlesinger added, the problem with the military was not that the senior officers were uncontrollable, but the opposite. After a lifetime of taking orders, generals and admirals were, if anything, too compliant.

Representative Les Aspin, the Wisconsin Democrat who was Chairman of the House Armed Services Committee, felt that he had played a role in selling Welch on the idea of a missile compromise in the first place. Several days after the rebuke, Aspin saw Cheney at a breakfast and took the Secretary aside.

"Jesus Christ, Dick," Aspin said, "Welch wasn't doing anything like that, and he always made it clear it was your decision."

Cheney responded with a knowing half-smile. "It was useful to do that," he said.

"Okay," replied Aspin, "I understand that agenda."

7

By THE TIME CHENEY HAD BEEN IN OFFICE ABOUT A MONTH, Crowe was beginning to see how the inner councils of national security decision making were going to work under Bush, and he wasn't happy. Much of the discussion at National Security Council (NSC) meetings was political. Decisions were made based on their likely impact on the Congress, the media and public opinion, and the focus was on managing the reaction. Crowe had serious doubts that these should be the main criteria for military and foreign-policy decisions.

Jim Baker seemed to think being Secretary of State was like running a big political campaign: Bush versus Gorbachev. Baker was looking for some dramatic arms control initiative to upstage the Soviets and make Bush more popular.

Another problem with NSC meetings was Brent Scowcroft's habit of engaging in prolonged academic discussions, picking through every angle. To Crowe, these were often a tedious waste of time. Bush himself brought one of these rambling talks to an abrupt end one day, remarking, "This subject is dying on its feet. Let's adjourn."

"Amen," Crowe said under his breath.

For all the impressiveness of his title, Crowe knew he occupied a tenuous position in the government, and it frustrated him. By law he was the principal military adviser to the President, Secretary of Defense and NSC, but only an adviser. He commanded no military forces, and technically neither the Chairman nor the four service chiefs were even in the chain of command, which ran from the President to the Secretary of Defense to the CINCs of the ten major warfighting commands. The Chairman directly oversaw only the 1,600 desk-bound officers, drawn from all four services, of the Pentagon-based Joint Staff. Any power he possessed was based almost entirely on his relationships with the President and the Secretary of Defense.

A January 14, 1987, memo signed by President Reagan effectively had inserted Crowe into the chain of command, directing that "communications between the President and the Secretary of Defense" and the ten CINCs "be transmitted through the Chairman of the Joint Chiefs of Staff." But advice and communications could be pretty thin gruel in a business where real command is the name of the game.

The specific, day-to-day demands of the job were feeling more burdensome than ever. Capitol Hill was sometimes a downright ordeal. Presenting the annual budget to the key committees, he had to sit for hours and listen while congressman after congressman postured on pet issues. At the end of one of these hearings, Crowe whispered to one of his aides, "I'm not going to go through this one more time." He went to Cheney the next day and said he had made a final decision to retire.

Crowe realized that if Bush pulled out all the stops and ordered him to stay, he might have no choice. He had to find a way to be firm in telling the President, without appearing to reject Bush or his administration.

Finally, he went to the White House and sat down with Bush. After explaining that he and his wife, Shirley, together had made the decision to leave, Crowe told Bush, "I'm going to regret this decision on occasion. I'm confident of that. But I'll tell you, fifty percent of my job, or sixty percent, I won't miss for five minutes."

Crowe had to finish out the spring and summer of 1989 before his term expired, and there were more than a few problems demanding his attention. Panama was near the top of the list. General Manuel Antonio Noriega, the strongman who ran the country, was a major irritant. Suspected of involvement in illegal drug trafficking, Noriega ran a notoriously corrupt regime. Although he once had been one of the CIA's key Latin American assets, the administration now viewed him as an outlaw and an enemy of U.S. interests. With the strategically important Panama Canal scheduled to pass from U.S. to Panamanian control at the end of the century, and 12,000 American military personnel and many of their families living in Panama, the Bush administration wanted Noriega out.

Crowe knew that the CINC responsible for Panama (known as CINCSOUTH), Army General Frederick F. Woerner, Jr., of the Southern Command, had a reputation as a wimp. Crowe liked and respected him, but he saw that Woerner, who'd never served in a senior Pentagon post, didn't understand Washington politics. The new assistant secretary of state for inter-American affairs, Bernard W. Aronson, was leading an effort to come down harder on Noriega, perhaps with military force if necessary, and Woerner was resistant. Woerner was opposed to aggressive U.S. military intervention in Latin America. Shortly after Bush's inauguration, Woerner had publicly stated there was a policy vacuum in Washington on Panama. Scowcroft himself had scolded Woerner, saying, "I want you to know the President was furious with your speech."

A few members of Congress who visited Panama to observe the May 7, 1989, elections there thought Woerner was almost pacifistic, allowing Noriega to threaten Americans. Southern Command staff people joked that they answered the phone in Woerner's headquarters, "Wimp Command." The legislators were urging Bush to fire him.

Crowe was present at a White House meeting when Scowcroft brought up the complaints.

"Gee whiz, Brent," Bush said, "if we changed everyone the congressmen complained of, I'd be out of a job in a week."

Everyone at the meeting laughed. Crowe was glad to see that Woerner's job seemed safe for the moment. Later, Crowe had what he considered a real come-to-Jesus discussion with Woerner, in which he explained the importance of assuaging visiting congressmen.

On Wednesday, May 10, Crowe was watching the evening television reports from Panama. Three days earlier, Noriega's hand-picked candidates had been soundly defeated, but he had nullified the election. The opposition candidates who'd had victory stolen out from under them had taken to the Via España in Panama City in a protest demonstration of honking cars that drew thousands. It was a rare bold action by the usually timid Noriega opposition. "Down with the pineapple," the protesters shouted in Spanish, using a nickname that referred to Noriega's acne-pocked face.

In response, the so-called Dignity Battalions (or Digbats, as they were known in the Pentagon), paramilitary pro-Noriega units, attacked the opposition candidates.

Opposition presidential candidate Guillermo Endara, 52, a 240-pound man with the benign face of an overfed boy, was hit in the forehead with an iron bar wielded by one of the members of the Digbats. The bodyguard of Guillermo "Billy" Ford, the opposition's second vice presidential candidate, was shot dead. Ford himself was shown on television as he was struck by a fist and then another. He staggered out of his car and stumbled along the sidewalk. Blood covered his eyes and soaked his white shirt. As another man came up and swiped at him with a pipe, Ford struck out blindly with his arms.

This film, and one of Endara in the hospital, ran again and again on American television. The image of the white-haired Ford, robbed of his elected post, bloodied and temporarily blinded, became an instant symbol of the state of lawlessness and chaos in Panama.

The televised coverage jolted Crowe, who went to the Pentagon that evening in civilian clothes. Five inconclusive reports of harassment of U.S. servicemen in Panama had already been received. The Chairman soon received word that he was to be at the White House later that night for a meeting with President Bush and the rest of the national security team.

Crowe was fed up with Panama. Nothing had worked—not the Justice Department's drug indictments of Noriega in 1988, not the aborted negotiation to drop the indictments if Noriega would give up power, not economic sanctions and not CIA covert action designed to unseat Noriega. Crowe had had a real problem with the now departed Elliott Abrams, Reagan's truculent assistant secretary of state for inter-American affairs, who had virtually called him a coward when Crowe had balked at using the military to throw Noriega out.

Crowe was a skeptic about all uses of force, not just in Panama. He knew presidents sometimes had ambitious, extravagant ideas about the goals they could achieve with military power. War, to Crowe's mind, was a nasty, unpredictable affair, not something to be treated as just another foreign-policy tool. He favored limited applications of force, small steps taken in pursuit of well-defined, achievable goals. The first serious military operation of his tenure, the April 1986 bombing of Libya, had taken just minutes to carry off and had smoothly achieved its goal of scaring Qaddafi back into his tent. Crowe had backed the 1987 decision to use the U.S. Navy to escort Kuwaiti oil tankers in the Persian Gulf, a mission with the limited, specific goal of protecting the free flow of oil shipments.

The goals in Panama were obvious: protection of U.S. citizens and interests, and installation of a friendly, democratic government. The question was by what means.

In April 1988, Crowe had approved a detailed examination of the secret contingency plans, called ELABORATE MAZE, that the Joint Staff had on the shelf in case the military had to be used in Panama. Both Crowe and Woerner felt the ELABORATE MAZE plans were unsatisfactory because they did not reflect the full range of possible scenarios.

He had had Woerner develop a new series of plans for Panama. One benefit would be to demonstrate to Elliott Abrams and the State Department that the Pentagon was ready.

The new plans had been given the overall codename PRAYER BOOK, though each had its own secret name:

POST TIME was a plan for the United States to unilaterally defend the Panama Canal in time of crisis by placing forces along its route so it could continue to operate. Crucial points like the locks and Madden Dam, a key water and power source for the canal, would be secured with military forces.

KLONDIKE KEY was called a "non-permissive NEO," meaning a Noncombatant Evacuation Operation conducted without the permission of the host country. It was a massive plan to take control of Panama City and use military and civilian aircraft, including aircraft carriers with helicopters aboard, to remove U.S. citizens. Because of the large number of U.S. noncombatants in Panama, many senior military experts felt this was too unwieldy a task to be carried off. But events in the Middle East had put everyone in the Reagan administration, including the President, on guard about possible hostage taking. So the plan was drawn up despite the doubts.

BLIND LOGIC was a much smaller plan to provide military specialists with civil affairs skills to assist the Panamanians in setting up a new government. This plan was to be executed only in the event a new civilian government requested assistance.

BLUE SPOON was a plan for offensive U.S. military operations against the Noriega-controlled military, the Panamanian Defense Forces (PDF). These would be conducted from Panama by the local U.S. Army commander, who would take command of a joint task force comprising units from all four services.

· · ·

At the White House meeting the night of May 10, Crowe saw that Noriega's decision to nullify the opposition victory was being perceived as a big setback to U.S. policy. President Bush was eager to do something to solve the Noriega problem. But he made what Crowe considered to be the key point: the U.S. could not run the risk of making Noriega an overnight martyr.

If the harassment of U.S. servicemen were to escalate to physical attacks on Americans similar to the attacks on the Panamanian opposition leaders, the situation would be intolerable, Bush said. Television pictures of Americans being clubbed and fleeing with blood-encrusted shirts would require immediate action.

Crowe said that he wanted to make sure the military forces were in a better posture to respond.

Knowing that Jim Baker had the most influence with Bush, Crowe watched to see where the Secretary of State now stood on Panama. As Reagan's Treasury Secretary, Baker had argued that Noriega wasn't worth so much attention. But later, Baker had been Bush's campaign manager when candidate Bush took a tough, public anti-Noriega line, opposing a plea-bargained deal. This had given a new high profile to the Noriega issue, and had implied a promise that, as President, Bush would find a solution.

"If we had known we would win the election by so much," Baker said now, only half-jokingly, "we would not have dug such a deep hole for ourselves."

While Baker was not yet anything like Elliott Abrams, Crowe could see he was taking on the activist coloring of his department, where, it seemed to Crowe, military solutions were too often viewed as the first resort rather than the last.

Bush said that he wanted to exploit the obvious anti-Noriega sentiment that was on the rise in Panama, and also wanted to see if the videos of Billy Ford being beaten up could not be used to build some anti-Noriega support within Latin America.

The tenor of the meeting was that the administration should find some measured, symbolic step.

That night Marlin Fitzwater, Bush's press secretary, read a mild public statement from Bush condemning the violence.

Over the next 24 hours Crowe and Cheney attempted to formulate a military recommendation to the President.

Like so many military plans, the carefully drafted, four-part PRAYER BOOK series did not apply to the situation at hand: the canal was not in danger, a full evacuation of civilians was not called for, there was no new government to assist, and an offensive operation against the Panamanian Defense Forces would be too extreme.

Crowe suggested to Cheney that they propose augmenting the U.S. forces in Panama with a brigade-size reinforcement of 2,000 to 3,000 troops. This could be done with some fanfare, sending an important psychological message to Noriega and the PDF. Cheney agreed.

Crowe called Woerner on the secure line. He first asked if Woerner needed or wanted some supplement to the rules of engagement —the guidelines for combat, dictating when force could be used and how much—so he could put his troops in a more aggressive posture.

No, Woerner said, adding that he had not had a single serious incident of undue use of force by his 12,000 troops and he wanted to keep the rules simple.

Crowe proposed sending the brigade-size reinforcement, but Woerner said he did not need it. When Crowe attempted to explain that they had to send some message, Woerner said an influx of thousands of troops could be an unneeded burden.

Things were moving pretty fast, Crowe said, and Woerner might have to accept some kind of force package for political reasons.

. . .

Crowe decided there was one more step that could be taken to prepare. A secret deployment of a small, super-elite special operations task force could be ordered. Soon after the failed Iranian hostage rescue operation of 1980, Desert I, the Department of Defense had created the Joint Special Operations Command, JSOC ("J-sock"), to conduct counterterrorist operations. Headed by an Army major general, JSOC was based at Fort Bragg, North Carolina, and had several tiers of operators. The top tier consisted of three elite Army Delta squadrons and the Navy's SEAL (sea-air-land) teams.

Each Delta squadron had 120 to 130 people with enough firepower to make any battle seem like a nonnuclear version of World War III. Delta assignments were for five years, and the average age of a member was about 30. Each was experienced and capable of moving covertly in most countries. Abroad, Delta members might dress as civilians, speak the local language, wear their hair long, do whatever else was necessary to blend into the culture or neighborhood. One squadron was always on alert, ready to travel within four hours.

SEAL Team 6, the Navy equivalent of Delta, was the most elite of the three formidable SEAL teams—the best of the best. Team members had an average age of about 20 and had to be in top physical shape because they might have to swim for hours before fighting on land. Based in Norfolk, SEAL Team 6 had hundreds of members divided into 30-man units; platoons of 14 could be deployed individually. Equipped with everything from advanced underwater breathing devices that make no bubbles to the latest high-tech surveillance equipment, SEAL Team 6 would add another dimension to the capabilities available to the United States as it poised to await Noriega's next move.

Dispatching these special forces to Panama would give the President considerable flexibility, and would put the military's best hostage rescue team on the scene. Crowe called the JSOC commander on the secure phone and alerted him that some of his forces might be needed.

Cheney approved Crowe's suggestion to recommend to the President that they dispatch a Delta team and part of SEAL Team 6 to Panama.

Crowe then called Fred Woerner in Panama. Once again, the general said he did not desire the new deployment the Pentagon wanted to send him. It was one of the few times in his career that Crowe had encountered a commander who resisted additional forces. Crowe indicated that a force package of some 2,000 troops plus a Delta team and a SEAL unit were likely to be coming, if the President approved.

Woerner was troubled by the push from Washington. The BLUE SPOON contingency plan called for a Delta unit to capture Noriega, and now a Delta unit was coming down. The United States would be one step closer to executing an armed intervention, a move Woerner still strongly opposed. He made it clear that he felt a snatch operation—conducted either as part of BLUE SPOON or independently—was just too risky. If it failed, it would represent a major escalation, putting all the U.S. citizens in Panama in jeopardy.

The likelihood of pulling off a snatch was remote, in Woerner's view. Noriega was hard for U.S. intelligence to track. Woerner only occasionally knew where Noriega had been, knew only rarely where he was at any given time, and never knew where he was going to be—a prerequisite to capturing him.

Through a secret source, Colonel Guillermo Wong, Noriega's military intelligence chief, the Southern Command had learned that Noriega had two plans to put into effect if he was attacked personally or sought by U.S. forces. One was to go to the hills and conduct guerrilla operations; the second was to take American hostages. Aware that an unsuccessful snatch operation could trigger the ultimate nightmare of hostage taking, Woerner thought to himself that the snatch option, in any form, was "Looney Tunes."

. . .

Although he had doubts about the wisdom of abducting Noriega, Crowe knew he had to consider that possibility. But before he reached his own conclusion, he needed to get a better idea of what would be acceptable to Cheney. Crowe felt he had not closed the loop with Cheney, had not come to know the man beneath the unrevealing surface. One day during a private discussion, Cheney had dropped his guard. "You know," he said to Crowe, "the President has got a long history of vindictive political actions." Cross Bush and you pay, he said, supplying the names of a few victims and adding: Bush remembers and you have to be careful.

What an important notion, Crowe reflected. *Bush remembers and you have to be careful.* Cheney's mask had momentarily slipped. Was it intentional—a warning to Crowe? Or a reminder for Cheney himself? Crowe was not at all sure. But apparently Cheney was afraid of Bush.

The new Secretary did not appear to be squeamish about the kinds of aggressive actions now under consideration for Panama. In his first two months in the Pentagon, he had insisted on being briefed about possible retaliation for the December 21 terrorist bombing of Pan Am Flight 103, which had exploded over Lockerbie, Scotland, killing 270 people. Libya, Syria and Iran were all suspected of involvement. He had approved plans for retaliation in the event the bombing could be traced directly to any of the suspect countries. Despite this early indication of Cheney's willingness to use force, Crowe couldn't be sure of the Secretary's views on a Noriega snatch.

In one session, Crowe mentioned the possibility to Cheney, saying it would be very risky and not necessarily wise. Cheney explored the details of this option, and said he favored it if an opportunity arose—if there was good intelligence on Noriega's whereabouts or if he did something openly provocative. But not, Cheney said, if such a snatch was going to have any political negatives.

On Thursday, May 11, Cheney and Crowe finished work on their recommendation to Bush: an announced troop deployment, plus a secret dispatch of a Delta squadron and part of SEAL Team 6. Bush agreed.

That afternoon, the President appeared briefly in the White House press room to announce that over the next several days he was sending an additional 1,881 American troops to Panama. Asked if the United States would look favorably on a coup attempt against Noriega, Bush sidestepped. "I've asserted what my interest is at this point. It is democracy in Panama; it is protection of the life of Americans in Panama."

At a news briefing later, Scowcroft was asked what the new forces were going to do about the election fraud. He said, "I don't remember the President saying the troops are there to restore democracy." The deployment was simply "a precautionary, prudent step."

The operation was code-named NIMROD DANCER and would consist of 1,716 Army troops and 165 Marines.

The next day, Friday, May 12, Cheney formally authorized the secret part of the deployment.

Most people cleared for access to details of this special operations deployment were told the units were being sent there for possible hostage rescue. Since Noriega and his Dignity Battalions might do anything to the Americans in Panama, it was considered a wise precaution to have the forces on hand to carry off a sophisticated rescue.

But there was another mission for the Delta squadron. A month before, a CIA operative named Kurt Muse had been arrested by the PDF for running a clandestine radio network which was part of the agency's covert operation to unseat Noriega. Intelligence reports said that a guard with a submachine gun was stationed outside Muse's cell with orders to kill him if there was any sign of hostilities by the Americans. The CIA was deeply concerned about Muse and wanted to avoid a repeat of the 1984 kidnapping and subsequent murder of their station chief in Beirut, William Buckley. In that episode, the agency's inability to locate and rescue one of its own had made it appear weak. So CIA Director William H. Webster pressed Cheney to have the military draw up a rescue plan for Muse that would be ready for execution on short notice.

Muse's wife was a Department of Defense employee in Panama, making Muse a dependent entitled by treaty to regular visits from an American attorney and doctor. They reported that Muse, who was being held in Modelo Prison across from Noriega's headquarters, known as the Comandancia, was being treated well. As Noriega's American hostage, however, he was very vulnerable.

A special plan, code-named ACID GAMBIT, was developed for a Delta team to rescue Muse in an operation that would take only nine minutes.

In operational terms, using Delta or the SEAL team to free an American hostage or prisoner was not much different from taking the heavily guarded Noriega from his bodyguards.

. . .

Crowe saw that the President—former CIA Director Bush—was very worried about the agency's captured operative. Bush also had made it clear that he wanted the military to be able to seize Noriega and bring him back to the United States for trial. The implications of going into a sovereign country and seizing its leader could be immense; but Crowe saw no sign that the consequences were being fully considered.

"I can't predict what the President will do," the Chairman told the JSOC commander on the secure telephone, "but get ready."

.   .   .

On Saturday, May 13, Bush boarded Air Force One to fly to Mississippi for a commencement address. He summoned the reporters traveling with him to his cabin to say that he had no quarrel with the Panamanian military, just with Noriega and his "thuggery." In his strongest public comments so far, Bush called on the Panamanian people and military to overthrow Noriega. "They ought to do everything they can to get Mr. Noriega out of there," he said. It was highly unusual for a president to call publicly for a coup, baldly declaring open season on a foreign ruler. When Bush was asked if there were any limits on what he meant, he said, "No, I would add no words of caution."

.   .   .

Crowe sent General Woerner a personal secret message proposing a plan for the U.S. military to conduct new exercises in Panama that would aggressively assert U.S. rights under the Panama Canal treaties. On May 17, Woerner sent a message back saying he was ready.

In a secure phone conversation, Crowe told Woerner that Bush had decided to authorize the exercises. "But understand you are to do nothing provocative," Crowe added.

Woerner had grown accustomed to executing a Panama policy that amounted to a sequence of subtleties and innuendos. He interpreted Crowe's new instructions to mean that the command should be intimidating, show resolve, create doubts in Noriega's mind about U.S. intentions, and act tough, *but* not pick a fight that would draw an armed response from the PDF. It seemed like a thin distinction.

In the following days, Noriega drew back. Woerner received intelligence reports, including some from the secret source Colonel Wong, showing that Noriega was telling his forces to be very careful during any encounters with Americans. They were not to give the Americans an excuse for a military response. According to one such report, Noriega warned, "Don't piss off the Americans."

.   .   .

Cheney realized that Woerner was an expert on Panama—perhaps too much so. The Secretary did not like the subtext of the Southern Command's reactions to events. When anything aggressive was proposed, such as new deployments or asserting the U.S. treaty rights, Woerner argued against it. The general always provided good reasons, but his heart didn't seem to be in a timely solution to the Noriega problem.

Cheney concluded that Woerner had gone native.

For Cheney, if push came to shove in Panama, the United States had basically two options: execute the BLUE SPOON offensive operations against the PDF, or snatch Noriega. Woerner was keen on neither. Furthermore, there didn't seem to be any circumstances when he would be.

. . .

Outgoing Army Secretary Jack Marsh had heard that there was going to be a game of musical chairs in the upper ranks of the military. Cheney was going to have to select a new JCS chairman. On May 30, when Cheney came over to join Marsh for one of the Army mess's famous catfish lunches, Marsh wanted to make sure Cheney considered an Army general for the post. So Marsh spoke to Cheney in glowing terms about one of his favorites—General Maxwell Reid Thurman.

8

JUST BEFORE LUNCHTIME ON JUNE 13, a small-framed man of average height with a large head and thick glasses rushed down the third-floor E-Ring corridor. If it hadn't been for his Army-green uniform and the four stars on each shoulder, he might have been taken for a Pentagon budget analyst.

A bachelor workaholic, he thought nothing of working himself, and his staff, nights and weekends. He spoke with piercing directness, and he did not accept excuses. There was perhaps no more intense man in the United States military.

General Maxwell Thurman, 58, was stopping by for a private lunch with Jack Marsh and Cheney. Marsh had arranged the lunch. It was a rare opportunity for Thurman, as he neared the end of his career, to speak with the Secretary of Defense. Commanding general of the Training and Doctrine Command—the Army's brain—since 1987, he had spent his life, 28 assignments in 36 years, as an Army officer, the last six as a four-star general.

He was scheduled to retire in two months and, like most four-star officers, was going to leave without having risen to one of the high-visibility posts, such as service chief or CINC. If he lacked public notoriety, Thurman made up for it within the Army, where he was somewhat of a legend, known variously as Mad Max, Maxatollah and Emperor Maximilian.

The Army Secretary's office was as large as Cheney's. In the center was the giant Lincoln Desk that had been built for Abraham Lincoln's son Robert, when he served as Secretary of War from 1881 to 1885. Cheney took his seat at the small dining table, directly beneath a vast 19th-century painting called *The Ragged Continentals,* depicting General George Washington with his somber, bedraggled troops at Valley Forge. Marsh sat at the head looking out the window to Arlington National Cemetery. He had always thought it appropriate that the Army Secretary and the Navy Secretary—whose office was one floor above—had this view of seemingly endless rows of white tombstones, a reminder of the true, measurable price of war.

As they began lunch, Thurman said right away that he would give his views "bark-off," with no diplomatic couching or coloring. He described how he had organized the Army's modern recruiting drive, building up the all-volunteer force and changing a hollow and dispirited army to a proud one.

Thurman knew that Cheney was under pressure from a number of quarters, including the White House, to get the military more actively involved in the drug war. "Look," Thurman said, "I don't know where you come out on this, Mr. Cheney, but there are a lot more opportunities in the drug war." This was a case where the military was dragging its feet.

The Defense Department could be much more aggressive in the war on drugs, he said. The intelligence capabilities, as Cheney well knew, were staggering. The ability to spy overhead with satellites and to tap into the world banking transactions was quite extraordinary. No drug lord could begin to compete if the military's espionage capabilities were turned loose. Routine radar surveillance could mean capturing many drug shipments.

At the same time, U.S. special operations teams could teach the local police and military how to overwhelm any drug outpost. The United States was not helpless fighting the drug war, Thurman said. There had just been no decision to use what existed.

Thurman got worked up as he delivered his monologue. It was a matter of seriousness of purpose, he said.

Cheney thought Marsh was right about Thurman. Here was a

no-bullshit, straight-ahead guy. Things clearly happened when Max was in charge. Where many senior officers saw obstacles or made excuses, Thurman saw possibilities. Although the general had an unfinished quality about him that made him wrong for the chairmanship, Cheney was pretty sure a CINC position was about to open up earlier than expected.

. . .

On July 6, Woerner received a call from Army Chief Carl Vuono, who said he wanted to come down to Panama to see Woerner. Why? Woerner asked.

Vuono, a good friend of Woerner's, wouldn't elaborate. He said only that he would be staying about an hour.

An hour? Certainly bad news, Woerner thought. But just a month earlier, he had been asked to extend his tour as CINC-SOUTH for another year, to the summer of 1991.

At the Southern Command headquarters, Vuono took Woerner into a small room so they could be alone.

"Fred," Vuono said, looking Woerner straight in the eye, "the President has decided to make a change."

Woerner felt ill, as if he had been kicked hard in the stomach. His 34 years in the Army, his whole life . . . "Why, Carl?"

"I don't know," Vuono replied. "The Secretary of the Army came and told me and said I couldn't tell you." Vuono explained he had told Marsh that Woerner was a close friend who'd given years of loyal service, and argued that Woerner deserved the courtesy of hearing about the decision face to face. But Woerner had to keep it secret.

Woerner pressed. Why was he being fired?

"I don't know why," Vuono repeated. "All I know is it is an irrevocable decision." Vuono proposed that they develop a reason —health, family, a job offer, anything.

Woerner would not hear of a cover story. He understood the rules: he served at the pleasure of the President and needed the support of the Chairman and the Army Chief. Vuono left 45 minutes later for his flight back to Washington.

Woerner kept the painful news to himself. He had promised to keep the secret, and there was no one he wanted to speak to about it anyway. It was often strange, he thought, the oaths an Army officer had to take. Imagine pledging to keep secret his own professional extinction.

When Woerner finally spoke by telephone with Crowe, both men pretended they did not know the news. When you are in Washington next, Crowe said, be sure to stop by.

The decision had been reached while Crowe was out of the country. When he learned of it, he had said to Cheney, "I wish you wouldn't do something like that without involving me."

"The White House did it," Cheney replied. He blamed the decision, as well as its suddenness and finality, on Scowcroft.

A few days later Woerner was in Washington. He went to Crowe's office.

"Fred," Crowe said, "I guess you know the President has decided to make a change. All I can tell you is that I know nothing. I was not consulted. The decision was made while I was in the Soviet Union." Crowe suggested they go up together to the third floor and see the Secretary of Defense.

Cheney pointed to the comfortable captain's chairs at his small conference table, and took a seat himself.

"The President has decided to make a change," Cheney said.

That sentence again, Woerner thought to himself, as if they had all been programmed. It told so much while it also masked so much. Cheney seemed relaxed, neither apologetic nor defensive, as he looked Woerner in the eye.

"After thirty-four years of service," Woerner said, bracing himself, "I believe I'm entitled to an explanation."

"This has nothing to do with you or your performance," Cheney said. "It's a political decision."

Why? Woerner asked. What does that mean?

Crowe sat like steel in his chair, silent.

Woerner pressed Cheney.

"Time for a change," Cheney said briskly. No matter how Woerner asked the question, Cheney would not amplify.

"You can call it anything you want," Woerner said. "In my terms I'm being relieved—the first time in my career."

Cheney said nothing. When Woerner had exhausted every way he could think of to ask the same question, Cheney said he wanted to arrange a timetable for the change of command.

Woerner's last day would be set two months away, they agreed, at the end of September.

Crowe and Woerner rose to leave. As the generals always seemed to do, Cheney reflected, Woerner had accepted the ax, saluted, and in the end was quite a gentleman.

Walking down the 27 steps to the second floor, Crowe and Woerner did not speak. Crowe did not say whether he agreed or disagreed. The decision had been made, the President had decided. That was the way. But Crowe felt bitter. Whenever *they*—the civilians—wanted, they could go merrily right around him. Crowe had had his own concerns about Woerner, but the dismissal was unjust. Woerner had been carrying out the essentials of the President's policy, which was still to avoid direct military confrontation with Noriega.

If the White House planned to change the policy, then they ought to face up to that, not slide around it by suggesting that some allegedly timid commander was the problem. But it was easier to fire Woerner, blame Woerner, make Woerner the issue. That was why Cheney couldn't give a reason. Most chilling to Crowe was the indifference that the Secretary of Defense seemed to have about the career of a four-star officer.

. . .

Later in July, Army Chief Vuono tracked down Max Thurman in Santa Fe, New Mexico. It was now less than a month before Thurman's scheduled retirement and he was sending out invitations to his retirement ceremony, making sure he included all the colleagues, friends, mentors and protégés he had accumulated over 36 years of service.

Vuono explained that Woerner was leaving the Southern Command sooner than expected—"an unprogrammed retirement," it was called. Would you be willing to take it, go down there for a couple of years? Vuono asked.

"Well," Thurman replied, "let me think about it for about ten minutes and I'll let you know."

"Let me know now," Vuono said.

"Okay," Thurman said, "I'll take it."

Thurman arranged a meeting with Woerner to begin learning about the command. "I want you to know I had nothing to do with this," he told Woerner.

"If I thought you did, I wouldn't be here."

Woerner was still shaken, but he had had some time to sort out his emotions and he was aware that some of them were contradictory. He understood the prerogative of the President and believed in it. But he worried that the military issues in Panama had become politicized, setting a dangerous precedent. He was sure he had been doing a good job carrying out the precise instructions of Bush, Cheney and Crowe. No more, no less. If the only way a commander could survive was to anticipate the political winds blowing in Washington and try to get out ahead of formal policy change, the military could be hopelessly contaminated.

. . .

Crowe and Cheney took their proposal to the White House that the Southern Command should begin a series of intensive exercises asserting the freedom of movement guaranteed to the U.S. military under the Panama Canal treaties. Some of the treaty rights had gone unexercised for years; it was time to send a clear message to Noriega. Woerner had authority to approve low-level training exercises called Category One and Category Two—movements of small numbers of U.S. troops. Category Three and Category Four exercises were defined as the severest provocations, involving hundreds of U.S. troops, and required notifying the President 24 hours in advance.

On July 17, President Bush approved the plan to have the Southern Command aggressively assert U.S. treaty rights by conducting these new exercises.

Three days later, Cheney announced that General Woerner was retiring. He would be replaced by General Thurman.

In a comfortable, brightly lit suite of offices behind a special security checkpoint in the Joint Staff's inner sanctum in the Pentagon, Lieutenant General Thomas W. Kelly roared into one of the telephones behind his desk. He was admonishing one of his immediate staff officers to be more watchful. Kelly, 56, a barrel-chested, take-few-prisoners three-star, was chief operational traffic cop for Crowe and the Joint Staff. As the director of the operations staff, or J-3, Kelly lived in the world of the immediate. If Qaddafi was stirring or Gorbachev had not been seen for a week or there was a coup on some Caribbean island, the problem landed automatically on Kelly's plate. He was responsible for making sure the U.S. military was positioned with the proper forces, plans and approvals to respond to just about anything that might happen.

J-3 was a coordination and information center. As director, Kelly lived between calamity and opportunity.

A tank commander by training and temperament, he would

insist on beer in a can and display his wisecracking, "so's-your-mother" style at the most formal cocktail party. But for all his tough-guy talk, Kelly had a sophisticated side. A Philadelphian with a journalism degree from Temple University, he was a smooth writer. As a one-star, he had worked for Crowe in Italy when the admiral was the CINC for Southern Europe. When Crowe phoned Kelly to recruit him to work on special operations for the Joint Staff, Kelly had said, "That's nice. I'm a tanker."

"What I need is somebody that can spell," Crowe replied.

Aware that the Category Three and Four exercises in Panama could flare up instantly into a confrontation that might require presidential decisions, Kelly had all his lines out. He knew that the plans for Panama were his most important contingencies for the moment and he hoped to minimize surprises for everyone.

Except for a few incidents that didn't amount to much—Kelly called them the "SouthCom Follies"—the U.S. exercises didn't seem to provoke Noriega's forces. Try as Kelly and his intelligence people might, they could not point to any positive proof that the PDF or Noriega was intentionally confronting U.S. forces. One American woman reported she had been raped, but it couldn't be traced to the PDF. A U.S. sailor claimed he had been taken by the PDF, then forced to kneel and say his prayers while someone pretended he was about to shoot him, but he couldn't pass a polygraph. There were shooting incidents around U.S. installations but they were traced to hunters. Kelly concluded that Noriega was carefully avoiding confrontation.

· · ·

On August 5, Army Lieutenant General Carl W. Stiner took his seat among the dignitaries at Fort Monroe, Virginia, a historic seacoast fortress near Norfolk and the headquarters of the Army Training and Doctrine Command. General Thurman's retirement ceremony had turned into a mere change of command, since he was going to be CINCSOUTH. Stiner, the commander of the Army's 18th Airborne Corps based at Fort Bragg, wanted to be on hand nevertheless. Thurman was an old friend, and Stiner didn't like to miss the informal get-togethers that took place after major change-of-command ceremonies.

Stiner, 52, a taut Tennessean, had one of the Army's premier commands, charged with responding to a short-notice crisis anywhere in the world. Any of the CINCs could call on the 41,000 troops of his Corps for help in carrying out contingency plans or responding to other emergencies. The modern airlift capability of the Air Force, ready to transport the 18th Corps on short notice, gave the men of Stiner's outfit a tremendous edge over most other U.S. forces. They could get to a crisis faster than any other American troops, unless Marines were already deployed in the immediate vicinity on Navy ships.

Before this assignment, Stiner had been commander of the elite Joint Special Operations Command and the 82nd Airborne Division. There was probably no general in the U.S. Army with more experience in quick-response warfare.

After the ceremony, Thurman stepped off the reviewing stand and approached Stiner. "Carlos," he said, poking his finger gently in the three-star general's chest, "you are my man for Panama. I hold you responsible for all contingency planning and any combat operations."

Stiner did not seem to fully understand.

"I need a man to plan and to execute contingency operations down there if they have to be executed," Thurman went on. "And I want you to go down there and take a look at this thing. Look at the staff."

"But you've already got a JTF down there," replied Stiner, referring to the Joint Task Force in Panama. General Woerner had designated an Army two-star in Panama to have command of the task force, which would mainly use the forces already permanently stationed there to respond to a crisis, and bring in reinforcements if needed.

"You absorb it," Thurman said. "I'm gonna hold you responsible."

"I understand that, yes sir."

"I've got a whole theatre to run," Thurman said. "And I'll handle all CINC duties and you take care of the contingency planning, the training of the forces that are there and the operations. They're all yours, all services."

Thurman had not commanded forces in the field for 14 years. As the CINC, he knew he was going to be an administrator and supervisor. He needed a warfighter and Stiner was the essence of the hard-nosed battle commander. Just as important, Thurman knew that as commanding general of the 18th, Stiner had all the best equipment, an operations staff three times the size of the CINC's staff in Panama, a big intelligence shop, and the best communications.

"Have you ever heard of Ulysses Grant Sharp?" Thurman asked. Admiral Sharp had been the Hawaii-based CINC of the Pacific Command (CINCPAC), with overall military command of the Pacific region, including Vietnam, at the start of major hostilities there in 1964.

"No, sir."

"Have you ever heard of Admiral McCain?" Thurman pressed. John S. McCain had been the CINCPAC from 1968 to 1972.

"Yeah."

"You notice Admiral McCain had a guy by the name of Westmoreland fighting in Saigon?"

"Yes, sir."

"Me McCain, you Westmoreland. Get your shit straight," said Thurman. "I can't give you any instructions, but if I am confirmed and I take the job and get down there . . ."

"Yes, sir," Stiner answered.

·   ·   ·

Stiner put his staff to work at once. Like Thurman, Kelly and Powell, Stiner had not gone to West Point; he held a degree in agriculture from Tennessee Polytechnical Institute.

Known for his aggressiveness and enterprise, Stiner was a very controversial figure. In 1985, he had been the special operations ground commander when the Italian cruise ship *Achille Lauro* was hijacked. In Sicily with the Delta team sent to seize the hijackers, he wouldn't take no for an answer when the Italians refused to surrender them. He had nearly fired on Italian forces, and then without Italian permission he had shadowed the plane carrying the hijackers to Rome. This prompted a serious protest from the Italian government and set back U.S.-Italian relations for some time.

Kelly thought Stiner was a great soldier, though tactless and too outspoken. As long as Stiner was not made ambassador to France, he could be handled.

·   ·   ·

After leaving his command, Thurman reluctantly faced an interim period that, borrowing the British term, he called a "garden leave." For the 50 days until he was scheduled to take over from Woerner, Thurman would be a general without a command.

"What do you want me to do in this fifty days?" Thurman asked Crowe after setting up a temporary Pentagon office. "You got any orders for me?"

"I want you to take a fresh look at everything," Crowe said. "No holds barred—fresh look, new eyes. Whatever you recommend, if we agree to it in the JCS, then you'll have to live with it."

Crowe said that the trend of events in Panama showed Noriega was heading over the cliff. His behavior was not predictable, and the push and shove was dangerous. "Noriega is proving he is an asshole," the Chairman said. "You're very much liable to have to go fight down there. And if you have to go fight—you better make sure you're ready." Crowe suggested that Thurman take a detailed look at the PRAYER BOOK contingency plans, pull them apart, report back on what was necessary. Get ready.

Yes, sir.

. . .

Crowe also went to Cheney and suggested that he put Panama on a wartime footing. The best way to do this, Crowe said, was to move the overall Southern Command headquarters out of Panama to some place like Florida. The CINC was giving too little attention to the rest of his command outside Panama, and a fighting command could be left in Panama that could focus exclusively on the problems there.

Big political problem, Cheney responded. No matter how it was dressed up, it would look like the United States was running. Just can't do it, no matter what the merits, the Secretary told his Chairman.

. . .

From his J-3 vantage point, Kelly watched Thurman's arrival with some wonder and much pleasure. "You don't have to do nothing to mobilize Max Thurman," Kelly said. "He is mobilized when he gets up in the morning, which is in the middle of the night." For some time, Kelly had thought that General Woerner's notion of keeping the warfighting Joint Task Force in Panama was byzantine. Southern Command didn't have the horsepower, staff or communications to run any large contingency operation. Kelly figured that Woerner had kept operational control in Panama so that he had a better chance of preventing the use of U.S. military force there.

Kelly explained all this to Thurman when the new CINC-SOUTH came by his office. It was immediately clear to Kelly that he was wasting his time because Thurman said he had already decided how to take care of it.

Stiner? Kelly asked.

Of course.

Very wise move, Kelly thought.

Both men realized that Bush's order to conduct exercises asserting the canal treaty rights could set something off in a second. Thurman wanted to know more about the PRAYER BOOK contingency plans and what General Stiner could really do. So he set off for Fort Bragg.

Stiner was not there, but Thurman had managed to get Woerner to send some Southern Command staff planners up to Bragg from Panama. They briefed him for about eight hours on the targets that would be hit, the intelligence and the sequence of events.

Thurman was appalled. The plans were built around the forces in place, and the reinforcement, if things really got bad, was expected to take five days! That guaranteed that operational security would be blown; Noriega would surely know that the Yankees were coming. It was contrary to two of the basic requirements of successful warfare: surprise and speed.

But the five-day buildup was intentional—all part of Woerner's strategic plan. Woerner felt that if the PDF leadership saw the United States mobilizing for offensive action or moving in an invasion force, there was a 50–50 chance they would overthrow Noriega on their own.

Even if that were true, 50–50 wasn't good enough for Thurman.

9

IN THE MONTHS SINCE HE LEFT THE WHITE HOUSE, Colin Powell had seen his life transformed. After living two years at the center of the policy storm, he was floating in calm, uneventful waters at Forces Command in Atlanta. When he relinquished the national security job to his successor, Brent Scowcroft, Powell had observed an old Army tradition—when relieved, you salute, leave the post, and *never* call back. He had not spoken with Scowcroft since.

There were occasional reminders he hadn't been forgotten. At the end of March 1989, he'd received a handwritten note from the President on one of Bush's personal heavy-stock note cards. Addressed simply to "Colin," it was a one-sentence congratulation for pinning on the "4th bright one,"—referring to Powell's fourth star. This was pure Bush: to recognize an important personal event, such as reaching the top Army rank, by dashing off a line or two. Powell set it aside for his scrapbook.

He was spending much of his time crisscrossing the country visiting the various units in Forces Command, a kind of umbrella organization comprising the service's entire strategic reserve of 1 million active-duty, Reserve, and National Guard troops. Powell was shocked to see it was business as usual, as if nothing in the world had changed. Communism was collapsing in eastern Europe, and the Army's freezers were still making ice for the Cold War. Listening to the commanders, officers and troops talk, and watching them operate, you would think the Soviet threat had not been altered one iota. Planning and training were still centered on the scenario of a large, World War II–style reinforcement of Europe—hundreds of thousands of U.S. troops—to counter a massive Soviet invasion.

There was a kind of free-for-all within the administration on the question of change in the Soviet Union, Powell knew. Cheney had publicly predicted that Gorbachev would "ultimately fail" and would likely be replaced by a leader more hostile to the West. The White House had openly disagreed.

For his part, Powell thought the Warsaw Pact was in jeopardy; it was an unholy alliance, and the Soviet Army was just an occupying force. The Soviet Union itself was changed almost beyond recognition. In a speech he gave that spring to a group of Army officers and contractors, Powell had said he "wouldn't bet on" Gorbachev's successor moving to threaten the West. "The bear looks benign," Powell had said. "If tomorrow morning we opened NATO to new members, we'd have several new applicants on our agenda within a week—Poland, Hungary, Czechoslovakia, Yugoslavia, maybe Estonia, Latvia, Lithuania and maybe even the Ukraine."

Powell told some close friends and associates that he had taken a big risk with this speech, particularly in contradicting Cheney. Powell was used to having his public statements combed for nuances, and now he said he expected to be zinged. But the speech made no waves. He saw that for the first time in years his words didn't make any difference. It was humbling, but also liberating.

On Sunday, August 6, 1989, Powell arrived at Belmont House, an estate outside Baltimore that had been turned into a conference center, for a three-day meeting of top Army generals called annually by Army Chief Vuono. The morning of the second day, Powell read with some distress a story in *The New York Times* headlined "Scramble On to Succeed Chairman of Joint Chiefs." It was accompanied by photos of Powell and the JCS Vice Chairman, General Robert Herres, and reported they were the leading candidates for the job. "General Powell," the story stated, "has

been keeping in touch with Mr. Cheney through frequent letters."
The implication was obvious—Powell was campaigning.

He had written only one letter to Cheney, and that was a routine quarterly report to the Secretary required of each of the ten CINCs. Apparently some officials wanted to send the message that Powell was engaged in some out-of-channels courtship of Cheney. Not only was he not lobbying for himself, he wasn't encouraging anyone else to push him either, though he was aware Frank Carlucci was promoting him to Cheney and to everyone all over Washington as the ideal candidate.

Powell's personal assessment was that he had lost out to Herres, who was backed by Admiral Crowe. Further, Powell assumed that Scowcroft would be uncomfortable with a former national security adviser coming in as Chairman and maybe second-guessing him. Nor was Powell sure that Cheney had the most favorable view of him. The two had worked together in 1987 and 1988 during the various congressional debates on support for the Nicaraguan contras, Cheney's pet cause. Representing the Reagan White House, Powell had concluded finally that the contras were of no military significance and had worked out a compromise with the Democrats. He suspected that Cheney thought he had not been sufficiently stalwart. For right-wingers like Cheney, the contras were a litmus test, and Powell imagined he probably had flunked.

Having closely observed or participated in the selection of dozens of people for senior military and civilian posts, including the three previous chairmen of the Joint Chiefs of Staff, Powell knew there was nothing scientific about the process. He had been at meetings in the Secretary's office or the White House when someone would mention a single fact about a candidate for a top job —perhaps his status as a "good guy," or that he had the backing of someone important—and it would transfix the group as it sailed across the table, instantly becoming the basis for his selection. Often there was nothing even approaching a talent hunt.

Since Powell had heard nothing from Cheney himself or from his numerous Washington contacts—there was not a single tom-tom sounding in the distance—he concluded it was over.

•   •   •

Even before he'd been confirmed as Secretary, Cheney had been thinking about Powell for Chairman. The new Chairman would be the fifth player in the national security team of Bush, Baker, Scowcroft and Cheney. They had to get the right person.

Cheney had twice talked at length with Frank Carlucci, the biggest Powell booster, who argued essentially that Powell was one of Washington's best problem solvers. No matter how large, small, routine or extraordinary the task, Powell was a right-hand man who delivered results, generally without ruffling feathers. For the last six years, as Weinberger's military assistant, Carlucci's deputy at the NSC and Reagan's national security adviser, he had probably not made a single major misstep. No one was more steeped in foreign policy, defense and military issues. Powell had strong views and would push for them, Carlucci said, but he knew when to follow orders and fall in line with the boss.

Carlucci also said that Powell seemed never to tire or lose his enthusiasm. He had remarkable endurance and could handle vast amounts of work.

Like nearly everyone, Cheney found Powell charming and likable. He recalled Powell's negotiations with the Democrats during the contra aid debate. Though Cheney had disagreed, he felt that Powell was carrying out President Reagan's wishes, not going off on his own. Now he wanted to find out for himself more about Powell, to make sure Powell would strengthen his hand at the White House, with the uniformed military, and in the building.

He was seeing confirmation of his belief that filling the top posts was perhaps his most important task. One of the problems in the building was the number of people at all levels who spent time trying to do someone else's job. Often, the military could be found trying to do civilian jobs, and vice versa. Cheney didn't want a chairman who would try to be Secretary. Given Powell's rather remarkable background in both Weinberger's office and the Reagan White House, the temptation might be there.

Over the summer Cheney arranged a short-notice stopover to see Powell at Fort McPherson, Georgia, the headquarters of Forces Command. One of the questions on his mind was whether Powell was susceptible to what Cheney called the "Haig Syndrome." In 1969, Army Colonel Alexander Haig had gone to work for Henry Kissinger in the White House, stayed in the political world for four years and returned to the Pentagon as a four-star general and Army vice chief of staff. Haig's rapid advancement, thanks to the patronage of Kissinger and President Nixon, had not gone down well at all in the Army or the building. Haig had worn his White House connection like a badge of honor, leaving a strong impression that the power had gone to his head.

Cheney drew an analogy to his own experience as a former White House chief of staff who became a freshman congressman. Many viewed it as a come-down, but he had never looked at it that way. He was comfortable as a freshman member, and tried to let everyone on the Hill know that he didn't miss his White House past or think he was more important because of it. He wanted to make certain Powell was similarly satisfied with his lot in life, and was not a disgruntled former presidential adviser overeager to get back inside the Beltway.

In Atlanta, Powell put on an impressive briefing that showed he was fully absorbed in the job at hand. His people seemed to love him, and he was tending to the nuts and bolts of being the Forces Command CINC—spending time with the troops, worrying about the National Guard and the Reserves. Over lunch at Powell's antebellum official residence, the two discussed the Army's future and their overall defense philosophies.

As he watched and listened, Cheney saw that Powell was feeling good to be back in the Army and had none of the post-Washington hang-ups, like unhealthy curiosity about power plays in the administration.

They didn't discuss the Chairman's job.

.   .   .

Cheney still hadn't finally settled on Powell. Mulling it over, he weighed Powell's drawbacks. One was that he was not only the junior CINC but the most junior of all the fifteen eligible four-stars. Even if Powell wasn't afflicted with Haig Syndrome, Cheney knew there would be some resistance in the military to the idea of choosing someone whose senior posts had mostly been in staff and political assignments. With this problem in mind, Cheney had looked hard at Bob Herres, the Vice Chairman, as another possible candidate. But Crowe had recommended Herres and, all other things being equal, Cheney did not like the idea of Crowe effectively naming his successor. Civilian control would be enhanced if the civilian leaders—the President and the Secretary of Defense—picked their own Chairman.

Cheney finally made his decision in favor of Powell. He did not share this with anyone until early August, when he quietly went over to the White House and talked to the President. His goal was to grease the skids and avoid a major struggle over the chairmanship within the administration. Cheney did not want Scowcroft, Baker or Sununu to come up with other names. He told Bush he'd looked at the entire pool of candidates—the CINCs, the four chiefs and the Vice Chairman. Both Herres and Powell were on the short list, he said. His own recommendation was Powell.

Bush was also high on Powell, but he wanted to be certain that the elevation of a man who six months before had only been a three-star did not offend those in the upper ranks of the military, where these seniority questions were taken very seriously. The President asked Cheney to talk to Powell specifically about that.

On the third day of the Army commanders' conference at Belmont House, Powell was in a meeting at about 2:30 p.m. when he was handed a note asking him to call Secretary Cheney. By 5 p.m., Powell, wearing casual civilian clothes, was seated in Cheney's office.

The Secretary went right to the point. You are on the short list for Chairman, he told Powell. Suggesting that he associated Powell with the two Reagan Defense secretaries, Weinberger and Carlucci, Cheney explained that it was a new regime. He was going to be a different kind of secretary. One hallmark of his Pentagon would be increased civilian control.

Powell made no argument, so Cheney popped the question: Are you interested in the job as Chairman? Is this a job you want?

Powell said he was, but added, "I do not seek the job. I'm happy where I am. If you pick someone else off the short list, I would not be upset at all. If you and the President want me, I'll do it."

Cheney ticked off what he believed were Powell's qualifications for the post: (1) you know the building; (2) you know the White House; (3) you have punched the proper tickets in the Army and have the credentials; (4) you know arms control—a topic that will be important in the coming years; (5) I know you, and worked well with you when I was in the House leadership.

The one problem was that Powell was the most junior of the eligible four-stars. Will you have problems being jumped over so many senior officers? Cheney asked directly.

Powell had the impression that the question came from the President. He replied that this was a fair question, but he thought he would have no problem dealing with the chiefs and CINCs. He knew most of them well, and had worked with them. He had carefully weighed the issue already, he said, and if he thought it were insurmountable, he would say so.

Cheney agreed, and said he wanted Powell for the job. "This will be my recommendation to the President."

Powell left the Pentagon feeling it was a done deal. Cheney wouldn't have put himself in the position of saying he was taking Powell's name to the President if there was any chance he would have to come back and say the President said no. He would have cleared the choice right up the line to the commander-in-chief before talking to him.

Cheney went back to the White House and reported Powell's answers to Bush. Bush approved his selection.

Cheney called Powell the next day, August 9, to say he had talked with the President and they both wanted Powell as Chairman. Cheney then formally offered him the job. Powell accepted.

One of Powell's first telephone calls was to Army Chief Vuono; the two had agreed previously that they would let each other know if they heard even a low-grade rumor about the debate over the next Chairman.

"You and I made a deal that I'd call you," Powell said, "and I'm calling you."

Vuono, who had been senior to Powell for the last 31 years, was now going to be the junior.

"The chiefs will support you," Vuono said, after offering his congratulations. "The only thing they want is to know what's going on. The only thing you do, if you're going to err, err on the side of keeping the chiefs too informed." He told Powell that as Chairman he would be the one to carry the chiefs' freight across the river to the White House. The chiefs would rely on him for this, Vuono said, because they did not attend the all-important NSC meetings.

Later that day, Cheney went to the Tank and informed the chiefs. Word of the Powell appointment immediately leaked out all over the building and to the news media.

Crowe called Powell in Atlanta to say congratulations. Since Powell had to come to Washington the next day for the official announcement at the White House, Crowe invited him and Alma to dinner.

The Powells arrived at Quarters 6, the Chairman's official residence, an unremarkable red brick house at Fort Myer, Virginia, at 7:30 p.m. As the couples talked about the personal details of the Chairman's life—the house, the aides, family, the protocol, the routine—Crowe looked listless, even sleepy.

But he bounced back when he started talking about his friend Marshal Akhromeyev. Now a top Gorbachev adviser, Akhromeyev had been in the United States just two weeks before to testify before the House Armed Services Committee and give some speeches. Crowe, who had accompanied his Soviet friend to Chicago, began offering Powell a few thoughts about the marshal, and the importance of having a direct line into the Soviet military.

"Oh, I've met Akhromeyev," Powell interjected, with a slight, dismissive shake of his head. Powell was determined not to treat the Soviet relationship as Crowe had—no tripping around the country with Akhromeyev. It didn't make public relations sense for the Chairman to be publicly chummy with a Soviet marshal when the Pentagon was trying to fund new strategic weapons like the Stealth bomber to meet the Soviet threat.

Crowe thought: there is not much you can tell a former national security adviser.

Later that month, Bush went to Kennebunkport, Maine, for a two-and-a-half-week vacation at his summer house on Walker's Point. While he was there, he received a friendly phone call from P. X. Kelley, the retired Commandant of the Marine Corps, who was also vacationing in the area. Bush invited Kelley over to Walker's Point for dinner and asked the former member of the Joint Chiefs how he thought Powell would be received among the upper ranks of the military, the officers who had more seniority than their new Chairman.

Kelley said that when he himself was the most junior member of the Joint Chiefs, doing his rotation as acting Chairman when the Chairman was out of town, the other chiefs would stand when he came into the Tank. "Don't worry about the Joint Chiefs," Kelley assured the President.

10

P OWELL HAD 40 DAYS before his Senate confirmation hearings. He decided he did not need to go off to the military equivalent of a nunnery to study how to handle the chairmanship. He had no secret plan for change, and he did not want to come crashing through the gate with new ideas. But he did want to look at the major operations that might have to be executed after he'd taken over.

He figured that there were several crises that might leap up and grab him with little or no warning, and he wanted to examine what military plans were on the shelf to deal with them. Plans would be his stock-in-trade in his new job. Powell knew he had an image among some senior officers as a pampered Washington general who had run only on the political fast track. They would be asking if this White House kid knew anything about the nuts and bolts of field operations.

Recognizing that Panama was a military crisis waiting to happen, he flew to Fort Bragg to examine the Panama plans. While he was there, a terrible storm hit, keeping him at Bragg for two days. Carl Stiner took advantage of the delay to brief Powell in extensive detail so he would understand that the 18th Corps was able to tailor force packages within 12 hours for just about any need that might arise in the world.

They went over the Panama PRAYER BOOK plans, including the BLUE SPOON plan for offensive operations against the PDF. Powell was surprised that it took so many days for the force buildup. Within a day or even hours, the entire landscape of a crisis could change. The plans did not take this into account. He made it clear to Stiner that the 18th Corps had to be able to move as rapidly as events. The new, lighter Army had this capability, but the existing plans did not exploit it. Things had to move much, much faster.

The plans offered no possibility of surprise, no invasion under the cover of darkness. Night-vision goggles and other technology gave U.S. forces the unmatched ability to launch a large operation at night, hitting multiple targets simultaneously. Night operations were the great advantage of the modern army. Hey, what gives? Powell asked.

He didn't see an urgent need to change the plans overnight, but he decided they ought to get working on a detailed review. They should see if it was possible to come up with a new concept that emphasized surprise, speed and the *night*.

Soon Stiner had five of his best officers down in Panama on two-month rotations, reworking the plans. He provided them with a direct satellite communications hook-up so he could talk to them and be right on top of each refinement they made.

• • •

During the latter part of August, Cheney received intelligence reports that came from an FBI source alleging that Colombian drug lord Pablo Escobar Gaviria, the multi-billionaire head of the Medellin cartel, was in Panama and was perhaps planning to move his base of operations there. Escobar, listed by *Fortune* magazine as one of the world's ten richest men, was the chieftain of the worldwide illegal narcotics industry. According to the intelligence, he apparently believed that Noriega could guarantee him more protection than he received in Colombia, where officials seemed to be getting serious about cracking down on the drug lords. Particularly good information for an area in which intelligence is usually spotty at best, thought Cheney.

The administration was due to announce a comprehensive plan

for its war on drugs and the President was going to address the nation on the subject in an evening speech on September 5. Cheney felt pressure to do something to assist with the drug problem. He could see Bush's frustration mounting.

One sign that the administration was leaning forward on drugs was a new, sweeping 29-page legal opinion from the Justice Department issued June 21, stating that the President had legal authority to direct the FBI to abduct a fugitive residing in a foreign country for violations of U.S. law. This could be done even if the arrest was contrary to customary international law, the opinion said. It overruled a 1980 Carter administration opinion that had concluded the exact opposite—that the FBI could not enforce U.S. laws abroad.

The opinion could apply to both Escobar and Noriega.

The new FBI intelligence on Escobar's whereabouts seemed like a much-needed break. Cheney asked Crowe to see if the JCS could come up with something that could be done to assist the effort to apprehend Escobar. Though the military apparently could not make such arrests, Cheney felt his forces could provide substantial assistance.

The President approved a tentative plan presented by Cheney and Attorney General Richard Thornburgh to apprehend Escobar. The first phase was to put "eyes" on the ground to conduct tactical reconnaissance of the location where Escobar was holed up according to the FBI informant. A special operations unit already in Panama could do this. It would confirm the FBI source's information, and Escobar would be quickly snatched. The military would provide intelligence, communications and protection, but FBI or Drug Enforcement Agency (DEA) agents accompanying the team would make the arrest.

Three strong arguments were presented for the operation. First, the arrest of Escobar would be a big bonanza in the drug war, making the point that there was no sanctuary—especially in Panama—for drug dealers. Second, it would scare the hell out of Noriega, who would surmise that he might be next. Third, White House speechwriters were looking for concrete examples of successes in the drug war for the President's upcoming speech, and the Escobar arrest would offer a stunning illustration.

In the end, the operation did not come off. The FBI had irregular access to its informant, who had provided only a general location where he claimed Escobar was staying. The special operations unit went searching for the house but was unable to find it. And there was also evidence that the report that Escobar was in Panama had been planted as part of an FBI sting operation against other drug traffickers.

Cheney was distressed they had not been able to provide more timely intelligence. He ordered the Joint Staff to increase its intelligence capability.

.   .   .

Because the Escobar arrest was not carried off, there was a blank space in the President's planned speech on the drug war. To fill it, Bush aides had the DEA lure a suspected drug dealer to Lafayette Park across from the White House for a crack sale on the President's doorstep. Holding up to the camera a sealed plastic evidence bag full of crack, the President told a national audience on September 5, "This is crack cocaine seized a few days ago by Drug Enforcement agents in a park just across the street from the White House. It could easily have been heroin or PCP. It's as innocent looking as candy, but it's turning our cities into battle zones, and it's murdering our children."

The Washington Post soon disclosed that the drug buy had been set up, an embarrassing revelation for the administration. All the publicity on the drugs put the spotlight once again on Noriega, an unpleasant symbol of American impotence in the face of illegal narcotics.

On his last trip to Washington before relinquishing command in Panama, Woerner had visited the State Department for a talk with Deputy Secretary Lawrence Eagleburger. The new assistant secretary for inter-American affairs, Aronson, joined the discussion and raised the possibility of a military solution in Panama.

Eagleburger, conveying the confidence of his three decades of foreign affairs experience, stated categorically, "We will NEVER invade Panama."

After a White House meeting in September, Crowe told the senior members of the Joint Staff: "I don't know when it's going to happen, I don't know what's going to precipitate it, but I am convinced that we are going to have to go in with military force into Panama to resolve the situation, and we need to be ready to do it."

. . .

On a rainy Wednesday morning, September 20, 1989, Powell went to Capitol Hill for his confirmation hearing at the Senate Armed Services Committee.

He had fixed in his mind some goals for the hearing. First, he wanted the committee to know he realized it was a changing world. Second, he wanted to say that, despite these changes, he did not want to oversee a hollowing out of the armed forces through budget cuts. Third, he didn't want to speak against Admiral Crowe. He wanted a hearing that made no news.

"Secretary Weinberger laid down certain criteria for the use of U.S. military forces abroad," Senator Nunn said to Powell toward the end of the uneventful hearing.

Powell half-smiled. He remembered well. In the spring of 1984, Powell was serving as the Secretary's military assistant when Weinberger drafted a major speech laying down six tests for use of military force. As soon as it was circulated for approval by the administration, bloody fights ensued. All the chiefs, except the Chairman, General John W. Vessey, Jr., were violently opposed. Reagan's national security adviser at the time, Robert McFarlane, stalled the speech until after the fall presidential election.

In the end, as was generally the case, Weinberger had his way. On November 28, 1984, he delivered the speech at the National Press Club. He felt it was the most important of his tenure. The tests were: (1) "The United States should not commit forces to combat overseas unless the particular engagement or occasion is deemed vital to our national interest"; (2) the commitment should only be made "with the clear intention of winning"; (3) it should be carried out with "clearly defined political and military objectives"; (4) it "must be continually reassessed and adjusted if necessary"; (5) it should "have the support of the American people and their elected representatives in Congress"; and (6) it should "be a last resort."

The speech, Powell knew, was part of Weinberger's titanic battle with Secretary of State George Shultz. State frequently pushed for military solutions to its problems, while Weinberger and the military, who actually had to carry out the use of force, were more cautious.

They were good rules, in Powell's view, but he wasn't sure they should have been publicly declared. This had the effect of chiseling them in stone, so that whenever the United States used force, somebody was going to object: wait a minute, you didn't follow one of the rules.

Nunn asked Powell, "Do you believe, as some so-called experts have said, that the Joint Chiefs under the Weinberger criteria are too reluctant and too reticent to use military forces abroad in certain contingencies?"

"My experience over the last several years," Powell answered, "is that the Joint Chiefs have been quite ready to recommend to the President the use of military force in situations." He cited the Persian Gulf escort mission, Libya and the 1983 Grenada invasion.

"So there is no hesitancy," Powell went on, "to use the armed forces as a political instrument when the mission is clear and when it is something that has been carefully thought out and considered and all the ramifications of using military forces have been considered.

"I do not sense that they go down the Weinberger checklist and say, 'Ah-ha, condition number three has not been met,'" Powell continued. "Secretary Weinberger's very famous speech and his guidelines are useful guidelines, but I have never seen them to be a series of steps each one of which must be met before the Joint Chiefs of Staff will recommend the use of military force."

The committee voted unanimously to confirm Powell. Within a day, the full Senate approved his nomination on a voice vote, a procedure reserved for the most uncontroversial questions.

11

ON SATURDAY, SEPTEMBER 30, Max Thurman took over the Southern Command from Woerner in Panama. The senior U.S. military officers and the attachés from the embassies of the other Latin American nations attended the change-of-command ceremony in Panama City. Afterwards, Thurman went right to work, receiving extensive briefings—"the dump," as he called it—on each country in his new area of responsibility. He worked a full day the next day, a Sunday. After supper, at about 9:30, he took a call from one of his assistants. The CIA station was reporting that it had received information from the wife of a fairly senior PDF officer—the name was unclear—that her husband was planning a coup against Noriega the next morning, and wanted the U.S. military to block some roads. The woman's information was vague.

"Okay," Thurman said, "you've got to break through all of that crap and get to the guts of whoever it is saying what they want to do. . . . Find out what the hell's going on."

Thurman went to his command center at the Tunnel, his secure complex in the side of a hill at Quarry Heights in Panama City. At about 2 a.m., two CIA men arrived.

"I've got bad news," one of them said. "We don't like the guy that's running it." They identified him as Major Moises Giroldi, a quiet, 38-year-old member of Noriega's PDF leadership. The CIA men had met first with his wife, then with him. As a major, one of the senior ranks in the PDF, Giroldi was in a position to carry out a successful coup. But they had discovered that he had helped Noriega crush a coup only 18 months earlier, in March 1988. Giroldi had turned in the coup participants, and Noriega had them jailed and tortured. Now this same guy was requesting U.S. military roadblocks at two key routes into Panama City, to block Noriega's troops.

Thurman suspected immediately that this was an attempt to drag him personally into some crazy sting operation, get him out front with military support, then expose him as a sucker, destroying his credibility in his first days of command.

So what is the Giroldi plan? he asked. What do the plotters plan to do with Noriega?

"They're going to talk him into retirement," one of the CIA men explained.

"Say what?" Thurman exploded.

"They're going to talk him into retirement. They hope he's not in the Comandancia when the coup gets going." Giroldi planned to seize the Comandancia, Noriega's headquarters, cutting the general off from his communications and staff, and then get in touch with him and convince him his rule was over and he ought to retire peaceably to the countryside.

"Let me see if I get this straight." Thurman said. "He's outside the Comandancia and they're going to talk to him on the telephone and ask him to retire gracefully?"

"Yes."

"It's preposterous," Thurman said. "Why wouldn't they grab him and do something with him? I've never heard of such a thing —that's cockamamie."

Just over 24 hours in command and now this. Thurman concluded he had better report to Washington. He reached General Kelly at home at 2:30 a.m. on his secure phone.

"Got a report for you," Thurman said. "There's a coup going down." He summarized what the CIA men had said, adding that the coup was scheduled for 9 a.m.—about six hours away—and that Giroldi said it was going to be announced 15 minutes in advance on the local television stations.

"What's your recommendation, sir?" asked Kelly, who had three stars to Thurman's four.

"Simple," Thurman said. "This is an ill-motivated; ill-conceived —they are going to talk this guy into retirement, hoping he's not there; ill-led—this guy doesn't know who is going to be in the coup; fatally flawed plan. I'd recommend you stay out of it. Stay out of it big time."

. . .

Powell, who had taken over the chairmanship of the JCS at midnight on October 1, without fanfare or ceremony, had spent Sunday at home waiting for his first duty day on Monday. He was asleep when Kelly called him.

"We have some indications in Panama there's going to be a coup," Kelly told his new boss.

Powell agreed to meet Kelly at the Pentagon within the hour, but first he woke up Cheney to tell him. Then he headed out into the rainy predawn to start his first day four hours early. Arriving at the National Military Command Center, the sealed-off part of the Pentagon where the Secretary, the Chairman and their top assistants often go to monitor and direct operations, he ribbed Kelly for getting him out of bed so early. They put a handful of officers on stand-by as a Crisis Action Team (CAT) to follow the situation and coordinate any use of force.

It sounds goofy, Powell said after he saw a summary on the coup. There seemed no reason for the United States to sign on. Neither Powell nor Kelly liked the idea of a snap involvement. Getting rid of Noriega was something to do on a U.S. timetable; not a half-baked coup with a half-baked coup leader, Powell said.

Because he wanted to take minimal action and not have the United States commit itself to anything foolish, the specific requests presented problems. A normal exercise could be staged by a company of several hundred U.S. troops on one of the roads the coup plotters wanted blocked. This was recommended and approved by Cheney. The second request, to secure the Bridge of the Americas, which traverses the canal into Panama City, would take U.S. forces close to Noriega's Comandancia headquarters and could not be masqueraded as a routine exercise. Powell did not recommend it.

. . .

One floor directly below Powell's office, Rear Admiral Edward D. "Ted" Sheafer was busy culling through the intelligence. Sheafer, 48, was the deputy director of the Defense Intelligence Agency for JCS support—Powell's intelligence officer. He was a longtime Navy intelligence specialist who had good lines into all the military intelligence agencies and the CIA. He used them that morning to put together an assessment for Powell. In intelligence language, Major Giroldi could easily be a "dangle" —a decoy sent out to mislead or trick—Sheafer said, adding, "Noriega might be trying to make us look like assholes." Giroldi seemed to be planning a coup against the Comandancia, not against Noriega. If it was genuine, it was based on the mistaken idea that seizing a building constituted seizing power. It was absurd, flaky, right down to the notion of retiring Noriega to the countryside with a full pension. Sheafer told his boss that the CIA was not on top of the situation.

Powell took Kelly and Sheafer up to Cheney's office. The White House was trying to set up a secure video conference with the Pentagon so President Bush could be briefed, but the equipment wasn't working properly. Scowcroft suggested that Cheney, Powell, Kelly and Sheafer should all come to the White House at 9 o'clock that morning to meet with the President.

Cheney and Powell took one car, and Kelly and Sheafer followed in a second. In the Oval Office, Powell summarized the situation: neither the leader of the coup nor the plan was reliable. He recommended the President hold off and await further information. If there is a coup, watch it develop before acting, Powell said.

The President agreed.

When the coup did not go off that day, Giroldi's wife passed word that it would start the next morning.

Cheney and Powell went through scheduled meetings with Soviet Defense Minister Dmitri Yazov, the first Soviet defense minister to visit the United States since World War II.

Before leaving the Pentagon for a dinner in honor of Yazov at Anderson House, a palatial old mansion on Massachusetts Avenue frequently used for the entertainment of foreign dignitaries, Powell spoke to Kelly. They agreed that the coup was probably just talk. Sheafer reported that they had equally fuzzy information about still another coup being hatched. Soon they were talking about Coup 1 and Coup 2.

"My guess is there won't be a coup," Kelly said.

. . .

The next morning in Panama, Thurman was up at five. At 7:40 a.m. there was shooting at the Comandancia, about a mile from Thurman's Quarry Heights headquarters. Thurman called Powell. "Allegedly, Noriega's in there but I can't attest to it because I haven't heard his voice," Thurman said. He liked to listen in himself to the electronic eavesdropping devices.

By 9 a.m., it was clear to Powell that a coup was under way, but there was still no definitive intelligence about whether Noriega was in the Comandancia. Powell phoned Cheney, who was on a bus with Yazov touring the Gettysburg Civil War battlefield in Pennsylvania, to tell him the coup had started.

Just after noon, U.S. forces in Panama blocked the road outside Fort Amador, under the guise of a routine exercise. The Panamanian Fifth Infantry based at Amador was the PDF unit closest to the Comandancia. Ten minutes later, local radio announced the coup.

At about 12:18 p.m., Thurman was notified that two Panamanian lieutenants identifying themselves as coup liaison negotiators were at the front gate of Fort Clayton. He gave approval for Major General Marc Cisneros, a two-star who headed the U.S. Southern Command's Army forces and was fluent in Spanish, to talk with them.

The lieutenants said that Noriega and his staff were inside the Comandancia under the control of the coup leaders, who were looking for an honorable way for Noriega to remain in Panama.

Cisneros said that the United States would take Noriega into custody if he was brought to Fort Clayton.

The lieutenants said they had no intention of turning anyone over to the United States. They wanted the Bridge of the Americas blocked.

Thurman got on the secure line with Powell at 1:30 p.m.

Powell had one intelligence report that Noriega was locked in a room where he had a telephone. Perhaps he was still in charge. Although the rebels did not seem to have Noriega under their full control, he had not appeared on television as he would be expected to do if he had put down the coup, so he was probably in some kind of trouble, Powell thought.

Thurman said he was not sure what was going on, either. The only thing he was sure of was that there had been shooting in the morning. For the moment, he was following standing Bush policy to avoid conflict or an escalation with Noriega or his forces. Since it was not a U.S.-sponsored coup, Thurman wondered what he could do. Could he apprehend Noriega?

"If they bring him to you," Powell said, "you can do it, but you don't have authority to go in and get him." A voluntary turnover was okay.

"Roger," Thurman said.

Powell worked out three options with Thurman:

1. If Noriega was brought to a U.S. base by the rebels, he could be accepted—"in a heartbeat," Powell said.

2. If U.S. forces could be used very discreetly and covertly to assist the rebels in bringing Noriega to a U.S. base, that too could be done on Thurman's authority. Thurman could tell the rebels, "If you need assistance to bring Noriega out [and] that will not involve a show of U.S. force, we'll do it." That would mean one or two U.S. soldiers helping, not much more.

3. If Thurman thought there was an opportunity to go get Noriega overtly with just a very small U.S. force, he could go ahead and plan that. But that would clearly be an escalation, requiring a new administration policy. This small-force option would have to be approved by President Bush. "We reserve that authority up here," Powell said. "I've got to go to the President." Powell added that communications to the White House were set up and he could get presidential permission quickly if Thurman thought it might work.

Having consulted with the lawyers at the JCS, Powell instructed Thurman to make sure that a U.S. law enforcement officer—FBI or DEA—was on hand to actually make the arrest. "I want a good bust," he said.

Though the coup held some promise at this point, Powell did not feel he should recommend that it be given any more U.S. support. At least not until Thurman came back with more information. Powell cleared all this with Cheney, who was back at the White House, still with Yazov. Cheney left the Soviet minister in an outer office while he briefed Bush, Scowcroft and Baker, and obtained presidential clearance for the options. Both Cheney and Powell now felt that it might be time to act and they wanted to make sure Thurman was ready—leaning forward, but not so far forward as to cross or fall over the policy line the President had set.

At about 2:30 p.m., Thurman passed up word that the coup had failed. It was over, Powell realized, and so were the opportunities, however inexact or fleeting they may have been. Noriega was soon on Panamanian television condemning the rebels and the United States for an attempt to "install a government of sellouts."

The White House moved quickly to distance itself from the coup, insisting that it was neither an American nor an American-sponsored operation. Press Secretary Marlin Fitzwater said that administration officials had only heard "rumbling" about the planned coup, they had not been directly informed.

"If we were, the President doesn't know about it," he said, "the Secretary of State doesn't know about it and the Secretary of Defense doesn't know about it."

Cheney arrived back at the Pentagon as employees were streaming out to fill up the parade ground overlooking the Potomac. They were gathering to witness Powell's full honor arrival, the military equivalent of an inauguration, scheduled for 3 p.m. It had turned into a fine Indian-summer day. There was a strong wind beating across the river.

The crowd cheered as Cheney escorted Powell to the reviewing stand. Inspecting the ceremonial troops, Powell stepped rapidly, and then Cheney told the assembled group that over the next four years he would spend more time with this new Chairman than with his family.

Powell appeared relaxed as he sat with his legs crossed. The only suggestion that he might have something on his mind was the folding and unfolding of his large hands. When it was his turn to speak, he described a painting hanging in a Pentagon stairwell, depicting the inside of a church. "A large church, with bright sunlight streaming through a beautiful stained-glass window. The church is empty except for a single family praying at the altar rail. The sunlight is falling on the family. There is a mother and father, and a young son and daughter, and the father is in uniform. You can sense from the painting that the family is praying together one last time before the father goes off to war.

"Every time I pass that painting a silent prayer comes to mind for all those who serve this nation in times of danger.

"Beneath the painting there is an inscription from the prophet Isaiah. The words read: 'And the Lord God asked: "Whom shall I send? Who will go for us?" And the reply came back: "Here am I, send me." ' "

Later in the speech, Powell said, "I am also very mindful today that the period we are entering may be the most historic period in the postwar era.

"President Bush and Secretary Cheney have set the proper course—to take advantage of every opportunity while exercising prudence and caution.

"And if we are successful," Powell added, "the men and women of our armed forces will pay only the price of eternal readiness, and not the tragic and precious price of life."

Marybel Batjer, Powell's former White House executive assistant, went up to him. Both her parents were ill, and over the past several weeks Powell and Armitage had taken turns touching base with her, one of them calling every day. She had heard the news about the Panama coup and she could tell that Powell was jittery.

How's it going with Cheney? she asked. She knew that Powell had had his worries about Cheney during the Iran-contra investigations. Cheney's uncritical support for Lieutenant Colonel Oliver North had bothered Powell.

Powell smiled. The coup was precisely what he and Cheney needed to break down the barriers, he told her. "The bonding process is working," he said. "There is nothing like a crisis for good bonding."

• • •

Pete Williams spent lots of time in Cheney's office that day as Powell, usually accompanied by his operations chief Kelly and his intelligence chief Sheafer, came in repeatedly to provide new information and updates for the Secretary. Williams was struck by how on-point Powell's summaries were. If a stranger had come into the room and been told that one person there was new to his job, he would never guess it was Powell. The new Chairman was utterly confident. He absolutely filled the room. There was a quality about him that announced, "Hi, get the hell out of the way,

I'm Chairman." Williams noted that Powell was working hard to control all the information flowing to Cheney.

"Do you have a dropline to me?" he asked Williams after one of these sessions, as the two walked down the corridor. A dropline is an automatic telephone link allowing two people to reach each other instantly; the push of a single button on one telephone console triggers a ring and light on the other end.

"No, sir." Although for protocol purposes Williams had the rank of a four-star, he liked to show respect when he addressed the Chairman. He had not had a direct line to Crowe and would never have thought of requesting one.

"I'll take care of it," said Powell.

. . .

Over the next two days, Wednesday and Thursday, both Republicans and Democrats in Congress attacked the administration for failing to exploit the coup attempt. Democratic Representative Les Aspin said, "We ought to be ready at any opportunity to use the confusion and the uncertainty of a coup attempt . . . to do something about Mr. Noriega."

Senator Jesse Helms, the North Carolina Republican and one of the Congress's chief anti-Noriega crusaders, called the administration a bunch of "Keystone Kops," and said, "After this, no member of the Panamanian Defense Forces can be expected to act against Noriega." On Thursday, Helms took to the Senate floor and delivered a speech in which he claimed, based on his own sources, that the coup leaders had offered to turn Noriega over but that the United States had declined.

"Occasionally," said Sam Nunn, "we have to foresee our policy of encouraging a coup might succeed, and we ought to be prepared."

Congressman Dave McCurdy, a moderate Oklahoma Democrat, said, "Yesterday makes Jimmy Carter look like a man of resolve. There's a resurgence of the wimp factor."

Editorials compared the incident to Carter's Iran hostage rescue mission and President Kennedy's fiasco at the Bay of Pigs.

George Will's column in The Washington Post, critical of Bush's handling of the coup attempt, was headlined "An Unserious Presidency."

At a White House meeting at the end of the week, deputy national security adviser Robert Gates gave a spirited defense of the CIA, and the intelligence on the coup. Because it had not been a U.S.-controlled and -sponsored attempt, there had been no way at the time to know whether Noriega was in custody. It was known only now that the rebels had had Noriega for at least two hours.

The missed opportunity prompted a reconsideration of the administration's objectives in Panama. Was the goal to overthrow Noriega? Was it to arrest him and bring him back to the United States for trial? To help establish a new government?

It was pretty clear that Bush's hard-line anti-Noriega rhetoric was not matched by specific plans or contingencies, either by the CIA or the military, Powell realized.

John Sununu was very agitated. This was a coordination issue—his primary task as White House chief of staff—and there had not been much to coordinate. He put his spurs into people very hard.

"Amateur hour is over," Bush declared. He told the National Security Council that Noriega would overstep some day and he wanted them to be ready. Nothing should be left to chance. "I want some follow-through planning," the President said.

. . .

On the afternoon of Friday, October 6, Bush went into Walter Reed Army Medical Center for removal of a benign cyst from one of his fingers. After the operation, a reporter asked, "Sir, how about Panama? Simply put, a lot of critics say you blew it."

"Well," Bush said, "what people—some people seemed to have wanted me to do is to unleash the full military and go in and, quote, get Noriega. I think that's what—the charge by those who are—feel as frustrated as I do about the results. But I think that's the allegation. So you say, What could a commander-in-chief have done? I suppose you could have gone to general quarters. But that's not prudent and that's not the way I plan to conduct the military or foreign affairs of this country."

Asked if he would use military force to help, Bush said, "I would not rule out any option. Any option. But you have to look at the facts at the time. And you've got to keep in mind the lives of American citizens, lives of your own troops, and what you're trying to do. But I wouldn't—certainly wouldn't rule that out."

At a morning news conference on October 13, Bush faced still more questions on Panama.

"I wouldn't mind using force if it could be done in a prudent manner," Bush said. "So, in other words, I'm not ruling out the use of force for all time."

He also said, "I have at stake the lives of American kids, and I am not going to easily thrust them into a battle unless I feel comfortable with it and unless those general officers in whom I have total confidence feel comfortable."

In answer to the question, "Has anybody been fired lately?" Bush replied: "No, and they're not going to be over this because they all did a good job—a good job. . . . And I haven't lost any confidence in our top people that are handling these matters, including—and I want to repeat it here—our military officers in Panama. None at all. And certainly not General Powell."

Powell, who followed every presidential statement closely, could have done without the "I-haven't-lost-any-confidence" endorsement. He knew well that such a sentiment was articulated when it was in question. "My God, what has happened to this town?" he thought to himself. He had seen emotional foreign-policy battles before, but never piling on of this intensity, and across the whole political spectrum. It was as if there was a lynch mob out there. He had been away from Washington only six months, but something had changed.

He thought he saw several reasons for the frenzy. First, it had been a slow news week. "Newsies," as Powell called them, abhorred a vacuum and always found something to fill it. Second, whenever there was a simple contradiction between rhetoric—as in Bush's earlier statement, "They ought to just do everything they can to get Mr. Noriega out of there"—and action, reporters jumped hard. Third, frustration with Noriega was at a fever pitch. Fourth and most important, perhaps, was the question of presidential image—lingering doubts about Bush as wimp. Nine months into his presidency, Bush still had not defined himself, and this failure left open a basic question: was the essential Bush indecisive and hesitant?

Powell felt that this was the wrong case on which to judge the Bush presidency. With some passion, he told the President that "there was no there there"—the rebels had not been sufficiently determined and they had had no real plan. U.S. participation would probably only have made it worse.

An old friend of Powell's, retired Colonel Harry G. Summers, Jr., who once had held the General Douglas MacArthur Chair at the Army War College, wrote a syndicated newspaper column on the episode. Under the headline, "Panama Coup Bumbling Is the Least of Our Worries," Powell read: "Last week, whether we realized or not, we had a glimpse into the abyss. Our national security decision-making process, the very heart and soul of our national defenses, was revealed to be in chaos. It was a frightening revelation. . . .

"If our national leaders bungled so badly on a minor crisis like Panama, what would they do in the face of a major threat? Would they still be shuffling papers and staffing options while enemy missiles were inbound?"

Summers named Baker, Cheney and Powell as the new "best and the brightest" and "veterans of crisis management at the highest levels. Yet they failed." He attributed this to the committee approach to command decision making—"a very bad case of arteriosclerosis at the very top—a potentially fatal clogging of the military command and control."

The columnist suggested that the President, the commander-in-chief, deal directly with the military as President Roosevelt had done in World War II.

Powell did not feel that was possible. Committee decision making, taking into account the perspectives of all the departments and agencies, was here to stay. But he did agree more could be done on the military end to make sure that the communications link from himself as Chairman to the CINCs and other combat commanders was more straightforward.

Cheney and Powell got together for one final scrub. They asked, if this *had* been the right moment, the right coup, one the United States could and should have supported, would they have been ready? The answer, unfortunately, was no.

If things were so bad that officers like Giroldi, a former close Noriega ally, had been willing to try to overthrow him, Cheney thought, others would try again. It was time to go back to the drawing board.

·   ·   ·

In Panama City, Thurman put his feet up, looked out his window, and identified a first step. If there was going to be a major fracas with Noriega, he had to get the U.S. dependents out of Panama. So he began issuing a series of requests to Washington for authorization to send the dependents home to the United States or to move them onto U.S. military bases in Panama.

He was summoned to testify at closed-door sessions of the Senate and House Armed Services Committees. After ten years of such appearances, Thurman felt confident about testifying; he'd learned the importance of doing his homework and dropping new tidbits to the legislators. In separate sessions of three hours each, he was faced essentially with a single question: Did we miss a golden opportunity? His answer was no. He presented the information that was available at the time of the coup, and the details from the after-action interrogation reports of those who had been eyewitnesses at the Comandancia. By stitching this together in a blow-by-blow narrative, he was able to show that at the time the coup liaisons were talking to General Cisneros, the coup was over inside the Comandancia.

"I'm going back to Panama and get me a good contingency plan," Thurman told the senators.

Thurman had read the papers. It was clear that nobody—not President Bush, Cheney, Powell nor he himself—could withstand another failure, or perceived failure.

Twenty-two years earlier, Major Max Thurman had spent a year at the Army Command and General Staff College at Fort Leavenworth. One of the lessons he learned there was that an officer had two jobs: first, to obey the explicit orders of his superiors; and second, to understand the implicit tasks that were part of those orders and make sure they too were accomplished. The higher up you went, the more implicit tasks you encountered.

The implicit task in Panama was simple: If it ever happens again, you better be ready. The "it" was not only a coup attempt, Thurman calculated, but anything that might suggest that George Bush, Max Thurman and everyone in between was not on top of things.

Thurman went to see Powell.

Is the planning on track with a new intensity? Powell asked.

A new intensity, Thurman promised. He was six years older than Powell, and until two weeks earlier had been senior to him. Thurman knew the rules and he was respectful, but it had been a long time since someone had ordered him around.

"You polishing up your plans and all?" the Chairman asked.

"Sure," Thurman said, "that's what we are doing. We get paid for doing that. We're busy at it. When I get it done, I'll report to you."

12

THURMAN ORDERED the more than 13,000 men and women under his command to wear their combat jungle fatigues with the irregular brown and green camouflage patterns every day. He had the soft-drink machines near the command's intelligence offices removed, so officers would no longer congregate there, making themselves targets for PDF spying. He intensified the major Category Three and Four exercises, sending anywhere from 150 to 500 men out on maneuvers around Panama in boats, helicopters, tanks, amphibious vehicles and aircraft. At least one helicopter exercise ran every night. These exercises were designed to appear random, but many involved actual targets that might be hit if offensive operations were ever ordered against the PDF.

One night during the week after the failed coup, Lieutenant General Stiner arrived at Howard Air Force Base in Panama aboard a C-20 airplane. He and his key planners and commanders were all wearing civilian clothes so they might slip in unbeknownst to the PDF.

Thurman met with Stiner and said that he wanted them to refine the BLUE SPOON contingency plan down to the finest details—"to a cat's eye," Thurman said.

Yes, sir, Stiner replied.

Then you and the 18th Corps will rehearse it every two months.

Yes, sir.

Every two months for the next ten years. "I won't be here but somebody will," Thurman added.

On October 11, Thurman's request for an additional deployment of military police was approved. Soon 24-hour-a-day police patrols were set up along some sensitive routes. Thurman ordered his helicopters to fly exercises to the headquarters of the PDF's Battalion 2000, an 800-man force considered Noriega's most potent and lethal, based at Fort Cimarron east of Panama City.

. . .

Powell was already intimately familiar with the PDF leadership. As Reagan's national security adviser, he had spent long hours examining the intelligence files of PDF officers, looking for alternatives to Noriega. He'd concluded that there was no one. The top 10 or 20 officers were committed to personal power and wealth. There was no way the U.S. could support these thugs. In Powell's view, only Colonel Eduardo Herrera Hassan, the former Panamanian ambassador to Israel, was a decent possibility; but he had been tainted, in the eyes of some Panamanians, by his involvement in several 1988 CIA coup plans that never got off the ground.

General Kelly's assessment of the PDF was even harsher. He felt there was sufficient intelligence to conclude that all the top leaders were murderers or torturers.

Powell was not sure they were all that bad, but with the prestige of President Bush and the United States on the line, how could the military risk participating, even indirectly or by implication, in the installation of another power-hungry self-seeker?

It couldn't, Powell concluded. He decided there was only one answer: the BLUE SPOON plan had to be made more ambitious. Any offensive operation against the PDF must be total; it must capture or drive out the entire leadership. Then legitimate civilian political leaders could take charge.

Powell issued a guidance to Thurman directing that the CINC-SOUTH be ready to respond to a contingency in Panama on two hours' notice with the forces already in place there. And for a full offensive operation against the PDF, the BLUE SPOON plan would have to be radically changed: Thurman would be given only 48 hours to mobilize for a large-scale attack—not the previous mobilization time of five days.

· · ·

During the week after the coup, Powell had ordered Kelly and Sheafer to set up a small, secret planning cell in the Pentagon, consisting of officers from Kelly's J-3 operations staff and Sheafer's J-2 intelligence staff. This cell was to work closely with Thurman and Stiner and their people to make sure that every detail was shared and coordinated.

Traditionally, operations and intelligence worked separately. Powell now wanted them in each other's back pockets. One key to a lightning offensive operation was making sure the U.S. forces knew everything possible about what they were attacking, as well as how they were going to attack, down to which squad would go through which door in which building. The planners were to make sure that each individual target folder—intelligence, maps, drawings, pictures, and all the specifics on the U.S. units assigned to hit that target—was up to date and briefed to those who needed to know. There would be more than two dozen targets.

· · ·

On Saturday, October 14, Carl Stiner went to the Ball Camp Baptist Church in Knoxville, Tennessee, for his daughter's wedding. During the reception afterwards, he was pulled away to take a call from the Pentagon. Stiner was to fly to Washington the next morning to give the Chairman an off-line briefing on progress to date on revising BLUE SPOON.

Stiner arrived at the National Military Command Center at the Pentagon, accompanied by Major General Gary Luck, 52, a short, gray-haired Army aviator and paratrooper. Luck was the commanding general of the Joint Special Operations Command (JSOC).

Stiner told Powell that substantial modifications in the BLUE SPOON plan were in the works. First, the conventional forces and the special operations forces were to be integrated under one commander—Stiner himself. He would give his orders directly to the various service commanders, including General Luck, whose special operations forces would be assigned to the most threatening PDF strongholds. These included the Comandancia, Battalion 2000 at Fort Cimarron, and the Modelo Prison, where CIA agent Kurt Muse was being held.

If he got the full 48 hours' notice, Stiner planned to bring in perhaps 11,000 additional troops to Panama to supplement the 13,000 at the Southern Command. He felt it was important to go with the full force, which would allow him to strike simultaneously the targets his planners had identified. Simultaneity should minimize casualties, fully engage all PDF units, and ensure that the PDF leadership was dislodged. Stiner said he didn't think there would be many fighters in the PDF—he planned to use special teams for psychological operations to frighten PDF troops and officers and encourage them to surrender.

The plan was set to be executed at night, Stiner said, and his instructions from Thurman were to rehearse so much that the Panamanians would grow numb watching ground and air exercises.

Powell asked what would happen if there was another coup attempt and the President decided he wanted to support it. He needed to be able to tell the Secretary and the President that the military had forces and a plan to receive Noriega from hypothetical coup leaders, or to abduct him.

The troops deployed during NIMROD DANCER in May could provide the short-notice force, Stiner said, and there were some special operations people on the ground in Panama who could respond to presidential orders. But Stiner emphasized that the in-country troops would not be enough to do all that was required. My recommendation, Stiner told Powell again, would be to go with the total BLUE SPOON plan.

Powell agreed.

. . .

The next day, October 16, Powell had Major General Luck into his office at 10 a.m. for two 30-minute dress rehearsal briefings. Five hours later, Powell and Luck presented themselves at the Oval Office with Cheney for presentations to President Bush on two top-secret special operations plans.

Cheney started the briefings by saying that he wanted the Pres-

ident to be aware of the special capability that could be in Panama
nine hours after he ordered its deployment: four hours to assem-
ble, and five hours to travel by plane.

The first special operations contingency plan was code-named
GABEL ADDER. Luck outlined how he could go to Panama, or
anywhere in the world for that matter, with a force of about 300
that could be used to rescue Americans or any other hostages. The
team could also be used to abduct one of the drug lords or Noriega
himself. Its specialty was forced entry into anything from a hostile
country to a barricaded building where hostages were located.

The team included:

• A Delta squadron capable of overt or covert strikes during
the day or night. All of it could be used at once, and smaller
portions could also be deployed.

• A package of 16 helicopters, code-named SILVER BULLET.

• Elements from SEAL Team 6 for any underwater work or
beach landing.

• Special intelligence teams to provide support for the operators. For example, one team of three listeners, code-named ROBIN
QUART, traveled with sophisticated equipment that could be used
to tap telephones without cutting into the wires, or to eavesdrop
on conversations from a distance without having to plant bugs.

• A medical unit, a communications unit and a command and
control staff.

In the second half hour, Luck presented the ACID GAMBIT contingency plan that could be used to extract Muse from Modelo
Prison.

A month before, Bush had received a personal plea for help
from Muse, in a letter smuggled out in a book. Powell was all too
aware of the impact American hostages had on presidents. Over-
reaction to the plight of Americans held captive abroad had become a pattern. Powell's approach to the hostage situations was
to try to keep the response measured, and if possible, presidential
emotions in check. But it was difficult. The CIA had created immense pressure for the military to develop a rescue plan, and Bush
had made it clear that he would order a rescue if there was clear
evidence that Muse's life was in danger.

Luck showed aerial photos of the prison and the route a helicopter assault would take. He presented a detailed scale model of the prison in a box that flopped open, showing the downtown neighborhood in which the prison was located, the terrain, and the prison itself, including guard posts, entrances, exits and the exact location of Muse's 8-by-12-foot, second-floor cell. Muse had been held in solitary confinement there for six months now.

Luck gave a minute-by-minute, at times a second-by-second description of how Delta forces would make the synchronized assault and proceed to Muse's cell by stunning the guards, perhaps not even killing any of them. Muse would be free and safely aboard a helicopter in nine minutes.

Cheney was not recommending an execution of ACID GAMBIT. The briefing was to demonstrate capability, and show that the Pentagon had responded to the requests for a plan from the President and the CIA. Cheney knew that Bush was under pressure on the Muse issue from CIA Director William Webster, who in turn was under pressure from covert-operations specialists. And the President was sympathetic, Cheney knew, to the CIA's desire to avoid at all costs a repeat of the murder of Beirut station chief William Buckley. Like Powell, Cheney was sure that Bush would order a rescue if Muse was in jeopardy.

Nonetheless, Cheney had been working hard for months to dampen any enthusiasm for execution of ACID GAMBIT. The first reason was that Muse was not in any great danger, and was being fed and treated well. Second, a rescue would put everyone else in Panama on notice that the United States possessed this quick-snatch capability and was willing to use it. Cheney thought that there were more valuable targets—the drug lords or Noriega himself—for a snatch. To blow the capability just on Muse would not be wise.

In addition, Cheney believed that a high-profile rescue at the prison, right across from Noriega's headquarters, would be a very direct affront to the PDF. As Cheney's lawyers had warned him, there would be unforeseeable consequences from a decision to violate the sovereignty of another nation in order to release a single person under arrest for violating the local laws. A war could start over one man. If the sole concern of the U.S. government was Muse, a rescue would be reasonable. But there were thousands of other Americans in Panama, and any one or any group of them could become hostages or prisoners.

· · ·

Some of the special operations forces dispatched to Panama in the spring had been sent back to the United States. Now Max Thurman wanted more. If he had to snatch Noriega or rescue Kurt Muse or some hostages on short notice, he needed the capability on the ground in Panama, not standing by at Fort Bragg waiting to be dispatched. By Friday, October 20, Thurman had requested and Powell had approved a secret deployment of a special operations team to Panama with Major General Luck commanding. Powell carried the deployment order up to Cheney, whose approval was required for *any* new deployment of troops anywhere in the world.

The reasons given for the deployment were: normal, prudent preparation for more Category Three and Four exercises; response to increased tensions; and enhanced capability to respond to emergencies. In addition, the exercises carried out by these forces, and others already in Panama, were superb rehearsals for actual operations.

Cheney was impressed by the contrast between Thurman and his predecessor, Woerner, who hadn't wanted more forces.

Without argument, Cheney signed the orders for the special deployment, code-named NIFTY PACKAGE, and consisting of: a Delta squadron, the SILVER BULLET package of 16 helicopters, and the three ROBIN QUART signals intelligence listeners, plus Luck and his staff of specialists. The only major difference between this deployment and the forces called for in Luck's GABEL ADDER rescue/abduction plan was that no SEAL Team 6 unit was included in NIFTY PACKAGE.

Delighted to receive the extra forces, Thurman sent them on a series of intense, high-adventure night exercises that only resulted in some dented helicopters.

· · ·

Army Chief of Staff Vuono worked to keep his hand directly in the Panama planning. He summoned Stiner and Luck, two of his own generals, up to Washington on October 27 for a full, private briefing on the changes that were being made to BLUE SPOON.

"This is a goddamn sophisticated plan here," Vuono said after hearing the outline. At the outset, more than 350 planes and helicopters would be flying close together in the airspace above Panama. He urged Stiner and Luck to make sure they were coordinated. "You've got to do as much rehearsal on something like this as you possibly can."

Yes, sir, Stiner replied. He was spending about one third of his time on planning and rehearsing for Panama.

To operate that many aircraft in such a small area at night, it was necessary to equip every pilot, co-pilot and aircraft crew member with super-sensitive night-vision goggles that would allow them to see almost as if it were day. With the goggles, they would be able to distinguish friendly U.S. troops from Panamanian forces, and avoid power lines, towers and other obstacles. To assist those wearing the goggles, there would be AC-130 gunship airplanes equipped with giant infrared searchlights. Circling quietly high above the ground, each could illuminate an area the size of several football fields.

"We'll own the night," Stiner told Vuono.

. . .

On Monday, October 30, Thurman signed a quarter-inch-thick document designated Commander in Chief Southern Command Operations Order 1-90 (BLUE SPOON). The plan was built around three principles—maximum surprise, minimum collateral damage (damage to nonmilitary targets) and minimum force.

That Wednesday, at 2 p.m., General Kelly and his J-3 planners went to Powell's office and gave the Chairman a detailed BLUE SPOON briefing. It was Powell's 30th day as Chairman.

Two days later, on Friday, November 3, Thurman, Stiner and Luck gave the BLUE SPOON briefing to the chiefs in the Tank, explaining how a light division-size force of about 11,000 additional troops could be brought to Panama quickly to help eliminate Noriega and his PDF. Luck said that since the ACID GAMBIT plan to rescue Kurt Muse was apparently not going to be carried out independently, he was going to incorporate it into the BLUE SPOON plan. If BLUE SPOON were executed, Luck explained, Muse would be in danger; accordingly, his rescue would have to be accomplished at the very instant of any offensive operations.

Also on November 3, the Justice Department issued a 28-page memorandum to Scowcroft which went well beyond the earlier ruling that the FBI could make arrests abroad. This new memo concluded that the Posse Comitatus Act, prohibiting the use of the military to make arrests in the United States, does not apply abroad. Thus the military could be used to arrest drug traffickers and fugitives overseas. The memo stated that such an interpretation "is necessary to enable certain criminal laws to be executed and to avoid unwarranted restraints on the President's constitutional powers."

An intelligence directive from the President also was issued around this time, authorizing the CIA to spend up to $3 million on a covert plan to recruit Panamanian military officers and exiles to topple Noriega. In effect, the CIA and the Pentagon were in competition to see who could first rid Bush of the Noriega problem.

The next week, Powell took the J-3 briefers up to Cheney to outline BLUE SPOON.

One of the targets was Rio Hato, a base 75 miles southwest of Panama City where Noriega's fierce, Cuban-trained *Macho de Monte* forces, which had put down the October coup attempt, were located. The plan called for the Air Force's new F-117A Stealth fighters to drop 2,000-pound bombs around the barracks, stunning and disorienting the PDF troops inside. Never before used in battle, the highly touted planes cost more than $100 million each. Employing the latest technological and design know-how, they were built to be virtually invisible to enemy radar and had ultra-precise targeting capabilities.

"Come on, guys," Cheney chuckled. "The Stealth—you're going to use the Stealth?" Cheney was mindful of the criticisms of the 1983 Grenada operation, when each of the services had done its best to get a piece of the action; the Stealth could be a high-profile bid by the Air Force for a bigger role in BLUE SPOON. "Why the hell do you want to use the 117?" Cheney asked sharply. "The last time I checked there was no serious air defense threat."

Stiner had requested it, Powell and the J-3 officers explained, because the F-117A would provide the best, most accurate night-time bombing capability. It had the most advanced laser guidance system, which allowed the pilot to direct his bombs to their precise targets with nearly perfect, pinpoint accuracy.

The F-117A was also going to be used to bomb one of Noriega's hangouts east of Panama City.

Cheney questioned them closely on this. If it ever came to execution, he asked, wouldn't they at least know whether Noriega was on the eastern or western side of Panama? And if he wasn't in the eastern part, then they wouldn't need to hit the target, would they?

That target was later dropped from the list.

.   .   .

Thurman and Stiner wanted still more forces prepositioned in Panama. The failed coup had pointed up the fact that with in-place forces only, the United States had no ready way to attack the Comandancia with heavy fire, and no way to prevent Noriega's Battalion 2000 from marching down ten miles from Fort Cimarron to rescue him at the Comandancia. In early November, Stiner requested a force package including:

• Four Sheridan tanks.
• An Airborne Armored platoon.
• Six versatile and powerful AH-64 Apache helicopters, which resembled flying spiders and had precision night-flying capability. Designed as a tank-killer, the Apache was heavily armed with Hellfire missiles, rockets and turreted 30mm chain guns (which use munitions that are fed in machine-gun style).
• Three OH-58 scout helicopters.

Thurman and Powell approved the request, and on November 7 Cheney signed the deployment order, which was given the code name ELOQUENT BANQUET.

.   .   .

Thurman was haunted by the criticism of the 1983 Grenada invasion, when communications had been so badly arranged that units could not talk with each other. The equipment, frequencies and procedures of each of the services had not matched, and there was no overall, joint communications plan. Now he personally examined the communications manuals, plans and orders in BLUE SPOON. The Communications-Electronic Operating Instructions (CEOI) made a stack three feet high.

"We're not going to repeat any of that bullshit, so get it down," Thurman ordered his planners, insisting on regular updates throughout the month. He wanted to be sure that the Air Force tankers, transports, and tactical aircraft were fully integrated for communication with the Army and the special operations units. When he was finished, he had examined and personally checked each page, and the CEOI was reduced to an inch-thick document.

Thurman also approved a plan to reduce the number of dependents in Panama to 500 families. Beginning November 16, all other dependents were to be shipped back to the United States.

. . .

During the week of November 20, Thanksgiving week, Stiner and a team of his planners flew down to Panama to check on the training and exercises. Once more they arrived at night wearing civilian clothes. Stiner wanted a detailed "backbrief"—an account of actions already taken—from every one of the U.S. commanders, covering what had happened each day since his last visit; no overall summaries would do. He listened patiently; no detail seemed to bore him. He was not satisfied with the aviation plan for night operations, a key part of BLUE SPOON.

Hoping to be back home at Fort Bragg for Thanksgiving dinner, Stiner had not even brought a uniform. But soon after he arrived, the U.S. Embassy in Panama City reported that a man had walked in at night claiming that by day he was working for the Medellin drug cartel. He said the cartel was fed up with U.S. support to the drug war in Colombia, where the cartel was getting hammered very badly, and was going to retaliate. His information was very precise: the cartel was in the process of planting or sending ten car bombs into U.S. installations. The bombs would be aimed at a full range of targets—officers, troops and dependents.

One target, the informant said, was the Gorgas U.S. Army Hospital, which was near Thurman's Quarry Heights headquarters. Partly perched on stilts alongside a mountain, with a parking lot underneath, the hospital was vulnerable. A single car bomb could cause havoc.

The walk-in source was given a polygraph test to determine if he was telling the truth. The results were ambiguous. A second test was administered and he passed.

When Thurman received the information in his headquarters, he called Stiner.

"Look," Thurman said, "what we're going to do is we're going to be ready now."

Yes, sir.

"You're stood up, my friend," Thurman said, meaning he was activating Stiner's Joint Task Force that instant, "so start operating." Stiner was now the warfighting commander of all the forces. If something happened and Washington ordered a military response, Stiner would be postured to provide it.

"You're in charge of everything," Thurman said.

Yes, sir.

"There's a single American killed," Thurman said, "we're going to blow him away. Mr. Noriega's going to go away."

Yes, sir.

Thurman sent off a message to Powell informing him of the emergency activation of the JTF.

Powell was not happy. Activation of a Joint Task Force was a decision for Cheney and Powell himself. Thurman commanded his troops in Panama and the rest of the Southern Command, but nowhere else. He could not unilaterally stand up Stiner, who was under the authority of Forces Command in the United States.

Powell called Thurman on the secure line.

"Very thoughtful," Powell said sarcastically. "Why don't you ask next time? And let me make the decision up here."

Faced with the threat of multiple car bombs, activation of the task force was obvious, Thurman felt. After the failed coup, after all the press criticism, after all the congressional second-guessing just seven weeks before, the President would have to respond militarily if there was a bombing. What choice would he have?

"Listen, my friend," Thurman told Powell, "if a bomb blows up down here, that is a trigger event."

Powell said probably so, but it would be for the President and Secretary of Defense to decide.

"If a goddamn bomb goes off," Thurman said, "we have ourselves a major problem, and particularly if Americans get killed."

While it was nice to have an aggressive commander, Powell thought, he would have to keep very close tabs on Thurman.

Powell reported to Cheney. The Secretary was worried about another Beirut-like car bombing killing dozens or hundreds. With 13,000 troops in Panama, a permanent presence—all there to protect U.S. interests—there was much more at stake. How could you not take seriously a report of car bombs in Panama sponsored by the Medellin cartel, Cheney wondered. Yeah, Max was acting aggressive, but that's probably what they needed, Cheney concluded. He decided to back Thurman fully. The Joint Task Force could continue to operate.

Thurman placed U.S. forces on maximum alert for a terrorist threat. The bases were virtually sealed. Everyone and everything coming through all the gates was subjected to what he called "rather fulsome inspections."

Thurman also put in a request for nearly all the dog teams in the U.S. military that had been trained in bomb detection. He got most of them. Criminal Investigation Division agents and physical security experts were also sent to Southern Command. Cheney approved these security deployments that week under the codename POLE TAX.

Stiner took command of all this security. "Shit," he said, trying to carry out Thurman's request for dogs to be sent down, "it doesn't have to be a trained dog. It can be any kind of dog." He had all the communications channels checked, set up more intelligence gathering and intensified night rehearsals.

At the Gorgas Army Hospital, U.S. forces conducted rigorous car inspections. Members of Noriega's Dignity Battalions turned out to protest, claiming that people were being obstructed from going to work. There was a big pushing and shoving match, but no shots were fired. U.S. troops had to be sent in to get the Dignity Battalions to leave.

Meanwhile, Powell and others began to wonder about the source who had appeared at the U.S. Embassy with these car-bomb claims. Powell began applying one of his favorite epithets, "goofy," to the whole situation. All week, night after night, the man had come to the embassy, insisting that he'd been in the cartel's inner councils all day. Powell concluded that if it were true, the cartel would not let him run off into the night like that. It made no sense. The intelligence capability of the entire U.S. military had been cranked up and there was not the slightest confirmation of the things he was saying.

The source was "boxed" on the polygraph a third time and he flunked gloriously. All the agencies and departments involved concluded that either he had just been lying or it was an elaborate sting to confuse or scare the United States.

At the end of November, after consulting with Powell, Thurman dissolved the Joint Task Force and sent Stiner home.

. . .

The individual unit rehearsals under BLUE SPOON were going well, but Thurman decided that during December he would conduct a Joint Readiness Exercise which would amount to a full rehearsal of the plan. Special operations forces, the in-country forces and some other units could rehearse in Panama, but most of the reinforcement units would rehearse in the United States.

In addition, night-readiness exercises were conducted at regular intervals in Panama, a practice that Thurman felt would help mask any large force movement if an actual operation were ever to take place.

The Muse rescue plan, ACID GAMBIT, was played out on an isolated Florida key, using a mock-up three quarters the size of the Modelo Prison.

. . .

Back in Washington, General Kelly pondered the radical transformation of the Southern Command that had taken place over just two months. The departed General Woerner had seemed unable to imagine the use of military force in Panama. Maxwell Thurman seemed to see a war coming.

13

LATE IN THE DAY ON THURSDAY, November 30, reliable reports came into the Pentagon that a 1,000-man rebel force had seized two air bases in the Philippines. Powell, who'd spent much of the day in budget sessions with the chiefs and the CINCs, was alarmed. There were constant rumors that someone was plotting a coup to end Philippine President Corazon Aquino's shaky three-and-a-half-year rule, but now the rebels had aircraft.

Powell went up to Cheney's office with maps and intelligence reports. The situation was murky, he told the Secretary. After reviewing the latest information, Powell went home for dinner.

Meanwhile, an interagency deputies' committee meeting had begun at the White House, with Powell's Vice Chairman, General Robert Herres, representing the JCS. The deputies continued to monitor the crisis as the evening wore on, breaking up their White House session but reconvening later by secure video hook-up. At one point, a request came in from the Filipino defense minister for U.S intervention.

Herres said that U.S. bases in the Philippines should not be used to intervene in civil strife, and Robert Gates, Scowcroft's deputy, was also reluctant about U.S. military involvement.

Shortly after 11 p.m., Powell returned to the Pentagon to take part in a formal NSC meeting, also to be conducted by video. Vice President Dan Quayle was going to chair the NSC because the President, accompanied by Baker and Scowcroft, was airborne on the way to Malta for a summit meeting with Gorbachev.

As reports of rebel bombing started coming in, Powell took his seat in the Crisis Situation Room at the Pentagon's National Military Command Center. Herres sat at his right. The CINC responsible for the Philippines and the rest of the Pacific region, Admiral Huntington Hardisty, in town for the budget discussions, was at Powell's left.

Cheney, at home with a flu he had picked up on a long trip to Europe, was not participating in the video conference, but a phone link from the command center to his home was set up so Powell could keep him informed.

Over in the White House Situation Room, Quayle was at the head of the table. Robert Gates sat to Quayle's right, and the Vice President's chief of staff, William Kristol, was to the left. The large video screen in front of them was broken up into sections, one each for Powell; a CIA representative; a Justice Department lawyer; Henry S. Rowen, the assistant secretary of defense for international security affairs; and the State Department representative, Deputy Secretary Lawrence Eagleburger.

"Look, we have no choice," Eagleburger said. "We have to go in, in some form. This is a democratic government that we have sponsored. There really should be no debate. There can be no debate." Eagleburger proposed that the Defense Department should figure out *how* to intervene, but there was no question something had to be done.

After about a half hour of discussion no one had seriously challenged Eagleburger's central point. Given the major role the United States had played in ousting the dictator Ferdinand Marcos, it had an obligation to stand behind the Aquino regime.

The crisis seemed to be growing more serious. Powell received reports that Aquino's presidential palace in Manila was being bombed and strafed. These were followed quickly by requests from the Philippine government that U.S. Air Force F-4s stationed at the nearby Clark Air Force Base bomb the two captured airfields, which the rebels were using to launch the attacks against the palace. The requests were accompanied by claims that intervention was required at once, and that it could tip the balance and save Aquino. Soon another request arrived, this one that the United States bomb a munitions depot that the rebels were apparently using.

Powell was concerned that the requests lacked precision and crispness. They were all coming to the Pentagon secondhand through the U.S. ambassador in Manila, Nicholas Platt, attributed to Mrs. Aquino or her Defense Secretary, Fidel Ramos. Powell smelled panic on the Philippine end.

At around midnight, Quayle received confirmation from Ambassador Platt that the request for intervention was coming directly from Aquino.

Quayle said they had to give President Bush a recommendation, and indicated that he thought Mrs. Aquino's request was legitimate and that the United States should comply with it. State and the CIA agreed.

Powell stressed the uncertainty of the situation, pointing out several times that they had reports but they could not be sure of anything.

What is our purpose? Powell asked. If we're going to do this, I've got to tell my guys what the mission is.

State and the White House responded that it was to support Mrs. Aquino and keep her in power.

What is the immediate objective we seek in bombing the airfields? Powell asked. He answered his own question: to keep the rebel aircraft from taking off. These Philippine aircraft were T-28s, old World War II trainers with propellers, he noted. There were other ways to keep them on the ground. He had some advanced F-4 fighter-bomber jets that, without dropping any bombs, could scare any T-28 pilot into thinking twice before taking off. "I think we can do this without getting ourselves into more trouble," he added.

The Filipino requests were too vague to translate into orders for the pilots of the U.S. F-4s, Powell said. He had no precise target information. "You don't call up a twenty-two-year-old or twenty-three-year-old kid . . . and say just go bomb here." Bombs are terrible things, he said, lethal and indiscriminate.

Powell had an Army officer's natural distrust of airpower. The big bombs always promised great achievement, but he had seen them fail too often—in Vietnam, for example. But he kept these thoughts to himself.

It was not only unclear what to bomb, he said, but he could not guarantee whose side the bombing would help. These were captured Philippine air bases, so there would be both rebels and loyalists all around. The United States would wind up killing some Filipinos. If we kill Filipinos, Powell said, *no one* in the Philippines will forgive us.

Anti-Americanism was always simmering just beneath the surface in that nation of 40 million people, so sensitive about its colonial past. Powell could even envision Mrs. Aquino attending the memorial service for the dead soldiers—whether rebels or loyalists—and denouncing the United States.

"Let's try something short of bombing," Powell proposed. "We can't stick our nose too far into a family fight."

After he had expressed his views, there was a lull in the video conference. He called Cheney to explain that something stupid was about to happen that could cause big political and public relations problems for the United States. There were lots of people who had never dropped bombs before about to make a decision to do just that. Powell said he could come up with an alternative.

Cheney said do it fast. He called Air Force One directly on his secure phone and urged that they wait for Powell's recommendation before making a decision.

Powell was still worried that their information was not good. It was probably coming from some scared kid on the scene. He began dictating an alternative, devising new rules of engagement to govern the behavior and responses of U.S. pilots. He laid out the following guidelines:

First rule: the U.S. pilots were to fly over the captured air bases and to demonstrate extreme hostile intent—in other words, to buzz the shit out of the rebel T-28s on the ground.

Second, if the T-28s or other rebel aircraft began to taxi on the runway, the U.S. pilots were to shoot in front of them—the classic warning shot across the bow.

Third, if at any point the rebels broke ground from the runway in a takeoff, the U.S. pilots were then to shoot the planes down.

Powell believed this would achieve the same purpose as Aquino's request: deter rebel aircraft.

General Herres and Admiral Hardisty both agreed with his proposal.

Powell had no time to ask anyone else's advice, as he normally
would. He didn't clear his proposal with any interagency committee and did not show it to any lawyer. Instead, he immediately
passed the suggested new rules to both Cheney at home and
Quayle at the White House.

Quayle had asked that a call be placed to Air Force One, so he
could talk to the President and forward a recommendation.

The NSC discussion resumed. Aware that he needed to buy time
for his alternatives, Powell threw out more questions and objec-
tions.

"If the purpose is to keep the planes from taking off," Powell
said, "why do we have to destroy them?" His plan had the added
virtue of less risk for the U.S. forces, at least initially, he argued,
and minimized the chances of anyone getting hurt. Mrs. Aquino
was asking for nothing less than a radical military intervention by
the United States. There were smaller steps that needed to be taken
first.

"We have interests in the Philippines that go beyond Mrs.
Aquino," Powell said. Suppose the coup succeeds? We don't want
to get off on the wrong foot with its leaders even before they take
power.

The group agreed to recommend Powell's plan to the President.

When Quayle got through to Air Force One, there was some
tension. Scowcroft seemed reluctant to delegate management of
this crisis to Quayle. The Vice President said there was no point
in re-creating the tactical picture for those who were with the
President somewhere over the Atlantic, because he had it fully in
hand in the White House Situation Room.

Quayle asked to speak with the President. Scowcroft said he
didn't want to wake Bush, who was getting a few precious hours
of sleep before the Malta meetings with Gorbachev. But Quayle
insisted, and Scowcroft finally relented and roused the President.

With Gates listening in at the White House end, Quayle told
Bush: we're giving you the unanimous recommendation that we
intervene, but in this way, and he proceeded to lay out Powell's
three rules of engagement. Bush approved.

By 1:30 a.m. Washington, D.C., time, the Air Force had
launched the F-4s.

A request came in from the Philippines that the United States bomb some armored personnel carriers which the Aquino government believed the rebels were using.

Powell said there was no way to tell which of the armored vehicles were being used by the loyalists and which by the rebels. They were not easily identifiable like the rebel T-28s.

Let's wait, he recommended.

Once the F-4 sorties had begun, there were no reports of any T-28s in the air or any new rebel bombing.

At about 2:30 a.m., Quayle called President Aquino. He wanted her to restate her request for assistance so that it would appear that the United States was providing what she had asked for, although in fact it had rejected her initial plea for bombing. This would allow her to save face, while the administration—well aware that support for Aquino was sacrosanct—could still say it had complied with her request.

Mrs. Aquino came on the phone to the Situation Room.

"Hello, Mr. Vice President," she said in a booming, confident voice.

Quayle asked if Aquino had wanted the United States to keep the rebel aircraft on the ground.

She said yes, that was what she wanted, and she reported that the F-4s had been successful so far.

"We're with you," Quayle told her.

White House Counsel Boyden Gray, who'd been called to the Situation Room to handle the legal implications of any decision to intervene, thought Aquino sounded more in charge than Quayle. But to Gray, the most important performance during those early morning hours was Powell's. Not only was the Chairman backstopping Quayle, but his had been the only voice to challenge the growing consensus that Mrs. Aquino's initial request for bombing should be approved.

Gray knew one seemingly remote country could leap up and play a disproportionate role in the fortunes of an American president. The Iran hostage crisis of 1979–80 had pretty much ended the Carter presidency. Six years later, the secret Iran arms sales had been the lowest moment of the Reagan administration. Gray felt that Bush would be interested to hear what had transpired that evening, and who had minded the store in the President's absence.

Powell was still concerned about the murkiness of the situation. He knew from all the past coup attempts in the Philippines that most of the military and other key players waited to see who would win before declaring themselves for either side. The Filipino military was an important political force, yet no one in the Pentagon or the White House knew where Defense Minister Fidel Ramos stood. When Powell raised that question, Quayle suggested he call Ramos directly.

Powell was not worried that Ramos would go over to the rebel side. He thought Ramos would sit out the coup—an action that might, intentionally or not, be fatal to Mrs. Aquino.

The Pentagon command center had a number of commercial phone numbers for Ramos, and Powell directed a Navy commander to pick up the commercial phone line and start dialing them systematically. It took 40 minutes to reach Ramos.

Powell wanted to make sure he did not get into a policy discussion with the defense minister. He asked Ramos for an assessment. Ramos painted a rosy picture—the rebels were a small group and the loyalists were in charge. Despite the initial bombing, Mrs. Aquino would not think of evacuating the palace, he said. She was going to stay.

Powell explained the U.S. decision to try intimidation and noted that from his end it seemed to have worked so far.

Ramos did not complain that the bombs had not been dropped as requested and said the Philippine government was appreciative of the U.S. efforts.

By about 3 a.m., everything seemed to be on track, and the discussion turned to what to tell the press and Congress. Powell took over the question, proposing they focus on the reformulated request that Quayle had prompted President Aquino to make. It was decided that this story would be put out, instead of the fact that the United States had denied Aquino's request to bomb the rebel planes.

At about 5:30 a.m., Quayle, Powell and the others concluded there was nothing more to do. Darkness had fallen in the Philippines and the T-28s could not operate at night.

Powell went home for two hours of sleep.

· · ·

Quayle and his chief of staff, Bill Kristol, left the White House with a few major impressions of the evening's decision making. It had been Quayle's first chance to act as a crisis manager for the administration, but they were both well aware that Bush had really made the final decision.

They noted how well the JCS had performed, and particularly Powell. Quayle had strongly supported Powell for Chairman over Herres, who didn't like the Strategic Defense Initiative, a pet program of the Vice President's. During this long night of decision making, Powell and his JCS had dominated the Defense Department input. To the surprise of both Quayle and Kristol, Powell, rather than Cheney's civilian representative Henry Rowen, had even controlled discussion of the purely political question of what to tell the press and Congress. Most important, Powell had come up with a less aggressive but no less effective way to solve the overall problem.

Pete Williams arrived at the Pentagon at about six o'clock in the morning to see what the media fallout was going to be. After he was briefed, Williams decided to make sure no one was peddling the story that Mrs. Aquino had wanted to bomb her own people. Soon calls began coming in from reporters who were trying to piece together the story. Some already had versions emphasizing that Dan Quayle had turned in a solid, steady performance filling in for Bush as crisis manager.

The news stories built on this theme. An article published the next day in the *Los Angeles Times* began, "Dan Quayle's moment in the sun came shortly after midnight," adding, "it was a chance to shine and one that he seized with gusto."

Powell thought the episode confirmed a few of his own notions about the use of military power.

The first was that there is no legitimate use of military force without a clear political objective—the bombing idea hadn't met that criterion.

Second was an idea Powell felt had been best expressed by the Athenian historian Thucydides (c. 470–400 B.C.): "Of all manifestations of power, restraint impresses men most." Powell liked the thought so much he kept it displayed beneath the glass covering his Pentagon desk.

Third was that a demonstrated willingness to use force—the tip of a rapier in someone's face—often did the job as well as, or even more effectively than, direct force itself. A neat, surgical application of a threat could work wonders.

· · ·

Powell was feeling very good after two months in the job. The pieces were falling into place as he worked his way through the daily run of problems and crises. More than anything, he was the action officer connecting the military forces to the political system, and the political system back to the forces.

And the forces were trained and ready. Powell wanted to be sure there was never a repeat of the post-Vietnam years. He himself had served two tours in Vietnam, where he'd seen some action but had worked mostly as an adviser and staff officer. In the early 1970s, after he had returned to the States, he'd felt a deep sense of rejection and inferiority as a professional Army officer. The country seemed to be erecting a barrier between itself and the military. The Pentagon was then moving to an all-volunteer force. As far as he was concerned, the decision to eliminate the draft meant the country had told the military, "We do not want to be with you guys."

The embattled Army turned inward in the 1970s, to try to solve its problems. Powell had a close-up view of the effort. In 1971, he was assigned to work as an analyst in the office of Lieutenant General William E. DePuy, the assistant vice chief of staff of the Army. In Powell's view, DePuy was the brain of the Army, the man who succeeded in repairing it after Vietnam. DePuy was tough and aloof, but intellectually open and willing to listen. Powell had never seen anyone who could solve a problem better. He would conceptualize it, make plans, organize to carry out the plans, supervise the execution and then encourage ruthless criticism of the project and of his own performance.

Later in the 1970s, while many in the Army were suffering from malaise, DePuy had overseen the drafting of a new how-to-fight doctrine. Training standards were established on everything from the minimum number of push-ups a soldier should be able to do to marksmanship scores to the time a platoon should take to make a river crossing. DePuy saw that an army had to perform thousands of discrete tasks, many of them boring and repetitive, but they added up to overall success or failure. The key was making sure they were performed well under the pressure of battle conditions.

Relentless training was at the heart of the new Army. To Powell, the most important result of the DePuy legacy was the creation of the National Training Center on 1,000 square miles in the Mojave Desert south of Death Valley. Beginning in 1981, Army combat units had been going there to spend two weeks straight, day and night, fighting an opposing force specially trained in Soviet tactics. The battle realism and live fire brought the soldiers and their officers as close to real war as possible. Mistakes were practically encouraged. "Learning through failure" became the unspoken motto of these rigorous exercises.

In Powell's view, DePuy had made war on the old Army, turning it into a ready force.

Army Chief Vuono, who also had worked for DePuy, was a believer in the gospel of training. Every month he made a trip halfway across the country to Fort Leavenworth, Kansas, to fire up the colonels and lieutenant colonels about to take command of major Army units. Speaking to an audience of about 70, Vuono would preach for two hours without notes. "Poor training kills soldiers," he said at one of these sessions that fall. "If the American Army is not well trained, you can't blame it on Congress, you can't blame it on the media, you can't blame it on the mythical 'they.' It's your fault, your fault, your fault and my fault because we didn't do our job. We can't have one youngster die because he or she wasn't properly trained, because if that happens, it's on our conscience, it's in our hands."

Powell felt another key to the Army's—and the entire military's —success was a mature understanding of public relations and politics, and how to use them. On December 13, he addressed the officers at the National Defense University in Washington, where he had studied 13 years earlier. He spoke at length about the responsibility of the modern military officer to understand the political and media components of their jobs.

The Chairman described how he worked on his relationships with reporters so they trusted him and accepted his explanations of events. "Once you've got all the forces moving and everything's being taken care of by the commanders," he said, "turn your attention to television because you can win the battle or lose the war if you don't handle the story right."

Politics, he said, is fundamental. "A great deal of my time is spent sensing that political environment. People sometimes say, well, Powell, he's a political general anyway. The fact of the matter is there isn't a general in Washington who isn't political, not if he's going to be successful, because that's the nature of our system. It's the way the Department of Defense works. It's the way in which we formulate foreign policy. It's the way in which we get approval for our policy."

14

LIEUTENANT GENERAL KELLY was at home on Saturday evening, December 16, when the phone rang at 9:25. It was the Southern Command's operations director, Brigadier General William Hertzog, calling from Panama City. He sounded agitated.

"We just had a guy shot," Hertzog said. "He might be dead."

Kelly asked for more information.

Hertzog said it was an off-duty Marine lieutenant. "We don't know what's happening right now. We're still working on it."

Fine, Kelly said. He hung up and began dialing.

Powell was at home at Quarters 6, up in the second-floor living area, which has a study, a TV room and a small dining room. The Powells spent most of their time there, away from the spacious, formal first floor used for official entertaining. All indications from intelligence were that it was going to be a quiet weekend around the world. Alma Powell was reading. The Chairman's private phone rang.

"General Powell," he answered.

Kelly reported the Panama shooting.

"Shit," Powell said. He asked Kelly to report further developments.

Soon Powell received a report that the Marine was seriously wounded, followed by a confirmed report that he had died at the hospital. His name was Lieutenant Robert Paz.

Powell called Cheney at home. "It is starting to build," Powell said.

Kelly went to his Pentagon office and was joined by his deputy for current operations, Rear Admiral Joe Lopez, a studious, low-key destroyer officer. They formed a small Crisis Action Team of a handful of Joint Staff specialists and began work immediately in the National Military Command Center (NMCC).

There were more details on the shooting. Paz had been one of four off-duty officers, unarmed and in civilian clothes, who had gone out into Panama City for dinner and had apparently made a wrong turn onto a street called Avenue A near PDF headquarters. Their car had been stopped at a PDF roadblock. They said PDF soldiers had tried to pull them from the car and aimed weapons at them, so the driver had attempted to speed away from the roadblock. The PDF had opened fire. Another of the officers had been grazed on the ankle by a bullet. Paz was wounded and later died at Gorgas Army Hospital.

Kelly was still personally tracking all the major incidents of Americans being abused or harassed in Panama. He had never been able to put his finger on anything conclusive establishing that Noriega or the senior PDF leadership was forcing a direct confrontation. Until now, no American serviceman had been killed by the PDF. As he read through the reports, Kelly saw that the Paz incident wasn't a clear-cut incident of unprovoked PDF aggression—the car had sped away from a legitimate roadblock, lending an element of ambiguity.

Earlier that evening General Thurman had arrived at Andrews Air Force Base outside Washington for a planned two-day blitz around town—the Pentagon, State, Congress. Thurman liked to explain his trips to the capital by taking out a piece of paper and listing his areas of responsibility as CINCSOUTH. In alphabetical order, the list went Argentina, Bolivia, Colombia . . . down to Uruguay, Venezuela. At the end he would coyly add Washington, D.C., which he designated as his last and perhaps most important area of operations.

From Andrews he had gone to his brother's house in town, had dinner and gone to bed. At 11 p.m. he was awakened and told about the shooting. He went right to the Pentagon, where he called Panama to talk with Hertzog. Intelligence now was showing that Noriega himself was in charge of managing the aftermath of the shooting incident.

Something always happens when I leave that goddamn joint down there, Thurman thought to himself. He could see events coming to a head. "It's time for me to go back," he announced and ordered up his plane. By 1 a.m., now December 17, he was headed back on the five-hour flight to Panama.

. . .

By 6 a.m. more reports were coming into the NMCC from Panama. Another, related incident had occurred at the same PDF checkpoint. Navy Lieutenant Adam J. Curtis and his wife, Bonnie, had been stopped about a half hour before the shooting and told to wait for a check on their identification. While waiting, they had witnessed the shooting. Blindfolded with masking tape, both were taken to a nearby PDF office and then to another building that turned out to be the Comandancia.

A senior PDF officer, at least a major, had overseen a four-hour interrogation of the Curtises, during which they were beaten and verbally abused. Lieutenant Curtis was kicked in the groin repeatedly and hit in the mouth. They were forced to stand against a cell wall with their hands over their heads. After half an hour Bonnie Curtis, 23, collapsed. When Lieutenant Curtis protested, paper was stuffed in his mouth. PDF members came in and said: let's kill them now, let's get rid of them. A gun was put to Lieutenant Curtis's head. The Panamanians fondled Bonnie Curtis's neck and the back of her legs. She was told that the repeated kicks to her husband's groin would ensure he would never again be able to perform in bed. At several points she was sexually threatened. She was put in a chair and interrogated about her husband's job, which the PDF claimed was with the CIA.

After four hours, the Curtises were abruptly released. They returned to the U.S. Naval Station about 2:15 a.m. and reported what had happened. The Naval Investigative Service was conducting extensive follow-up debriefings of the couple.

Kelly wondered if the PDF was coming apart. Had the situation in Panama reached a point of dangerous instability? Previously Noriega had been meticulous about not having a direct face-off that would show senior PDF involvement and a lack of discipline.

This was not a matter of a single sergeant or officer out of control. It was a regime out of control. Had Noriega lost authority over his troops? Was the PDF in the process of becoming a renegade force?

The detention and harassment of the Curtises was reported in detail to Powell and Cheney. Cheney said that he wanted to have a meeting in his Pentagon office at ten o'clock Sunday morning to review the options. He called Scowcroft and said that he thought there would have to be a meeting with the President later that day.

Thurman arrived back in Panama at about 6 a.m. and went to his headquarters to review the situation.

At 8:30 a.m. Powell went to the Pentagon and sat down with Kelly and the Crisis Action Team. Kelly reported that Noriega was really scrambling on this one. Noriega had issued a communiqué blaming the shooting incident on the four U.S. officers, alleging that the men had broken through a PDF checkpoint in their car and shot at Noriega's Comandancia, wounding three Panamanians, including a soldier and a one-year-old girl.

The three officers who had been with Paz had been fully debriefed. Noriega's communiqué was total bullshit, Kelly said. The U.S. signals intelligence listeners had heard Noriega himself on the telephone and radio working out false stories to shift the blame to the Americans.

Powell talked with Thurman on the secure line. Thurman already had his more than 13,000 troops on so-called Delta Alert, the second-highest state of readiness. It sharply limited the movement of U.S. personnel and dependents. Thurman said that Noriega's actions were about as inflammatory as could be. He reminded Powell that just two days earlier Noriega's appointed legislature had named him "maximum leader for national liberation" and declared that Panama was "in a state of war" with the United States. Thurman said that the PDF bullies had soaked up all the rhetoric and were giving Noriega what he wanted.

Thurman said he saw three options: (1) do nothing militarily—just protest; (2) execute some portion of the BLUE SPOON offensive operations against the PDF and try to snatch Noriega; (3) execute the full BLUE SPOON plan.

"Do nothing and we'll pay a horrendous price," Thurman said. "Because all that will do is elevate his stature in the minds of his major thugs that are aiding and abetting him." The killing of Paz in cold blood required an answer.

The snatch job on Noriega puts you in harm's way, Thurman said, rejecting option two. They were tracking Noriega and knew his whereabouts perhaps 80 percent of the time. If the U.S. military went after him and missed him, and he still had his PDF, no American in Panama would be safe.

Thurman recommended option three—do it all, demolish the PDF, and get it over with. We are rehearsed, he said. The Southern Command would never be readier.

After about ten minutes, Powell said, "Okay, fine, got your pitch on it. . . . I've got to go brief Cheney." Powell was clearly reserving his opinion. "I'll get back to you later."

Powell went up to Cheney's office, where the two sat down alone just before 10 a.m. Powell thought it was critical that he get a sense from Cheney about what was possible. He did not want to go charging off with a military recommendation that was going to be rejected, that was not in the band of politically acceptable options. But as usual, Cheney seemed mainly to want to listen.

There was a lot of premeditation in what the PDF was doing to Americans, Powell said. "It was not a snap judgment by the PDF." The Chairman said that the BLUE SPOON plan was good. They had rehearsed 100 percent; they might never be more ready.

Cheney nodded, showed no reluctance and left Powell with the impression that they both were of the same mind.

Powell said it was important to conduct such an operation— any military operation—on their own timetable. He was for recommending the execution of the full BLUE SPOON plan.

Cheney did not disagree. He seemed open to all possibilities, but said he wanted to hear what the others had to say.

At this point they were joined by Assistant Secretary Henry Rowen; Richard C. Brown, the deputy assistant secretary for inter-American affairs; spokesman Pete Williams; Rear Admiral Owens, Cheney's military assistant; Dave Addington, Cheney's civilian special assistant; and Kelly and Sheafer of the Joint Staff.

After the latest reports about the death of Lieutenant Paz and the beating and harassment of Lieutenant Curtis and his wife were summarized, Cheney said he wanted assessments and recommendations. He went around the room asking each man for his opinion.

Seeing that military action was clearly under consideration, several of the civilians wondered whether that was wise. They asked if the killing of Lieutenant Paz, apparently the main issue, constituted a sufficient smoking gun to justify military action.

"All I know is that he's dead," Powell answered. It was the most serious incident in Panama in 25 years.

The civilians pushed. Would the facts as now presented hold up under the scrutiny that would inevitably come? Was Powell sure? Did Noriega's claim that the U.S. officers had fired first have any merit? Did speeding away from the checkpoint give the PDF justification for shooting?

Powell and the others said they were checking everything but it looked as if the Noriega claim was provably untrue.

The civilians pressed. Was this the catalytic event? Should it be?

Most seemed to agree that the answer might largely turn on the certainty of the information.

When it seemed each man had had his full say, Cheney thanked them all politely.

Whatever the outcome, Williams realized, they were in a crisis. He told Cheney that he had spoken with the Southern Command public affairs officer in Panama, who said that Lieutenant Curtis was coherent and could go on television and explain what had happened to him and his wife. Williams saw this as an interesting possibility.

"Let it pass," Cheney directed. "We don't want to whip things up." Cheney told Williams to draft a statement saying precisely what had happened to Paz and the Curtises, and he wanted to look at it before it was released.

. . .

Cheney asked Powell to stay behind so the two could talk alone again. He realized now that Americans—military and civilian—were seriously at risk in Panama. That changed the entire situation.

Powell agreed.

They talked about the mess in Panama. It had been that way for a long time, but frankly, Cheney said, they now had an obligation, if they were going to have their guys there.

They could not allow this kind of thing to happen, Powell said. It was probably time to act.

Yes, Cheney said. And not just Noriega. The whole PDF. They

had finally reached a point where they could justify U.S. military intervention.

Powell said that he would very quietly call the Joint Chiefs together, get their views and make sure they were on board.

. . .

Though by law the Chairman is the principal military adviser to the President and his Secretary of Defense, the other chiefs are also presidential military advisers. Powell wanted them to have more, not less, access to the system, but wanted that access to pass through him. He would go to the White House meetings; he would inform the chiefs of what was under consideration; and he would convey their views to the President.

Now, however, Powell did not know what the White House was thinking. He had not spoken with President Bush, or with Scowcroft or Baker, so he was not sure what might be coming from above. It was time to see what might be coming from below.

Powell did not want to call the chiefs into the Pentagon, where they would almost certainly be noticed. A Sunday meeting of the JCS would alert the press. Instead, he sent word to each of them that he wanted them for coffee at his quarters at 11:30 a.m. Vuono lived just down the street at Quarters 1 and had been on alert; Chief of Naval Operations Admiral Carl Trost, who had been informed of both the Paz killing and the harassment of the Navy couple, was contacted at chapel at the Navy Yard in Washington; Marine Commandant Al Gray was standing by; and General Welch was also anticipating trouble.

The four chiefs gathered in the first-floor study at the back of Quarters 6. Alma Powell had begun redecorating and the walls of the small corner room were a fashionable light orange, with pictures and memorabilia of the Chairman's Army career on display.

Powell greeted each man warmly—Al, Larry, Carl and Carl. They all took seats and coffee was served. Kelly briefed them for about ten minutes, providing the latest on the killing of Paz and the harassment of the Curtises. He could see from the chiefs' looks and questions that the plight of the Curtises had caught everybody's attention more than the shooting. Here were Noriega's men mistreating a family, a woman, a noncombatant. The Curtises were totally innocent. By no stretch had they provoked the PDF. They had just happened to witness the Paz shooting. Kelly very quickly summarized the BLUE SPOON plan, with which the chiefs were all familiar since they had been briefed the previous month.

Powell told them he had met with Cheney and Cheney's staff earlier that morning. Both the Secretary and he were inclined to recommend to President Bush later that afternoon that BLUE SPOON be executed. Noriega has pushed us about as far as we can tolerate, the Chairman said. But he and Cheney wanted their views, not just on the military side, but also on the political side. What advice did they individually or collectively wish him to convey to the Secretary and President?

Carl Vuono said that BLUE SPOON was a good plan—complex, yes, but it would achieve the objective of wiping out the PDF. Any attempt to dilute the plan, to throw in some lesser options, had to be resisted. He had vivid memories of Vietnam, where the civilian leadership hadn't been willing to commit the force necessary to accomplish the military objectives. Panama, unlike Vietnam, had to be done completely and with sufficient force to ensure that the troops did not get bogged down. The force was ready, well trained, fully rehearsed. The units were not undermanned, underled, or inexperienced as in Vietnam.

From a military perspective, Vuono said, the operation was fully supportable and sufficient to achieve the assigned task.

General Al Gray was fidgety. "My world is divided into acceptable and unacceptable acts," he said. "This is unacceptable." The situation would not get better and it was time to act, he said forcefully. He was totally in favor of military action, and he was sure the Panamanian people wanted Noriega out. They would be dancing in the streets if the United States acted to remove him.

Kelly silently observed that though Gray seemed 100 percent supportive, he spoke with bittersweet enthusiasm. Gray's Marines competed with the Army to be the ground force of choice—for the missions, for funding, for respect. Panama was a classic candidate for a Marine landing; it was a small country, virtually all coastline. But BLUE SPOON was almost exclusively an Army operation. Surprise and speed dictated an airborne operation. Marines transported on ships often took too long to arrive; and their presence en route or offshore was difficult to hide.

Wearing a sheepish expression, Gray said that he had a Marine Expeditionary Unit (MEU) of several thousand men heading back from Hawaii. They had just completed a deployment and could not be better trained. The MEU was also special-operations-capable. All Gray had to do, he said, was see that orders were issued for the ships to make a hard right turn and they soon would be ready over the horizon. The Marines could be off the west coast of Panama in several days.

"That's good to know, Al," Powell said, "but I can't change the timelines or the plan now."

Everyone in the room knew that it would take the Marines too long to get there.

Gray responded with what Kelly thought sounded like a Marine Corps commercial, touting his versatile force, which carried enough supplies for 30 days.

Restraint was not Gray's strong suit, but he tried to hold himself in. Privately, he felt that these Army light forces that parachuted out of the sky were a sham—a demonstration of the hollowness of the Army. The Army Rangers were light enough to get there quickly, yes, but also light enough to get in trouble if combat lasted more than several days. They came with only several days' supplies and ammunition.

Gray said that if the fight in Panama got mired down, his Marines would be handy.

Powell made it clear that BLUE SPOON had been designed to ensure quick success: a total of 24,000 U.S. troops against the 16,000-member PDF, only 3,500 of whom were combat-capable; superior equipment, night capability, surprise, superior soldiers. Powell had a notion that when weapons and men were thrown into battle, the combat amounted to teenagers fighting duels. And the American teenagers were much better.

As a final matter, Gray suggested that some amphibious ships with Marines be moved, just in case, off the coast on the Atlantic side of Panama. Since such ships would also be off the coast of Nicaragua, they would be ready if the Sandinistas tried anything.

General Gray had been doing most of the talking. Finally the Chairman cut him off, saying, "Well, this is pretty well settled, but we'll keep it in mind."

The Navy had ships in the Caribbean and the Pacific on drug-interdiction operations, Admiral Carl Trost knew. They could have been called in. There was some symbolic appeal to the idea of showing the force of a carrier battle group or an amphibious ready group, but he didn't think they would be needed or could have much of an impact. A token force of some 800 Navy people would be involved in BLUE SPOON, including some SEALs and troops on small boats. Trost was willing to concede it was predominantly an Army–Air Force operation.

The Chief of Naval Operations felt that the United States, for practical purposes, had control of Panama with the 13,000 troops already there. It was just a matter of dumping Noriega and a couple dozen of his senior officers, and neutralizing the rest of the PDF. He found much private amusement in one aspect of BLUE SPOON. Thousands of Army troops were going to be dropped in by parachute. Some of the early parachute drops made good sense to him, but the rest of the troops could as easily arrive in airplanes on the airstrips that the U.S. forces by then were going to control. The admiral was pretty certain this was all designed to make sure that the maximum number of troops received their combat jump badges. He silently counted many unnecessary broken legs from the parachute drops.

It was evident to Trost that this was not going to be anything resembling a fair fight. Once, years ago, he had hit a rattlesnake with a shovel. It might have been overkill but the shovel got the job done. He did not begrudge the others their shovels.

It also occurred to Trost, though he did not say it, that this would answer the often-lodged criticism that the chiefs were a bunch of wimps who didn't want to fight and never thought or planned ahead. BLUE SPOON was going to show these detractors. Trost simply told the others that he strongly supported BLUE SPOON.

Characteristically, General Welch listened quietly, not saying a great deal, coming to his own conclusions. This was a very, very important meeting, he thought. For good reason, the chiefs were traditionally conservative on the use of military force. They did not typically support interventions that were hasty or primarily political. He thought the execution of BLUE SPOON would be both.

Welch said he agreed that the mistreatment of the Navy couple was more indicative of an environment of chaos than was the shooting of the Marine. He wanted to make sure both actions were not the work of some errant PDF soldiers.

Powell and Kelly said that they were as sure as they could be. Not only the accounts of the Navy couple, but the intercepted signals intelligence on Noriega showed he was personally covering up for his own organization.

In that environment, Welch responded, the choice for the United States was either to get out of Panama entirely or get in all the way. Given the international responsibility to protect the Panama Canal, the United States could not retreat to a Panama equivalent of Guantanamo Bay, the only remaining U.S. enclave in Cuba. So in that sense there was no choice.

Still, Welch, holding his audience with a careful pause, said they had to understand and consider the downsides of a massive invasion.

Powell and the others seemed to want to hear what he had to say.

The first downside, Welch said, was that they had to expect that the other Latin American nations would, at the least, posture against what the United States was doing. U.S. policies in the region could be set back years. The issue would likely be whipped up by the media. There was no way the United States realistically could expect any public expressions of support from Latin American friends.

Though Powell agreed, he replied that the Latin American leaders privately would be as delighted as anybody to be rid of the Noriega embarrassment.

Nonetheless, Welch said, it was a downside that had to be faced. In addition, the reaction was likely to be negative in other countries where the United States had large bases, such as the Philippines.

A second downside, Welch said, was the possibility that the PDF might be far more resistant than expected. The United States had to be prepared to commit whatever force was necessary for whatever time was necessary to clear up the situation. BLUE SPOON includes what we think is a totally adequate force, Welch said, and that could lead the President or anyone else to conclude that that is the limit of the commitment. That could be a big problem. He hoped a quick fix had not been promised.

A third downside, Welch pointed out, was that there would be critics who would say that the Department of Defense was running out of enemies and had seized on this opportunity to demonstrate the need for military force.

Fourth, Welch said, was the David and Goliath problem—the real possibility that popular feeling, due partly to the impact of the media in this country, would see Noriega as the little guy, unfairly overwhelmed.

And fifth, they had to be sure that they didn't have a Gulf of Tonkin situation, Welch said, referring to the ambiguous nature of the 1964 North Vietnamese attacks on U.S. ships, which had led to a congressional resolution granting President Johnson extraordinary authority to respond in Vietnam. This time, Welch said, the American military had to be certain that the provocation was genuine, that they had a situation in Panama they couldn't live with, that they couldn't ask their people down there to live with.

It was a long list of negatives, and it was not clear where Welch was going with his argument.

He finally summarized. As long as they went in with their eyes open to these downsides and were committed enough to overcome them as events unfolded, he supported the operation. There was no other solution, he said.

Powell took the floor. He and Kelly were going over to see the President, he said. My recommendation is going to be that we execute BLUE SPOON. "I want to make sure that we're all agreeing." He went around the room once again asking for final recommendations.

All four chiefs said they were with him.

Carrying large poster-board maps showing the assault points in Panama, Powell and Kelly climbed into the Chairman's car and were driven to the White House.

That Sunday was a beautiful wintry day. The city streets were decked out for Christmas. It was a time for family and peace, perhaps the most difficult season in which to recommend an offensive military operation to the President, Powell reflected.

Kelly and Powell were wearing casual civilian clothes as they trooped through the White House up to the second-floor residence for a two o'clock meeting with Bush. One of the Bushes' many Christmas parties, this one for some of their closest family and friends, was winding down on the first floor. Carolers in 18th-century costume were singing off to one side and a few hangers-on lingered.

Cheney, who had attended a few Christmas parties since his morning meeting at the Pentagon, arrived. Baker, Scowcroft, Bob Gates and press secretary Marlin Fitzwater also came in. Bush was wearing a white shirt, blue blazer, gray slacks, brown shoes and a pair of bright red socks, one emblazoned with the word "Merry," the other with "Christmas." Kelly thought they were the most God-awful socks he'd ever seen.

Powell noted to himself that the only key players missing were Vice President Quayle and Chief of Staff Sununu. Normally Powell wouldn't have gone to such a meeting without an advance read on the positions of the various players, but events had carried them so quickly that he had not had a chance to find out where people stood.

Kelly gave a seven-minute summary of the facts they had gathered about Lieutenant Paz's death and the harassment of the Curtises. The latter incident had been overseen, he said, by a senior PDF officer. Kelly could tell that Bush and the others were more disturbed by this event than by the shooting of Paz. Sticking to the facts, Kelly, who favored an invasion, laid it on as heavily as he could. He said these two actions were unprecedented, even in Noriega's Panama.

Powell presented only one option to the President: BLUE SPOON.

Why don't we just go get Noriega? Bush asked. Take me through why we shouldn't do this with a smaller force.

Reeling off all his arguments about the need to destroy the PDF, Powell said that the massive use of force was in fact *less risky* than a smaller effort. This was the prudent course, he told Bush. The choice, effectively, was pay now or pay later. You go down there to take Noriega out and you haven't accomplished that much because he would be replaced by another corrupt PDF thug.

"You're going to have American blood spilled," Powell warned, but probably more would be spilled with a small force than if they used a major blow to take the PDF down.

Powell said he would need at least 48 hours' advance notice to prepare and marshal the forces and air transportation for BLUE SPOON. The ideal H-Hour was 1 a.m., late enough to surprise the PDF but leaving five hours before daybreak to decapitate them. Also, a 1 a.m. start would be close to high tide, a real benefit for the Navy SEALs. At low tide, some of the landing areas would be vast mudflats, so mucky that not even the hardy SEALs could trudge through them. Another benefit was that only one plane was scheduled to land after 1 a.m. at Torrijos international airport, a key target.

BLUE SPOON would be a complete take-down of the PDF and the Panamanian government. "We are going to own the country for several weeks," Powell said, underscoring that this plan was not a surgical strike, or a simple in-and-out operation. Bad things will happen, Mr. President, the Chairman said. There will be casualties, ours and theirs, military and civilian. "We will do everything we can to keep them at a minimum."

Scowcroft inquired about casualty levels.

"We are going to hurt people," Powell responded. "There will be loss of life and there will be chaos. We are going to be taking down the law enforcement operation." He avoided naming a specific number. He said he could guarantee rapid success but could not give a specific time of how long it would take.

"Don't ask us in two days when we are coming home, Mr. President," Powell said. "The PDF could surrender at the first landing and be out there with 'Welcome Yankee' signs, or there could be nasty firefights for weeks."

Bush probed. He had all kinds of questions that challenged the plan, some of them very specific; for example, how long it would take to get from one road to another. "Well, I don't know," the President said at one point.

Powell feared that the meeting was drifting like a sailboat tacking back and forth across a bay, and he didn't know where it would end up. After answering the questions put to him, he concluded: "My recommendation is that we go with the full plan. I can tell you that the chiefs agree with me to a man."

When Powell was finished, Cheney spoke up. "I support what the Chairman just recommended to you," he told Bush.

Kelly had the impression that Cheney's relative silence meant he'd talked with the President separately before the meeting, and felt that since his position was already on the table, he didn't need to say a lot.

But, in fact, Cheney had not spoken privately with Bush. It was simply that after the failed coup, it had become clear to him that the President wanted this problem solved. It had been up to Powell, he felt, to carry the ball by outlining the military plan.

"I think we ought to go," Baker said. "As you know, the State Department has been for this for a long time, but these are the downsides of doing it."

The Secretary of State then made a tour of the world, predicting the responses the invasion would prompt. The Organization of American States would feel an obligation to denounce the interference, he said, but that was predictable. Individual Latin American governments and Third World nations would feel the same obligation. Mexico would take a real shot for sure. Even the allies, the friendly governments of Western Europe, would give the United States some flak just because it would be a good opportunity to bash Uncle Sam. The Soviets would also make their usual negative statement. But overall, Baker said, he did not think that any nation's heart would be in the criticism, and he anticipated that privately most of these governments would send back-channel word that they were neutral or even pleased.

Baker said that State could handle the notification process with other governments—the allies, the Soviets. The President, of course, would want to make many of the calls.

Scowcroft reentered the fray. As Powell saw it, Scowcroft was doing Bush's sharpshooting.

What about the casualty levels? Scowcroft asked again, raising his voice.

Powell said no number could be given.

Damage levels?

Again it was hard to say, but a large force was planned and the damage would be extensive, though they were not going to go in just to shoot up the place, Powell said. Each of the 28 targeted assault points was there for a reason—concentrations of the PDF, possible Noriega hangouts, the main power distribution center, and Madden Dam, which controlled much of the water in the canal and had to be protected. Loss of Madden Dam could render the canal unusable for up to a year. The CIA man Kurt Muse was targeted for rescue—the old ACID GAMBIT rescue plan had been incorporated into BLUE SPOON.

Would Noriega be captured?

The best special operations people would be on his trail.

One of the President's stated goals in Panama was to bring about democracy, Scowcroft noted. Would this do it? And how?

The plan was to secretly swear in Endara, the winner of the May election, as president just before the invasion.

Soon they turned away from the BLUE SPOON plan itself, and began to ask about the aftermath. At this moment, Powell thought it finally looked as if Bush were going to approve. The sailboat had finished its tacking and was heading directly to its destination.

Someone asked about the public and press reaction.

Marlin Fitzwater, who had said very little, now remarked that he thought both would generally be positive. "Of course, you're going to have that element in the press that will criticize you," he told Bush. But he himself did not think that would be a major problem.

After an hour and 40 minutes, Bush said, as if to summarize the view of Noriega that had emerged, "This guy is not going to lay off. It will only get worse."

In Powell's own mind, the six key questions had been asked and answered. Was there sufficient provocation? Powell thought yes. Has the PDF changed and gone out of control? Again yes. Would BLUE SPOON resolve the problem? Yes. Would the plan minimize damage and casualties? Yes. Would it bring democracy? Yes. And public and press reaction? Probably positive.

"Okay, let's go," Bush said. He looked at Powell, and said very quietly, "We're going to go."

"Roger, sir."

Kelly felt an immediate rush to his gut, the first time in his two years as director of operations. They were committing young Americans to combat and some of them were going to die. The safety had been taken off the loaded guns.

Because BLUE SPOON required a 48-hour minimum advance notice, H-Hour was set for 1 a.m. Wednesday, December 20.

Who could know about the decision without compromising operational security? someone asked.

The minimum number of people essential to successfully carry out the operation, Bush directed. He made it clear that he meant the absolute minimum.

. . .

Powell and Kelly were quiet in the car going back to the Pentagon. "I want you to get this information out," Powell said, referring exclusively to the key operations people in the commands that would be involved. "I don't want an order published. I want you to just call people on the [secure] telephone." Powell said that the Vice Chairman, General Bob Herres, and the current director of the Joint Staff, Lieutenant General Michael P. C. Carnes, could be told the next day.

Both Powell and Kelly pondered how long the secret could be kept. They hoped to make it through the Monday evening news without some direct information leaking. They thought something would get out on Tuesday for sure, but perhaps the leak would be late enough or unclear enough that they would still have a chance for some kind of surprise at H-Hour.

Back at the Pentagon, Powell called the four CINCs who would be immediately involved.

One was Max Thurman. Powell told him that BLUE SPOON had been approved but the formal order would not come until the next day.

"Roger."

Powell also called the CINC of the Special Operations Command, General James J. Lindsay, and the Forces Command CINC, General Edwin H. Burba, Jr.

At the U.S. Transportation Command headquarters at Scott Air Force Base, Illinois, General Hansford T. Johnson was not anticipating an execution order. Several months earlier he had left the Pentagon, where he had been director of the Joint Staff under Admiral Crowe, and he still had good contacts back in Washington. Earlier that Sunday morning he and his people had received informal word to "spin up" their airlift capability for BLUE SPOON. Some of Johnson's staff people had told him they would not be able to find the pilots fast enough for an execution. But in the afternoon they were told it wasn't going to happen and to get unspun. When Powell's call came through, Johnson was a little surprised to be hearing from the Chairman.

"The President has authorized me to tell you we're going to execute BLUE SPOON," Powell said.

"We are prepared to go," Johnson said, in spite of the warnings of a pilot shortage.

Powell called each of the chiefs to inform them of Bush's approval. He apologized to Vuono for failing to show up at his Christmas party that afternoon. Cheney also had been a no-show.

As a final matter that night, Powell made sure that the key special operations units were dispatched. The lead Delta squadron, code-named AZTEC PACKAGE, and a SILVER BULLET package of helicopters probably would be left back in the States for any terrorist contingency elsewhere in the world. Otherwise, much of the military's special operations capability was going to be sent to Panama, more than 4,000 men. Many would be involved in tracking and, if all went well, apprehending Noriega in the first hours of the operation.

An order was issued dispatching 20 special operations scout and attack helicopters to Panama on giant C-5 cargo planes. They were to be unloaded at night and hidden in hangars until H-Hour.

. . .

Kelly knew one way he could enforce "opsec," operational security. Back in his office at the Pentagon, he called in the Crisis Action Team for Panama and told them to go home. Next, he called in the public affairs officer for the Joint Staff, Navy Captain Erwin A. Sharp, and told him to go on his scheduled Christmas leave.

When everyone had cleared out, Kelly summoned his deputy for current operations, Joe Lopez, and four junior officers on his Latin American team, and sat them down on the leather couches and chairs in his office.

"We're going to execute BLUE SPOON," Kelly said, swearing each to maximum secrecy, and instructing that every step was to be carried out with opsec foremost in their minds.

Kelly received a call from General Lindsay, commander-in-chief of the Special Operations Command. Lindsay said he thought it was a terrible name for an operation. "Do you want your grandchildren to say you were in BLUE SPOON?" he asked Kelly.

It could have been worse, Kelly thought. One of the Panama contingency plans was named BLIND LOGIC. Other operations had been given equally strange names over the years. One general had executed a STUMBLING BLOCK and a LIMA BEAN. Kelly tossed around ideas for a new name with Joe Lopez. "How about JUST ACTION?" Kelly proposed.

"How about JUST CAUSE?" Lopez countered.

They agreed that would be much better. The name was sent up the chain of command and approved.

A fax had arrived from Panama, reporting on the Naval Investigative Service's debriefings of Navy Lieutenant Curtis and his wife, Bonnie. Bonnie Curtis's detailed account of her treatment was even worse than what had been reported to President Bush, Cheney and Powell. The two-and-a-half-page summary, stamped received at the JCS December 17 at 12:37 p.m., said of Mrs. Curtis's questioning: "The interrogator made a few lewd comments like, If you don't tell us the truth, I will stick my finger up inside you, Don't you want me to put my nine inches inside you?"

Powell went back to Quarters 6. There were a few more calls to make sure that each of the key people knew what the others were doing. After the calls, suddenly with time on his hands, he let the enormity of the decision sink in. They were going to war. He'd personally known, but heard and read more, about the self-doubt the commander feels on the eve of battle. Now such misgivings struck him hard, and thinking through the plans again did not make the doubts yield or go away. BLUE SPOON was an incredibly complex plan, requiring precision—one miscue could set off a string of others, like a pile-up on the freeway.

The F-117As arriving from their Nevada base would be bombing at Rio Hato, a key PDF base, one minute before the Ranger drop there. That was very close. Late 117As or early Rangers would mean disaster. The AC-130 gunships would have only ten minutes to "prepare"—demolish—the Comandancia before infantry attacked it. Powell wondered if the SEAL teams were wired together properly and fully integrated with the rest of the plan.

And where was Noriega? Did he know? Would he suspect anything? Would he find out?

15

WHEN POWELL WENT INTO THE PENTAGON very early Monday, December 18, he felt uneasy. He went upstairs to bring Cheney up to speed. Cheney himself did not feel much in the way of jitters. He knew when he had accepted the job as Secretary that it might entail using force, and sending men to die. When he had arrived at the Pentagon, he had asked for and read the classified after-action reports of the major uses of the U.S. military since Vietnam. He had been in the Ford White House during the 1975 evacuation of Southeast Asia, and during the *Mayaguez* incident that same year, when a U.S. merchant ship was seized by Cambodians and Marines were sent in to rescue the crew. By the time of the invasion the crew had already been set free. Forty-one Americans had been killed in the operation. He had seen firsthand the tendency of the people at the top—the President, the national security adviser, the Secretary of Defense—to meddle needlessly and counterproductively in military operations.

In the reports on the 1983 Beirut bombing and the Grenada operation, he had read about more of this same tendency. The one remedy, Cheney had decided, was a clean, clear-cut chain of command—as short as possible. And no meddling from the top. Stay out of their hair.

As the chief intermediary between the uniformed military and the White House, Cheney felt he could do as much as anyone to reduce interference, and keep the chain of command short. But he was not going to sit it out. He would make sure he understood and approved of the plan, so he could answer any questions that might come from the White House.

That morning, Cheney asked a lot of questions. It seemed to Powell that Cheney wanted to know all the details, right down to the squad level.

Later, Powell called in Kelly and began his own interrogation. He wanted to review each element, every single event of the plan.

"Why are you doing this?" Powell asked in a very confrontational way, referring to one of the special operations targets.

Kelly thought to himself: well, shit, I ain't doing it, for one thing —it's the guy down there, Thurman or Stiner. But Kelly gave the best answer he could to that question and to a whole series of others as Powell went through the plan.

Powell was concerned that they might be doing some things just for show. After preaching the importance of a sufficient force or "mass" during the operation, the Chairman was now looking for excesses. He spoke of reducing risks and damage.

In Kelly's opinion, it was as if Powell had reached into his desk and brought out a wire brush—and he was now scrubbing everything and everyone, including himself. Necessary and inevitable, Kelly concluded; there was a lot at stake. The leader's great fear before battle was not just a personal fear or fear of failure, but a larger, moral kind of fear. Kelly could see this in Powell, the Custer Syndrome or something like that. Powell was afraid that he was going to get a bunch of people killed because of stupidity.

Kelly had his own worries. He was thinking about his retirement, and didn't want to leave in disgrace.

Powell's wire brush found several excesses. As Cheney had suggested during an earlier review of the plan, there was no need to attack a Noriega hideout on the coast of Panama because there was no indication he was going to be using it.

Powell wanted to know more about the F-117A Stealth fighters and their planned use at the Rio Hato PDF barracks.

Two 2,000-pound bombs were going to be dropped about 50

yards from the barracks, Kelly said. This "offset" bombing might break a few windows, stun the troops in the barracks, and perhaps cause some electrical fires, but not do a great deal more.

Who says? Powell wanted to know.

That's what the weapons effects experts claimed anyhow, Kelly said, knowing that those people wouldn't be held responsible for the results. Kelly had talked with Carl Stiner about the offset bombing, and he knew that Stiner was having his own little crisis of confidence in the F-117As, which had not yet been combat-tested. Fifty yards was not much of a margin for error.

Powell realized that the United States had to put Panama back together as quickly as possible after the invasion. This would require popular support from the Panamanians, which meant killing as few as possible of the kinds of people—PDF privates—who would be asleep in the barracks and who Powell hoped would surrender. He ordered the offset distance be increased dramatically. The bomb targets were moved to points about 200 yards away from one barracks and 250 yards from another.

As Powell went through this process, he felt somewhat more comfortable. He knew that he was just following the lessons of his military experience. As a new major in 1966 he had taught precisely this subject—operations and planning—at the Army Infantry School, Fort Benning, Georgia.

By that evening Powell felt a momentary sense of contentment.

. . .

Stiner had arrived in Panama that Monday night dressed as usual in civilian clothes. At 10 p.m. he gathered all his commanders down to the battalion level, 30 officers in all, and stood up before them. "This is it," he said. "This is a go." Security, he said, is of the greatest importance. They could tell their own operations and intelligence officers, in other words only those with top-secret clearance.

Stiner was worried about leaks. U.S. servicemen and servicewomen lived all over the place in Panama; some even lived at the same installations as PDF troops. Stiner asked for recommendations on when, in light of the need for opsec, the lower-ranking officers and the troops should be told. It was agreed to wait until the next night—8 p.m. for the officers, just five hours before H-Hour, and 10 p.m. for the troops. The troops would be brought in, briefed and then sequestered so they could load ammunition and get ready to go. None would be allowed access to telephones. Stiner ordered that there was to be no increased level of activity, no signal of any kind.

. . .

Cheney was also worried about leaks. He decided that he would not have Pete Williams notify the media pool, the small group of reporters who would cover the invasion for all the news oganizations, until after the evening television news shows the next night. This would be less than six hours before H-Hour, making it impossible for reporters to make it to Panama in time for the start of JUST CAUSE.

The Secretary raised his worries with Powell. Almost everything leaks, he remarked. What happens if the cover is blown? If it becomes public? Does Max have, on the ground in Panama, the capability to go ahead and start the operation? If on Tuesday night we turn on the tube and there's word that the Americans are coming, can Max go ahead early with what he's already got on hand?

Powell checked and then assured Cheney they could go early.

Later that night, after the Monday evening news shows, Tom Kelly sat at his large desk in his windowless office. Too quiet, he concluded. H-Hour was still some 30 hours away. It was too silky. Things weren't going wrong. With each minute passing he felt a sense of foreboding. Something was supposed to go wrong. Though all the training, planning, all the money, all the worrying each detail into the ground was designed to prevent the misstep, a misstep was expected. He realized that he was counting on a fuck-up. Then he could throw himself into the fray, straighten things out, fix it. Instead, all his energy was going into waiting. He preferred the fixing.

. . .

At 7 a.m. the next day, Tuesday, December 19, Powell called in his chief public affairs aide, Army Colonel Bill Smullen, told him the operation was going to occur and pledged him to secrecy.

"I want to maintain as much normalcy as possible," Powell said. Looking at his schedule for the day, he saw he had a noon lunch with Naval Academy midshipman Tom Daily. At the Army-Navy football game several weeks before, Daily had approached the Chairman with a friendly wager on the outcome. Powell had accepted and Navy had won. Daily's prize was lunch with the Chairman at the Pentagon, which was set for this worst of all possible days, just before the largest U.S. military operation in years. Okay, Powell said, I'm going to go through with the lunch. It lasted 45 minutes.

Later that day, Powell had another nonessential appointment on his schedule, this one with Tiffani Starks, the teen-aged daughter of an Air Force lieutenant colonel Powell knew. Tiffani had chosen Powell as the subject of a high school paper she'd been assigned to write on a famous person. Powell decided to keep the meeting, which was scheduled to last 15 minutes. When Tiffani and her father showed up at the Chairman's office at 4:30 p.m., Powell's time was becoming tight. I can't give 15 minutes, he told the staff. Cut it to five. Tiffani came in and Powell answered her questions about what had motivated him to stay in the Army, and whether he ever had thought he'd make general.

The day was otherwise filled with pre-invasion meetings and briefings. Cheney and Powell went to the White House to update Bush. On the question of whether to use the F-117A Stealth fighter, Bush replied, "If that's the best plane, use it."

Cheney wanted more and more information. When he'd taken over from Crowe, Powell had noticed that Kelly and the key operations staff regularly used to go to Cheney's office to brief military assistant Bill Owens on various matters. Powell had cut this off, making it clear that he would provide the Secretary and his staff with operational and other information. Now, just hours away from H-Hour, Powell found himself too busy to be tending constantly to Cheney's every need. The operation now mattered more than his desire to be the lone channel to the Secretary.

"Go up there and tell him anything he wants to know," Powell told his operations people.

.   .   .

Around 5 p.m. Powell had the chiefs into his office for a final runthrough. Cheney came down to join them. For Cheney, it was a satisfying symbolic moment. It showed he was keeping the chiefs involved. He felt that the chain of command was just right, running as it did from him to Powell, rather than to the chiefs as a committee.

"Don't worry about initial reports," Marine Commandant

Gray told Cheney. "It's a night-time operation and things will always go wrong. Things will happen. But by morning, you'll have a successful operation."

Powell was glad they had finally stopped messing with the plan. He turned his attention to worries about the news media. Word had come that reporters for CBS and NBC had stories that some kind of operation was about to happen, but neither had any idea of its dimensions. On CBS, Dan Rather led off the news saying, "U.S. military transport planes have left Fort Bragg, North Carolina, home of the Army's elite 82nd Airborne paratroopers. The Pentagon declines to say whether or not they are bound for Panama. It will say only that the Bragg-based 18th Airborne Corps has been conducting what the Army calls an 'airborne readiness exercise.' "

NBC reporter Ed Rabel said, "United States C-141 Starlifters flew into Panama this afternoon, one landing every ten minutes. At the same time these aircraft were arriving, security was tightened around the airbase. U.S. soldiers could be seen in full combat gear on roads around the base." At the end of his brief report, Rabel noted, "No one here could confirm that these aircraft were part of a U.S. invasion group. But tensions on both sides are high this evening over the possibility of a U.S. strike."

Powell watched the television reports. Mighty close but no compromise. He realized he would wind up having to thank some reporters.

Kelly was still astonished that it had not leaked. There was already a lot of aluminum flying through the air to Panama.

Powell, home for dinner, told Alma he was going back to the Pentagon and didn't know when he would return. He knew she had noticed all the movement and the phone calls, but he hadn't told her what was happening; he never did. The Powell family policy was to keep their home life as separate from military business as possible.

Powell returned to the Pentagon after dinner and took a nap.

The building was eerily quiet. In the Crisis Situation Room at the National Military Command Center, there were about 15 people working in an atmosphere of hushed excitement and tension. Secure phone lines to the Southern Command had been activated. The television set was tuned to the three networks and CNN. On a screen on one wall were the latest data on the status of JUST CAUSE.

Kelly and Sheafer sat at the center of the room's long table. Kelly was running things, checking periodically with Thurman, whose twangy voice would issue from a loudspeaker so everyone in the room could hear. Kelly was pounding hard on the key question of Noriega's whereabouts. They had lost him at around 6 p.m. Goddammit, we want him, Kelly was saying. Where is he? The United States had been working on tracking Noriega for more than a year. There were three to four dozen people in Panama specifically designated as the Noriega Tracking Team. And yet he'd slipped away.

At 11:30, Thurman reported over the loudspeaker that Noriega was possibly in the city of Colon, which was the last place he'd been spotted by his trackers.

Up from his nap, Powell arrived at the Crisis Situation Room at 11:52. He was wearing a black sweater with four stars sewn on each shoulder, and his green Army pants. His shirt was open at the neck, where his white T-shirt showed.

. . .

Down in Panama, two U.S. soldiers who had somehow found their way outside of Stiner's lock-up were overheard mentioning H-Hour by a PDF eavesdropper, who reported up the chain to Noriega.

"The Americans aren't coming," Noriega said. "They wouldn't do a thing like that." He arranged to have a meeting at the Comandancia the next morning at eight o'clock to review the situation.

U.S. listeners picked up part of a conversation in which some-one from the PDF said, "The ballgame starts at one."

Stiner was convinced that this referred to the H-Hour, and that the operation had been compromised. He picked up the direct line to Thurman.

"We need to advance the timing," Stiner said, explaining that it looked as if some of the PDF knew.

"How much advance do you want?" Thurman asked.

"How about thirty minutes?"

"Okay, do it," Thurman said, passing the information to Washington, not asking approval.

But there were complications. The rescue of Muse and the attack on the Comandancia had to be precisely coordinated. A swing bridge had to be placed over the canal so four Sheridan tanks could be moved onto a hill where they could hit the Comandancia with direct fire. There was a ship in one of the canal locks and it had to be cleared out before the swing bridge could be moved into place.

Stiner picked up the phone again to Thurman.

"I can't do it in thirty minutes," Stiner reported. "How about fifteen?"

"Fifteen's okay too," Thurman said.

At 12:07 a.m. Thurman officially sent out the order to JSOC that it should execute its Muse rescue mission at H minus 15, or 12:45. At 12:18 he directed the same execution time for the attack on the Comandancia and for the Navy SEALs' mission at Puenta Paitilla Airport, where they were to come ashore and disable Noriega's private jet, a possible escape vehicle.

A report of a female U.S. dependent wounded by the PDF at the U.S.-controlled Albrook Air Force Station in Panama City came in to Powell and the others over the speaker in the Crisis Situation Room at 12:29. In the next five minutes they listened to reports from Thurman about gunfire at Fort Amador, and machine-gun fire at the strategically located Bridge of the Americas across the canal, as well as at Albrook.

President Bush had informed Cheney and Powell that the point of no return would be achieved once Endara agreed to be sworn in as president of Panama and to request U.S. intervention. If Endara would not play, they had to check with him personally, Bush said.

Thurman was heard from again at 12:39. The swearing in of Endara as the new president of Panama had been completed.

Although some units had moved into place in advance, official execution of JUST CAUSE took place at H minus 15. At exactly the moment of execution, Thurman's voice came over the speaker, reporting a gunfire exchange in the vicinity of the Comandancia. The PDF was firing at the helicopters coming in for Muse at the nearby Modelo Prison.

Divided into task forces with names like Task Force Red, Task Force Bayonet and Task Force Semper Fi, the troops so carefully prepared for this moment by Thurman and Stiner were swinging into action at spots in and all around Panama. Task Force Bayonet, for example, was assigned the job of securing Fort Amador, the Comandancia and PDF sites throughout Panama City. Task Force Red was responsible for the adjacent Torrijos and Tocumen airports and for Rio Hato.

Around the time the operation began, President Bush arrived in the Oval Office wearing a dark blue sweater over his shirt and tie. He signed a short order authorizing the armed forces to apprehend and arrest Noriega and other persons in Panama currently under indictment in the United States for drug-related offenses.

At 12:57, gunfire was reported on the Atlantic side of Panama.

At 1 a.m., the military officially moved up to the highest defense readiness condition, called DEFCON 1, signifying that hostilities were under way. At the same time, a report came in to the Crisis Situation Room that the commander of the PDF's military Zone 3, one of seven military zones, was staying out of the fight.

· · ·

From his experience in the Ford White House, Cheney knew the human reaction to this kind of crisis. The situation would build and everyone would stay up all night to hear the latest news on events they could do nothing about. Then, when the moment of action or decision arrived, they would all be exhausted and in the worst possible shape to make judgments. So Cheney had gone up to his office after dinner and fallen asleep in a small bunk room there. After several hours, he rose. For the first time, he used his office shower.

He then went down to the Crisis Situation Room, where he saw that Powell, Kelly and Sheafer were already set up. It was two minutes after one o'clock. He moved in next to Powell at the center of the long table.

Almost immediately, a second report came in from SOUTH-COM concerning the PDF Zone 3 commander. Great news: the commander had ordered his unit to stand down. This was significant, as it meant several companies were out of action on the PDF side.

At 1:07 there was a report that U.S. troops using a loudspeaker to order the PDF troops in the Comandancia to lay down their arms had been met instead with return fire. Just two minutes later, CNN reported that U.S. troops had attacked Noriega's headquarters.

At 1:11 Powell and Cheney listened as the news came over the loudspeaker that the Delta team was on the roof of the Modelo Prison. Two minutes later, word came that Muse was out.

At 1:14 the PDF was reported to be retreating at one of the areas of battle, Albrook Air Force Station.

At 1:17 SOUTHCOM said the Comandancia was calling for reinforcements.

At 1:19 the Rangers were reported to be parachuting into the key target area of Rio Hato.

The PDF commander of the 5th Company at Balboa had shut down his operation, Thurman reported at 1:23.

The next report said the Marines at the U.S. Embassy were taking fire from rocket-propelled grenades.

Just before 1:30 SOUTHCOM issued a few positive reports. All the Rangers had dropped onto Rio Hato, and the Bridge of the Americas was secure.

There was a report that the helicopter carrying Muse away from the Modelo Prison had crashed, and it looked as if the crew and Muse might be dead. Disappointment was written all over Powell's face. Muse was the guy they were going to rescue for the President, and now his helicopter had gone down.

At about the same time, word came that U.S. troops had broken into Noriega's most likely hideout, a beach house, and found it empty. This intensified the pessimism in the room. They'd reached a real low—no Muse, no Noriega.

Powell knew there was an apartment near Colon that was another Noriega hangout. He felt too much time had elapsed between hitting the beach house and the apartment, and he called Thurman to let him know.

"When are we going to take down the apartment?" Powell snapped.

"We're working on it," Thurman replied.

Soon Thurman was back with the news that they'd taken down the apartment and it too was a blank. A third downer in a very short period.

· · ·

Over at the White House, Bush turned on the television set in his study. At 1:40 Marlin Fitzwater appeared on the screen. "The President has directed United States forces to execute at one a.m. this morning pre-planned missions in Panama to protect American lives, restore the democratic process, preserve the integrity of the Panama Canal treaties and apprehend Manuel Noriega.

"Last Friday," Fitzwater told the reporters gathered before him, "Noriega declared a state of war with the United States."

"Has General Noriega been captured yet, Marlin?" a reporter asked.

"We don't know how long it will take, but that is our ultimate objective," Fitzwater said. "It has not happened at this time."

"Marlin," another reporter asked, "can you tell us who's got operational control?"

"Operational control is in the Pentagon."

· · ·

Just before 2 a.m., Powell and Cheney received word from Thurman that all was quiet at the U.S. Embassy, and that everything was going okay at Tocumen Airport. The mission at Tocumen was to seize the airport and neutralize a PDF company based there. An hour before, AC-130s and AH-6s had opened fire on the infantry company's compound, and three minutes later, Rangers had parachuted in to eliminate PDF resistance.

Minutes later there was a report that the commander of the PDF's Zone 6 had ordered his troops to abandon posts before the Americans arrived.

At 2:20 a.m. word came that Muse had survived the crash and was safe. Instantly, the atmosphere became buoyant, almost joyful. Powell and Cheney knew they'd accomplished a main objective.

Powell picked up the phone and called CIA Director Webster. "Just wanted you to know we got your man out and he's safe," Powell said, now bursting with optimism.

Cheney called the White House. In his first call across the river shortly after arriving at the Crisis Situation Room that night, he had talked to Scowcroft. After that, at the President's request, Cheney's calls were all put through directly to the President, about one every half hour. Now he told Bush that Muse was out and safe. What's more, the Delta team had done the job in record time, even better than the best practice time.

SOUTHCOM reported at 2:40 that the Comandancia was in flames.

A sour note was struck at 2:49, when Cheney and Powell listened to Thurman report that Noriega was still at large. Except for this large problem, the operation generally seemed to be going well and was on track. Shortly after 3:00 they learned that PDF forces at Colon, Tocumen Airport and near the Costa Rican border had fallen. The PDF was surrendering left and right, without a fight. Within a half hour, the Comandancia fires were out.

Powell listened, made notes and talked quietly to Cheney. Neither was trying personally to manage the operation. Both felt they had to let Thurman and the others do their jobs. Although he was glad about all the reports of success, Powell knew that war—particularly war fought in darkness—is a funny thing. It was likely that bad news, especially really bad news, would be the slowest to work its way up the chain to him. He was also aware that the first information to reach him was liable to be wrong.

More bad news did come. Three platoons of Navy SEALs who had moved into Puenta Paitilla Airport before H-Hour to disable Noriega's private jet had met heavy PDF resistance. Of the attacking platoon of 15 men, four had been killed by PDF fire, and seven were wounded. Although the SEALs had succeeded in disabling the aircraft, the deaths of these elite fighters shocked those gathered in the Crisis Situation Room.

The Noriega question tugged at Powell throughout the night. At 3:39, they received a signals intelligence report that the dictator had fled and was still safe. The report was based on an intercepted phone conversation. An hour and a half later, SOUTHCOM said another intercept indicated that Noriega was hiding in a reinforced house, location unknown.

Cheney continued to give the President half-hour updates. The Comandancia had been reduced to rubble. The key military targets had been overrun, and much of the organized PDF resistance had been eliminated. At 4 a.m. Bush went to bed.

About 4:30 a.m. Powell started to prepare his end—all the military details—of a public briefing that he and Cheney would be giving in a few hours. He looked over the large operational maps they were using in the NMCC. The maps had far too much detail for a simple show-and-tell—the language of monks, he called it. And the special operations missions, which shouldn't be revealed to the public, were identifiable. He knew his briefing had to be good, and these graphics weren't going to cut it. Powell called in the Pentagon's expert mapmaker and ordered up some instant simplifications.

He took his notes and went into a little room off to the side of the Crisis Situation Room which had a map of Panama on the wall. Army Brigadier General Tom White, Powell's executive assistant, brought him a cup of coffee. The Chairman sat there for 15 or 20 minutes, in a kind of trance, alternately making notes and studying the map. He remarked to an aide that the American public's opinion of the operation would start its rise or fall on the basis of his and Cheney's presentation. When Powell was done, he went down to his office bathroom, took off his sweater and put on a tie and Army jacket.

One advantage of the post-midnight H-Hour was that the administration would be able to take an early time slot on morning television and provide its own description of the operation before the news day began. Given the massive influx of U.S. troops, there was a virtual guarantee that some early successes could be reported.

The plan called for the President to address the nation at about 7 a.m., followed by a briefing and press conference at the Pentagon by Cheney and Powell.

. . .

At 6:30 a.m. Bush returned to the Oval Office. An 11-paragraph speech had been prepared. There was not enough time to put it on the TelePrompTer. He would have to read from a typed version with his own notes written in the margin. By 7:20 Bush was before the cameras. He gave a very broad overview of the situation. "General Noriega's reckless threats and attacks upon Americans in Panama created an imminent danger to the thirty-five thousand American citizens in Panama," he said.

"The United States intends to withdraw the forces newly deployed to Panama as quickly as possible."

He reminded his audience of "those horrible pictures of newly elected [Panamanian] Vice President Ford, covered head to toe with blood, beaten mercilessly."

Bush said, "I took this action only after reaching the conclusion that every other avenue was closed."

Immediately afterwards, Cheney and Powell appeared at the Pentagon press room to brief reporters and answer questions. Cheney delivered a seven-paragraph statement that echoed the President's.

Powell took the podium as Kelly stood by the newly drawn maps.

"There will be details that I cannot get into for purposes of operational security," Powell said. Speaking without notes and taking much more time than Cheney had, he moved confidently over the geography of Panama and the details of the operation, matching units to missions and locations. He preserved enough of the language of monks to show he knew his forces—the 193rd Infantry Brigade, 7th Infantry Division, 82nd Airborne Division, the 16th Military Police Brigade, etc.—making no less than 16 references to various units.

He began with a report of success. U.S. forces had taken the prison at Gamboa, "within which there are some PDF personnel who had been put in jail as a result of the coup attempt earlier in the fall, and we now have some forty-seven, forty-eight very happy prisoners who have been released." The electrical distribution center was secure, he said, as was Madden Dam. A PDF infantry company on the north side had been neutralized. The Bridge of the Americas across the canal had been taken, and the area around Howard Air Force Base was secure. The same with Rio Hato, the Comandancia, and the Torrijos international airport. "We also took special actions to immobilize the PDF Navy," Powell said. Reports of U.S. hostages were being checked.

"We have not yet located the General," Powell said, tight-jawed. "But, as a practical matter, we have decapitated him from the dictatorship of this country and he is now a fugitive and will be treated as such."

The American Embassy had taken some fire but nobody was injured.

So far, he said, preliminary information indicated that nine Americans had been killed in action and 39 wounded.

Most of the questions were addressed to Powell.

To one on Noriega, he replied: "He's demonstrated incredible ability to survive catastrophe. And we'll see over time whether he survives this catastrophe."

"This reign of terror is over," Powell also said.

"For the most part, organized resistance is over," he went on, declaring that many of those still out in the street "are just thugs and rabble rousers."

There were more questions on Noriega.

"We're looking for him. He's not running anything, because we own all of the bases he owned eight hours ago."

At the end of the session, when the questioning was over, Powell stepped to the microphone and said: "Could I just say that I hope you recognize how complicated an operation this was, and how competently it was carried out by the Armed Forces of the United States. We all, the Secretary and I, all of our associates, deeply regret the loss of American life. But that's sometimes necessary in pursuit of our national interests and in the fight for democracy."

.   .   .

Alma Powell had not known her husband was going to be on television that morning, but a family member had called to alert her. Normally very critical of his performances, she called him later that day at the Pentagon. "That was good," she said.

.   .   .

Powell began receiving calls from Army commanders from all over, offering their forces, pledging their readiness and enthusiasm.

Among those who called was the commander of the 101st Airborne Division at Fort Campbell, which had been put on secret alert to move into Nicaragua if the Sandinistas tried a military move. Powell would have had early warning of such a move, thanks to a program called TENCAP—Tactical Exploitation of National Capabilities—which harnessed the latest intelligence for immediate use in Panama. Using satellite and ground intercepts of radio and other communications, U.S. intelligence officers were able to monitor Cuban and Nicaraguan reaction to JUST CAUSE, to determine if those countries might somehow come to Noriega's aid.

In addition, satellite imagery and photos gathered by reconnaissance aircraft were sent from Fort Bragg via satellite to terminals at Southern Command. This link provided Thurman and Stiner with reconnaissance photos of Tocumen Airport, for example, and imagery reports on other critical sites in Panama, including the Comandancia, Fort Cimarron and Rio Hato.

By December 21—D-Day plus 1, as it was called in Pentagonese —almost all of the key goals of the operation had been achieved. The various task forces had done their assigned work, securing the key target sites. The JCS ordered the execution of BLIND LOGIC, the operations plan from the original PRAYER BOOK series to help run the new civilian government of Panama. The canal, closed down during the battle, was reopened for daylight operations. A snag that received heavy media attention, the PDF's holding of U.S. hostages—among them some journalists—at the Marriott Hotel, was resolved on this second day of the operation when the hotel was taken by U.S. soldiers and the hostages were evacuated.

There was international grumbling about the United States going into Panama. At a press conference on Thursday, the day after the operation, Bush was asked about tough Soviet condemnation of JUST CAUSE. The President said he wanted to send a wire or telegram to Gorbachev saying, "Look, if they kill an American Marine, that's real bad. And if they threaten and brutalize the wife of an American citizen, sexually threatening the lieutenant's wife while kicking him in the groin over and over again, then, Mr. Gorbachev, please understand this President is going to do something about it."

.   .   .

The failure to capture Noriega, along with other problems, including an outbreak of looting in Panama City, resulted in some bad press for the operation on Thursday and Friday. These days were the low point for Powell, but by the time he went home on Friday night, D plus 2, things were looking up. Noriega still hadn't been found, but the situation otherwise seemed to be under control. He wasn't surprised to find that many of the newspaper stories he saw that weekend, especially Saturday, were a little outdated and downbeat. Over years of media watching, Powell had learned that newspapers generally lagged 12 hours behind events. He read one article that fingered him by name as the man who'd recommended the Panama invasion.

I'm being set up, he said to himself, both disturbed and amused. Someone at the White House or State was trying to dump Panama off on him, Powell thought.

On Sunday, when more positive stories appeared, Bush visited the Pentagon. "Boy, Colin," he said to Powell, "things sure were grim yesterday. But now they sure look better."

.   .   .

The elusive Noriega, still at large, was the most serious stain on the operation. The United States announced that it had put a $1 million bounty on him, hoping that a PDF member or some other

Panamanian anxious to end the Noriega era would step forward. Powell began referring to the capture of Noriega as "this last little irritant," and continued to emphasize that Noriega had been eliminated as a leader. He had come to view the hunt for the fugitive general as a kind of crusade.

There were reports that large stashes of drugs and strange religious paraphernalia had been found in Noriega's home, and Powell took to calling Noriega "a dope-sniffing, voodoo-loving thug." (The alleged drugs found in Noriega's hangout turned out to be tamales containing slips of paper with the names of Noriega's enemies written on them. This was apparently part of a ritual to neutralize foes and had nothing to do with drugs.)

Prior to the operation, the conventional wisdom in the Pentagon was that Noriega would go down shooting rather than let himself be captured. Now just finding him was turning into an obsession.

"We will destroy his Robin Hood image," Powell declared in his office on December 23. To a reporter who persisted with questions about the importance of capturing Noriega, Powell retorted, "Stick it."

The next day, Sunday, December 24, at about 3:30 p.m., a car drove up to the residence of the Vatican's representative in Panama, the Papal Nuncio. General Noriega, wearing a T-shirt and carrying two AK-47 semiautomatic rifles over his shoulder, emerged from the car, went inside the nunciature building and requested political asylum.

Powell knew this did not solve the problem at all. Noriega could stay in the residence indefinitely, creating a diplomatic standoff.

The Chairman expected Thurman and Stiner would come up with some ideas. He warned them to be careful, but determined that it would be best if he did not know what they might concoct.

Stiner knew he would have to respect the double sanctity of the Papal Nuncio's residence as both embassy and Church property. But there were ways to put pressure on the Church. A visiting archbishop was taken on a tour of Noriega's former house and office. He was shown some of the things that U.S. soldiers had found there: witchcraft materials, a library of books on Hitler, albums of pornographic and torture photos and a large poster of all the Catholic priests in Panama and other high Catholic officials in Central America that suggested they were on a hit list.

The Nuncio, the Reverend Sebastian Laboa, met with Thurman

and Stiner. He gave them a handwritten note that said if shooting
started inside the nunciature, they were authorized to conduct an
emergency assault to rescue as many people as possible and to
minimize death and suffering.

Stiner went to his headquarters and picked up the hotline to
Kelly at the Pentagon. He asked Kelly for new rules of engagement
that would permit his forces to enter the Nuncio's residence if
requested or if shooting started.

The request was passed to Powell and Cheney, who approved,
and within an hour Stiner had his new authority.

The next day, Wednesday, December 27, Thurman and Stiner
ordered the troops to blast the nunciature with ear-splitting
heavy-metal and other music, to prevent anyone from eavesdropping on SOUTHCOM's negotiations with the Papal Nuncio. It
could be heard for several blocks.

Other troops acted as if they were preparing the building for an
assault. Tall grass and brush in the neighborhood was cut down
to improve the view; street lights were shot out; barbed wire was
laid in the streets; patrols of a dozen men paraded around the
embassy walls; other soldiers took up posts in a parking garage
some 50 feet from the back of the embassy; an Army Black Hawk
helicopter landed several times nearby to unload troops and
equipment; light tanks and armored personnel carriers blocked all
the streets in the area.

Still, Noriega did not budge.

On Friday, December 29, Powell was watching a CNN report
that U.S. troops had entered the residence of the Nicaraguan ambassador to Panama. The camera revealed a sign the size of a
manhole cover showing unmistakably that it was the ambassador's residence. On the sidewalk outside the house, Powell spotted
the distinctive cracks made by U.S. armored personnel carriers.
He was furious. Invading an embassy was out of bounds. International convention made such buildings absolutely immune; they
were the equivalent of national property. The Iranian students had
done this kind of thing in 1979 when they had invaded the U.S.
Embassy in Teheran.

Powell called Thurman for some answers.

When there was no immediate reply, Powell knew there had
been a screw-up. He raised the issue with Cheney.

"Well, okay, let's get it worked out," Cheney replied calmly,
"but let's not come down hard on our guys."

When Thurman at last called back, he explained that they had intelligence that indicated the residence was full of weapons. The search had yielded four Uzi submachine guns, 12 AK-47s, six grenade launchers—the rocket-propelled type—and 17 bayonets. And, Thurman added, it was not clear it was a diplomatic residence.

"It's undeniable," Powell snapped. "I just saw it on CNN. Stop bullshitting me. We did it."

Well aware that Thurman was spring-loaded, Powell had been able to live with some of the CINCSOUTH's excesses. But now things were going out of control. Powell had a heart-to-heart talk with his commander about the need to make sure that they did not tarnish a brilliant operation through some minor incident in the aftermath. Powell now started to pull back some authority to Washington.

· · ·

At 8:44 p.m. on Wednesday, January 3, 1990, Noriega walked out of the nunciature in his military uniform and surrendered to members of Delta Force. When he was handcuffed, he shouted and cursed at the Nuncio, who was standing nearby. Apparently, Noriega had expected to be treated as a head of state, or a prisoner of war, and now he blamed the Nuncio for misleading him. The Nuncio blessed Noriega, who was taken by helicopter to Howard Air Force Base, where a DEA agent arrested him.

At 9 p.m. Cheney called Bush. Forty minutes later, Bush walked into the White House briefing room to read a six-paragraph statement announcing the arrest.

"The return of General Noriega marks a significant milestone in Operation JUST CAUSE. The U.S. used its resources in a manner consistent with political, diplomatic and moral principle. . . .

"I want to express the special thanks of our nation to those servicemen who were wounded and to the families of those who gave their lives. Their sacrifice has been a noble cause and will never be forgotten."

The smoke eventually cleared concerning Noriega's movements before he gave himself up. The U.S. trackers had lost the general around 6 p.m. in Colon. At the start of JUST CAUSE, Powell learned, the general had been at a brothel at Tocumen. When Noriega heard gunshots, he climbed into his trousers and jumped into an escape vehicle. Taking a well-traveled highway into Panama City, he disappeared into the city, where he moved from one hiding place to another, to houses of various friends and associates.

On January 5, Powell flew down to Panama to visit the commanders and the troops. The next day, in a meeting there with reporters, he emphasized the political result of the operation. "The most important mission we accomplished is that we gave the country back to its people."

Why such a large force? he was asked.

"I'm always a great believer in making sure you get there with what you need to accomplish the mission and don't go in on the cheap side."

What do you think the impact of the operation will be on the debate on the cuts in the defense budget?

"Thank you for the question," Powell boomed. "I hope it has a great effect. I hope it has enormous effect. . . . And as we start to go down in dollars and as we see the world changing, don't bust this apart. . . . Don't think that this is the time to demobilize the armed force of the United States, because it isn't. There are still dangers in the world."

He knew this statement would attract little or no attention. Nonetheless, he felt, Panama was truly manna from heaven.

He flew home glad that the operation didn't look any different on the ground than it had from the Pentagon. There was no sign of buried secrets. The politicians and the media would have little alternative but to declare it a success. A CBS poll released that day showed that 92 percent of Panamanians supported the U.S. military action.

The next day, Saturday, Powell was out in the garage behind Quarters 6, immersed in one of his favorite pastimes: fixing up an old Volvo.

In the weeks and months after the operation, Panama resurfaced now and then in the news, often in reports of previously unrevealed flaws.

After complaints from reporters who were shut out of covering JUST CAUSE as the operation was under way, the Defense Department's public affairs staff admitted it had botched its handling of the press pool. In a memo to the CINCs on this subject, Powell wrote that "otherwise successful operations are not total successes unless the media aspects are properly handled."

An Army paratrooper was charged with unpremeditated murder for killing an unarmed Panamanian civilian at a roadblock on the fourth day of the operation, but was acquitted in a military court.

SOUTHCOM's initial death counts for the operation, released in mid-January, were 314 Panamanian military fatalities, 202 Panamanian civilians and 23 U.S. troops. The CBS News show "60 Minutes" ran a report that as many as 4,000 Panamanian civilians had died in the conflict. Investigations by other organizations in Panama and the United States indicated SOUTHCOM wasn't far off the mark, although it probably had overestimated Panamanian military deaths while underestimating the civilian total. The SOUTHCOM numbers were generally accepted.

When *Newsweek* magazine reported that as many as 60 percent of U.S. casualties may have resulted from "friendly fire" from U.S. forces, the Pentagon announced for the first time that friendly fire accounted for two of the 23 U.S. deaths and 19 of 324 U.S. injuries.

· · ·

Powell settled back into a peacetime rhythm. Panama, the largest U.S. military action since Vietnam, was behind him. Now the focus was back on the military needs of the post–Cold War era. He spent many hours in his office, being briefed, working the phones, trying to come up with a strategy for change. He was sure that the best way to proceed was to trust his gut instincts, but he also had a collection of rules and maxims he used as a practical roadmap for each day of decisions. Many were on a list he'd drawn up, which he both handed out to visitors and kept in the center of his desktop, on display beneath the glass cover:

COLIN POWELL'S RULES

1. It ain't as bad as you think. It will look better in the morning.
2. Get mad, then get over it.
3. Avoid having your ego so close to your position that when your position falls, your ego goes with it.
4. It can be done!
5. Be careful what you choose. You may get it.
6. Don't let adverse facts stand in the way of a good decision.
7. You can't make someone else's choices. You shouldn't let some one else make yours.

8. Check small things.
9. Share credit.
10. Remain calm. Be kind.
11. Have a vision. Be demanding.
12. Don't take counsel of your fears or naysayers.
13. Perpetual optimism is a force multiplier.

To the left of that list was an aphorism not for public consumption that the Chairman had written out by hand on a piece of paper: SOMETIMES BEING RESPONSIBLE MEANS PISSING PEOPLE OFF.

There was yet another axiom Powell tried to live by, especially in his professional life. He occasionally confided it, but it wasn't written down. Powell didn't need to remind himself of that one: "You never know what you can get away with, unless you try."

PART TWO

16

IN EARLY APRIL 1990, the Saudi Arabian ambassador to the United States, Prince Bandar bin Sultan, received a call from his uncle, King Fahd.

Fahd reported that Iraqi President Saddam Hussein had just phoned to say that he wanted someone to come to Iraq to see him personally and discuss an urgent matter relating to America. Fahd wanted Bandar to undertake the mission. Bandar had been directly involved in the 1988 United Nations negotiations arranging a cease-fire in the eight-year Iran-Iraq War, and Saddam Hussein had agreed to receive him as the emissary.

Bandar, 41, had an absolutely unique position in Washington. Most ambassadors spent their time on ceremonies and the fringes of real power. Bandar had long-term friendships with Bush, Baker, Cheney, Scowcroft and Powell, having plied his backslapping irreverence and directness with all of them. This gave the Saudi royal family a channel into the upper reaches of the American government. Until Bandar had become ambassador in 1983, the Saudis had worked through obscure State Department officials. Bandar insisted on dealing with the top, cultivating personal relationships with those already there and with dozens of others who someday might be.

In 1981, before becoming ambassador, he obtained Vice President Bush's assistance in pushing President Reagan on a large arms sale package to Saudi Arabia. During the first Reagan term, Bush and Bandar had lunch several times a year. Bandar felt that Bush had a balanced view of the Middle East and was not emotionally or exclusively attached to the interests of Israel.

An Arab Gatsby who gave big parties and extended himself to any individual or group important to his country, Bandar had taken Vice President Bush seriously, even when Bush was dismissed as a weak number two to Reagan. In 1985, at a time when Bush was being widely criticized as ineffective, the prince threw a party for the Vice President with singer Roberta Flack for entertainment. Bandar even went fishing with Bush. He knew that personal relationships pushed things through the pipeline faster than anything else. A Saudi fighter pilot for 17 years and a favorite of King Fahd's, Bandar still walked with a fighter jock's swagger. He fit right into the tough-guy, cowboy-boot side of the Bush administration. Bandar spoke perfect English and was steeped in American habits.

Working political and media circles with cigars, gifts, invitations, information, off-color stories and practical jokes (a full-size blow-up doll of a naked woman for one Jewish journalist he had befriended), the prince was smooth and attentive. He could be both boyish and ruthless.

Fahd's latest request suggested that Bandar would have an opportunity to act as intermediary between Saddam and the United States, just the kind of task he enjoyed. He left immediately for Iraq in his private jet. At the airport on April 5, he was met by Saddam Hussein's personal secretary, who pointed the way. But security personnel told both Bandar and the secretary that Saddam was in a different location than planned. The personal secretary told Bandar that they were not allowed to know Saddam's whereabouts. The other senior government officials—even Saddam's brother, the chief of intelligence—did not know. Only the security people knew in advance where to find their leader at any given moment. This arrangement made it difficult, if not impossible, for any other high-ranking Iraqis to overthrow Saddam.

When Bandar sat down with Saddam, the Iraqi president said

he had requested the meeting because officials in the United States were grossly overreacting to his April 1 speech. In the widely publicized talk, Saddam had discussed his chemical weapons capability and threatened to burn half of Israel if he was attacked by Israel. The West, Saddam had said, "will be deluded if they imagine that they can give Israel the cover to come and strike. . . . By God, we will make the fire eat up half of Israel if it tries to do anything against Iraq."

The State Department had called the speech "inflammatory, irresponsible and outrageous." On April 3, the White House had issued a statement calling the remarks "particularly deplorable and irresponsible." President Bush that same day had publicly said, "This is no time to be talking about using chemical or biological weapons. This is no time to be escalating tensions in the Middle East. And I found those statements to be bad. . . . I would suggest that those statements be withdrawn."

Saddam told Bandar that his words had been misunderstood to mean he intended an offensive strike against Israel. He acknowledged to Bandar that he wished his speech had been different. It had been delivered to members of his armed forces at a public forum where emotions were running high, with people clapping and screaming. As they both knew, he said, it never hurt in the Arab world to threaten Israel, and so he had done it. Nonetheless, he had threatened to attack *only if* he was attacked. A surprise strike by Israel was always possible. In 1981, Israel had launched a preemptive air strike destroying the Osirak nuclear research reactor to the south of Baghdad, and the memory lingered. He did not want to provoke another attack, he said.

The Iraqi leader knew that the recent execution of a British journalist, Iranian-born Farzad Bazoft, in Iraq was also bringing him criticism from the West. But, Saddam said, the journalist had been spying, and they had found direct links between him and Israel.

"If I am attacked by Israel now," said Saddam, "I would not last six hours. When I was attacked the first time [1981], I was in a war [with Iran] and I could always say I was in a war. And now if I'm attacked, people will not understand why this happened." He would be embarrassed by another attack. There was an Arab summit meeting coming up, and Bandar knew Saddam was a proud man.

"I want to assure President Bush and His Majesty King Fahd that I will not attack Israel," Saddam stressed. In return, he said that the Americans would have to work with Israel to ensure that Israel would not attack Iraq.

Since neither Iraq nor Saudi Arabia had diplomatic relations with Israel, Saddam was asking Bandar, who regularly had direct contact with Bush, to send the message and receive a reply through the United States.

"Do you want us to mention this to Bush as our observation?" Bandar asked, "Or is it a message from you to President Bush?"

"It's a message from me to the President," Saddam replied.

Bandar said he would carry the message back to the United States.

There was a pause in the conversation. Then, almost out of the blue, Saddam referred to what he called "the imperialist-Zionist conspiracy."

"By the way," he said, "we have to be very careful about this conspiracy because the imperialist-Zionist forces keep pushing this theory that I have designs over my neighbors. I don't have designs over my neighbors."

Saddam did not name these neighbors, but Bandar interpreted him to mean the small Arab Gulf states such as the United Arab Emirates and Kuwait.

"Well, Mr. President," Bandar said, "your brothers, your neighbors don't suspect you. And if you tell me now that you don't have designs, then there is no reason for either of us to worry about it at all."

"No, no," Saddam said, "but it's important that we don't allow the imperialist-Zionist rumormill or forces to get between us."

Saddam then turned to justifying his verbal assault on Israel, though he continued giving assurances that he would not attack the Jewish state. Israel was the natural lightning rod for creating a crisis atmosphere, he said. It had been two years since the Iran-Iraq cease-fire, and the Iraqi people were getting relaxed. "I must whip them into a sort of frenzy or emotional mobilization so they will be ready for whatever may happen."

Bandar left after four hours. He prepared an 18-page memo for his own records that summarized his discussion with Saddam. Bandar also reported to King Fahd, who told him to prevail on his personal relationship with the White House and pass the message directly to Bush. No intermediaries.

Saudi Arabia shared more than 500 miles of its northern border with Iraq. A friendly, stable Iraq was very much in Fahd's interest. For years he had been vouching for Saddam, who shunned the moderate Arab camp. Iraq, like Syria and Libya, was an outlaw state frequently tied to terrorist organizations and accused of flagrant human rights abuses.

The Iran-Iraq War had provided an opportunity for the Saudis to bring Iraq closer to them. Bandar had acted as middleman between Iraq and CIA Director William J. Casey so Iraq could obtain highly classified satellite information about Iranian troop movements during the war. The Saudis had also signed a contract with the French for Mirage jets to be delivered to Iraq, and done countless other large and small favors for Saddam.

Bandar felt that Saddam appreciated the assistance, but he also sensed that Saddam hated the dependence.

Four days after his early April meeting with Saddam, Bandar was in the Oval Office to see Bush.

"His Majesty," Bandar began, "sent me here to give you a message that I got from President Saddam to you, which is he assures you he has no intention of attacking Israel." It was a direct message, Bandar said, not a Saudi interpretation, not King Fahd's thoughts but exclusively Saddam's. Saddam was saying he would respond if attacked by Israel but he would not initiate an attack on Israel.

Bush seemed flabbergasted. "Well, if he doesn't intend it, why on earth does he have to say it?"

Bandar reminded Bush of the 1981 Israeli attack on the Iraqi reactor. Saddam's been hit before, Bandar said. Some Israelis were saying a new Iraqi reactor that had been built should be hit, that it would have to be done sooner or later. So there were grounds for nervousness.

Bush was skeptical.

Saddam is suspicious there is a conspiracy against him, Bandar said.

Bull, Bush said. There is no conspiracy against him. It's his behavior that worries people.

Saddam is paranoid, Bandar said, like most military, security-conscious dictators. Little things mount up. Bandar told Bush that the British journalist Bazoft had the telephone number of an Israeli official in his pocket when he was arrested and he had been seen outside the Palestinian Liberation Organization headquarters before the Israelis attacked it. Bandar reported on Saddam's other points—his worry about the Arab summit, not wanting to be embarrassed. Bandar said that in his view, Saddam had been shaken by the reaction in the West and by President Bush's own statements, and the Iraqi now was just trying to calm everything down and do the right thing.

Bush said he would think about it all, but the bottom line was Saddam should not have made the verbal attacks he did.

Two days later Saddam contacted King Fahd and the Iraqi ambassador to the United States, Mohamed Mashat, asking if there was any response from Bush. The Iraqi leader, having given his assurances that he would not attack Israel, wanted explicit assurances from Bush that Israel would not strike Iraq.

It was mid-April when King Fahd told Bandar to go back to Bush again.

Bandar requested an immediate meeting that day. Bush was very busy, but he could always give Bandar a few minutes.

At the White House, Bush only had a little time to talk between meetings so the two stood off to the side.

"You know, Mr. President," Bandar said, "they really are serious about this and they want to assure you." Saddam and the Iraqis would not attack Israel. "And they would like to have assurance that Israel will not attack them because they're getting nervous."

"I don't want anybody to attack anybody," Bush said. He just wanted people to settle down, in the region and elsewhere, he said. "We will talk to the Israelis and I will get back to you. But everybody must just cool it."

Bush also indicated that he was baffled by Saddam. "If this guy really doesn't mean it, why the heck does he go around saying these things?"

The White House then contacted the Israelis, who said if Iraq did not launch anything against them, Israel would not launch anything against Iraq. The United States then passed that Israeli assurance directly to Saddam.

Bandar also passed along his understanding of these assurances to King Fahd, who called Saddam with the report.

17

THREE MONTHS LATER, early in the week of July 16, 1990, in a second-floor office in the innermost ring of the Pentagon, a stocky, balding, well-dressed man was working the phones like a bookie. The red, gray and green secure phones allowed him to discuss top-secret codeword material with the National Security Agency, CIA, National Photographic Intelligence Center and other U.S. intelligence units in and out of the Pentagon.

Walter P. "Pat" Lang, Jr., a 50-year-old retired Army colonel, was the Defense Intelligence Agency's national intelligence officer for the Middle East and South Asia, the senior Pentagon intelligence civilian for the region. He reported to the head of the DIA, a three-star general overseeing about 5,000 civilian and military personnel who coordinate intelligence for the Army, Navy, Air Force and Marines. The agency is charged with bringing unified intelligence summaries to the JCS and the Secretary of Defense, free of service bias. Lang was one of the people who directly received and evaluated raw intelligence, then relayed it in digested form to the highest level in the Pentagon, including Cheney and Powell. Lang not only had hands-on knowledge of satellite photos and communications intercepts, but was a Middle East expert fluent in Arabic. He had traveled to Iraq half a dozen times and had served in the early 1980s for three years as the defense attaché in Saudi Arabia.

This morning, Lang was hunched over the morning satellite photos of his region. Where there had been empty desert in southeastern Iraq, north of Kuwait, the day before, he saw the beginning of a brigade of an Iraqi tank division of T-72 tanks, the top-of-the-line heavy tanks supplied to Iraq by the Soviets. The photos also showed all kinds of equipment being loaded on rail lines, equipment that could only belong to the Republican Guard, the most elite units of President Saddam Hussein. These units existed primarily to protect the regime in the capital of Baghdad, and normally stayed nearby, in central Iraq. Why had the tanks been moved hundreds of miles? The photos from the high-resolution satellites were so detailed that Lang could identify the tanks as belonging to the Hammurabi Division, named after the Babylonian king who devised the first formal legal system. He knew, from following the battles of the eight-year Iran-Iraq War, that there was no more potent division in all of Iraq.

Iraq had been complaining bitterly that Kuwait was exceeding its oil production quotas set by the Organization of Petroleum Exporting Countries (OPEC), driving the prices down. Though Kuwait had once been part of Basra Province in Iraq, it had been granted independence in 1961 by the British. Various border disputes and animosities continued, but for practical purposes Iraq had acquiesced to Kuwait's status as a nation when it permitted Kuwait's admission to the Arab League in 1963.

To Lang, the military logic was overwhelming: the movement of this unit meant Saddam intended to use force somehow. But Lang needed to see more. One day's photos were not enough to start raising alarms.

The next morning's photographs were even more disconcerting. The whole of the Hammurabi Division, all 300 tanks and more than 10,000 men, was in place near the Kuwait border. A second division, the Medina Munawwrah, or Medina Luminous Division —another crack armored unit of the Republican Guard—was showing up on the border. The third day, a third division—the In God We Trust Division—could be seen moving into the region above Kuwait.

By July 19, more than 35,000 men from the three divisions were within 10 to 30 miles of the Kuwait border. The tanks were in the classic coiled pattern, all facing outward for maximum defense; the coil also made refueling and administration easier.

Over the years, Lang had closely followed Iraq. In 1986, during the Iran-Iraq War, he had seen Iraq turn a major corner militarily. The sprawling nation of nearly 18 million people in an area larger than the state of California was no longer a Third World military power. Its 1-million-man army was the fourth largest in the world. Iraq was now a major conventional power.

Most of the other Middle East experts in the CIA and other intelligence agencies had disagreed. DIA had a reputation for extravagant puffing of the military threat posed by other nations. But in 1987, Lang saw his view confirmed as Iraq waged increasingly sophisticated warfare, killing as many as 20,000 to 30,000 Iranians in a single battle. In the last major ground battle of the war, the Iraqis killed 65,000 Iranians. At that point, Lang felt, Iraq could have moved its army anywhere into Iran. The Iraqis had chosen to consolidate their gains and had made peace in 1988, wisely so, in Lang's view.

The sudden placement of three divisions on the Kuwaiti border was perplexing to Lang. In the fall of 1989, a secret National Intelligence Estimate representing the assessments of all the U.S. intelligence agencies, including the DIA and CIA, concluded that, while Saddam wished to dominate the Gulf region, he was unlikely to employ his military to do so because the eight-year war had so severely strained the country's economy.

There was something else that did not make sense. During the Iran-Iraq War, U.S. satellites had revealed that Iraq conducted scrupulous rehearsals of operations and battles in vacant parts of the desert. Lang could find no rehearsal indicating Saddam would take the three divisions just moved to the Kuwaiti border to battle, or anything resembling it. This suggested to him that Saddam did not intend to commit the forces to immediate battle. So, the intelligence summaries forwarded up the chain of command at this point stressed the extraordinary nature of the troop movements but did not forecast they would be used.

Powell read the intelligence summaries showing the Iraqi movement of 35,000 troops in three days. Troubling but not alarming, he concluded. General Kelly and the JCS intelligence analysts were saying it looked as if Iraqi leader Saddam Hussein was using the deployment as a threatening lever in the ongoing negotiations over oil. They thought that Iraq might seize a single Kuwaiti oil field or take two small islands in the Persian Gulf it coveted.

Earlier in the month, the Chairman had spent six days visiting Morocco, Egypt, Jordan and Israel. The heads of state and other senior officials all had downplayed the prospect of Middle East hostilities in the near future, and Powell had returned reassured of continuing stability in the region.

But he still had some concerns about Iraq. Saddam had just had himself declared President for Life by the powerless legislature. It was reminiscent of Noriega having himself named Maximum Leader. Powell wanted to take some preliminary planning steps. During his three years as Weinberger's military assistant, one of the constants in crisis management was the JCS's unpreparedness. They never seemed tuned in, fully ready, certainly never enough on top of the situation to meet the Secretary's needs and answer his questions.

Powell called Army General H. Norman Schwarzkopf, 55, the commander of the U.S. Central Command, the CINC responsible for the Middle East and Southwest Asia. Because the Gulf countries did not wish a visible U.S. presence in the region, Schwarzkopf's CENTCOM headquarters was at MacDill Air Force Base in Florida. CENTCOM was largely a paper command. Its commander had a staff of 700, but in a crisis fighting units would have to be assigned to him from all over the world.

A burly, aggressive and outspoken former West Point football player (class of 1956), Schwarzkopf was known as "The Bear," and "Stormin' Norman." At 6 foot 3, he looked like a taller version of the actor Carroll O'Connor of the old TV series "All in the Family." Army Chief Vuono called him "H. Norman Cigar" —Vuono felt there was as much smoke as fire behind his fierce exterior.

He was a terror as a boss, often furious when unhappy or dissatisfied, infamous for shooting the messengers who brought bad news. Schwarzkopf also sometimes exploded when Pentagon civilians with little or no military experience made proposals he found militarily unsound. When the Army undersecretary had proposed robot infantrymen and radio-controlled armored cars several years earlier, Schwarzkopf had launched into a desk-thumping tirade.

He was familiar with the Middle East, having spent two years as a teenager living in Teheran. His father, a two-star Army general, had been sent there by General George Marshall to set up an Iranian national police force.

Powell had come to know Schwarzkopf about five years earlier when they both had quarters at Fort Myer, Virginia. They had grown close two years later when Powell was the national security adviser and Schwarzkopf was the Army's operations deputy, or "little chief." The CINC for the Central Command was a post held alternately by Army and Marine generals by agreement of the chiefs. But in 1988 the Navy had attempted to put an admiral in, arguing that since 1987, when it had begun escorting Kuwaiti tankers through the Persian Gulf, the Navy's maritime mission had been the command's centerpiece. Having a general in Florida running operations thousands of miles away at sea was absurd, they argued.

Powell thought it would be a mistake to let the Navy take over. CENTCOM had been created to coordinate and command a rapid deployment of ground forces to the Middle East. In a real crisis the problem would be on the ground. He carefully lent his support to the Army's candidate, Schwarzkopf.

Schwarzkopf was one of the dozens of four-stars Powell had leapfrogged to become Chairman, but since then he had become one of Powell's favorite CINCs because he had adjusted to the twin realities of a diminished Soviet threat and a smaller U.S. force. Powell also appreciated Schwarzkopf's glandular qualities. When he felt Powell was wrong or had pissed someone off, he said so.

Now Powell asked Schwarzkopf for an evaluation of the Iraqi troop buildup, and the general said it looked at most as if Iraq was poised to launch a punitive but limited strike into Kuwait. Powell said that he wanted Schwarzkopf to draft a two-tiered plan for possible U.S. responses to any Iraqi move against Kuwait, which held 10 percent of the world's oil reserves. The first tier was what U.S. forces could do to retaliate against Iraq; the second was what the United States might do defensively to stop any Iraqi move. Powell promised to "pipe"—send directly and immediately —to Schwarzkopf any special high-level intelligence or information he learned in Washington. They agreed to schedule a day soon for Schwarzkopf to come to the Pentagon to brief the chiefs in the Tank.

At a press breakfast on July 19, before the intelligence about the Iraqi troop buildup had leaked, Cheney was asked about Iraq's threats to Kuwait over the oil question. "We would, in fact," Cheney replied, "take seriously any threat to U.S. interests or U.S. friends in the region."

In the meantime, the United Arab Emirates (UAE), the small Persian Gulf oil state which also was being bullied by Iraq for overproducing oil and driving down prices, asked the United States secretly to supply two large KC-135 aerial-refueling tankers. The tankers would allow the UAE to keep patrol planes in the air around the clock. Schwarzkopf, Powell, policy undersecretary Paul Wolfowitz and Cheney recommended that the United States agree to the request. The State Department was initially opposed but finally was talked into approving it on Saturday night, July 21, and the White House gave a final okay.

A short-notice U.S. Navy exercise with the United Arab Emirates was announced, pulling two U.S. ships out of port to join four other ships in the Gulf. This exercise was basically a cover for the KC-135s. On July 24, Pete Williams publicly confirmed the presence of the KC-135s, as well as the naval exercise, portraying the actions as a signal of support for the UAE and Kuwait. The UAE was furious and cabled Washington that it had wanted the actions kept secret, with no public declarations. Evidently the Arab states were still jumpy about getting too close to the U.S. military.

. . .

Meanwhile, Pat Lang continued to monitor Iraq. At the rate of almost a division a day, Saddam had moved five additional divisions—four infantry and one special operations division—to positions north of Kuwait. Within 11 days, eight divisions had been amassed. Each had moved 300 to 400 miles. Giant heavy-equipment transport trucks carried the tanks, protecting their delicate tracks for use in battle. In all, Saddam had 100,000 troops on the border. Moving that many men and troops would have been a considerable military achievement for any nation. Since these were the maneuver units normally kept in the center of Iraq for use in any contingency at any border, Saddam was accepting some risk by using them for this single mission.

. . .

With one hour's notice, on July 25, Saddam summoned the U.S. ambassador to Iraq, April Glaspie, to his office. Glaspie, a career diplomat, did not have time to obtain any new instructions from the State Department.

U.S. policy toward Iraq was muddled. Bush administration officials had been talking tough about Saddam's threats against Israel, the movement of Iraqi SCUD missile launchers closer to Israel, and Iraq's efforts to illegally import components for nuclear weapons. At the same time, the administration had blocked congressional efforts to impose economic sanctions on Iraq or cut U.S. food assistance. Baker's most recent public comment on U.S-Iraq relations was optimistic, saying there was a "possibility of improvement, and we want to encourage that possibility."

Glaspie, 48, who had been ambassador since 1988, was suspicious of Saddam. She had claimed to colleagues that she intended to keep the "thug" in place.

"What can it mean when America says it will now protect its friends?" * Saddam asked, in an apparent reference to Cheney's statement that the United States would stick by its friends in the Gulf. "It can only mean prejudice against Iraq. This stance plus maneuvers and statements which have been made has encouraged the UAE and Kuwait. . . .

"The United States must have a better understanding of the situation and declare who it wants to have relations with and who its enemies are."

Glaspie said, "I have direct instruction from the President to seek better relations with Iraq."

"But how?" Saddam asked.

Glaspie said that more talks and meetings would help. She remarked that she had seen an ABC News profile of Saddam and his interview with Diane Sawyer. "That program was cheap and unjust," Glaspie said. "And this is a real picture of what happens in the American media—even to American politicians themselves. These are the methods the Western media employs. I am pleased that you add your voice to the diplomats who stand up to the media. Because your appearance in the media, even for five minutes, would help us to make the American people understand Iraq.

* The direct quotes are from an Iraqi translation of the meeting made from a tape recording. A U.S. official said Ambassador Glaspie's own official report of the meeting to the State Department corresponds with the Iraqi version, but Glaspie later said that only 80 percent of the meeting had been published by the Iraqis.

This would increase mutual understanding. If the American President had control of the media, his job would be much easier."

Later in the meeting Glaspie told Saddam, "But we have no opinion on the Arab-Arab conflicts like your border disagreement with Kuwait." She went on to say that the United States would insist on a nonviolent settlement. "I received an instruction to ask you, in the spirit of friendship—not in the spirit of confrontation —regarding your intentions."

Saddam said that through the intervention of Egyptian President Hosni Mubarak he had agreed to talks with the Kuwaitis.

"This is good news," Glaspie said. "Congratulations." She added that she had planned to postpone a trip to the United States the following week, but with this good news, she would leave Baghdad on Monday.

· · ·

Powell was relieved when he saw the cable Glaspie sent to Washington on her meeting with Saddam. It seemed to suggest that there was room for negotiations between Iraq and Kuwait. All the Iraqi troops on the border certainly indicated that something strange was going on. But his days seemed to be filled with people and documents reporting strange, inconclusive goings-on. It was in some respects a world filled with fuzzy, blurred pictures, and his approach was to let time fine-tune them.

As he monitored the flow of information, Powell remained cool about the prospects for trouble. He knew what a field army had to do to prepare for combat, and the Iraqi Army was not acting as if it were really going to attack. Four things were missing: (1) communications networks were not in place—intercepts showed the traffic levels were too low for an invasion; (2) artillery stocks were not in place for offensive action; (3) other needed munitions were not there; and (4) there was an insufficient logistics "tail"— supply lines—capable of supporting attacks by armored tank forces.

· · ·

Friday, July 27, was a fairly routine day for Powell—several foreign visitors and a meeting of the Defense Planning Resources Board, one of the Pentagon's many policy committees and oversight groups. He also was going to attend the Marines' weekly evening parade and a reception hosted by Al Gray at the Marine Barracks, a summer Friday night ritual.

Saudi Ambassador Prince Bandar had asked to stop by and see him at the Pentagon at 4 p.m. Powell and Bandar had known each other for more than a decade. They had played racquetball when Bandar was a major in the Saudi Air Force assigned to Washington in his pre-ambassador days and Powell was in one of his early Pentagon assignments.

Powell was somewhat wary of Bandar, a specialist in out-of-channel solutions and relationships. In Bandar's office in his lavish ambassador's residence, he kept 15 to 20 locked attaché cases containing the details of covert operations or confidential arrangements with individuals and countries. Bandar's fingerprints were all over the Iran-contra affair; he had been the go-between with the Reagan administration arranging the controversial $25 million in secret Saudi funding for the Nicaraguan contras; he had worked with Reagan CIA Director William J. Casey to set up the assassination of a suspected Middle East terrorist leader in Beirut with a car bomb which instead killed at least 80 bystanders and not the terrorist leader; he had arranged a huge, secret, $3 billion Saudi purchase of ballistic missiles from China.

Bandar worked hard to keep in touch with the five key people in the administration—Bush, Baker, Scowcroft, Cheney and Powell. No more politically oriented group could be running the U.S. government, he felt. To a certain extent he found the five interchangeable—each half statesman, half warrior, half politician, half of everything. A very lethal inner circle, capable of playing at the highest level of political gamesmanship, he had once remarked. Of the five, he judged Powell probably the most cautious.

This Friday afternoon, Bandar told Powell that Saudi King Fahd was being assured by everyone in Iraq and the Middle East that Saddam was not going to invade Kuwait. Saddam had given personal assurances to Mubarak of Egypt and King Hussein of Jordan. It isn't going to happen, Bandar said confidently. Saddam was saying it was only a military exercise of his crack divisions. Saddam's summons to U.S. Ambassador Glaspie was a positive sign, he said. Clearly, the dispatch of the KC-135s to the United Arab Emirates had caught Saddam's attention. Though the official Saudi position—Bandar said he had instructions on this from his government—was that the UAE was wrong to ask for the aircraft, the Saudi government believed that once asked, the United States was correct to provide the planes. Bandar said he personally felt the UAE had done the right thing.

Powell agreed that Saddam was saber-rattling. His information supported that view.

The crisis has peaked and will be resolved peacefully, at least for the moment, Bandar said. This week, this year is okay. But he predicted later trouble from Saddam.

Bandar and the Saudis held Kuwait in deep contempt, generally viewing the Kuwaiti ruling family and leadership as a mercantile class with little national identity. Their land was a business before it was a nation. When Bandar was out with close friends and had to visit the washroom, he would say, "I've got to go to Kuwait."

Confident that there was no immediate crisis, Bandar was planning to leave for Europe the next week and take his family on an around-the-world August vacation, including stops in Singapore, China, Bali and Hawaii.

Powell said he too expected August to be quiet and was planning to take some leave.

"Well, Colin," Bandar said, "it looks good. Everything looks on track. Of course, if he escalates this, you may have to come help us all." The Saudis had spent tens of billions on American arms, additional airfields and vast military installations. The implied contract had for years been that the United States was the protector.

"Let's pray he doesn't escalate it," Powell said.

"Well, what would you do if he did?"

Powell waved him off. His eyes were very careful.

What would be your recommendation? Bandar pressed.

"I have no view," Powell said. "That would be up to the President."

Bandar, probing and testing, pushed a third time. As a former national security adviser, as the Chairman, how would you look at it? Come on, Colin.

"In the hypothetical," Powell said, "if I was asked, should we go, I would say no. If I was told, I'd go, but I'd go to win. I don't want to go to lose."

Bandar said that he hoped it didn't come to that.

"I hope, too."

• • •

Since the deputy national security adviser Bob Gates was out of town, no deputies committee meeting on the Iraqi-Kuwaiti situation had been held. Robert Kimmitt, the undersecretary for political affairs at State, called a deputies committee meeting that same Friday, July 27, at the State Department.

A general feeling of optimism characterized the meeting. Bandar's positive interpretation of the Saddam-Glaspie exchange was circulating. President Mubarak had sent a personal message to President Bush, repeating his forecast of no imminent trouble and cautioning the United States to stop both saying and doing things to try to influence the situation. Let the Arabs handle it, Mubarak said. This message was carrying great weight with the White House, where Scowcroft interpreted it as saying, Hey, relax.

A direct message from Baker to Iraq was drafted and circulated. Restrained in tone, it assured Saddam that the United States was trying to get along with Iraq and attempting to establish a way to work with him, and that Iraq must reciprocate.

Paul Wolfowitz, on behalf of Defense, objected to the message, and urged something stronger. If a stiffer message could not be sent, he said it would be better to send nothing. But the general feeling was that Saddam was not going to cross fellow Arab Mubarak.

CIA Deputy Director Richard Kerr said that the level of buildup made it hard to dismiss the possibility of military action, but his experts noted the strong counterarguments: Iraq's real enemy was to its west—Israel. And it would be unprecedented for one Arab state to attack another.

Baker's restrained message was sent.

At the Pentagon later, Wolfowitz was trying to figure out how the situation might be influenced indirectly. He proposed moving the so-called MPS ships, Maritime Pre-positioned Ships, at the U.S. base on the island of Diego Garcia in the Indian Ocean, the closest supply base to the Persian Gulf but still 3,000 miles away. These ships held 30 days' food, ammunition and supplies for a Marine unit of more than 16,000.

Powell was opposed to such a show of force. What for? What can it accomplish? What's the mission? he asked.

The Chairman did not normally like to use his forces as a signal, and didn't want some bright idea by the civilians to get them committed with no clear objective in sight. Also, Powell didn't want to get started on a vague objective, and then midway through the mission have the military told what the administration *really* wanted to accomplish. Moving MPS ships signaled a commitment of ground forces, and no one was talking about that. Sending the KC-135s to the UAE had not accomplished much, he noted, and in retrospect he thought it had been a mistake. The announcement had scared the hell out of the UAE, not the Iraqis. And deploying the MPS ships would leak to the news media, and then the administration would have to provide an explanation.

Wolfowitz felt this attitude undervalued the impact such a show of force could have on the diplomatic moment. There are benefits in ambiguity, he believed.

Kuwait had not requested any help, Powell noted. MPS ships were not an acceptable solution. Where would the Marines land?

Wolfowitz conceded. The Kuwaiti ambassador had come to see him in the Pentagon earlier that week and talked about how worried he was. Wolfowitz had given the ambassador every opening to ask for assistance, but he had not done so.

Hard to help someone who doesn't want to be helped, Powell felt. Kuwait had not moved any of its small army of 20,000 to meet the Iraqis at the border.

No MPS ships were deployed.

.   .   .

On Monday, July 30, Pat Lang sat down to write a top-secret electronic-mail message to the DIA director, Lieutenant General Harry E. Soyster, and the other division heads within the agency. The secure internal electronic-mail system, called E-Mail, provided a means of quick, nearly instantaneous communications by computer with the boss. Soyster would decide whether to give it further circulation.

"I have been looking at the pattern of reinforcement along the Kuwaiti border," Lang typed on his Zenith 386 computer. "There is some artillery and logistics moving; aircraft are moving. There is absolutely no reason for Saddam Hussein to do this, it doesn't make any sense if his aim is to intimidate Kuwait. He has created the capability to overrun all of Kuwait and all of Eastern Saudi Arabia. If he attacks, given his disposition, we will have no warning.

"I do not believe he is bluffing. I have looked at his personality profile. He doesn't know how to bluff. It is not in his past pattern of behavior.

"I fear that Kuwait will be so stiff-necked in answering his demands that they will not fulfill his minimal requirements.

"In short, Saddam Hussein has moved a force disproportionate to the task at hand, if it is to bluff. Then there is only one answer: he intends to use it."

The interpretation that Saddam was trying to intimidate did not pass Lang's common-sense test. Kuwait did not have the intelligence capability and satellites to see the large Iraqi force on its border. Only the United States would know for sure, and Saddam could not know whether this intelligence would be passed on. So, if the 100,000 troops were only a show of force, a demonstration, it was being lost on the audience it was designed to influence—Kuwait.

He finally pushed the key sending the message on its way.

There were too many people involved in preparing formal intelligence papers that went through too many hands and committees, Lang felt. These papers tended to iron out the differences into a whole that in the end said nothing. The general rule in intelligence was never be wrong. An analyst didn't have to be right, but it was a great curse to be wrong. So the formal papers and national estimates hedged.

Lang wanted his new analysis to serve as a thunderclap. The horrible truth, he realized, was that when the policymakers had some idea or interpretation in their minds, intelligence assessments, even thunderclaps, would not move them. The mind-set *not* to believe could be a potent force. And, after all, he could not prove this force was going to be used.

He had another motive. Earlier in the month he had spent two days at a Rand Corporation seminar in which the participants examined an Iraqi threat against Kuwait. They had decided that the only effective way to forestall such a situation would be to get the President of the United States to warn Saddam that if he stepped over the border, the United States was going to come get him. Lang did not include this suggestion in his message; he was an intelligence officer and it was not his job to make policy recommendations.

Soyster told Lang he did not believe his assessment. The DIA director just did not find it conceivable that Saddam would do something so anachronistic as an old-fashioned land grab. Countries didn't go around doing things like that any more. But Soyster knew the message from Lang could not be ignored. He ordered copies hand-carried to Cheney and Powell, and appended a margin note saying he wanted them to see Lang's conclusion.

Powell considered Lang's interpretation a mere personal assessment. It was not based on any new hard information. Iraqi communications and munitions were still at insufficient levels, and no Iraqi airpower was in place to support a ground attack.

CIA Deputy Director Kerr, too, told Powell that an invasion could be launched, but the CIA had not yet put this down in a written intelligence report. This suggested to Powell that it also was an educated guess. Again it was apparently a personal conclusion, and Powell didn't see any firm facts backing it up.

After Lang had sent his message, he was dispatched to give the Kuwaiti ambassador in Washington a briefing on the buildup. He described the situation in great detail and asked him, "Well, are you going to do anything?"

"What can we do?" the ambassador replied.

· · ·

At his regular noon press briefing on Tuesday, July 31, Pete Williams was asked about a story on page 16 of that day's *Washington Post*. "Have the Iraqis moved 100,000 troops to the Kuwaiti border?"

"That would get into intelligence information which we just can't discuss," Williams said.

The reporter pressed, "You've not refused in the past to give the information, you've refused to say how you got it. You can't confirm that the troops are there?"

"I've seen reports about the troops there," Williams replied, following the administration line that the issue be downplayed, "but we've never discussed here numbers or made any further comments on that. I think the State Department has some language they've been using about obviously being concerned about any buildup of forces in the area, and can go through, as we've gone through here, what our interests in the Gulf are, but we've never really gotten into numbers like that or given that kind of information out."

· · ·

When Lang arrived at his office about 6 a.m. on Wednesday, August 1, some of his staff were waiting for him. They directed him to the latest pictures of the Kuwait-Iraq border which had arrived at DIA moments before.

All three Iraqi armored divisions had uncoiled and moved dramatically forward to within three miles of the Kuwait border. It was breathtaking, a beautiful military maneuver. Hammurabi and In God We Trust had taken up positions near the main four-lane highway heading into the center of Kuwait. Hundreds of tanks were on line—all facing toward Kuwait, spaced some 50 to 75 yards apart. It was a genuine line of death, miles long. Artillery had moved in behind the tanks.

The Medina Luminous Division had moved around to the western side of Kuwait. These tanks also were on line, stretched out for miles.

Command tanks had taken the traditional battlefield position in the rear of the line in the center of each division.

He had been wrong about there being no advance warning, Lang realized. Here it was. Saddam was being very deliberate. As Lang's eyes raced over the images, he realized that armored units could not more vividly advertise their intent. It was as if a gun had been loaded and aimed, and a finger put on the trigger. Now he was watching the muscle in the finger tighten; it was happening in slow motion before his eyes.

The photographs also showed that the Iraqis had moved some 80 helicopters closer to the border in a classic air-land assault posture.

Lang drafted a top-secret, highest-priority flash warning message describing the situation and forecasting an attack that night or the next morning. A special top-secret bulletin was put out to senior officials in the Pentagon. The whisper raced through the building among those who were cleared: it was going to be a long night for the Middle East staffs.

That morning Powell read a CIA assessment that said all indicators showed that Saddam was going to invade. Powell knew that this assignment of intent was a big deal. The CIA tried to avoid crying wolf too often. Now the DIA warnings landed on his desk. Not only had Saddam moved his tanks on line overnight, but the communications, artillery, munitions, logistics and air-power were in place. A crossover point had been reached militarily. Powell realized, however, that in a totalitarian regime, the only way to be sure of intent was to know what was in the leader's mind, and neither CIA nor DIA had good human sources in the

Iraqi government. He was no soothsayer. But a field army of great capacity had sprung to life before their eyes. Kuwait—my God, Powell thought, Iraq could have sent the local police force to take over.

Later in the morning Powell attended a meeting with Cheney on nuclear command and control. Among the subjects discussed was fail-safe procedures worldwide in the U.S. military to make sure there was no unauthorized detonation of nuclear weapons. Afterwards, Powell went to a luncheon hosted by the visiting president of Togo, the small West African country.

Schwarzkopf briefed the Joint Chiefs and Cheney in the Tank that afternoon. Giving a status report on the location of the 100,000 Iraqi forces, he said they were positioned in a way to give Saddam lots of options—not just an attack. He did not predict an invasion or border crossing.

Cheney agreed that everything Saddam had to do to prepare for an invasion was exactly what he also had to do if his intention was simply to scare the Kuwaitis. There was no way to distinguish between the two. The bluff was only credible if Saddam did all the things he had done: uncoiled the tanks, moved them to the line, and moved in all the communications, munitions and logistics. Saddam might suspect the United States would pass its intelligence information to Kuwait, and the figure of 100,000 troops had been in *The Washington Post* the day before.

Schwarzkopf said that there was little or nothing he could do. There were only 10,000 U.S. military personnel in the region, almost all naval forces. CENTCOM had no ground forces nearby.

Briefly, Schwarzkopf referred to the Central Command's Operations Plan 90-1002, a top-secret contingency plan for moving about 100,000 ground troops to the region over three to four months. "Ten-oh-two," as it was called, had its origins in the early 1980s when the JCS had drafted standard battle plans to fight the Soviet Union or Iran. It included a detailed transportation and logistics plan. On Day 1, according to the plan, tactical F-15 fighters could be sent to the region; by Day 7 the most ready ground force, the so-called Division Ready Brigade of some 2,300 troops from the 82nd Airborne, would be on the ground; on Day 17, the Marines would arrive from the United States and be joined up with ammunition, supplies and equipment that would be sent on the MPS ships from Diego Garcia; not until Day 27 would the first heavy tanks start arriving.

There was one big hitch. All of this assumed 30 days' advance warning for preparation before the actual commencement, or C-Day, of the deployment.

Powell found the field commander's perspective sobering. But there was also an air of incredulity in the Tank. It was difficult to believe that Saddam would use or need 100,000 troops to invade Kuwait, a country that could be taken over with much less force. It was too much for too little. No one, certainly not Powell, could say for sure what Saddam was going to do. Absent any indication, it seemed there was no immediate response for the U.S. military to take.

But Powell himself now no longer believed that Saddam was bluffing. He suggested that Cheney sound the alarm at the White House. This was the moment to mobilize the President, perhaps get him to issue a presidential warning to Saddam through secret diplomatic channels. We've got to do something, Powell told Cheney.

They pushed the White House. As far as Powell could tell, either the White House had another idea about how to handle the problem, or the suggestion just fell through the cracks.

• • •

General Tom Kelly still judged an invasion to be unlikely, despite the intelligence. And Operations Plan 90-1002 was not ready. It had been updated only by junior staff officers and given none of the high-level attention and analysis the Panama BLUE SPOON plan had received. About 60 percent of Kelly's time was being spent on the drug war. Every day there were small deployment orders—two or three men being sent to some country for liaison or training or some essentially passive activity to help other nations fight narcotics trafficking. Kelly, expecting to retire the next year, did not have his heart in the small details of a war on drugs that was not his operation.

At 4 p.m. Powell went to an award and farewell ceremony that Cheney was hosting for his departing military assistant, Rear Admiral Bill Owens, who was leaving at the end of the week. Owens was effectively skipping two-star rank and going to three stars to take over the prestigious Sixth Fleet in the Mediterranean.

Schwarzkopf went back to Florida.

Cheney wasn't alarmed. He didn't take the CIA or DIA warnings as absolutes. There seemed to be a continuing flow of such warnings. Almost weekly, a message arrived in his office warning of a coup in the Philippines. And everyone out there in the Middle East—Mubarak of Egypt, Fahd of Saudi Arabia, King Hussein of Jordan, the Kuwaitis themselves—was saying that Saddam would not invade. It was all a ploy, they said, a move to obtain leverage.

Cheney was also a little put off by the United Arab Emirates' response to the assistance that the Pentagon had provided. America's friends in the region like the UAE wanted it both ways—protect us but don't let anyone know. The attitude seemed to be, you guys hang around the neighborhood but keep the ships and planes that protect us over the horizon.

. . .

About 9 p.m. Cheney received a phone call at home from Rear Admiral Owens. The Iraqi forces had crossed the border into Kuwait at both tank lines. Hundreds of main battle tanks were racing south and east toward Kuwait City.

Cheney wasn't entirely shocked. He told Owens to keep him informed.

Powell also received a call at home. The Chairman decided to stay home and get updates. Vice Chairman Admiral David Jeremiah went to the Pentagon for the night. General Kelly was called about 9:10 p.m. and 20 minutes later was in the Crisis Situation Room overseeing a team of operations specialists and intelligence analysts. He sat in the center of the long table in the front. Before him were three large projection screens. One screen had a time log that scrolled up, marking key events, communications and intelligence. Another was tuned to CNN's 24-hour news coverage because Kelly wanted to know what was going out publicly. He knew that if it wasn't correct, Powell would want to take steps to fix the impression.

Kelly kept open a secure line to Schwarzkopf at the Central Command headquarters in Florida. Iraqi tanks made it to Kuwait City in about three and one half hours. The DIA had sent a major who was an intelligence specialist to the U.S. Embassy in Kuwait City several days earlier. He was able to funnel out both human intelligence and signals intelligence to describe the virtual sacking of the city. Kelly was concerned about the U.S. Embassy in Kuwait as fighting went on all around it. The small Kuwaiti Army was putting up a fight, but it was hopelessly outnumbered.

Scowcroft had already returned to his home in suburban Maryland when he received his call. He was astonished. He had been sure it was all bluster. Saddam had been talking tough for months, but the talk had been about oil and oil prices, and about a few territorial disputes, not the basic sovereignty of Kuwait. There had been nothing substantial in Saddam's most immediate rhetoric or declared aims to suggest that Iraq was treating the government of Kuwait as illegitimate—the rhetorical foundation he would have expected Saddam to lay before taking this sort of dramatic action. Scowcroft felt that there were some pretty obvious downsides for Saddam to invade his neighbor, and world reaction would be strong.

Scowcroft returned to the White House and informed Bush. The President said he wanted something done right away. Since Bob Gates was on vacation, Scowcroft called an emergency meeting of the deputies committee by secure video link and chaired it himself from the Situation Room.

A public statement was drafted and Scowcroft gave it to Bush for approval. At 11:20 p.m. a statement was issued that strongly condemned the invasion and called for "the immediate and unconditional withdrawal of all Iraqi forces."

Scowcroft, legal counsel Boyden Gray and Treasury officials went to work on a plan to freeze Iraqi assets in the United States and prohibit any transactions with the aggressor. Since it was clear that Kuwait was being overrun, a second plan was drafted to freeze Kuwaiti assets so that Saddam could not get at any portion of the estimated $100 billion in investments held abroad by Kuwaitis. Both plans were reduced to emergency executive orders for Bush to sign.

With the deputies committee, Scowcroft pressed for more actions that would demonstrate that the United States was taking the Iraqi invasion seriously.

What about ground forces? he was asked. That would be the ultimate demonstration of seriousness.

No, Scowcroft said. He wanted something that (a) could be moved very, very quickly and (b) would not be an immediate, visible presence. He proposed a squadron of Air Force F-15 fighters—about 24 planes that could be offered to Saudi Arabia if the kingdom would accept them.

The others—Kimmitt from State, Wolfowitz and Jeremiah from the Pentagon, and Kerr from the CIA—agreed.

Scowcroft also called an NSC meeting for first thing in the morning. The Pentagon reported that General Schwarzkopf was in town and he might be a good resource to have at the meeting because he knew the disposition of all the forces in the Middle East.

Schwarzkopf, however, was already back at his headquarters in Florida. About 2:30 a.m., Powell called Kelly in the Crisis Situation Room. Call Schwarzkopf, Powell directed, and tell him I want him back in my office at 7 a.m. because there's an 8 a.m. NSC meeting at the White House I want him to attend.

Kelly picked up his secure line to Schwarzkopf.

"Sir," Kelly said, "Tom Kelly. The Chairman just called and said he would like you in his office at seven a.m."

Long pause.

"Yes, sir, this morning."

Long pause.

"Yes, in four and one half hours."

.   .   .

At about 4 a.m., Scowcroft went to sleep in his office. He awoke about 45 minutes later and by 5 a.m. was at Bush's bedroom door in the residence, so the executive orders on freezing the assets could be signed.

Powell arrived at the Pentagon at 6 a.m. At about 6:50 Schwarzkopf also appeared and the two had a closed-door meeting until 7:30, when they left for the White House.

The full National Security Council gathered at 8 a.m. in the Cabinet Room. In addition to Powell and Schwarzkopf, Cheney and Wolfowitz were there. Kimmitt was sitting in for Baker, who was in Siberia meeting with his counterpart, Soviet Foreign Minister Eduard Shevardnadze.

Before the meeting began, Schwarzkopf had to be asked to put away his top-secret maps and slides. Bush was going to answer a few questions from a media pool so he could be seen on television stating his concern about the invasion.

"We're not discussing intervention," Bush told the reporters.

"You're not contemplating any intervention or sending troops?" one of the reporters asked.

"I'm not contemplating such action," he said.

Scowcroft believed that Bush didn't mean what that sentence said. He was talking off the cuff. Clearly it was too early to rule out anything; the statement would have to be corrected later.

Bush said there was no evidence that any other countries in the Middle East were threatened, but he said that he wanted to "have this invasion be reversed and have them get out of Kuwait."

He also said, "I'm sure there will be a lot of frenzied diplomatic activity. I plan to participate in some of that myself."

Powell noticed yet again the sharp contrast between Bush and Reagan. Bush had spent eight years watching Reagan operate, and delegate. Unlike Reagan, Bush wanted the details, all the details. He wanted to be the player, the guy who made as many of the calls as possible. It was not a matter of one style being good and one being bad, Powell told himself. It was just different. On occasion, Powell had to remind himself that the people had elected Bush, not his advisers. The net result was that principal military adviser Powell had a much smaller role under Bush than national security adviser Powell had under Reagan.

When the reporters left, Scowcroft began running down an agenda, attempting to be discreetly directive, but the President immediately took charge of the meeting.

CIA Director Webster opened with an intelligence briefing. Kuwait had been overrun by more than 100,000 troops, well beyond what was needed. The Iraqi forces in Kuwait were being resupplied and reorganized, in some cases just ten miles from the Saudi border. They could easily continue their march and punch through meager Saudi defenses. Saudi Arabia had a military of less than 70,000 and only one small unit stood between the Iraqi units and the vast Saudi oil fields. He presented the situation as serious but not grim.

Next, Bob Kimmitt summarized the diplomacy. The U.N. Security Council had met most of the night and had condemned the invasion; the Arab League was being convened; but no one had yet joined the United States in freezing Iraqi and Kuwaiti assets.

The President said they needed to think about additional economic sanctions. He had acted quickly to freeze the assets and he

indicated with pride that he did not think Saddam or others normally accustomed to the slow-moving American bureaucracy
would have expected such fast action.

Bush, the former U.N. ambassador, wanted to make sure the
United Nations was moving forward on additional measures.
U.N. Ambassador Thomas Pickering, who had arrived from New
York City on a 6:30 a.m. flight, said they were. The President and
Scowcroft had talked with Jim Baker, who was working with the
Soviets.

Bush, the former ambassador to China, asked if the Chinese
government would come through in support. He indicated he expected some help since he had tempered his criticism of the previous year's slaughter of students in Tiananmen Square.

Scowcroft and State were working the situation.

Bush said that he wanted the diplomatic effort to be massive
and he ordered that nothing be left undone that might add to the
pressure and help organize world opinion against Iraq.

Treasury Secretary Nicholas Brady next explained that Iraq
would be getting potential oil profits of about $20 million a day
from Kuwait production. In all, Iraq now held 20 percent of the
world's known oil reserves. If Saddam were to take over Saudi
Arabia, he would have 40 percent.

Bush, the former Texas oil man, seemed horrified that Saddam
might get Saudi Arabia. He engaged in an extended analysis of the
impact on world oil availability and price. Could the United States
and others slap an embargo on Iraqi oil? Would Saddam withhold
Iraqi and Kuwaiti oil? Or would he try to flood the world market?
What would be the impact on U.S. oil reserves?

With just 20 percent of the world's oil, Saddam would be able
to manipulate world prices and hold the United States and its allies
at his mercy. Higher oil prices would fuel inflation, worsening the
already gloomy condition of the U.S. economy.

Powell thought to himself that there was lots of loose talk and
speculation about oil, but Bush had the advantage over everyone
else because he had been an oil man and knew the market.

Sununu suggested that they ought to try to stop Iraq from selling Kuwaiti oil on the open market and gaining an immediate
benefit from the invasion.

The marketing of oil could normally not be stopped with economic and political pressure, Cheney said. On the immediate mil-

itary situation, the Secretary of Defense informed them that U.S. Air Force KC-10s, large tanker planes used for aerial refueling of other aircraft, had been moved to Saudi Arabia.

An attack air package, Powell added, referring to the squadron of F-15s, was on alert to go to Saudi Arabia if the Saudis gave their approval.

Energy Secretary James Watkins, the former Navy chief, pointed out that Iraq moved its oil in pipelines through Turkey and Saudi Arabia. The retired admiral suggested that the pipelines might present interesting opportunities as targets. They were Saddam's economic lifelines. Could they be hit with air strikes?

Powell said they could. He didn't know how much Iraqi oil the two lines carried or how permanent their shutdown would be. But as a military matter, he noted, lineal targets—straight lines like roads, railroad tracks and pipelines—were not desirable. They could be too easily repaired and put back into action.

A question was raised about the possibility of shutting down Iraq's entire oil export business, not just the pipelines but the refineries and terminals and pumping stations.

Cheney said that wouldn't make a lot of sense. Saddam's move on Kuwait was, among other things, an attempt to meddle with the world's oil supply. The United States could not respond by bombing the world's oil supply.

Scowcroft worried that the debate was wandering and unfocused. They could too easily talk themselves into doing nothing. "We don't have the option to *appear* not to be acting," he said.

Cheney said that the marriage of Iraq's military of 1 million men with 20 percent of the world's oil presented a significant threat. They ought to distinguish between defending Saudi Arabia and expelling Iraq from Kuwait, he said, suggesting he favored the protection mission.

"So the problem is not unlike ERNEST WILL," Scowcroft said, referring to the operation of protecting Kuwaiti oil tankers in the Gulf in 1987–88.

"But the military requirement would be much greater," Cheney said.

Powell said that the Iraqi military had conducted a very professional operation. The Chairman then introduced General Schwarzkopf, who put up his maps and charts showing the region and the Iraqi attack routes.

Two tiers of responses were possible, the general said. The first tier could be single retaliatory strikes. Since the U.S. Army and Air Force had no forces in the region for immediate action, any strikes would have to be carried out by U.S. naval aircraft based on carriers in the region. Possible targets for such air strikes included the Iraqi Army in Kuwait; military or strategic targets in Iraq itself; economic targets in Iraq such as the pipelines running to Turkey and Saudi Arabia; and Iraqi oil tankers at sea. These would be limited, punitive strikes. Such attacks could not be sustained very long and probably would not accomplish much in terms of hurting the Iraqi military or economy, Schwarzkopf said.

Tier Two, Schwarzkopf continued, was the execution of Operations Plan 90-1002 for the defense of the Saudi Peninsula. That would take months and involve 100,000 to 200,000 military personnel from all the services. This could not be executed unless Saudi Arabia or some other country allowed the United States to set up a series of bases—an unlikely prospect given past Arab reluctance to permit it.

Sununu continued to press on the possibility of some kind of economic move. Isn't there some way to organize to prevent Iraq from selling not only Kuwaiti oil but its own? he asked. "Whose check does Iraq get?"

Economic embargoes historically haven't worked, Richard G. Darman, the budget director, said. The international trade system does not respond to declarations of embargo or the closing of borders, he added. The market responds to price, and in an embargo, the price goes up and the incentive to violate the embargo increases.

Right, the President said. Iraq would just find a new middleman. Where there was a buck to be made, someone would buy and sell the oil, Bush said. "Like my Texas friends."

It was important to keep the moderate Arabs out in front during this crisis, Kimmitt remarked.

Darman said he thought their objectives were unclear. Given what Schwarzkopf had presented, the invasion of Kuwait was accomplished and he didn't see how it was possible to eliminate Iraqi oil from the market.

"What do you mean?" Bush asked.

It was not clear to Darman if Bush was referring to his comment on accepting the invasion of Kuwait, or on the possibility of keeping the oil off the market.

Darman replied to the President on the oil market issue. He said that an embargo needed an enforcement mechanism. He knew this implied a military operation, such as using the Navy for a blockade, a bigger step, perhaps, than the President wanted to take.

"But we just can't accept what's happened in Kuwait just because it's too hard to do anything about it," Bush said. He did not indicate that he was eager to use the military for that, or for any purpose.

Cutting the pipelines would have an economic impact, Darman said, but that would have to be done early.

Powell felt that everything was being left up in the air. He posed a question: "Don't we want just to draw a firm line with Saudi Arabia?" That country was the real U.S. interest.

Pickering remarked that such a firm line would leave Kuwait on the other side, in the hands of Iraq.

The meeting ended on this very inconclusive note.

. . .

Boyden Gray left feeling that the military now had a real opportunity. It seemed to him that Bush was certainly going to do something. Over the years, Gray had seen Bush charged up many times —in some respects it was a natural state for him—but rarely this much. The slower, matter-of-fact atmosphere of the night before, the mood that had prevailed at the executive order drafting session, was gone. Bush was now betraying the traits of a cornered man. But Gray thought this was when the President was at his best, as he was in a tennis match when he was down 4 to 1 in the final set.

Darman thought the situation was pathetic. Given the vital U.S. interests in the region and Saddam's past aggressions, it was just short of dereliction that U.S. intelligence hadn't had a clue this was going to happen and that the military didn't have an adequate and updated contingency plan. Seeing the Army-green uniforms of Powell and Schwarzkopf, Darman was concerned that the military would want to put troops on the ground in the Middle East. That could lead to another Vietnam, he feared.

Paul Wolfowitz, who had watched and listened from the sidelines, worried that they might talk themselves into paralysis. There was a terrible circularity to the situation: the administration could not do anything without Arab support; they were not going to get Arab support; therefore nothing could be done.

Powell had watched Bush carefully, and he did not think it was at all clear what the President was going to do or whether he would accept the loss of Kuwait. He knew that Bush was flying off to Aspen, Colorado, to give a speech later that day and meet with British Prime Minister Margaret Thatcher. She would no doubt have strong opinions and a strong influence on Bush.

Cheney was also puzzled about what Bush might do. The Secretary felt a little unprepared. He didn't have any practical military options to lay before the President.

Scowcroft was alarmed. Iraq was a major threat to the vital interests of the United States. This went back to the Carter Doctrine of 1980, when President Carter had said in his State of the Union address that "an attempt by any outside force to gain control of the Persian Gulf region will be regarded as an assault on the vital interests of the United States of America. And such an assault will be repelled by any means necessary, including military force." Saddam was no less hostile or threatening than any outsider. The principle seemed to apply.

The national security adviser saw another, larger principle at stake. The Vietnam Syndrome was alive and well—the military didn't want to use force unless everyone approved. Cap Weinberger's six conditions for the use of military force epitomized this paralysis. Weinberger's conditions virtually required a national referendum before force could be employed. Waging war was impossible without a galvanizing event such as Pearl Harbor, or a moral or emotional crusade.

Scowcroft believed the United States could choke on such strictures. For Scowcroft, war was an instrument of foreign policy, pure and simple. President Bush had demonstrated this in Panama. The administration had not gone out and taken a vote or attempted to drum up support. Instead, Bush had used his authority as commander-in-chief of the armed forces. The public and congressional support had then followed.

After the meeting, Scowcroft went back to the Oval Office with the President.

Though Sununu, Darman and some of the others had expressed

their concern about the economic consequences of the invasion, Scowcroft indicated to the President that the meeting had seemed to miss the point about the larger foreign-policy questions.

Mr. President, Scowcroft said, I think you and I are the only ones who really are exercised about this.

Before completing their discussion, they had to rush off to Aspen, Colorado, for Bush's speech. Before they left, however, the President had a private meeting with his counsel, Boyden Gray. Bush wanted to be sure about his legal authority to deploy or use military airpower—Tier One options.

. . .

Cheney and Powell had to dash up to the Hill to brief Sam Nunn, Les Aspin and six other senior members of defense-related committees, on the "force of the future" and the Pentagon's plan to reduce the size of the military by 25 percent in the next five years. It was built around Powell's concept of a "base force" below which the United States could not safely go. Getting the chiefs to go along had been like fitting a size-ten foot into a size-eight shoe, Powell felt. But he had prevailed.

It seemed ironic to Cheney that the invasion and the briefing had come together in a single morning. He told the legislators the United States no longer needed to prepare for global conflict on short warning. Now the imperative was to deal with regional contingencies, and here was one—Saddam's invasion of Kuwait. The congressional leaders seemed to like the new idea for the force of the future and expressed approval. But most of their questions were about the invasion.

In the afternoon at another press conference in Colorado, Bush shifted some ground from the early morning: "We're not ruling any options in, but we're not ruling any options out."

Two hours later, Bush talked with King Fahd of Saudi Arabia. From his service as the U.N. ambassador and CIA director, Bush had good relations with the monarchs in the Middle East—the "friendly royals," as they were often called in the CIA. He and Fahd both knew they could pick up the phone to talk.

The immensely wealthy Fahd, 69, was known as a super-cautious, tentatively pro-Western monarch who tended to pursue his foreign-policy goals through financial diplomacy—in short, pay-offs. The two spoke for nearly half an hour. Fahd had lots of questions about what the United States thought Saddam was planning and what Bush could do to help the Saudis. They agreed that the attack on Kuwait was unacceptable, but did not settle on a course of action.

Returning to Washington on Air Force One, Bush also spoke with King Hussein of Jordan and President Mubarak of Egypt, who were together meeting in Alexandria. The two Middle East leaders passed the phone back and forth as each spoke with Bush. Their message was, give us more time and let the Arabs try to handle this.

. . .

Pete Williams wanted more information and knew that the Joint Staff—the "J-boys," as he often referred to them—would be the best immediate source. There was always something there—a plan or an analysis or someone who had spent his life on the problem. It was just a matter of working his way through the bureaucratic labyrinth. He went down to General Kelly's office that afternoon. He usually found that Kelly had a way of getting in your face and making it clear he was the man with the stars on his shoulders. His pronouncements were delivered as matters of fact.

General Kelly was pessimistic. "There's nothing we can do," he said. With no heavy ground forces—tank divisions—in the area, there was no effective way to meet Saddam's thrust. Kelly said that the military did not want to get involved in a land war in Southwest Asia, thank you anyway.

"We hope you political types aren't dreaming," Kelly added. "This isn't going to be Panama. . . . If we're thinking of taking on the Iraqis in any way, I want to voice a note of caution." Frontal tank warfare was a "big nasty thing," said Kelly, who had spent much of his career as a tank commander. "We can't have a land war."

. . .

Cheney had been scheduled to go to Colorado with Bush that afternoon, but he had canceled. Instead, he called a meeting in his office of his top civilian and military advisers. About 15 people gathered, an unusually large meeting for Cheney, who liked small groups of two, three or four.

General Kelly started out. Here is the story of how Iraq took

Kuwait, he said. Kelly's tone of voice reflected his professional admiration for the rapid, precise, massive and technically brilliant Iraqi operation.

Okay guys, Cheney said, what do we do?

Powell told him the chiefs and Schwarzkopf were working on options.

Cheney seemed incredulous there were so few options.

It's hard, Powell said. They were dealing with a huge, instant invasion that was now over and complete. Saddam's initial mission was accomplished.

There was a growing tension in the crowded office.

"I need some options I can show the President," Cheney said.

Powell reiterated that they were working on it. Both he and Kelly wanted it made clear they were not going to come up with some half-baked proposals. Powell didn't want the U.S. military to deliver a few pinprick surgical strikes. What would they do after that? There wasn't much that could be done from this distance, and the Pentagon would look impotent and weak.

What about a surgical strike on the pipelines into Saudi Arabia and Turkey? someone asked.

Kelly said that would be fruitless. Bombing could not be that precise. When and if they were hit, the lines would be repaired easily. The losers in such a mission would be Saudi Arabia, Turkey, or both, since it would lead to retribution. It would be provocative and impractical. Saddam would then have his reason to attack them.

There was a suggestion that perhaps it was time to take out Saddam's chemical and nuclear facilities, since that was the serious long-term threat from Iraq.

The idea was quickly dismissed as a serious escalation.

Pete Williams and Dave Addington, Cheney's special assistant, stood up and left the meeting before it had ended, hoping to signal the other backbenchers that it was time to depart. Cheney did not like large meetings, they knew, particularly if a fight was brewing.

When Cheney and Powell were finally alone, the Secretary said he felt blocked. The President did not need political advice. Both he and Bush needed military options, and they did not seem to be forthcoming.

Mr. Secretary, Powell said, it's 6,000 miles-plus away. We don't have any ground forces and an air strike would be pissing into the wind and might provoke what we don't want—an assault on Saudi Arabia.

It was one of the tensest exchanges the two had ever had.

• • •

Kelly didn't know what he was supposed to do. The JCS and his operations people first needed a statement of the military goal and mission. What was it they were supposed to offer a plan for? Reprisals against Iraq? Liberation of Kuwait? Defense of other Arab states? He hadn't seen any guidance from the political level —from either the President or the Secretary of Defense. Absent a mission, discussion of options was pretty abstract. He set up a schedule called a watch bill that assigned officers to rotate shifts so key J-3 staff would be on duty in the Pentagon 24 hours a day. But soon he and his staff were sitting around twiddling their thumbs, waiting for their mission.

Powell went over the remarks the President had made that afternoon in Colorado. It was his habit to excavate Bush's public statements. The Chairman had to know the President's policy, and this President tended to lay out at least some of his thinking in speeches and comments to the press. Sometimes the policy came out carefully and incrementally. Other times Powell discovered surprises.

The Aspen statements seemed measured. Bush had said that he had spoken with King Hussein and President Mubarak: "They asked for restraint. They asked for a short period of time in which to have this Arab solution evolve. . . . [They said] Let us try now, as neighbors and Arabs, to resolve this. And I made clear to them that it had gone beyond simply a regional dispute because of the naked aggression."

• • •

Cheney was stewing. The fall of Kuwait was all by itself a threat to U.S. interests, and the President was entitled to a full range of options, including military options. He called in Admiral Bill Owens, who was on his next-to-last day as Cheney's military assistant.

"What can the Navy do?" Cheney asked. He wanted some ideas for an immediate, punishing surgical strike on Iraq. He had in mind something that might really send a message to Saddam Hussein, something that might be accomplished with standoff weapons fired from tens of miles away so no U.S. forces would get hurt.

The Navy had the capability of launching deadly Tomahawk cruise missiles, Owens said. The so-called T-LAMs—Tomahawk Land Attack Missiles—could be preprogrammed for targets into Iraq.

Cheney said he wanted the numbers and details, and he ordered Owens to make a foray to his Navy friends on the fourth floor and come up with something. At once. Go down and bang on the system and find out what we can do and how fast we can do it. There was always stuff cranking around over there; it was a matter of locating the right office or file cabinet. The JCS wasn't responding.

Cheney made the same request of his junior military assistant, Air Force Colonel Garry R. Trexler, directing him to find out the Air Force plans or ideas.

Cheney called this "pulsing the system." Sampling the various services and using the informal ties was precisely what Cheney was sure Powell had done many times as military assistant to Cap Weinberger. Cheney felt that like any senior official in government running a large department, he needed multiple sources of information. There was no way he was going to let himself be captive of the JCS or Colin Powell.

. . .

When Bush and Scowcroft returned to Washington, they resumed their discussion about that morning's inconclusive NSC meeting. For Scowcroft, there was too much drag—the attitude that this is too hard, the problem is halfway around the world, the military and administration have budget problems and maybe the situation was not so bad.

Bush agreed it was deadly serious.

Mr. President, Scowcroft said, I don't think you ought to be the one. Let me present the case for action and then we can see what happens.

They scheduled another NSC meeting for the next morning, and Scowcroft went off to write out some of his thoughts.

That night Powell hosted a dinner at Quarters 6 for British Admiral Sir Benjamin Bathurst, the NATO commander of the English Channel forces. Conferring, meeting and socializing with dozens of foreign senior commanders was a routine and time-consuming part of the Chairman's life. Admiral Jeremiah and 30 other guests were there. Powell threw his arms around Jeremiah in an affectionate embrace at one point during the cocktail hour. He seemed very happy with his new Vice Chairman. Powell looked relaxed. He was affable, but in his toast at dinner, he said that the Iraqi invasion was very sobering—"a cold washcloth in the face."

Powell completed his dinner without a single interruption about the crisis. He told those at his table that he had been humbled many times in his life. One weekend, he said, when he was Reagan's national security adviser, he was attending the wedding of the daughter of his friend Vernon Jordan. The church was filled with politicians and journalists, "newsies," as Powell called them. After he and Alma had taken their seats, Powell's vibrating beeper silently went off, signaling him to call the office. He raced out of the church. The newsies and everyone else noticed, but they were all trapped in the church. He went to his car and got on the phone to the White House to learn that there had been an assassination attempt on the Turkish president, Turgut Ozal. He had made some calls to ensure the system was responding properly.

When he came back into the church about ten minutes later, everyone was straining to read the seriousness of whatever had called him away. He had played it for all it was worth, strutting in grim-faced and important. As he sat down, Alma leaned over to ask what had happened. Powell whispered his hot inside information.

"Colin, for godsakes," she said, "I heard that on the radio three hours ago."

After the laughter, Powell said the air could get thin in the policy stratosphere, and it was good to have a little imaginary oxygen mask off to the side of his head. When he thought everything was going fine and he was in control, he would take it and breathe a little to come back to earth. That day, he noted, instead of an oxygen mask he had Saddam Hussein.

.   .   .

The next day, Friday, August 3, the National Security Council met again at the White House. Clasping his notes, Scowcroft began: "We have got to examine what the long-term interests are for this country and for the Middle East if the invasion and taking of Kuwait become an accomplished fact. We have to begin our deliberations with the fact that this is unacceptable. Yes, it's hard to do much. There are lots of reasons why we can't do things but it's our job."

Wolfowitz thought Scowcroft had, right then, changed the entire focus. It even seemed to stem Sununu's tendency to take shots at any option under consideration and to question any uncertainties he could identify.

Darman felt that Scowcroft's introduction was a plea for the cabinet to unify, to fall in line.

The President indicated that he agreed with his national security adviser. The participants discussed economic sanctions, and the ways the administration might work with the allies and the United Nations to erect a wall around Saddam to isolate him.

They discussed a CIA report arguing that the invasion posed a threat to the current world order and that the long-run impact on the world economy could be devastating. Saddam was bent on turning Iraq into an Arab superpower—a balance to the United States, the Soviet Union and Japan. Control of 20 percent of the world's oil would give him more than enough leverage. There was also an ominous assessment of Iraqi capability: the CIA believed that Saddam could easily swing his armies in Kuwait south and be in Riyadh, the Saudi capital 275 miles away, within three days.

Scowcroft stated that there had to be two tracks. First, he believed the United States had to be willing to use force to stop this, and that it had to make that clear to the world. Second, he said that Saddam had to be toppled. That had to be done covertly through the CIA, and be unclear to the world.

Bush ordered the CIA to begin planning for a covert operation that would destabilize the regime and, he hoped, remove Saddam from power. He wanted an all-fronts effort to strangle the Iraqi economy, support anti-Saddam resistance groups inside or outside Iraq, and look for alternative leaders in the military or anywhere in Iraqi society. He knew that covert action would be difficult if not impossible given that Saddam ran a police state and brutally repressed any dissent or opposition. Still, he wanted to see what could be done. If ever there was a case for covert action undertaken in the national interest, he said, this was it.

Bush said that he wanted Cheney, Powell and Schwarzkopf at Camp David the next day to brief him on the military options.

. . .

Later that day in the Pentagon, one of the chiefs told Powell that Rear Admiral Owens and others on Cheney's staff were calling their parent services to dig out the surgical-strike plans on Iraq for the Secretary. Powell bounded up to the Secretary's suite on the third floor and into Owens's office, where Powell himself had sat for three years.

"I don't like freelancing out of this office," Powell told Owens, a slim, mild man who was now on his last day in Cheney's office. "Don't you ever do that again." The Chairman was waving his finger in Owens's face. Powell had visions of Lieutenant Colonel Oliver North's Iran-contra operations. Like North, Owens was going out of channels and playing to the short-term requests and emotions of the boss. It was a path that could lead both boss and country down the drain. That hand from the past was not going to touch Powell if he could help it. He felt he had contained such impulses while in this very office under Weinberger. He had survived Iran-contra and had come into the Reagan White House in the aftermath to help clean up the NSC as the deputy security adviser. Untainted by that scandal, he was not going to let some equivalent out-of-channels dealings flourish while he was Chairman.

Owens, caught between the two most powerful people in the Pentagon, didn't tell Powell that he had been following Cheney's orders.

"We will give you any important thing you want," the Chairman said. All he wanted, he said, was that all information and options from the services to the Secretary come through him and the Joint Chiefs. He said, "The last thing I want is to execute something someone dreamed up that I just heard of."

Calming down, Powell reminded Owens that the military assistant had to absorb the pressure coming from the Secretary. Don't do silly things to meet an immediate need, Powell admonished. Absorb the pressure and do it right. The Joint Staff was working, the chiefs were working, Schwarzkopf was working.

Owens took the rebuke quietly.

Powell still held to his views that the use of force was immensely tricky. He deplored the attitude that you could just drop a few bombs, launch a few Tomahawk missiles, and keep the attack "surgical" and limited. The very word "surgical" and the concept behind it drove Powell nutty. It was the modern military illusion, the brass-balls approach some people wanted to take when the country was in a pinch with a Saddam: let's launch one of these that will show him what we can do, and no one on our side will get hurt. Pure fantasy.

Powell met with the chiefs that afternoon. There was a new dynamic. The new Air Force chief, General Michael J. Dugan, and the new Chief of Naval Operations, Admiral Frank B. Kelso II, both had only a month on the JCS. Vuono and Gray—the ones with Army and Marine ground forces—were now the old hands. The very large question on the table was: What was the ultimate result that the United States wanted as a nation? It was unclear for the simple reason that President Bush had not decided, or had not yet told them his decision.

The chiefs and services had to act together on this, Powell said. Work a consensus, work with Schwarzkopf, no one-service solutions, no freelancing.

. . .

That afternoon, Scowcroft arranged for Prince Bandar to come to the White House.

Bandar had been in London when he received word of the invasion of Kuwait some 40 hours earlier. He immediately ordered his private jet to take him back to the United States. As he sat on the plane recrossing the Atlantic, he tried to digest what had happened. He flashed back to his meeting with Saddam less than four months earlier and Saddam's search for assurances that Israel would not attack Iraq. As soon as Bandar was back in Washington, he had his staff retrieve the 18-page memo recounting the meeting. As Bandar read the words, he said to himself, My God, this guy was setting the stage to attack. Saddam had sought and received American and Israeli assurances he would not be attacked. He had protected his western flank with Israel, freeing him to do what he wanted on the east with Kuwait. Bandar's conclusion was that he and the Bush administration had been set up. It was only reinforced when he learned that Saddam did not have a single soldier on the western flank.

Bandar was very concerned when he arrived at the White House to see Scowcroft on Friday.

Scowcroft had a more positive view of Bandar than Powell did; as national security adviser he had found Bandar a pretty clear channel. Bandar had repeatedly demonstrated that he had direct access to King Fahd, and could provide a nearly instantaneous read on the king's attitudes. If anything, Bandar seemed to come down on the U.S. side on most matters. Accordingly, Scowcroft made sure Bandar had direct access to Bush when necessary.

During this meeting, Scowcroft said he was speaking for the President. The Saudis had not given an answer on the U.S. offer of a squadron of F-15s, and Scowcroft knew that such a non-answer was, for the moment at least, a Saudi no. He said that Bush was willing to up the ante. The Bush position was that the United States was *inclined* to help in any way possible.

Bandar reminded Scowcroft that only a decade before, when the shah of Iran had fallen from power, President Carter had told the Saudis, let me send over a couple of squadrons of F-15s to Saudi Arabia as a gesture. His Majesty had agreed. When the planes were in the air, halfway over, Carter had announced they were unarmed. Bandar said the consequences had been devastating to the Saudis and lived on. Frankly, he said, we're worried. Do you guys have the guts or don't you? "We don't want you to put out a hand and then pull it back," the ambassador said, "and leave us with this guy on our border twice as mad as he is now."

"Let me tell you, we won't do that," Scowcroft said. "We're serious and we'll do what is necessary to protect you." But he added that the Saudis would have to demonstrate that they too were serious and would accept U.S. forces.

At that moment, President Bush dropped into Scowcroft's office.

"This is your friend?" Bush said to Bandar, clearly referring to Bandar's earlier pleas for assurances for Saddam.

Bandar chuckled.

"Do you remember?" Bush asked. "This is the guy you came to me telling me he's okay."

"Water over a dam, Mr. President," Bandar said. He acknowledged that both the Saudis and the United States had been used.

Bush turned to the problem at hand. He said he was upset that Kuwait had not asked for help from the United States until apparently a half hour or a few minutes before Iraq invaded. He was scared that the Saudis, who might be next on Saddam's list, would ask too late and the United States would not be able to help.

What sort of help can be provided, Bandar asked. How many aircraft? What sort of weapons? If it was going to be considered, King Fahd would have to know precisely.

Bush and Scowcroft said they didn't have those answers. Cheney and Powell would have to provide them.

Bandar pressed and alluded sarcastically to Jimmy Carter's unarmed F-15s. Bush seemed almost hurt, as if there was some doubt and the Saudis suspected his resolve. He seemed to be taking the questioning personally.

"I give my word of honor," Bush finally told Bandar, "I will see this through with you."

Bandar felt his hair stand up. The President of the United States had just put his personal honor on the line.

. . .

Scowcroft called Cheney and said that the President wanted to help the Saudis. Show him the best we have, Tier Two—the massive operations plan. "Get Bandar in and brief him on what we can do for him." The President did not want any half measures. He had given his word. This was as serious as anything they might undertake. To convince the Saudis, the President wanted Cheney to show Bandar the top-secret satellite photos. They would demonstrate the peril as Saddam massed his forces in the direction of Saudi Arabia.

Cheney made the arrangements for Bandar to come to the Pentagon later that afternoon. But first, Cheney had to have what he considered a come-to-Jesus meeting with Powell about the necessity of getting the military options to the President.

The Secretary and the Chairman sat down alone. There could be no more stalling, foot dragging or even the appearance of either, Cheney said. Serious talk was coming out of the White House, and they had to present the military alternatives. It was time for military advice commensurate with the seriousness of the situation. The President would be better served if there was more military advice. The Pentagon had to stick to its knitting, Cheney said firmly.

"I can't do it unless I know what the pattern is," Powell replied.

Cheney explained they now had it. Scowcroft had just called to say the President wanted them to brief Bandar on Tier Two—Operations Plan 90-1002. According to the orders of the President, Bandar was to see the latest top-secret overhead photography.

The tension soon drained away. Both men knew that they needed each other.

. . .

Before the Bandar briefing, Cheney pulsed the system some more. Lang, the DIA's Middle East specialist, had written another of his electronic messages that day reviewing the possible outcomes of the crisis. Chief among them was the high likelihood that the Saudis would turn inward and refuse visible assistance, although their large country was protected only by a military of less than 70,000 men. They were turning down requests for overflights of U.S. military planes, and had also denied a U.S. request to augment coverage of the region by U.S. AWACS (Airborne Warning and Control System) radar planes.

Cheney called Lang to his office. Lang seemed to be the only analyst who had taken the Iraqi troop buildup of the previous weeks with the seriousness it had evidently deserved. Cheney said he wanted to talk about the Iraqis. He had one essential question: "What are these people really like?"

Lang, who had been pumping up the intelligence community for several years about the Iraqi threat, was delighted at the opportunity. "They are formidable," he said. "They have a very capable military and a developed industrial base. They are modern for a Third World country. They are nationalistic. They are dangerous." He backed up his analysis with statistics and anecdotes.

. . .

Cheney had known Prince Bandar for years and liked him. He was intrigued that a mere ambassador was able to have such a wide impact in the U.S. government, Washington and the world; Bandar also acted as the de facto Saudi connection with Prime Minister Thatcher, the Soviets and the Chinese. But Cheney worried that the prince had his own agenda. Left to his own devices, Bandar would attempt to manage the foreign policy of the United

States, Saudi Arabia and, for that matter, any and all countries. In short, Cheney considered Bandar a little bit off the wall and not necessarily a 100 percent clear channel to King Fahd. Messages might get distorted for other purposes that Cheney might not even be able to imagine.

When Bandar arrived in Cheney's office in the afternoon of August 3, he took a third seat in a captain's chair at the small round conference table with Cheney and Powell. Paul Wolfowitz and NSC Middle East expert Richard Haass also joined them.

"The President has instructed me to brief you on what the United States can do to help the kingdom defend itself," Cheney said. He added that if the United States came in it would be with a hell of a lot, and promised that if invited in to defend the kingdom, it would be a very, very serious commitment. The United States was clearly in a position to fly a mission off one of the aircraft carriers and drop a few bombs on Saddam's head, but that would just make him mad, Cheney said. That wouldn't solve any real problem. The key would be forces on the ground.

Cheney knew that Bandar had been on the telephone to Saudi Arabia, and was about to go there to speak directly to the king. He wanted to make sure the ambassador received the message loud and clear.

To emphasize the problem the Saudis were facing, Cheney and Powell produced copies of the high-resolution overhead photography and pointed out the three Iraqi armored divisions that had been the initial thrust into Kuwait. One was moving through Kuwait to the Saudi border; the others could follow. Still more Iraqi divisions were taking places behind the armored units in the same way they had before the invasion of Kuwait two days earlier. The streak of divisions was like a sword pointing down at the kingdom, which appeared to be in grave danger.

It took Powell about ten minutes to summarize Operations Plan 90-1002, noting that it included more than four divisions, three aircraft carriers and many attack squadrons. He allowed Bandar a peek at the large book with the top-secret plan and charts showing the movement of forces over the months. "That's a rather large force," Powell said.

"How many are you talking about?" Bandar asked.

Powell said 100,000 to 200,000 in the theater.

Bandar let his breath out audibly. "Well, at least this shows you're serious, and this may make it clear to you why we did not want that tactical fighter squadron."

This is serious, Powell insisted.

"We agree you need to be serious," Bandar said, trying for the upper hand. If this kind of force was there in Saudi Arabia now, Bandar said, the kingdom would be able to take aggressive actions such as shutting down the Iraqi pipeline. Without a defensive force of this size, His Majesty's hands were tied because Saddam could come in and overrun Saudi Arabia. Bandar said he agreed with the plan, and favored it. He promised to convey to the king and to his father, the Saudi defense minister, what could be done.

Bandar made clear that he and other Saudi officials were attempting to talk to Saddam to get a statement of his intentions, and they were not having much success. According to Bandar, King Fahd had not been able to reach Saddam for the first ten hours after the Kuwait invasion. When they had talked, Saddam was dismissive, saying that the movement of his troops to the Saudi border was an exercise. The vice president of the Iraqi Revolutionary Command Council had then come to meet with King Fahd and had indicated he could not shed light on Saddam's intentions.

Bandar described a controlled state of panic back home—controlled, he said, because as everyone knew, royalty never panics. He once remarked, "Composure is very important in our culture, even if it doesn't make sense."

There had been three serious border incursions by the Iraqis, who had crossed five or more miles into Saudi territory, Bandar said. The Iraqi chief of staff had told the Saudis these were mistakes by his troops and had vowed the first time to cut off the arm of any Iraqi soldier who put his finger over the border. After the third incursion, the Saudis had not been able to reach any Iraqi authority on a telephone hotline that had been set up between the two countries. Following one incursion, the Iraqis had withdrawn, but only after blowing up a bridge they had used on a well-marked route.

As Bandar rose to leave, Cheney said that if the Saudis invited the U.S. forces and President Bush approved, they could send General Schwarzkopf or somebody to coordinate, making sure that, for example, the U.S. Air Force jets landed where the Saudis wanted.

Bandar assured them that he would be an advocate for an immediate American deployment. He then left.

Wolfowitz expressed surprise at the suddenly serious mood on both sides. He proposed that they ought to start alerting the U.S. forces, particularly the airborne troops that would go first, given the obvious receptivity of Bandar.

"He blows smoke," Powell said. "I don't think it's time to start alerting the 82nd Airborne." After all, one brigade of the 82nd was always on alert.

Cheney agreed, but he told Powell he wanted Schwarzkopf to bring the key commanders from each of the services up to Camp David. He knew that personal contacts were essential for the President. People didn't exist for Bush until he had met them. It was important that the President be given eyes-on personal knowledge of the men who might be running such an operation, Cheney said. He asked Owens to arrange for one of the large White House helicopters, the so-called white tops, to take them all to Camp David the next morning for the presentation to Bush.

· · ·

Later in the day, Cheney was getting a haircut in the Pentagon barber shop when Owens tracked him down. Sununu's office had said no to the helicopter request, Owens reported.

Typical crap out of Sununu's office, Cheney thought. He felt that Sununu had adopted an imperial role for himself as chief of staff. When Cheney had held the job under Ford, he had worked assiduously to stay in the background and avoid the mantle of assistant President. Sununu had donned it. Once, Bush had been late for a cabinet meeting, and Sununu had plunked himself down in the President's chair—a small impropriety, but to Cheney it symbolized the self-importance Sununu brought to his post.

As Secretary of Defense, Cheney had control of more helicopters than anyone. He ordered Owens to use their own choppers for the flight.

· · ·

Bandar called King Fahd to report. Fahd wanted to be assured the threat from Iraq was real. They both knew that Kuwait had delayed asking for assistance from the United States because the

Kuwaitis suspected the Iraqi threat was being used as a guise to get American troops on their soil.

The satellite photos supported the case that the kingdom was in serious trouble, Bandar told Fahd. The threat was genuine.

"Have you seen—with your own eyes—have you seen the overheads?" Fahd asked.

"Yes sir."

"Then tell them to come and bring the overheads."

18

ON AN OVERCAST SATURDAY MORNING, August 4, Cheney, Powell, Wolfowitz, Schwarzkopf and several of his top commanders flew up to Camp David.

Cheney was comfortable with Operations Plan 90-1002. It was the only one they had and he did not want to reinvent the wheel in the midst of a crisis.

They all went into the retreat's big lodge, with its modern conference room. Bush, Quayle, Cheney, Sununu, Webster and Wolfowitz sat on one side of the 25-foot conference table. On the other side were Baker, Scowcroft, Powell, Schwarzkopf, Fitzwater and Richard Haass. Five small model airplanes were arranged down the middle of the table.

Webster opened with an intelligence update. The CIA director did not usually receive a lot of attention in such meetings because most senior officials felt his briefings were a mere summary of the various classified reports and analyses that had already circulated to them.

This morning his report spoke for itself: an unnecessarily large Iraqi force of more than 100,000 was in Kuwait. Some of these

Iraqi soldiers were approaching and massing near the Saudi border—a possible grim foreshadowing of what happened before the Kuwait invasion. The only thing standing between Saddam and the vast Saudi oil fields was a battalion of the Saudi National Guard, fewer than 1,000 men.

Cheney called on Powell, who said that General Schwarzkopf would give an expanded version of the Tier Two option discussed earlier, Operations Plan 90-1002. "The plan is do-able," Powell said. "It will achieve the mission of defending or repelling an attack. Should there be a subsequent decision to move north to Kuwait" under the same plan, that would be "do-able but expensive." Under any circumstance, "some [Reserve] call-ups would be required to sustain this force over the long term."

Summarizing, he said: "There's a deterrence piece and a war-fighting piece. The sooner we put something in place to deter, the better we are. What we can get there most quickly is air power. The Navy's in position. There's more moving. Within a month, we could have a large field army in Saudi Arabia. It would be hard to sustain, though, for a long period. There is not much left for elsewhere" in the world should a new crisis develop.

The Chairman reminded them that, given the size of the force that would be necessary to meet the threat, and the distance it would have to travel, this was not another Panama.

What about the Iraqi Air Force versus the Saudi Air Force, asked Sununu, who was sitting between Quayle and Webster.

Iraq has 1,127 aircraft, Schwarzkopf replied. Limited quantities of good ones. The Iraqi Air Force is predominantly used for defense.

Schwarzkopf's Air Force commander, Lieutenant General Charles Horner, said the Saudis had 60 U.S.-supplied F-15s and 115 older F-5s. He noted that during the invasion of Kuwait, the Saudis had refueled but refused to rearm the small Kuwaiti Air Force, which had put up a futile day-long fight.

Schwarzkopf began his presentation by saying that though the Iraqis had a large army, "They're not ten feet tall." He said their forces included:

• A total land force of 900,000, consisting of 63 divisions; but only 8 of them, the Republican Guard, are really the focus of our concern.

• In all, 5,747 tanks, of which 1,072 are the Soviet-supplied T-72s. Most of the T-72s are in Kuwait now.

• About 10,000 lightly armored vehicles, of which only 1,600 are the advanced type.

• Some 3,500 pieces of artillery, but only 330 are self-propelled; the rest have to be towed.

• A total of 3,000 heavy-equipment transporters for moving tanks. This is a remarkable number, he said. The whole U.S. Army has only 500.

"We would not have to worry about the air force after a fairly short period. The navy's not a problem."

Summing up, the general said that the Iraqi strengths were obviously the size of their land force, and their chemical weapons, which they had used in the Iran-Iraq War and in 1988 against some of their own citizens, Kurdish rebels in northern Iraq.

Their weaknesses included: centralized command and control; dependence on foreign countries for spare parts; and lack of experience in deep operations away from the front in battle because they were accustomed mainly to frontal attacks like those used by Iran in the Iran-Iraq War.

Schwarzkopf said it would take 17 weeks to get the full deterrence piece of Plan 90-1002—totaling some 200,000 to 250,000 Army, Navy, Air Force and Marines—into the region.

The warfighting piece or offensive capability, he warned, was something very different. Army commanders traditionally speak of desired attacker-to-defender ratios of 3 to 1, 4 to 1, even 5 to 1, he said. In an offensive mode the United States would be the attacker, and in this case the plan called for six and two-thirds divisions on the ground, about 150,000 on the U.S. side. Against the Iraqi force of 100,000, this wouldn't yield the traditional ratio, but better U.S. equipment, as well as better tactics, control of the air and sea, and many other factors—an economic blockade, possible forces from other nations—would make an attack possible.

On this warfighting piece, Schwarzkopf said, it would take 8 to 12 months to put in place the U.S. force needed to kick Saddam out of Kuwait.

Powell reflected to himself that it was crucial to state these long timelines. For all practical purposes, Saddam's whole army of

900,000 was available to fight anything the United States might put on the ground in the region. So the deterrence piece and the warfighting piece would both be difficult, perhaps more than difficult. The President had to know that up front. Powell didn't want the military presenting any pipe dreams about how easy it would be.

Schwarzkopf continued to underscore the U.S. limitations. Sixty percent of the Army's logistics support personnel are in the reserves, he said. The United States would be dependent on supplies of fuel from the nations in the Middle East. Munitions shortfalls could be expected if shooting started.

Discussion briefly turned to a possible air campaign—going in with nothing but airpower, the obvious U.S. advantage. Hundreds of planes could be made available for this, Schwarzkopf said, describing how those forces could be moved in within days and weeks.

Cheney and Powell made it clear they were not at all comfortable with airpower only.

Powell felt that he had accomplished one thing at least: Cheney had become an absolute believer in the need for ground power.

In his own mind, Cheney saw ground power as the key back-up to airpower. It was necessary, he felt, to adopt a skeptical approach to *all* the components of any deployment. Defensive or offensive U.S. air superiority might do what was needed right off the bat, and he hoped it would, but no one could be sure. Of course, the Air Force would say it could take care of everything, but Cheney knew he couldn't buy into that view, or present it to the President. In any event, any defense or offense would have to include ground combat forces.

Cheney turned their attention back to a possible ground defense. What about Iraq's chemical weapons? What would it be like to try to operate in the chemical protective gear U.S. forces would have to wear in the Saudi desert during the month of August? he asked.

Schwarzkopf said that the units that might be deployed had all trained at the National Training Center in the California desert, in summer conditions that were somewhat equivalent. "The equipment is very uncomfortable," he said. "It degrades fighting ability. But we have practiced with it a lot."

When the talk turned again to the possibility of an air campaign, Cheney warned, "From previous history, air campaigns have frequently not achieved the results predicted for them."

"I'm not an airpower-only advocate," Schwarzkopf said, but added, "There are four favorable factors that suggest air may be particularly important here. One, it's a target-rich environment— easy to see things. Secondly, Iraq has no experience operating under air attack." During the eight years of the Iran-Iraq War, the Iranians had had no substantial air force to use, so the Iraqis were used to operating under clear skies.

"It could cause great disorder and disarray," Schwarzkopf continued. "Three, we have sophisticated munitions with more precision than ever before. Four, there could be quite a significant morale effect on the Iraqis in the rear who have never been subjected to danger in the past."

But there are no guarantees, Schwarzkopf said.

Powell said he saw the issue as deterrence—stopping Saddam from coming into Saudi Arabia. "If you want to deter, don't put up a phony defense, don't create a phony deterrence," he said. This was one of the largest land armies in the world; it had to be met with a land force. "If you do it, do it real and do it right."

There was concern expressed that any fighting would endanger the holy Muslim sites in Saudi Arabia, a development that would rock the Arab world. Islam's two most revered places were both in Saudi Arabia—Mecca, the birthplace of Mohammed, and Medina, his burial site.

Where is Mecca? Sununu asked.

It was pointed out that Mecca was on the other side of Saudi Arabia, some 700 miles southwest of Kuwait.

"The Saudis worry whether we're really serious," Scowcroft told them. "We can do a lot in the air but what we really need is a ground force. Air can bug out in a hurry. This plan is very heavy on air up front."

Prince Bandar had been worried about the United States just sending one fighter squadron, Cheney said, but he reported that Bandar had been impressed that the plan outlined the day before had seemed serious.

Bush entered the discussion. "My worry about the Saudis," he said, "is that they're going to be the ones who are going to bug out at the last minute and accept a puppet regime in Kuwait. We should be asking them how committed they are."

"It's a chicken-and-egg problem," Scowcroft said. "They can't go out front until they know whether we can be counted on."

"But this is like if your homeland is about to be invaded," the President replied, "you grab a pitchfork and go to the border."

"But this is the Middle East," Scowcroft said. He reminded them that the Kuwaitis hadn't mobilized when they were threatened.

"What about this withdrawal announcement?" the President asked, referring to a statement issued by the Iraqis the day before claiming their forces were going to begin leaving Kuwait in two days.

Everyone at the table seemed to agree this announcement might be enough to get the Arab states circling the wagons, saying everything is going to be fine, and insisting that the United States butt out.

"Don't underestimate Saddam Hussein," Scowcroft said. "He's capable of pulling out a brigade and giving the Saudis an excuse."

This led the discussion back to the unanswered questions: What did Saddam really want? What were just his tactical moves? What were his ultimate objectives?

"There are three things the Iraqis want from a puppet government," Sununu said. "One, the assets; two, debt forgiveness; three, control of oil."

Schwarzkopf corrected him slightly, saying that the conditions before the invasion boiled down to: adjustments of the Iraq-Kuwait border in favor of Iraq, debt forgiveness, payment of $4 billion and control of two tiny Kuwaiti-controlled islands, Warba and Bubiyan, at the northwest corner of the Gulf. Saddam wanted the uninhabited islands because they blocked Iraqi access to the Gulf.

On the question of whether Iraq would withdraw, Schwarzkopf said, "They sent in lots of Iraqi special forces in civilian clothes they might be planning to leave in behind."

"Even if the Iraqis go all the way back," Powell said, "it's going to be a different emir and a different situation." Powell's point was that the head of the Kuwaiti state would be a changed man, and the status quo in Kuwait and elsewhere in the region had been forever altered.

"This is all designed to be attractive to the Arab League," Scowcroft said. Arab League meetings were generally designed for the purpose of showing Arab unity, kissing and making up. "Kuwait is not popular among the Arabs," Scowcroft added.

"That's why our defense of Saudi Arabia has to be our focus," Bush finally said.

Powell was delighted that the President seemed to agree with him, but he was still uncertain about what Bush might decide.

The meeting was adjourned, but the top officials—Bush, Quayle, Sununu, Baker, Scowcroft, Cheney, Powell, Webster— were asked to stay behind for a "principals only" get-together. In this smaller group, some very sensitive intelligence on the Saudis was presented. Gathering intelligence on friends and allies of the United States is one of the most risky enterprises conducted by the various U.S. intelligence agencies. But today's friend might be to-morrow's enemy—friendships are a matter of degree. In any case, the intelligence agencies were under orders to cast a wide net. Information was often more available on friends than neutrals or enemies, because the United States supplied communications and cryptographic equipment to many allies, and because of the shared airwaves and the sheer proximity of U.S. intelligence operatives in friendly nations. To gather this intelligence, the agencies used everything from the simplest methods, like phone tapping, to the most exotic, such as electronically measuring window vibrations of buildings to pick up conversations inside, to human sources within friendly governments.

The intelligence report showed that the Saudi leaders were get-ting cold feet, and as had so often happened in the past, it ap-peared they were giving some consideration to buying their way out of the threat by offering billions of dollars from their oil revenue to Saddam. The Saudis had been willing to pay blackmail before.

Among those gathered, there was a pessimism about the Arabs in general. Everyone heaped blamed on them. They could not be relied on; they would pay off the thief at their throat. There was even some talk that this whole crisis be put on the backburner and downplayed; the United States, after all, had limited power and could not help those who did not want to help themselves.

Despite this negative note on which the meeting ended, it was decided that the President would call King Fahd to take a sound-ing and make a pitch.

Cheney and Powell left Camp David about lunchtime. Cheney

stopped back at his Pentagon office, where some of his aides were hovering, eager to hear what had happened. "What the hell do you want?" he asked half-joking, declining to provide any details. He loaded up a bunch of papers and went home.

.   .   .

Scowcroft stayed on at Camp David with the President while he called the Saudi king. It was time for some pressure. Bush told the king that Saddam was piling up forces near the king's border. The Saudis had to act.

Fahd said that Saudi Arabia did not need ground troops to defend itself. The Saudis only needed help with airpower and perhaps some equipment. He also said that Prince Bandar had reported to him on the previous day's briefings from the Pentagon. I understand you are going to send a team to brief me on the latest overheads and on what your capabilities are to help us defend ourselves, the king told Bush. "Where's this briefing team you're going to send?" he asked.

Bush did not have the foggiest idea what the king was talking about. He didn't know anything about such a plan; it had not been discussed with any of his advisers.

"I did not know you were expecting one, but we'll put one together," the President told Fahd.

Fahd said, yes, he wanted a team, a low-level technical or management team.

Afterwards, Bush and Scowcroft realized that the team idea was all the king and Bush had agreed on, and it was not clear what kind of team would be best. Who should be sent? For precisely what purpose? When? A round of telephone calls followed as Bush, Baker and Scowcroft conferred with others about the possibilities. Cheney replied that all he had offered to Bandar the day before was a coordination team so that U.S. forces, if invited in, would arrive in the right spots.

Bandar thought that he had mentioned the idea of a team to Scowcroft. Scowcroft didn't recall.

"I want to do this," Bush told Scowcroft. "I want to do it big time." And later he added, "I want to send somebody personally. It has to be with the understanding they will not come back with no decisions having been made." The President wanted to use the team to increase the pressure on King Fahd.

Bush raised the possibility of sending Scowcroft. A low-level person would leave the Saudis in the comfortable position of not having to make a decision. But Scowcroft or a high-level, high-visibility team would make it more difficult for the king to delay, or say no. They decided they had to send an offer King Fahd could not refuse.

Bush continued his personal diplomatic activity. He spoke with President Turgut Ozal of Turkey and Canadian Prime Minister Brian Mulroney, two leaders who had already voiced strong opposition to Saddam's invasion.

The President also spoke with the Kuwaiti Emir, Sheikh Jabir al Ahmed al Sabah. A taciturn man who has headed Kuwait's large ruling family since 1978, the emir had escaped by car to Saudi Arabia just minutes before invading Iraqi soldiers arrived at his palace to take him prisoner or kill him.

With the emir, Bush was sympathetic and emotional. He made a vow to the exiled Kuwaiti leader: the United States would help win back his country and would ensure that he was restored to power.

. . .

When Powell heard about the Bush-Fahd conversation concerning a "team," he immediately saw Bandar's hand. The prince had been working overtime. Bush's inclination to help and Cheney's suggestion that Schwarzkopf be used to coordinate a possible operation had been transformed into a "team" to make a presentation to the king. Powell called it "convenient confusion" on Bandar's part. Bandar had once again cleverly moved the two nations into each other's arms.

The question for Bush remained not only whom to send, but what exactly to offer Fahd. The king had already stated a disinclination to accept U.S. ground forces, a key part of Schwarzkopf's Operations Plan 90-1002.

Scowcroft worried that the team might be doomed to failure. He had a series of conversations with Bandar. If the team wasn't going to get results, he told Bandar, the President would send a lower-level State or Defense official. But if it had a chance of succeeding, if some U.S. official could persuade the king or provide the margin of difference, Bush would send someone senior like himself or Cheney. At the same time, he wanted to know if it was possible for the king to agree to accept the U.S. forces before the President selected someone to send. In other words, could they make sure it was a done deal before the President sent his man?

Bandar said the king was not yet ready; intense discussions were going on within the royal family. He himself was leaving for Saudi Arabia that afternoon to join them and add his arguments for accepting U.S. forces. He promised that after he had arrived in the kingdom and talked with the king, he would call Scowcroft.

Meanwhile, Bush decided that Cheney should head the team if the Saudis would accept him. He was senior enough to act as the President's personal representative; and as Secretary of Defense, he could speak with complete authority on military matters.

At about 3 p.m. Scowcroft called Cheney at home and explained how the early Bandar discussions had been molded and stretched by Bandar into the notion of a team. But this might help the situation by forcing the king's hand, Scowcroft said, and the President wants you to head the team. There was, however, some doubt for the moment about whether the king would accept someone as highly placed as Cheney because it would make it almost impossible to say no.

Stand by, Scowcroft told the Secretary of Defense. Saddam might help force the Saudi hand by continuing the buildup on the border and by refusing to supply the Saudis with an explanation of his intentions. Saddam's silence was scaring the Saudis to death.

About an hour later, Cheney called his spokesman, Pete Williams, who was at home waxing his car. He told Williams to pack his bags, they were going to Saudi Arabia the next day. "I'm not certain we're going, but it looks like it," Cheney said. "We'll know for sure at ten a.m. tomorrow."

· · ·

Williams packed and went to the Pentagon Sunday morning to be ready for the 10 a.m. decision. He read the morning papers and watched the Sunday talk shows.

Schwarzkopf, summoned from Florida again, arrived in the Secretary's office. As they were awaiting word from the Saudis, Scowcroft came over to the Pentagon. Cheney, continuing his education on Iraq, had invited a group of experts up for a briefing. They included DIA intelligence officer Pat Lang, former U.S. Ambassador to Iraq David G. Newton, and two other experts.

Lang focused on the Iraqi military, while Newton talked about the internal situation in Iraq.

"If anyone is telling you the Iraqis are not capable," Lang said, "don't believe them. They are tough as hell. They can go clear to Dhahran [an oil city on the Saudi Gulf coast]. Saddam is not bluffing." Saddam had a lot of late-model military equipment.

Cheney said he wanted to know what Iraq was like, and what Saddam was like. "I want to know how this looks from the Iraqi side."

Ambassador Newton spoke for about 30 minutes. He had served as ambassador in Iraq from 1984 to 1988 and knew quite a bit about the country. He was well aware that Cheney and other U.S. policymakers lacked firsthand reports on Saddam's decision making. U.S. intelligence had one source in Saddam's inner circle, but he was not at the regular meetings of the Iraqi president's advisers. There was no true inside knowledge.

The invasion had taken Newton by surprise. When other Arab leaders like King Hussein and Mubarak had said categorically, Look, Saddam told me he's not going to do this, there was good reason to believe they were right. The Arabs had a kind of heads-of-state club whose members tended to believe one another's personal statements as absolutes. Newton had concluded that the massing of Iraqi forces on the border had been coercive diplomacy. Now he was concerned that the United States would fall victim to its own "rational man syndrome," a tendency to analyze foreign leaders as completely rational decision makers. In a one-man operation like Iraq's that was not the way to make predictions.

Newton told Cheney that Saddam was "a tough, ruthless, hard-nosed, intelligent and sometimes brutal leader who is used to getting his own way." Saddam's political history emphasized physical survival. He would not tolerate political opposition, and had killed opponents—although Newton was of the opinion that some of the stories about Saddam's executions were exaggerated. Since most Iraqis believed Kuwait was part of Iraq, Newton said, Saddam's smash-and-grab job would be popular, but in any case, public opinion would not determine what Saddam did.

Saddam was a believer in the practical use of force, Newton added. He was indifferent to the suffering of others and justified his actions as serving the higher purpose of the Iraqi state. He was cold-blooded.

Iraq might be exhausted by war and desirous of a kind of peace dividend, and the citizen army full of draftees with ten years of service who wanted to return home, but the Iraqi Army was no pushover.

Newton, who had met four times with Saddam, said that the Iraqi president thought he was tougher than the United States, and did not respect democracies.

The experts also told Cheney and Scowcroft that Saddam did not have a Masada Complex, he was not suicidal. His objective was power, and he had the flexibility and manipulative skills of a person who tries to maximize power.

. . .

Scowcroft talked on the telephone to Bandar, who was now back in Saudi Arabia. The national security adviser felt that it was crucial to get a high-level team over there. It must succeed. If it failed, that would amount to an invitation for Saddam to invade. It would demonstrate conclusively to the Iraqi leader that the United States and Saudi Arabia were not standing together, that the United States would not support or defend the Saudis, that the Saudis did not want a U.S. protective umbrella.

About noon, Bandar indicated to Scowcroft that the king would not accept someone at Cheney's level. The king wanted someone at a lower level, apparently to make it easier to say no. It was precisely what Scowcroft had feared.

But Bush decided what the hell, let's send someone anyway. It was agreed they would dispatch General Schwarzkopf. Since the general was now going to head a team, not support a Cheney mission, he would have to bring along some of his senior officers and planners. He would fly back to Florida for the third time in four days, pick them up, and leave straight from there for Saudi Arabia on his own plane.

The intelligence that was coming in showed that Saddam was not withdrawing his forces from Kuwait. Instead, more and more Iraqi troops were arriving there.

. . .

In Saudi Arabia, Bandar was told that the king had ordered Saudi scouts to cross the border into Kuwait to see if they could see the Iraqi troops that Bandar had reported. The scouts had come back reporting nothing. There was no trace of the Iraqi troops heading toward the kingdom.

Bandar explained again to the king that he had seen the overheads. There was a debate among the king's advisers. Much doubt was expressed. Bandar said the king ought to see for himself. The doubt was all the more reason to give the okay for the American team to come make their presentation, Bandar argued, and they might as well accept Cheney, not some lower-level representative.

King Fahd finally agreed.

Bandar called Scowcroft. The Cheney mission was approved, he said. "Come ahead and send him."

Scowcroft was pleased, but he also wondered about the Saudis' change of heart. Bandar felt that Scowcroft had panicked. These things always took time to work out. There was always some back and forth.

The two agreed that this did not necessarily mean the king had made the more important decision to accept the U.S. forces. Bandar could not provide absolute assurance on that. But by the end of the conversation, Scowcroft felt that they should take the risk of sending Cheney.

The President agreed.

Scowcroft called Cheney again. "They will accept you," he said. "It's a go."

Departure time was set for 2:30 that afternoon. Cheney was taking Gates, General Schwarzkopf and half a dozen others.

Before he left, Cheney spoke to Bush, who was still at Camp David. There was no time for formal, written instructions. The President outlined the mission verbally. Get the king to agree to accept U.S. forces, he said, get that invitation, persuade him. Prove that the administration will commit fully to a defense and will not back down. If King Fahd invited the U.S. forces in, Bush would send them en masse and they would stay as long as necessary, but not longer than the Saudis wanted.

Powell didn't get word that Cheney was off to Saudi Arabia until Cheney was almost in the air. As he ran over the events of the past several days in his mind, the Chairman was unable to pinpoint precisely when the President had decided that this major deployment was what he wanted to do. There had not been a piece of paper that laid out the decision or the alternatives, or the implications. There had been no clear statement about goals. The one thing that was clear was that the President was deeply, even emotionally, concerned about the fate of Saudi Arabia.

Powell felt he had played his proper role, laying down the necessity of doing it right—ground troops, airpower, Operations Plan 90-1002. Schwarzkopf was en route to Saudi Arabia with Cheney and with his copy of "Ten-oh-two," which outlined the deployment of 250,000 troops, airmen and sailors.

That afternoon, Powell was watching CNN as Bush returned from Camp David and stepped off his helicopter on the White House lawn. Bush went to the microphones to comment on the diplomatic activity—talks with the leaders of Turkey, Japan, Canada, France, Germany, and with the now deposed emir of Kuwait. "What's emerging is nobody seems to be showing up as willing to accept anything less than total withdrawal from Kuwait of Iraqi forces, and no puppet regime," the President said.

"Are you going to move militarily?" he was asked by one reporter.

"I will not discuss with you what my options are or might be, but they're wide open, I can assure you of that." Bush was clearly angered. "Iraq lied once again. They said they were going to start moving out today, and we have no evidence of their moving out."

When he was pressed by the reporters, Bush snapped, "Just wait. Watch and learn."

Waving his finger, growing visibly hot, he said, "I view very seriously our determination to reverse out this aggression. . . . This will not stand. This will not stand, this aggression against Kuwait."

"Uh-oh!" Powell said to himself. The President had now clearly, categorically, set a new goal, not only to deter an attack on Saudi Arabia and defend Saudi Arabia but to reverse the invasion of Kuwait. Powell was stunned. He had not been consulted. He had not spoken with Bush since the Camp David meeting the previous morning.

It was true that Bush had said the first day after the invasion that he wanted it reversed, but it had not been set in stone. Now here it was, a personal and emotional declaration.

Powell had seen presidents get off helicopters and pop off like this before. At times it was an accident, at times it was intentional. Maybe Baker, Scowcroft or Cheney or someone had advised or recommended this. Maybe it was something the President had been brooding about. But Powell knew that he certainly had not been part of it. There had been no NSC meeting, no debate. The Chairman could not understand why the President had laid down this new marker, changing radically the definition of success. It was one thing to stop Saddam from going into other countries like Saudi Arabia; it was very much another thing to reverse an invasion that was accomplished. In military terms, it was night and day. A defense of Saudi Arabia might be accomplished without a fight. Schwarzkopf had told Bush that it would take 8 to 12 months to build U.S. forces up to a level adequate to kick Saddam out of Kuwait. Reversing an invasion was probably the most difficult military task imaginable, and Powell, the number-one military man, had been given no opportunity to offer his assessment.

This angry statement was much more than Powell had expected from Bush. Powell marveled at the distance Bush had traveled in three days. To Powell, it was almost as if the President had six-shooters in both hands and he was blazing away.

.   .   .

Powell went to the White House that evening for an NSC meeting. Bush, he saw, was still one determined President. He was worked up, his mind made up. If Cheney obtained an invitation, the President was going into Saudi Arabia. Powell attempted to tailor his comments and advice to this obvious given. At the meeting, he made four points:

• Saddam did not want and could not withstand a war with the United States. He was ruthless but not irrational. He would be able to see that he would lose a full-scale shootout with the American superpower. In any event, it was important to make Saddam think he did not want a war with the United States, so they had to get forces there.

• As he had said before, sufficient force had to be sent, no phony defense, no phony deterrence. Operations Plan 90-1002 would guarantee control of the air and sea. Ground forces had to include several heavy divisions to be both a credible deterrent and a credible fighting force.

• A token force—elements of the 82nd Division Ready Brigade —had to be sent immediately as a demonstration of commitment.

• The deployment had to be visible so Saddam could see it and know that any attack into Saudi Arabia would put him in ground combat with Americans.

Bush seemed to like Powell's points and had no quarrel with them. Whatever it takes to do the job, he said.

The reports from the intelligence agencies were becoming more and more hysterical, Powell felt. As they showed more concern, he found himself becoming less concerned. Powell believed Saddam was gambling. The Iraqi leader thought he could get away with Kuwait, thought it was worth the gamble. Kuwait was his target—small, unpopular and an afterthought in the region. Its riches were a source of resentment to the have-nots in the Arab world. Saddam would know that Saudi Arabia was another matter entirely. Attacking Saudi Arabia would be overreaching; it would be a direct assault on the oil-dependent West.

Baker, like Powell, realized that there had been no debate on whether to make the deployment. Likewise, there had been no discussion about the level of force. The deployment had been decided by George Bush; the level of force was being decided by Operations Plan 90-1002.

Baker liked to solve problems with negotiations and deal-making. He was well on the road to negotiating away the Cold War, and he hoped there soon would be an opportunity to use diplomacy in this new crisis.

Later, Baker worried to several of his closest aides that the White House was speeding, not thinking through what it was doing. Saudi Arabia was a vital national security interest, he believed, and the intelligence showed it was threatened. But Baker knew about moving troops. The first arrivals would be only several thousand. He had grave reservations. "These young men could be slaughtered if Saddam Hussein attacked," he said.

19

CHENEY'S PLANE, a comfortable modern jetliner very like the Vice President's Air Force Two, had left Andrews Air Force Base about 2:30 p.m that Sunday. Accompanying Cheney were General Schwarzkopf, who had made his fourth trip to Washington from Florida in five days; Bob Gates of the NSC; Paul Wolfowitz, the undersecretary for policy; Pete Williams; Charles W. Freeman, Jr., the U.S. ambassador to Saudi Arabia, a career foreign service officer who spoke Arabic; and a CIA expert from the National Photographic Interpretation Center with the latest top-secret satellite photographs.

The CIA man was so concerned about security he acted as if he'd surgically bonded the pouch of photos to his knees.

Cheney said he wanted to walk through a practice run of their presentation to King Fahd. He would open with general remarks, then the CIA man would brief the king on how Iraq had accomplished the invasion and on the Iraqi capabilities assembled near the Saudi border. Schwarzkopf would give his presentation on what the United States could do to help to deter and defend, and he himself would close with a summary.

Cheney said he planned to say the following: The United States has a longstanding relationship with Your Majesty and the Saudi Kingdom. We will only come in if you want us. We will only come in for as long as you want us. We are not coming to establish a permanent military presence. But we will stay as long as we can do the job. This will not be a weak or partial presence. It will reflect the President's commitment to the full defense of your country. We won't pull and run on you.

The CIA man brought out a dozen photos and began a technical interpretation. They showed rows of hundreds of Iraqi tanks dug into the desert, with sand embankments on the front and two sides of each tank. Stabilizing and camouflaging the tanks in this way is a standard defensive tactic. But they could back out and move forward in a short time if the Iraqis decided to mount a quick offensive. There were roughly 70,000 Iraqi troops near or advancing on the Saudi border. The photos also showed seven ground-to-ground SCUD missile launchers outside Kuwait City, aimed south at Saudi Arabia.

Cheney realized the agency man's presentation was not going to set the world on fire. Act One of the New World Order shouldn't begin with a technician demonstrating his prowess at reading the tea leaves from overhead photography. Photo interpretation is an obscure subject, and not terribly convincing. Only the experts can tell what the blobs, dots and shadows mean. It was not a presentation that would impress King Fahd.

Scrub the CIA briefing, Cheney said. Schwarzkopf and he would incorporate the information in their own remarks.

As for Schwarzkopf, he had a three-inch-thick, blue vinyl three-ring binder marked "Top Secret" that contained Operations Plan 90-1002. When the general opened it, Cheney went to his own compartment. He already knew the plan.

The day the President pushes the button, executing the plan, Schwarzkopf said, this is what happens. On Day 1, C-Day, the F-15s would be sent. Then in daily increments the various land, sea and air forces would be alerted and deployed. It would take 17 weeks to implement the plan, though it could be stopped at any point. "One of the lessons of Panama was send a big force and get it done quickly," Schwarzkopf said. Because of the distance to the Middle East and the size of the force that was called for, it would take a full 120 days.

There was no discussion of alternatives. None were presented. Williams observed that once Schwarzkopf opened that little blue binder, they all just marched right through it. The White House called to report that Bush had made a public statement and wanted Cheney to have a transcript. Williams took it down and then read it to Cheney. It was the President's "This-will-not stand" remark, his pledge to reverse the invasion.

Well and good, Cheney thought, but he didn't have any forces on the ground to stop Saddam from going into Saudi Arabia, let alone reverse the accomplished invasion. The American shirt tail was flapping and Cheney wanted to focus on the problem at hand —defending Saudi Arabia. "Thanks for the information," he said matter-of-factly. "It's good to know that."

The Secretary wanted to refine his presentation. He invited Gates, Wolfowitz and Ambassador Freeman in to his compartment individually and as a group. Each stressed that Cheney was swimming against a strong current. It was unheard of for the Saudis to ask the United States for forces. Wolfowitz said that Cheney would be asking the Saudis to confront a decision they had spent their lifetimes shying away from. It would be a radical departure to accept forces of any size.

Freeman said Fahd was a master of indecision. The Saudis could spend days and weeks arguing among themselves. Royal family deliberations could make the American Congress seem fast.

They also told Cheney that the biggest worry might be that the Saudis would agree to accept an American deployment but insist on an upper ceiling or cap of so many troops, perhaps much lower than the 250,000 called for in the Operations Plan.

Cheney said that he was going to push to get the deployment started and then deal later with any limits the Saudis might try to impose. During the Iran-Iraq War, the United States had frightened the Saudis with CIA intelligence reports alleging that Iran was coming across the narrow Persian Gulf to attack them. The Reagan administration had formally requested permission to deploy U.S. Air Force fighters to stop these expected attacks. The Saudis had refused. The attacks never materialized, and the Saudis concluded that the United States used intelligence for its own political and strategic purposes, this time to attempt to get Gulf basing for U.S. forces.

After he'd listened to all the advice, Cheney said that they had to be careful. We don't know Saddam is going to invade Saudi Arabia, he said, so let's not go in there and suggest it is inevitable, or that we have inside knowledge. He wanted a hard sell on the capability of the U.S. force that could be sent, and on the political commitment from the President. He wanted a soft sell on the intelligence. The Kuwait invasion spoke loudest about Saddam's willingness to overrun his Arab neighbors.

· · ·

After a 16-hour flight, at about 1 p.m. Saudi time on Monday, August 6, the Americans arrived in Jiddah. They were taken to very elaborate quarters. Their meeting with the king had been scheduled for two hours later, but word came that His Majesty, a night person, preferred to delay it six to eight hours. Unbeknownst to Cheney, Fahd was checking with Muslim religious leaders to see if they would tolerate a U.S. deployment.

The journey to Saudi Arabia, equivalent to two back-to-back transatlantic crossings, had taken a major whack out of Cheney. He seized on the down time to take a nap.

· · ·

Fahd ibn Abdul Aziz, King of Saudi Arabia and Custodian of the Holy Places of Mecca and Medina was his preferred title. Fahd's realm was very secretive and conservative, consisting of an area one quarter the size of the United States with only 14 million people. The king had been a playboy in his youth. CIA reports said Fahd used to take teenage girls for lovemaking sprees on his Boeing 747 jet. But the king had finally settled down. He basically had run the kingdom as crown prince in the late 1970s before succeeding to the throne in 1982.

That evening, Cheney, Gates, Schwarzkopf, Wolfowitz and Ambassador Freeman were conducted to the royal family's private council room in the summer palace. Fahd and half a dozen key members of his government and the royal family, including the foreign minister and the deputy defense minister, were there. Saudi Crown Prince Abdullah was off to one side.

Prince Bandar was going to do the translation for both sides.

Cheney expected that at the end of the presentation, the king would say: thank you very much, we'll get back to you. He would then send Cheney off to sit and wait while the Saudis made up their minds.

The meeting began with small talk about Fahd's long relationship with Bush. When Bush had been CIA director in 1976, Fahd, who'd run Saudi intelligence for 13 years as interior minister, was overseeing Saudi foreign policy as crown prince.

Ordinarily at these royal meetings, the king would open with a lengthy statement. This evening he turned to Cheney rather quickly.

The Secretary began by reminding his hosts that the United States had come to the assistance of Saudi Arabia in 1962 against Yemen and Egypt. He cited the protection of oil tanker shipments in the Gulf in 1987–88 as another example of the United States backing its allies in the region. "It's not a commitment that we take lightly," Cheney said. "Saudi Arabia faces what may be the greatest threat in its history."

After a pause, he continued, "The President sent me out here to reaffirm what he told you on the phone. He stands personally behind the American security guarantee. . . . Saddam Hussein has used lies, deceit and naked aggression to already change the balance of power. He will only become more dangerous if he goes unchallenged. . . . The President's engaged in active diplomacy. He's contacted all the major arms suppliers" used by Iraq.

France, the Soviet Union and China had all agreed to take action, Cheney said. Secretary of State Baker was going to Moscow, where a joint statement would be issued; President Bush had spoken personally with the leaders of Great Britain, France, Germany, Turkey, Japan and Italy.

"If this is not countered, there will be grave consequences for Saudi Arabia, and serious consequences for the United States," Cheney said. He had carefully selected his adjectives—"grave" for the Saudis and "serious" for the United States—to indicate it was Saudi Arabia that had its ass on the line.

"We all have to cooperate to see that this man does not succeed," Cheney said. He proposed a two-part strategy: first, cooperation to defend Saudi Arabia against a future attack; second, the strangulation of Iraq. "Economic measures are important, but in future months, as Saddam Hussein begins to feel the pressure, he could lash out and attack." So it was important to carry out both parts of the strategy at once: defense and strangulation.

Cheney then introduced Schwarzkopf. The general showed King Fahd the satellite pictures of Iraqi tanks on the way to the

Saudi border. "If you put it all together," he said, "this is one division of the best forces that Iraq has. Some place between there"—he pointed out the 50 miles—"and Kuwait City, there are two more of these divisions. After having taken Kuwait City, they moved units in to free up these so they could go to the border. But of even more concern, there are three more divisions moved down from the Basra area. We're watching carefully to monitor what's going on. There's a large amount of resupply."

The pictures clearly explained why Saudi scouts sent into Kuwait had not been able to find the Iraqi forces Bandar had said he'd seen with his own eyes in the initial overheads. The Iraqis, as was their style, were moving their command, control and communications units ahead of the mass of troops. These units were so small, the scouts had missed them.

The pictures also showed the SCUD launchers pointing menacingly south.

Remembering Cheney's order to use caution, Schwarzkopf said, "We think Saddam Hussein *could* attack Saudi Arabia in as little as forty-eight hours. We don't know what he's going to do." Schwarzkopf mentioned that the Iraqis had 22 aircraft loaded for combat at one air base, as well as tankers that would give them additional range. "We don't know what the purpose of that is. It could be just against the U.S. fleet."

Fahd said he did not see the ambiguity. "They have forces in position that are not needed just for Kuwait," he said. "Therefore they must have other objectives." Fahd seemed disgusted. "We used to think Saddam Hussein tells the truth. He told us, he told the U.S., he told Mubarak he wouldn't attack Kuwait, but the opposite happened. So we know his bad intentions are there. As long as the right preparations for the right response at the right time are done, that is the best way to roll back these Iraqi actions. And I am grateful this is being done."

The pause for translation was making it easy for the notetakers to record the meeting, but the exact meaning of the king's last statement was not clear. It seemed that Fahd was moving in the direction Cheney wanted to take him.

"It's right," Cheney said, "that we can't read Saddam Hussein's intentions. He can move faster to attack than we can to defend. In the case of Kuwait, we watched the forces build up and the emir waited until he was attacked before he asked for any help. If you wait for unambiguous warning, it will be too late for us to help you. We have to come much further to defend than he to attack.

"We do not want to start a war any more than anyone else, but [we] believe that preparations are the best way to prevent a war. If a war should come, we would stand with you in defense of Saudi sovereignty and take the war to the enemy."

Cheney also said, "The President asked me to assure you that we will stay as long as you want us. We will leave when you no longer need us. We will stay until justice is done but not stay a minute longer. We are not seeking bases but you are a long way away. We need to make joint preparations now."

Schwarzkopf described Saddam's forces. They're not ten feet tall, he said again, but they are a very tough opponent. The Iraqis are not good in the offensive role, he said. Their chief weakness is a very centralized command system; the officers at all levels wait for the next order. "In the military, we say, 'If you cut off the head, the body won't function.' "

The U.S. naval forces already in the Gulf area were on heightened alert and it was Schwarzkopf's opinion that that was probably the reason Iraq had its planes on alert. The aircraft carrier U.S.S. *Independence* and another half dozen ships were being brought into the region.

Bringing U.S. forces would entail a 7,000-mile journey for those coming by air, and 12,000 miles by sea. Fighter air squadrons would come first, followed by light ground troops. Schwarzkopf then went through a week-by-week description of the buildup. By week 17, it would be a very large force—many Air Force planes, Navy ships, two tank divisions and two other divisions.

"What's the size of a division?" Crown Prince Abdullah asked.

Schwarzkopf said 18,000. No one asked for the total number of troops and personnel, so Schwarzkopf did not have to give the 250,000 figure. He did say he was convinced that after the 17 weeks, the force could defeat anything that came against it.

"After 120 days, we could build up a force that, together with Saudi forces, could kick them into the sea or anywhere else you want to." Schwarzkopf did not offer the 8–12-month estimate for a full offensive option he'd given to Bush only two days earlier.

Abdullah then asked a couple of questions about the maps, trying to distinguish between actual and hypothetical Iraqi troop placements.

"The President asked me to emphasize four things," Cheney said. "The United States is prepared to commit a force to defend Saudi Arabia that can do the job. Though Saddam Hussein possesses a large army and enormous military might, the United States can put in enough force so that Saddam Hussein will be deterred. Should deterrence fail, our forces together will suffice to defeat him.

"The second point the President asked me to repeat: to be successful, we have to have forces in place. We can't wait until Iraqi forces cross the border. Time is of the essence.

"Third point: After the danger is over, our forces will go home."

Under his breath in Arabic, Abdullah interjected, "I would hope so." Bandar did not translate this.

"Because of our cooperation," Cheney continued on the third point, "your forces will be better able to defend your country after we leave. And we will be able to return more quickly if we're needed."

Fahd said, yes, almost like a joint training exercise when the United States leaves equipment behind—a standard U.S. practice.

Schwarzkopf joked, "I think I might want to think about that a little bit."

Fahd seemed to be looking for a long-run, concrete benefit from such a deployment.

Cheney picked up on it. "Our position would be much easier now if there were equipment in place." He continued with his presidential message. "Fourth, it will be far more dangerous if we wait. If we fail to deal with Saddam Hussein now, he will only grow stronger and more threatening. I'd like to receive your approval to proceed with introducing U.S. forces. We want to work with you so that this can be an international force, including forces of regional countries, but urge you not to wait for this to be organized before you agree to the deployment of U.S. forces."

"Our cooperation with the United States is not out of the desire to attack others or to be aggressors," Fahd said, adding that the basis was the threat to Saudi Arabia and mutual interests. As if thinking aloud, the king continued: "We did not create the problem. The problem was created for us. One has to ask why Saddam Hussein creates these forces." Fahd noted that Saddam spent all this money on armaments, instead of things that are for the good of his people. "No one is seeking to create a problem for him. . . . This shows how shallow he is. Why should he attack Kuwait—it's a small country—and create oppression?

"It's not just his aggression against Kuwait but [he] aspires to something larger. . . . Because he's egotistical, he thinks he really knows it all. [He] makes the big mistake if he really believes that, and I think he does.

"If we do anything with our American friends, we do it only in self-defense, not as aggressors—shows how deep the relationship is between our two countries. That in itself shows these two countries consider each other's interest and security.

"We do not do it for aggressive purposes. People all over the world are saying, what will the United States do for Saudi Arabia? I am very pleased what I heard just now. We have to work to implement the arrangements to achieve that." Fahd then turned to his entourage and asked, "Does anybody have any comments?"

A lively exchange in Arabic ensued between the king and Crown Prince Abdullah. Bandar did not translate. On the U.S. side, only Ambassador Freeman understood what was said.

"We have to do this," Fahd said. "The Kuwaitis waited, they waited too long and now there no longer is a Kuwait."

"Oh yes there is," Abdullah shot back, "there is still a Kuwait."

"Yes," Fahd replied, "and all the Kuwaitis are living in our hotel rooms."

After this, the king turned to Cheney. Bandar resumed translation. "Mr. Secretary, we approve of the principle. Let's believe in God and do what has to be done. We will proceed with the details.

"I don't care what other people say," the king added. "The most important thing is to proceed to protect our country together with the Americans, also bringing some people from other Arab countries who are our friends."

"I think that would be excellent," Cheney said.

"Very good," Fahd said. "Some of them have said in the past they're ready and willing. Some of them are countries that are friendly to you and us, like Egypt and Morocco."

"I'm very pleased with your approval of our plan," Cheney said.

The king said they didn't have the luxury of time; they faced immediate dangers. What needs to be done quickly must be done at once, he said.

Cheney was pleasantly surprised. He had been worried that an international force including other Arab nations might be so important to the Saudis that they would insist it be put together before anything else.

"The United States has no ulterior motive," Fahd said. "We have taken this country from bushes and stones and built it to a nation that is equal to few in the world. We've invested billions of dollars to build this nation. It looks like we've been at it for hundreds of years but actually only for a very few. I wish you would have time to see for yourself how we have built things in the middle of nowhere. You could see where the billions of dollars of oil income go. It doesn't bother me what other media may say. People who see the facts honestly will acknowledge what we have accomplished. What matters to me is what the people of Saudi Arabia think. And as long as they live a decent standard of living, it doesn't bother me what people may say about me."

The Custodian of Mecca and Medina continued with the history, the sort of speech that normally would have been expected at the beginning of the meeting. "Twenty-two years ago, where you sit was formed a desert. I was the minister of education. We had no more than 33,000 students, five high schools. Now, in a short time, we have seven universities and 37 junior colleges. [We] have gone from 33,000 to 2.7 million students. . . . Who would have believed? From nothing to 2,200 factories."

Why such success, the king asked. Because, he answered, they always went into joint ventures with people and countries who knew what they were doing. "We're not afraid to learn from people who are better than we are. The Saudi people have no complexes. We want to cooperate with other people." He offered to send Cheney some videos describing this transformation and he also encouraged Cheney to return and see for himself.

Fahd said he laughed at reports that most of the Saudi income went to the royal family. "Read in one place that I have an income of $40 billion a year. The whole income of the country is only $40 billion. Many preposterous things are said, but I don't care what's said outside. What I care about is the welfare and well-being of the Saudi people."

In a direct shot at King Hussein of Jordan, who traced his own ancestry directly to the Prophet Mohammed, Fahd said, "We do not claim that our ancestors are holy. We're just one family of the Saudi people.

"We believe strongly in our God. We believe he knows the truth and that he will guide us.

"In closing, I want to thank the President, the Vice President, his administration, both houses of Congress, you personally. You've come here with one objective, which is to help Saudi Arabia. [I] hope that these problems in our part of the world can subside and I still owe you a visit to the United States and I am holding to it."

Cheney said that President Bush was eager for the king to visit. "This has been a truly historic meeting," Cheney added.

"No doubt it is," Fahd replied.

The Secretary said he would be going back to Washington right away to brief the President on this conversation. "General Schwarzkopf will work with your officials to work out the details. We will leave a team behind."

"It's good to leave a team. The quicker the work gets done, the better. The less we give to the media, the better."

"I will give word to the President," Cheney said. "He will start moving forces right away."

Back in his room, Cheney told his aides, "They've invited us in." He phoned the President, who took the call in the Oval Office where he was meeting again with Prime Minister Thatcher.

King Fahd has approved the deployment, Cheney said.

Bush sounded quite happy.

Cheney said he was formally asking the President's approval to begin moving the forces.

"You got it. Go," Bush said.

.   .   .

Cheney called Powell to tell him that they were authorized to start the deployment.

Powell was surprised to hear the Saudis had agreed.

General Kelly and his operations staff had spent much of the weekend in the building—first working to prepare for a deployment, and then waiting. Kelly had been told that there was movement at the political level but it hadn't quite been settled. About 4 p.m., the mission came. They were ordered "to defend against an Iraqi attack on Saudi Arabia and be prepared to conduct other operations as directed." The immediate order was to execute Operations Plan 90-1002.

The first unit sent would be 48 advanced F-15 jets from the 1st

Tactical Fighter Wing at Langley Air Force Base, Virginia. The Division Ready Brigade of 2,300 men from the 82nd Airborne Division—the troops in the highest state of readiness—would be next.

The initial planes and troops could not arrive until the morning after next, Wednesday, August 8.

Powell was concerned. The Division Ready Brigade was an extremely light force. In the eyes of some military experts, it was little more than a massive airport security detail. The brigade, the 48 jet fighters, the naval airpower in the region and the small Saudi Army were no match for Saddam's six divisions. It was naked vulnerability, prime time for Saddam to strike.

. . .

Cheney was aware that Powell believed Saddam did not want to go to war with the United States, that way down deep, Saddam would be frightened, that he had a healthy respect for U.S. military capability and would conclude that a war would be suicidal. But Cheney disagreed. Perhaps, he thought, Saddam had a very different concept of what could constitute victory. Just standing up to the United States or inflicting a bloody nose on Uncle Sam might be a significant political gain for Saddam. Perhaps even worth the price that would be paid in a war.

Saddam was not suicidal, Cheney thought, but some degree of conflict with the United States might not necessarily be a bad thing for him. He thought Saddam's position might resemble Egyptian President Sadat's in the 1973 war, which had begun when Egypt and Syria launched a surprise attack on Israel. Sadat didn't have to beat Israel to "win" that war—all he had to do was get across the Suez Canal and demonstrate he was willing to try to take the Sinai Peninsula back from Israel. Though it was a military defeat for Egypt, Sadat proclaimed victory; he'd made his point and the episode had won him status as an Arab leader. Cheney was sure that fighting was at least a real possibility in the Gulf.

Before leaving Saudi Arabia the next morning, Cheney met with Bandar and his father, Saudi Defense Minister Prince Sultan, to review the bidding. Bandar already had information from his network. "My friends Kissinger and Crowe are predicting failure," he said, adding that the Saudis had been up all night discussing the matter.

"Look," Bandar continued, "there's no backing away from the decision. It's a done deal, not just because the king said it." He suggested they try to conceal it, proposing the two countries "just say it is a joint exercise. Saddam is not crazy. He is foxy and evil. But let's employ some of his tactics and not advertise what we are doing." Bandar said he was deeply worried about the first arrivals; they would be so few in number that they could not provide any kind of defense. Could they not hide what they were doing until there were enough troops to defend the kingdom?

Cheney responded that he did not know how this could be done. The President could not mislead the American people, Bandar knew that. This was a big decision for the President and his best opportunity was to lay it out straight. If he did not, the news would leak and he would be demolished. You know the American system, Cheney reminded Bandar. It wouldn't work.

Bandar said it was just a tactic. "Let's play dead like a desert animal and then rise up," he said.

After more discussion, both sides agreed to delay any announcement of a troop deployment until the first troops were actually on the ground in Saudi Arabia—Wednesday morning in the United States, Wednesday afternoon and evening in Saudi Arabia. As Cheney prepared to leave, he was thinking that the agreement might be soft. With Bandar, with the Saudis, you never knew what you had. His worry was compounded when Schwarzkopf contacted the senior general in the Saudi defense ministry to begin coordination of the deployment. The Saudi general wanted to reopen discussions and talk about whether the United States was going to send troops at all.

Schwarzkopf, concerned that the invitation was off, told the general he understood it had been decided and that they were supposed to start deploying immediately. Skeptical, the Saudi said he would check. He did so and came back to Schwarzkopf very surprised. Schwarzkopf was right about the deployment.

Cheney finally departed Saudi Arabia for Cairo, where he was taken by small plane to see President Mubarak in Alexandria. He informed the Egyptian president about the coming U.S. deployment to Saudi Arabia. Would Mubarak please grant permission for the nuclear aircraft carrier U.S.S. *Eisenhower* to go through the Suez Canal? Mubarak said fine, but when? Tonight, Cheney said. Mubarak agreed. The Egyptian president didn't agree to send troops, but did later when he spoke to President Bush.

Cheney left Egypt to return to the United States. When he was over Italy, he received a call directly from the President, who was still dialing the world seeking more support and troops.

"Dick," Bush said, "I just got off the phone with King Hassan of Morocco. I'd like you to stop in and see him."

Landing charts for Morocco were immediately faxed up to Cheney's plane.

Since his year as CIA director, Bush had been close to Hassan, who now had ruled Morocco for 29 years. The king owed his longevity on the throne in part to the CIA, which had long provided friendly-head-of-state security assistance and training that helped him stay in power. In return, Hassan allowed U.S. intelligence agencies free run of his strategically located country at the western entrance to the Mediterranean Sea.

At the palace, Cheney saw Hassan first in a group meeting, then privately. Between the two discussions, the king took a call from Libyan leader Muammar Qaddafi. All the regional heads of state were talking to each other. When Cheney and the king were alone, Hassan did not reveal what the Libyan leader had said. Cheney told Hassan that the Saudis had agreed to accept a significant number of U.S. troops. The President would welcome Hassan's support. Hassan said that he was ready to contribute Moroccan troops immediately.

Afterwards, Cheney and Gates went to the U.S. Embassy in Rabat and called Scowcroft on the secure phone to discuss the speech the President was planning to give announcing the decision. Scowcroft was attempting to define precisely the action and the reasoning.

Cheney said King Fahd had asked that President Bush make it clear in any public statements that the Saudis had requested the U.S. presence.

Scowcroft assured him that that point would be included in the speech.

Cheney finally landed in Washington at 6 a.m. on Wednesday, three hours before the President's speech. A draft had been faxed to him and he had reviewed it. The speech drew on some World War II analogies: Iraq had "stormed in blitzkrieg fashion through

Kuwait," and "Appeasement does not work. As was the case in
the 1930s." The deployment was cast in terms of a principled
moral crusade, and the speech explicitly said that the mission was
defensive.

. . .

At 9 a.m. on August 8 Bush appeared on national television from
the Oval Office, looking tired and drawn.

"In the life of a nation," he began, "we're called upon to define
who we are and what we believe. Sometimes these choices are not
easy. But today as President, I ask for your support in a decision
I've made to stand up for what's right and condemn what's wrong,
all in the cause of peace."

His voice was a bit scratchy and his rhythm off. His facial
expression did not seem to match his words of high purpose.
Holding to his "this-will-not-stand" position, the President said,
"We seek the immediate, unconditional and complete withdrawal
of all Iraqi forces from Kuwait."

But he explained that the military would not be used offensively
for this purpose. "The mission of our troops is wholly defensive.
Hopefully, they will not be needed long. They will not initiate
hostilities, but they will defend themselves, the Kingdom of Saudi
Arabia, and other friends in the Persian Gulf."

A nervous smile flashed at several inappropriate moments. Bush
stuck his fist in the air when he spoke of "unity of purpose."

At a noon press conference, the President repeated the point
that the military mission was not to drive the Iraqis out of Kuwait.

At 1 p.m. Cheney and Powell appeared at a Pentagon press
conference.

"I would, at the outset though," Cheney said in a subdued
manner, "emphasize for all of you—especially those of you who
remember the Panama operation in December—that this situation
is different." Because it was an ongoing operation, he said he
couldn't answer many questions about what units were going,
when they were going and their strength. He outlined his trip to
Saudi Arabia in six paragraphs, then turned the conference over
to Powell.

Powell made an unusually direct appeal to the media. "I also
would ask for some restraint on your part as you find out infor-

mation," the Chairman said, "if you would always measure it against the need for operational security to protect our troops. That should be uppermost, I think, in all our minds."

To a question concerning the vulnerability of the initial troops, Powell stretched the point. "I think they are pretty secure," he said. He mentioned the airpower from the *Independence* and *Eisenhower* battle groups, and the Saudi armed forces with AWACS aircraft and their "top-of-the-line fighters." The Chairman added, "So I'm reasonably sure that we can get in in good order without presenting any vulnerabilities."

But privately, Powell was still concerned about the vulnerability of his initial forces. Many in the world, apparently including Saddam, thought somehow that the United States could deploy tens or hundreds of thousands of troops instantaneously. Of course it wasn't true. Powell didn't even have the Division Ready Brigade of 2,300 in Saudi Arabia yet. In the first three or four weeks, his troops would be naked and excruciatingly vulnerable. It was a secret that needed to be guarded at almost any cost. Lives depended on it.

. . .

DIA officer Pat Lang was sent out to brief Prince Bandar at his elegant, sprawling residence in Virginia. The former British commandos who acted as Bandar's personal security guards escorted him into an ornately decorated room where he put up a map of the region. For an hour, Lang went over in detail what had happened during the Kuwait invasion and how Saddam was massing the same elite force of eight divisions on the Saudi border.

He crisply described how nearly 800 T-72 tanks were on the battle line and could move unimpeded into eastern Saudi Arabia and duplicate the Kuwait success. "We are powerless to stop them," Lang said.

"Oh, God," Bandar said, "Oh, God. Do *they* know this?" Does Saddam realize he can overrun Saudi Arabia this easily?

"I think they suspect it," Lang replied, "but they don't know it." He added that reading Saddam's mind had become the question of the day, and that so far everyone had flunked the test.

. . .

Pete Williams, who had the top security clearances and was as trusted a Cheney aide as any, did not know exactly how many troops were scheduled for deployment. He was hearing from other senior Pentagon civilians and military officers that 100,000 or 150,000 might be the final number, but not the accurate figure of 250,000. Whenever he asked Powell, the Chairman was vague. Powell seemed almost paranoid about the numbers and the locations of the troops.

From the White House, Sununu put out the figure 50,000, which was published Thursday, August 9, and attributed to an unnamed senior administration official.

. . .

When General Vuono saw the low ball figure, he was distressed. The operation, now dubbed Desert Shield, could sour on the question of expectations and credibility. With the White House and political leadership concealing facts and risks, creating false hopes for a small, short-lived operation, he heard echoes of Vietnam. The Army chief recognized that Operations Plan 90-1002 put the military in for the long haul—months and months, if not longer. No one knew how long the deployment might last. If the media and therefore the public didn't feel they were getting the facts, there was no chance of maintaining public support. Such a massive deployment could not be concealed; orders were going to units in dozens of states. "The big question is the political will question," Vuono told his staff. A Vuono aide soon leaked the real number of up to 250,000 to the Associated Press, which ran a story.

Vuono also detected an initial complacency in the Army operations staff. He went to see them, reminding the staff that once the Army had a heavy tank division on the ground in Saudi Arabia, they might become involved in high-intensity, central-front warfare—the stuff they had trained for and worried about in Europe for decades.

The Army is going to be tested, he said, adding sternly, "Anticipate, coordinate and verify."

. . .

On that Thursday, retired Air Force Chief Larry Welch and his wife Eunice were scheduled for a 15-minute farewell courtesy call with Bush, a thank you to Welch for 37 years of service. When they arrived, they were asked if they could stay for lunch with the Bushes. Brent Scowcroft joined the two couples in the residence for lunch.

Barbara Bush and the President both talked at some length about their children and family. Welch noticed that Bush seemed entirely relaxed. He had watched Bush enough to realize that when the President was on the verge of making a decision, he became intense, outspoken, often launched a frenzy of public statements. Once the decision had been made, Bush would pull back and loosen up.

Welch had written part of the initial contingency plan for the Gulf deployment in the early 1980s. He was well aware that the desert would be extremely taxing and that the Saudis would be very restrictive. It would be a Gatorade, not a Budweiser deployment. Welch felt that the risks of failing to defend Saudi Arabia far outweighed the risks of sending the force. But an attempt to push the Iraqis out of Kuwait would be another thing entirely, he felt. It would reduce Kuwait City to the ruins of Beirut. Any effort to restore the status quo would likely fail because the status quo was gone forever.

"You're doing the right thing, Mr. President," General Welch said.

Bush didn't dwell on the Gulf. He preferred to talk about his family. He, Welch and Scowcroft all said they were glad to have an officer as strong as the new Air Force chief, General Michael Dugan, Welch's successor.

. . .

On Sunday, August 12, Cheney appeared on NBC Television's "Meet the Press." "The fact of the matter is that the United States has a significant military force in the area this morning," the Secretary said without any specifics. "There's more on the way."

Pressed for numbers, he replied, "I would not want to put an upper level on that. . . . No one should assume this is easy or is going to be wrapped up very quickly or without a significant U.S. effort." Of course, he knew the real timelines—17 weeks to defend and perhaps 8 to 12 months for a full offensive capability. But no one was even hinting that the nation had started down that road.

Bush decided he would go to the Pentagon. On Tuesday, August 14, Cheney and Powell held a one-hour rehearsal in the Tank of a briefing for the President. The next day, Wednesday, Bush visited the Tank.

Powell was alarmed about all the troops and military force he was beginning to pour into the Gulf, without any clear notion of where the buildup would end. Where was it all leading? The question had been on the Chairman's mind since that Sunday afternoon ten days earlier when he'd watched the President get off his helicopter on the White House lawn and state unequivocally, "This will not stand." It seemed to him like a crucial moment, perhaps a definition of a new mission. If the invasion of Kuwait were going to be reversed, what did that mean in practical military terms? How much force was needed and what kind of action should they be planning for?

It seemed to Powell that the military was rolling down a highway, uncertain which off-ramp it was supposed to take. After the Tank session, Bush, Cheney and Powell went to Cheney's office.

I want to tell you how the buildup is going, Powell told the President. It was his first chance to talk to Bush since the deployment had been ordered. He showed the President a chart that illustrated graphically, week by week, the U.S. forces going into the Gulf. The chart ended on December 1, the closure point for the mission, when 250,000 troops would be there.

We have our mission to deter and defend, Powell said. There will be no question you can defend Saudi Arabia at the end. We have no other job, Powell said, and this is what the future looks like to December 1, when we will be completed. We're at risk now, but we are deterring.

"If you want me to do more, the curve goes up. If you want more, I need to know whether it's two miles or three miles down the road that I get off and exit here."

At some point Schwarzkopf will report to you, mission accomplished, Powell told Bush. What we need, Mr. President, is for you to tell us before that mission is accomplished what you want us to do next—so if we have things in the military supply pipeline, do we stop the pipeline or keep it going, or whatever?

Powell wasn't looking for an immediate new mission from the President. He was not pushing for a decision, just inquiring whether they had or were going to get a new military mission.

There was no response from Bush, but Powell felt that he had, at least, put the President on notice that a decision would have to be made soon.

Later, Bush spoke to Pentagon employees at the River Entrance overlooking the Potomac. With Cheney and Powell standing behind him, he said:

"Saddam has claimed that this is a holy war of Arab against infidel—this from the man who has used poison gas against the men, women and children of his own country; who invaded Iran in a war that cost the lives of more than half a million Moslems; and who now plunders Kuwait. Atrocities have been committed by Saddam's soldiers and henchmen. The reports out of Kuwait tell a sordid tale of brutality."

It was a fiery attack on Saddam. "It is Saddam who lied to his Arab neighbors. It is Saddam who invaded an Arab state. And it is he who now threatens the Arab nation," Bush said, his voice rising.

Standing near Bush before the crowd, Cheney thought to himself that it was far too personal an attack, harsh and overdone, ratcheting up the rhetoric way too much. The text of the speech had come over from the White House only an hour before and there had been no chance for Cheney or anyone else in the Pentagon to suggest changes.

Cheney later mentioned his concern directly to Scowcroft. Saddam now had roughly 200,000 troops in Kuwait to the 20,000 of the United States—a 10 to 1 advantage. The possibility of a slaughter still could not be ruled out and Cheney did not want some debate-team flourish by the President to provoke Saddam.

Though Bush had gone to Kennebunkport trying to take his summer vacation, Cheney had canceled two weeks of fishing scheduled to begin that day. He did not see how the Secretary of Defense could be ordering hundreds of thousands to the Saudi desert and then go fishing.

At the end of the week, Bush signed a top-secret intelligence "finding," authorizing CIA covert actions to overthrow Saddam. The CIA was not to violate the ban on involvement in assassination attempts, but rather recruit Iraqi dissidents to remove Saddam from power.

.   .   .

On Friday, August 17, Cheney left for Saudi Arabia and a four-day swing through other countries in the region. He planned to visit Bahrain, Oman, the United Arab Emirates and Egypt to obtain more support. Attempting to duplicate his success with the Saudis, he was seeking landing and staging rights for U.S. forces, particularly Air Force fighters, bombers and cargo planes.

There was one scare when some reports came in that the U.S. Navy had boarded an Iraqi tanker. Cheney was concerned that some Navy officer way down the line was going to start a war. It took half an hour to get through to the Pentagon to learn that the Navy had only fired across the bow of the ship.

Visiting the U.S. units already in Saudi Arabia, Cheney was dramatically reminded of their precarious situation. Everyone seemed consumed with logistics, transportation and just getting settled. The atmosphere was like the first night at camp. Suppose there was a fight before all the U.S. forces got in place? Were they assuming the initial deployment would deter Saddam?

Cheney called Powell on the secure line. Is Schwarzkopf making certain that we are ready for any short-term contingency? he asked. What if Saddam just moves a little further and comes into Saudi Arabia? What if he goes for the oil fields?

Powell agreed they were vulnerable. But if Saddam was going to move into Saudi Arabia, why hadn't he done it earlier? Powell said each day the United States is better off.

There was another problem on the ground in Saudi Arabia. Too many officers and staff people had been sent in the initial waves, and the commanders were urgently requesting more privates and troops who could fight.

When Cheney returned to Washington, he and Powell flew to Kennebunkport on Wednesday, August 22, to brief the President and discuss the next steps.

It was a bright sunny day at Walker's Point, a beautiful piece of oceanfront real estate. Cheney and Powell joined Bush, Scowcroft, Sununu, Gates and Larry Eagleburger around a small circular garden table overlooking the craggy Maine coast. Baker was in Wyoming on vacation, attempting to put on an August-as-usual face.

Cheney and Powell sought Bush's final approval to call up some 50,000 reservists. Certain critical military specialties such as logistics, transportation, medical services, construction and intelligence were concentrated in the Reserves. Frustrated by President Johnson's refusal to fully mobilize the military in the Vietnam War by calling up the Reserves, the Pentagon had intentionally organized the services so that the specialists that would be required in a large deployment were in the Reserves. This would force a president to use the Reserves for any major military action, making it difficult if not impossible to slide slowly into war without the public's participation.

Having committed to the large operation in the Gulf, Bush, Powell and Cheney knew the Reserve call-up was inevitable. Bush now authorized it.

The United Nations, which already had approved economic sanctions against Iraq, was now considering a resolution approving a blockade. The immediate question was whether to wait for the U.N., or go ahead unilaterally and board Iraqi ships. The Navy had stopped some Iraqi vessels, but had not yet boarded any.

Cheney could see that it was a huge decision for the President. Bush was clearly eager to assert the right of the United States to act by itself and wanted to demonstrate some muscle. Two days earlier, he had been asked by a reporter whether he was prepared to stop Iraqi tankers. He had replied with one of his dares, "You just watch. You just watch and see." Nonetheless, Cheney recommended that the President not rush to board ships, but wait for the United Nations.

Powell pointed out that shooting up a ship for a short-term gain would not be worth it. The ship was part of the capillary system of supply and not at the heart of the problem. From Wyoming, Baker had made it clear that was his view also.

Bush was skeptical the U.N. would come through. When he was U.N. ambassador in 1971–72, the Soviets had blocked everything the United States tried to do. But this was a new era. He decided he would wait for a ruling from the U.N. Security Council.

Powell informed the President that, for the first time since the deployment had begun, the situation was not dicey. There were some 35,000 troops in Saudi Arabia or on the way, and another 20,000 U.S. sailors were on ships in the region. General Schwarzkopf, of course, was not satisfied, but Powell never expected a commander to be satisfied. There were now about 200,000 Iraqi troops in Kuwait. The situation was improving each day, though no one would be really comfortable until the tanks of the 24th

Mechanized Division were fully in place. Saddam probably would not attack now, Powell said, because he had not taken the chance when he really had the upper hand during the first two weeks, when the U.S. forces had been considerably smaller.

Yet, Powell said, the Iraqi military was still capable of inflicting tremendous damage. He had pulled together lots of intelligence and updated work from the Joint Staff. One big factor was the Iraqi ground-to-ground missile force, including large quantities of the Soviet-supplied SCUD-B, which had been modified to have a range of 615 kilometers. Intelligence was not sure how many the Iraqis had, but the estimates said 800 to 1,000. Chemical weapons could be placed on some of the missiles. The Iraqis didn't always get the fuel-to-air ratios correct, making missile performance erratic. The performance of the SCUD depended on a number of factors, such as whether the wind was blowing the right way.

Saddam's forces in Kuwait were digging in. As the United States brought in heavy armored forces, two of the world's large armies eventually would be facing off. If there was conflict, it would be major land warfare. This was nothing like the liberation of Grenada or Panama.

Bush asked Powell for his view—not just his military advice, Bush added, but on what course of action to take. The President wanted an overall assessment. Powell said they were doing fine defending Saudi Arabia.

By the end of the meeting, Powell saw that Bush was somewhat sobered. Talk of liberating Kuwait was no longer on the front burner.

In the following days, the President toned down his public attacks on Saddam.

On Saturday, August 25, the United Nations Security Council voted to give the navies of the United States and other countries the right to use force to stop trade with Iraq. It was the first time in the U.N.'s 45-year history that individual countries outside an umbrella U.N. command were authorized to enforce an international blockade, an extraordinary diplomatic victory for the administration.

Bush, who had sweated out the U.N. vote, was euphoric.

．　．　．

At the Joint Staff, General Kelly made an assessment of the situation three weeks after the start of the deployment. First, the Air Force deserved a gold star for its performance in achieving what looked like early air superiority in the region. Kelly's major concern was what he called "the mind-set of this beast Saddam." He had reviewed the intelligence reports from the Iran-Iraq War. Though they were not absolutely reliable, they had the grim ring of truth. In addition to the well-publicized reports that Saddam personally had executed senior advisers and ministers who disagreed with him, there was information showing how he treated his senior military commanders. Iraqi Army generals who lost 20 kilometers to the Iranians during the Iran-Iraq War had been executed, according to the intelligence. In the Iraqi Air Force, generals had been executed if they lost a certain number of planes. Consequently, they had made sure the planes weren't flown much, leaving Iraq with mostly inexperienced and untrained pilots.

But given his mind-set, Saddam might well use his chemical weapons, and there was some intelligence that he could soon have biological weapons as well. The biggest problem, Kelly concluded, was that Saddam, his military and the Iraqi people were used to doing without, used to the pain and suffering and deprivation of an eight-year war. In fact, Kelly felt Iraq could last longer at these things than the United States.

· · ·

A delegation of 16 senators, ten aides and eight military escorts left for Saudi Arabia on August 31 aboard a C-137 jet. The next day their first briefing was given by General Schwarzkopf at his temporary headquarters in Dhahran. The general put a map on the wall. He said, here are the Army units, the Marines, the Navy ships, the Air Force, the Saudi forces and the Iraqis. There was no discussion of contingency plans or options.

Later, one of the senior U.S. generals commanding troops in the Gulf told some of the senators very privately that the U.S. side was not ready to fight and would need at least another ten days. The senators then visited Marines in forward positions nearer Kuwait and had lunch—the latest version of the field ration, called MRE, for Meals Ready to Eat. Troops joked that MRE stood for Meals Rejected by Ethiopia.

Later that afternoon the delegation flew to Bahrain and a small group attended a palace dinner hosted by Emir Sheikh Isa bin Sulman al Khalifa, the leader of the small emirate. The emir inquired why the United States allowed the Iraqis to appear on CNN to criticize America and American policy.

On Sunday, the group visited Navy ships, including the battleship U.S.S. *Wisconsin,* then went back to Saudi Arabia for a meeting with King Fahd, who had nothing new or startling to say. Later that evening the senators were supposed to meet with senior Kuwaiti officials. The emir of Kuwait, who was in Saudi Arabia, declined to meet with them.

The senators were furious. Here the United States had undertaken this massive military deployment in part to help Kuwait, and their exiled leader wouldn't meet his potential saviors. Republican Senator William Cohen of Maine was incredulous. It was not as if the emir had pressing government responsibilities, given that his country had been stolen from him.

The Kuwaiti officials sent to visit the senators were really the second team, Cohen could see. Cameras filmed the discussions. Cohen and the others didn't know whether to laugh or cry when they learned that the filming was being done by the American public relations firm of Hill & Knowlton, hired by Kuwait to do some image-polishing.

On Monday, September 3—the Labor Day holiday in America and the fourth day of the grueling trip—the senators flew the two hours to Cairo and linked up with a House delegation for a meeting with Mubarak. The Egyptian president delivered a two-hour tirade against King Hussein of Jordan, who was staying out of the Arab coalition against Saddam. Mubarak also disclosed that Saddam had tried to bribe him to keep Egypt out of the anti-Iraq coalition. In the afternoon they flew 1,500 miles to Abu Dhabi, the sheikdom that is the capital of the United Arab Emirates, for meetings with His Highness President Sheikh Zayed bin Sultan al Nahayan.

The sheikh delivered a long monologue about the courage of the Kuwaitis. Daniel Patrick Moynihan, the New York Democrat, seated on a beautiful couch alongside his fellow senators, grew increasingly uneasy. He moved to the edge of his seat as His Highness expounded on the magnificence of the brave Kuwaitis.

"Your Grace," Moynihan finally shouted, his hand in the air as in his days as U.N. ambassador. "Your Grace," he repeated in his melodramatic voice.

All eyes were on Moynihan. "Your Grace, the Kuwaitis left their wives. They left their servants. They took their money and stuffed it in Swiss bank accounts. That is not my definition of courage."

The sheikh disagreed. He said the Kuwaitis were heroic and in need. His entourage nodded in agreement with their leader, who also noted that the Kuwaitis had been taken by surprise.

"Your Grace," Moynihan answered, "a warrior nation is never taken by surprise."

Cohen whispered to Moynihan, "What about Pearl Harbor?" The United States had also been surprised by the Iraqi invasion, he reminded him.

The next day the delegation flew back to the United States. Cohen felt as if he'd been presented with a sound and light show. There had been no real news or information about what really mattered—the decisions or options the President was facing in seeming isolation, with only a handful of advisers.

. . .

The next day, Wednesday, September 5, Bush invited 30 senators and congressmen, most of whom had traveled to the Gulf the previous weekend, to the White House.

Cheney, who attended the meeting, felt that the August congressional recess had been a tremendous advantage. The administration had been able to spend the month doing what needed to be done, rather than explaining itself on Capitol Hill. But Bush and Cheney, both former congressmen, knew that it was important to have congressional goodwill.

Every senator and congressman who spoke at the meeting praised Bush's handling of the crisis, and expressed support for the military and diplomatic moves.

"Mr. President," Cohen said when he had a chance to speak, "there is a photograph in The New York Times this morning showing a Marine being helped by his comrades. I don't have to quote Shakespeare for us to see that if this Marine had been felled by a bullet and not the sun, there would be a wholly different reaction in this country.

"Mr. President, I'd suggest that you convene a special session of Congress and that we deal with the law of the land in the War Powers Act, and that you get a vote while you have the support of Congress for this operation."

Cohen said that he was making this suggestion for the sake of the President, for the sake of unity between the administration and the Congress, for the sake of the troops in the desert who deserved a government unified, and for the sake of Congress, which was so deft at avoiding its responsibility.

"Mr. President, I hope you will resist the calls that are being made for an offensive action," he said.

"When there comes a point that there is blood in the sand," Cohen said, "the Congress—which is following its constituents now—will again do so, and follow them in the opposite direction.

"We visited the Kuwaitis, we saw the Kuwaitis and we realized that Kuwaitis are willing to fight—until every U.S. soldier has dropped."

Bush politely acknowledged his points and moved on.

20

POWELL WAS UP EARLY ON SUNDAY, September 16. He had just returned the night before from Saudi Arabia and was jet-lagged. During his whirlwind tour, the troops had bombarded him with questions in front of reporters about when they would be going home, and he wasn't happy that he did not have a satisfactory answer. At 6 a.m. he heard a report on CNN about statements Air Force Chief General Michael Dugan had made about the plans for war against Iraq. The report, based on a story published that morning in *The Washington Post,* sounded weird. Powell went looking for his *Post* on the doorstep outside Quarters 6, but it hadn't arrived yet.

About 40 minutes later the paper came, and Powell began reading the story, prominently stretched across the entire top of the front page. Under the headline, "U.S. to Rely on Air Strikes if War Erupts," Powell read: "The Joint Chiefs of Staff have concluded that U.S. military air power—including a massive bombing campaign against Baghdad that specifically targets Iraqi President Saddam Hussein—is the only effective option to force Iraqi forces from Kuwait if war erupts, according to Air Force chief of staff Gen. Michael J. Dugan."

With mounting surprise and alarm, Powell read that Dugan said the other chiefs as well as General Schwarzkopf shared Dugan's view that " 'air power is the only answer that's available to our country' to avoid a bloody land war that would probably destroy Kuwait.

"Until two weeks ago," Powell read, "U.S. target planners had assembled a somewhat conventional list of Iraqi targets which included, in order of priority: Iraqi air defenses; airfields and warplanes; intermediate-range missile sites, including SCUD ground-to-ground missiles; communications and command centers; chemical, nuclear and munitions plants; and Iraqi armor formations. . . .

" 'That's a nice list of targets, and I might be able to accept those, but that's not enough,' Dugan said. He asked his planners to interview academics, journalists, 'ex-military types' and Iraqi defectors to determine 'what is unique about Iraqi culture that they put very high value on. What is it that psychologically would make an impact on the population and regime in Iraq?' The intent, he added, is to find 'centers of gravity, where air power could make a difference early on.'

"Israeli sources have advised that 'the best way to hurt Saddam' is to target his family, his personal guard and his mistress. Because Saddam is a 'one man show' in Iraq, Dugan said, 'if and when we choose violence he ought to be at the focus of our efforts'—a military strategy known as decapitation."

Powell read Dugan's comments about Iraqi capabilities. "Their air force has very limited military capability," "they did not distinguish themselves in the war against Iran" and they have "an incompetent Army."

The predominance of airpower was the overriding theme, a kind of one-service, Victory-Through-Airpower approach. While Dugan admitted that "there are a lot of things that air power cannot accomplish," and that the Air Force had "great difficulty in driving people out of the jungle" in Vietnam, he added that "there's not much jungle where we're going." The article said that "Marine and Army ground forces could be used for diversions, flanking attacks and to block an Iraqi counterstrike on Saudi Arabia. . . . Ground forces may be needed to reoccupy Kuwait, Dugan added, but only after air power has so shattered enemy resistance that soldiers can 'walk in and not have to fight' house-to-house."

The piece closed with comments Dugan had made to an F-15

squadron about American support for the operation: " 'I think they'd support this operation longer than you would think. . . . The American people will support this operation until body bags come home.' "

To Powell, the story read as a public shot across his bow during a most sensitive phase of the deployment, and against the joint consensus Powell had worked so hard to maintain among the services and the chiefs.

It gave a status report on the deployment of U.S. forces to the region and their general readiness for battle, including numbers and types of specific aircraft—details Powell had worked hard to keep out of the media.

This is going to be bad, Powell thought. He noted that the *Post* said Dugan and five of his generals had been interviewed for some ten hours "during a trip to and from Saudi Arabia last week." Talking to reporters for so long in such close quarters was a dangerous and foolish thing to do, Powell knew, and any junior public relations officer knew it. He couldn't believe Dugan had done it. Powell was well aware that Dugan had put a premium on mending Air Force relations with the media, which he felt had been hurt by his predecessor Welch. As part of the campaign, Dugan had had his public affairs people print up laminated Rolodex-size cards with an "on TARGET CONTACT LIST" of the phone numbers of 31 top Air Force officials, "to assist reporters and editors to prepare accurate stories on Air Force issues." In recent weeks, Powell had congratulated Dugan several times about his media policy, but he'd also repeatedly cautioned him to remember that the President was the decision maker. The Air Force chief obviously had been swept up with seeing the troops, and had gone seriously overboard with his new age of openness.

Powell called Cheney at 7 a.m., knowing the Secretary was up early even on Sundays.

"Have you read the *Post*?" Powell asked.

Cheney said he hadn't.

Powell told him about the story, and said he thought it was bad.

Cheney retrieved his copy of the newspaper and read the story twice. Furious, he called Pete Williams at home.

Cheney also talked to Scowcroft, who was going to do a taping of the talk show "Face the Nation" at 10:30 a.m.

Scowcroft was not prepared to say airpower could win a major conflict. It never had. He was aghast that the Air Force chief was pushing that line, particularly in such a rambling way, showing a lack of self-discipline. Scowcroft could hear that Cheney was angry, and rightly so, he thought.

"At a minimum," Scowcroft told Cheney, "I think I have to say, at this point he does not speak for the administration."

Cheney agreed.

On "Face the Nation" Scowcroft made his point: "General Dugan is not in the chain of command and does not speak for the administration." Meanwhile, Cheney went out for a two-hour walk along the C & O Canal, which runs next to the Potomac. He had been a runner, but was forced to give it up when his knees went bad. A daily walk was his main form of exercise.

Pete Williams talked to Powell. The Chairman wanted to know what Scowcroft was going to say. What was Cheney going to say? What had Williams heard? What was Williams going to say? It was obvious Powell was worried.

Back home from his walk, Cheney read the story again. He was still steaming; he called Williams, who came over with a copy of a *Los Angeles Times* story, written by another reporter on the trip. Cheney and Williams compared the two stories and saw that they tracked very closely. There was little possibility Dugan had been misunderstood or misquoted.

Cheney called Camp David where Bush was playing tennis. Don't pull him off the court, Cheney said, leaving a message. Bush called back after the match. He had already seen the story in the *Post*. It seemed a little bizarre, but Bush thought it might be an intentional, crafty attempt by the Pentagon to scare Saddam.

No, Cheney said, unfortunately it was not a ploy. Cheney said the comments were so extreme that he might find it necessary to relieve General Dugan. "Do you have a problem with that?" Cheney asked.

No, Bush said, whatever Cheney wanted to do, he would have Bush's support.

Bush still wasn't too upset about it, but he could tell that Cheney was hopping mad.

That night Cheney called his new military assistant, Rear Admiral Joe Lopez. Have General Dugan in my office in the morning at 8 a.m., Cheney directed. He then called Williams and said he was thinking about firing Dugan.

"If I did it, think about what I should say and what the reaction might be," the Secretary told Williams.

Williams had always thought it was a very bad idea for Dugan to take such a strong personal role in working the press. "I'm the top Air Force public affairs guy," Williams remembered Dugan saying. Senior people like the Air Force chief needed public affairs professionals to provide insulation. He had argued, to no avail, against Dugan bringing reporters with him on the Saudi Arabian trip. Williams was also amazed that there had been no heads-up in the system. Neither Powell, Cheney nor Williams himself had been alerted in advance that these stories were coming. That, he realized, was part of the problem—someone in the Air Force should have seen the potential danger and made a discreet call of notification.

. . .

Cheney thought long and hard. Policing the four-stars was part of his ongoing job managing the building. Dugan was not the first, nor would he likely be the last, officer to step out of line. Dugan was a good man who had been off to a great start as chief. It would be a hell of a way for him to end his distinguished career. But Dugan's comments were way over the boundary. The new chief was obviously a loose cannon.

Cheney filled two yellow legal pages with key excerpts of the articles, then turned to a third to summarize his reasoning. Under the heading "Problems," he jotted down the following:

1. You displayed egregious judgment.
2. The discussion of operational plans and a priority listing of targets.
3. It makes you the self-appointed spokesman for the JCS and the theater commander.
4. A bad example for others, especially in the Air Force.
5. Treats the prospect of casualties in a cavalier manner.
6. You said we would violate the executive order banning participation in assassinations.
7. The potential revelation of classified information about the size and disposition of our forces.
8. You denigrated the role of the other services.
9. Raises sensitive matters of diplomacy, including obtaining targeting information from Israel.

Before 8 a.m. the next morning, Cheney had Deputy Secretary Don Atwood and Powell in his office. It is my intention to relieve Dugan, Cheney said.

There followed some discussion of the downsides and impact. A firing certainly would draw attention to some Dugan statements in the articles that had not been picked up by other major news organizations that morning; real scoops tended to die unless backed up by official reaction.

Cheney made it clear that he was convinced he had to act. Neither Atwood nor Powell offered any strenuous arguments against it.

Powell left, but Atwood stayed in Cheney's office.

When Dugan arrived, Cheney went through the major points in the articles point by point, asking Dugan if he'd actually made the statements attributed to him.

Yes, Dugan said, he had basically said those things.

Cheney told Dugan he would have to relieve him of his responsibilities as Air Force chief. So that there was no ambiguity about the reasoning, Cheney read out his list of nine reasons why he was taking this action. Cheney also said that Dugan's remarks and tone had suggested disdain for the quality of the Iraqi forces.

If you, the Air Force chief, don't take them seriously, then you're not the right guy to lead the Air Force in the future, Cheney said. You're relieved.

Dugan said little.

Neither the Secretary of the Air Force, Donald Rice, nor General Schwarzkopf had been consulted on the decision.

Cheney put in a call to Bush, who was in a meeting. He asked Bush's secretary to carry to the President at once a message that Dugan had been relieved. Cheney did not want Bush to be surprised.

Later that morning Cheney went to address a meeting of the Air Force Association, a private group with 200,000 members nationwide. Cheney decided not to announce the firing to this group; he wanted Dugan to have a few hours to tell people before word leaked out.

It was a moment of supreme awkwardness for Cheney when he walked into the association meeting and received a big cheer.

. . .

Previously scheduled to participate in a 12:30 p.m. press briefing
at the White House, Cheney arrived early and took over Bob
Gates's closetlike office so he could use the desk there to write out
a statement on the firing. At the White House and later at the
Pentagon, he carefully summarized his reasons. Cheney aimed no
harsh rhetoric at Dugan, opting to let the act of firing speak for
itself. During the Pentagon briefing, he used the colorless word
"inappropriate" four times to characterize Dugan's actions. Although Cheney made it clear he had spoken to Bush and others,
he said he'd ultimately made the call. "It's basically my decision,
my responsibility, and I've exercised it."

· · ·

In retirement, General Welch heard from retired and active-duty
officers. It was clear that the service had been damaged. Welch
was not worried about how the rest of the Air Force would treat
Dugan. No one would say anything to hurt him, Welch was sure.
The old blues would make sure Dugan was taken care of.

No one in the Air Force had said "that damn Cheney" about
the firing. But Air Force people *were* asking one big question
about the incident: Had Cheney's decision to relieve the chief
somehow discredited airpower?

21

ON SEPTEMBER 21, the sixth week into the U.S. deployment, Saddam's Revolutionary Command Council issued a bellicose statement saying, "There is not a single chance for any retreat. . . . Let everybody understand that this battle is going to become the mother of all battles."

Satellite photos and other intelligence presented to President Bush showed that Iraq was systematically dismantling Kuwait, looting the entire nation. Everything of value was being carried back to Iraq; the populace was being terrorized, starved, beaten, murdered. Kuwait would soon become a perpetual no-man's-land, Bush was told. He could see much of it with his own eyes.

U.S. intelligence claimed that Saddam had 430,000 troops in Kuwait and southern Iraq. His forces were digging in, moving into even more defensive positions. This made an offensive attack by Saddam into Saudi Arabia less likely. In order to attack, the Iraqis would have to dig out and move into the so-called killing zones—swatches of open desert miles wide—where the United States could obliterate troops and tanks with superior airpower and Schwarzkopf's own ground forces. Though the United States had less than half as many troops in the theater as Iraq, Cheney and

Powell told Bush they now felt quite sure the U.S. and allied forces could defend Saudi Arabia.

Friday, September 28, was the Day of the Emir. Bush had the exiled emir of Kuwait, who was visiting the United States for the first time, into the Oval Office for a meeting. Scowcroft joined them for the hour-long meeting. Though the emir did not directly ask for military intervention to liberate his country, Scowcroft could see that that was his subliminal message. Bush then took the exiled leader to meet with the cabinet and later to have lunch with the cabinet members in the White House residence. That afternoon, Cheney and Powell met with the emir privately.

Afterwards Bush said that Kuwait was running out of time. It certainly wasn't going to be around as a country if they waited for sanctions to work. The emir himself, the stories of destruction supported by intelligence reports, left an indelible mark on the President, both Cheney and Powell could see. Bush was personally moved. Iraq will fail and Kuwait will endure, Bush said.

At the same time, Powell realized that Schwarzkopf in Saudi Arabia was growing increasingly uneasy. Schwarzkopf had chewed out Kelly on the phone once when Powell had requested some information within 30 minutes. Kelly was not afraid, and had barked back that he was just conveying Powell's order: "I didn't give it to you, the Chairman did." But Schwarzkopf had just about everyone else intimidated. Schwarzkopf needed to be consoled not about the hard tasks that might lie ahead but about his uncertainty as to what Washington might order. He was increasingly nervous about the scale of the Iraqi buildup and was asking questions about U.S. objectives and force levels. Though his stated military mission was still only the defense of Saudi Arabia, Schwarzkopf was aware of repeated presidential statements moving the mission close to the liberation of Kuwait.

At times brooding in his daily secure phone conversations to Powell in the Pentagon, Schwarzkopf was regularly looking for clues, or asking directly, about the next step. Were they going to hold to the defensive mission? Or were they going to build up the forces to do more?

"Norm, I'm working on it," Powell had been telling him.

In their regular 5 p.m. meetings, Cheney and Powell spent much time on these questions.

"You know," Powell told Cheney in early October, "we're

going to have to get a decision." The President had to tell them
whether to continue deploying forces, or to stop, well before the
cut-off date of December 1, when they expected to have in place
all the forces and supplies needed for the defensive mission.
"When I put the last thing in the funnel, two weeks later it will
come out in Saudi Arabia. We need to know when to stop putting
things in the funnel." Powell reminded Cheney that he had not
participated in a full policy review or a discussion of the options
and their merits.

Cheney didn't give much of a response.

Powell started jotting down some notes. He felt that containment or strangulation was working. An extraordinary political-
diplomatic coalition had been assembled, leaving Iraq without
substantial allies—condemned, scorned and isolated as perhaps
no country had been in modern history. Intelligence showed that
economic sanctions were cutting off up to 95 percent of Saddam's
imports and nearly all his exports. Saddam was practically sealed
off in Iraq and Kuwait. The impact could not be measured in
weeks, Powell felt. It might take months. There would come a
point a month or six weeks before Saddam was down to the last
pound of rice when the sanctions would trigger some kind of a
response.

Paul Wolfowitz, the undersecretary for policy, told Powell that
he felt strangulation was a defensible position as long as it meant
applying sanctions indefinitely. Saddam had to know he was facing strangulation forever. To adopt a policy that said, or implied,
that sanctions would be in effect for one year or 18 months would
give the Iraqi leader a point when he could count on relief. He
would have only to tell his people to hold out another so-many
months. Wolfowitz said he thought it was a hard call; probably
55 percent of the merit was for one side, 45 percent for the other.

.   .   .

Powell went to Cheney to outline the case for containment. He
had not reduced his arguments to a formal paper; there was no
memo, no plan, nothing typed up. All he had were his handwritten
notes. Until they were sure sanctions and strangulation had failed,
it would be very difficult to go to war, Powell said. If there was a
chance that sanctions might work, there might be an obligation to
continue waiting—at least to a certain point. To do something

premature when there was still a chance of accomplishing the political objectives with sanctions could be a serious mistake.

"I don't know," Cheney responded. "I don't think the President will buy it." Cheney thought that containment was insufficient, and did not see any really convincing evidence that the sanctions were going to guarantee success. The President was committed to policy success. Containment could leave Kuwait in Saddam's hands. That would constitute policy failure. It would be unacceptable to the President.

Powell wanted another dog in the fight. He was concerned that no one was laying out the alternatives to the President. Bush might not be hearing everything he needed to hear. A full slate of options should be presented. Several days later Powell went back to Cheney with an expanded presentation on containment.

"Uh—hmm," Cheney said, noncommittal. "It certainly is another way to look at it."

Powell next went to see Baker to talk about containment. The Secretary of State was Powell's chief ally in the upper ranks of the administration. They thought alike on many issues. Both men preferred dealmaking to confrontation or conflict. And both worked the news media assiduously to get their points of view across and have them cast in the most favorable light. Baker was very unhappy about the talk of using or developing an offensive military option. He wanted diplomacy—meaning the State Department—to achieve the policy success. He informed Powell that he had some of his staff working on an analysis of the advantages of containment. This should force a discussion of containment within the Bush inner circle, Baker indicated, or at least it would get out publicly.

But no White House meetings or discussion followed. Powell felt that he'd sent the idea up the flagpole but no one had saluted or even commented. He could see, all too plainly, that the President was consistent and dug in, insisting that Kuwait be freed. Bush had not blinked, and frustrations were obviously mounting in the White House. After more than two months, neither the United Nations resolutions, nor diplomacy, nor economic sanctions, nor rhetoric appeared to be forcing Saddam's hand. Powell had too often seen presidential emotions drive policy; Reagan's personal concern for the American hostages in Lebanon had been behind the Iran-contra affair. Powell decided to go see Scowcroft in the White House.

Scowcroft indicated he was having a difficult time that Powell, as a former national security adviser, would understand. He was trying to manage and control an incredibly active President. Bush was out making statements, giving press conferences almost daily, up at dawn making calls, on the phone with one world leader after another, setting up meetings. Scowcroft found himself scrambling just to catch up. On a supposedly relaxing weekend Bush talked with or saw more people related to his job than most people did in a normal work week.

After listening sympathetically, Powell turned to the question of the next steps in the Gulf. He said he wondered about containment and strangulation, the advantages of economic sanctions.

Scowcroft knew Powell's attitude because Cheney had hinted at it. But now Powell was indirect. He did not come out and say, in so many words, this is my position.

"The President is more and more convinced that sanctions are not going to work," Scowcroft responded. He made it clear that he had a solid read on the President. Bush's determination was undisguised and he had virtually foreclosed any possibility that his views could be changed.

Powell could see that Scowcroft agreed with Bush, and was strongly reinforcing the President's inclinations. As national security adviser, it was his job. As the overseer of the administration's entire foreign policy, he had to mirror the President. But the security adviser also had a responsibility to make sure the range of alternatives was presented.

Scowcroft was substantially more willing to go to war than Powell. War was an instrument of foreign policy in Scowcroft's view. Powell did not disagree; he just saw that instrument much closer, less a disembodied abstraction than real men and women, faces—many of them kids' faces—that Powell looked into on his visits to the troops. In the West Wing of the White House where Scowcroft sat, the Pentagon seemed far away, and the forces even further away. Powell knew that. He had been there.

Powell told Scowcroft that if there was an alternative to war, he wanted to make sure it was fully considered. If there were any possible way to achieve the goals without the use of force, those prospects had to be explored.

Scowcroft became impatient. The President was doing everything imaginable, he said.

Powell left. He had become increasingly disenchanted with the

National Security Council procedures and meetings. Scowcroft seemed unable, or unwilling, to coordinate and make sense of all the components of the Gulf policy—military, diplomatic, public affairs, economic, the United Nations. When the principals met, Bush liked to keep everyone around the table smiling—jokes, camaraderie, the conviviality of old friends. Positions and alternatives were not completely discussed. Interruptions were common. Clear decisions rarely emerged. Often Powell and Cheney returned from these gatherings and said to each other, now what did that mean? What are we supposed to do? Frequently, they had to wait to hear the answer later from Scowcroft or the television.

The operation needed a field marshal—someone of the highest rank who was the day-to-day manager, Powell felt. The President, given his other domestic and political responsibilities, couldn't be chief coordinator. It should be the national security adviser. Instead, Scowcroft had become the First Companion and all-purpose playmate to the President on golf, fishing and weekend outings. He was regularly failing in his larger duty to ensure that policy was carefully debated and formulated.

Sununu only added to the problem, exerting little or no control over the process as White House chief of staff.

As a result, the President was left painted into a corner by his own repeated declarations. His obvious emotional attachment to them was converting presidential remarks into hard policy. The goal now, more than ever, was the liberation of Kuwait at almost any cost.

. . .

"Why don't you come over with me and we'll see what the man thinks about your idea," Cheney said to Powell on Friday. Cheney had a private Oval Office meeting scheduled with the President. It was time reserved for the key cabinet members—"the big guys," as Powell privately referred to them. These included just Bush, a cabinet member and Sununu or Scowcroft. Normally, Powell was not included.

At the White House, Cheney and Powell went to the Oval Office to see Bush and Scowcroft. At this meeting Powell made his pitch for containment but pulled away from the brink of advocating it personally.*

* Described in the Prologue, pp. 41–42.

• • •

Powell's thoughts that containment had not been fully shot down by Bush were soon corrected. Within days, Scowcroft told Cheney that Bush wanted a briefing right away on what an offensive operation against Saddam's forces in Kuwait might look like. This planning was being done by Schwarzkopf and his staff in Saudi Arabia, so Powell passed the word to Schwarzkopf to send someone to Washington.

Over the Columbus Day weekend of October 6–8, Army Chief Carl Vuono flew to Saudi Arabia to see Schwarzkopf. They'd been friends since they were teen-aged cadets together at West Point in the 1950s. Schwarzkopf had been a class ahead, but Vuono had been promoted a little faster, so on three occasions during their careers Schwarzkopf had worked for Vuono. Vuono considered Schwarzkopf one of the most difficult, stubborn and talented men in the Army.

When they went off for a private talk, Vuono could see that Schwarzkopf was upset. The CINC, all 6 foot 3, 240 pounds of him, seemed about to explode out of his desert fatigues. He was precisely halfway through the 17 weeks he'd told the President he would need to put the defensive force in place. Now Washington was beginning to talk offense. Les Aspin had said publicly that the administration was "looking more favorably on an early war option." *The New York Times* had reported that the word around the Pentagon was that the offensive would begin on October 15. Worse, Powell had just told Schwarzkopf in a secure phone conversation that Bush wanted a briefing right away on what an offensive operation against Saddam's forces in Kuwait would look like.

Schwarzkopf was furious. They had to be kidding. He was not ready to present such a plan. He had received no warning, and he didn't want to be pushed prematurely into offensive operations. Now he was afraid some son-of-a-bitch was going to wake up some morning and say, let's get the offense rolling. He had two more months' work to do on defense, and he had told the President in August it would take 8 to 12 months to be ready for offense. That meant next March, but now in October they wanted an offensive plan that they could carry out right away.

Powell had told him that everyone understood it would be a

preliminary plan. He gave the Central Command about 48 hours to get someone to Washington with a briefing. Schwarzkopf couldn't leave Saudi Arabia so he would have to send a subordinate.

After listening to Schwarzkopf for four hours, Vuono felt as if he'd been through a psychotherapy session. He could see that his old friend felt very lonely and vulnerable. Vuono promised to do what he could.

On Wednesday morning, October 10, Powell received Schwarzkopf's chief of staff, Marine Major General Robert B. Johnston, at the Pentagon. In the afternoon, Cheney, Wolfowitz, Powell, the other chiefs and Kelly went to the Tank. They were all in the most restricted group cleared for top-secret war plans. It was absolutely essential that word not leak out that the Pentagon was considering an offensive operation. It might be an invitation for Saddam to attack before the full defensive force was in place.

Johnston, a stiff, deferential, buttoned-down Marine with extensive briefing experience, began by reminding them that the Central Command had deployed its forces in accordance with the President's deter-and-defend mission. But if the President tells us to go on the offense tomorrow, he said, here's what we would do. Though we haven't had a lot of time to think this through, and we're not prepared to say in detail this is the right plan, this is our best shot at it.

The plan was broken into four phases, he explained. The first three were exclusively an air campaign, and the fourth was a ground attack.

Phase One would be an air attack on Iraqi command, control and communications, attempting to sever Saddam in Baghdad from his forces in Kuwait and southern Iraq. Simultaneously, air-power would destroy the Iraqi Air Force and air defense system. In addition, Phase One would include an air attack to destroy Iraqi chemical, biological and nuclear weapons facilities.

Phase Two would be a massive, continuous air bombardment of Iraqi supply and munitions bases, transportation facilities and roads, designed to cut off the Iraqi forces from their supplies.

Phase Three would be an air attack on the entrenched Iraqi ground forces of 430,000 men, and on the Republican Guard.

The phases would overlap somewhat. As early as a week after the beginning of the first air phase, the Phase Four ground assault

would be launched on the Iraqi forces in Kuwait. One of Johnston's slides was a map with three large arrows showing the three
attack points where coalition forces would hit the Iraqis. One
arrow represented U.S. Marines in an amphibious assault from
the Gulf; another was the U.S. Army on the ground attacking
directly into Iraqi lines; and the third was an Egyptian ground
division, also going straight into enemy forces, while protecting
one of the U.S. flanks.

Cheney, Powell and several of the others asked question after
question. Could they count on the Egyptians to protect the American ground troops? What about back-up forces if the Iraqis coun-
terattacked?

Powell and Vuono wanted to know if it was possible to move
the U.S. forces out to the west along the Iraqi border and then
come up on the Iraqi Army from the side and behind. Could the
U.S. forces be repositioned fast enough so the Iraqis would not
know?

The initial terrain analysis showed that the Iraqi desert was too
soft and wet for the support vehicles to carry the necessary supplies, Johnston said.

Kelly was sure that the straight-up-the-middle plan briefed by
Johnston was not going to cut it and would not survive a serious
review. Two of the main rules of war were "Never attack the
enemy's strength" and "Go where they are not." The plan needed
mobility.

Cheney felt pretty good about the three phases of the air campaign. The planning looked detailed and complete. Even after the
Dugan firing, the Air Force was basically saying they would take
care of it all. Cheney didn't believe it, but he could see airpower
would have a tremendous advantage in the desert. In addition, the
plans anticipated that targets missed on the first run would be hit
again and again as necessary.

The Phase Four ground plan, however, looked inadequate to
Cheney. The offensive U.S. Army and Marine units would be sent
against a potentially larger defensive Iraqi force, depending on
what remained of Saddam's troops after the bombing. Even to a
civilian like himself, Cheney reflected, it looked unwise.

Cheney remarked that many of the U.S. forces like the 18th
Airborne Corps were lightly armed and might have to fight heavily
armored tanks. There were no reserve forces for back-up. He also

questioned whether the U.S. ground forces could be kept supplied with food, fuel and munitions for a long period.

He noted that the ground plan called for the U.S. forces to make their assault straight into the Iraqi entrenchments and barricades, the Iraqi strength. Why go right up the middle? he asked.

Johnston deflected most of the questions. The plan was preliminary, he reminded them, and the questions reflected the caveats from Schwarzkopf that were listed in the last slide. By the time Johnston reached the last slide, however, the Phase Four plan was pretty much shredded. That slide said that Schwarzkopf felt an attack now on the Iraqi force twice the size of his, even with U.S. air, naval and technological superiority, was loaded with problems. "We do not have the capability on the ground to guarantee success," Johnston said. Schwarzkopf felt that he would need an additional Army Corps of three heavy armored divisions for a proper offensive option.

Cheney concluded that an attack with the U.S. forces now in place and based on this plan would be a risk of a high order.

Johnston said there was a window of opportunity of some six weeks, from about January 1 to February 15, when offensive action would be most desirable. After that, the weather and Muslim religious holidays would conspire to make combat more difficult. Heavy rains would begin in March and the temperatures could rise to 100 degrees or more. But they could work around the weather. It could not and should not determine their timetable, he said.

On March 17, the Muslims would start the observation of Ramadan, one month of fasting from sunrise to sunset, and in June would be the annual pilgrimage to Mecca, Johnston noted. The timing could present another complication for Arab states in the anti-Saddam coalition.

Cheney recognized that he had an obligation to present this brief to President Bush. The President needed to know exactly where Schwarzkopf was, the status of the deployment, and what might happen if offensive operations were ordered. The President, Scowcroft and Sununu at least had to be educated on the magnitude of the task. Cheney did not want to walk over to the White House one day, months down the road, to say, "Here's the plan, bang, go." The President had to comprehend the stakes, the costs and the risks, step by step.

By now Cheney had come to realize what an impact the Vietnam War had had on Bush. The President had internalized the lessons—send enough force to do the job and don't tie the hands of the commanders. In a September 12 speech in California, Cheney had said, "The President belongs to what I call the 'Don't screw around' school of military strategy."

Though this perhaps was inelegantly stated, Cheney was certain that the President didn't want to screw around. That meant a viable offensive option.

Schwarzkopf, in Saudi Arabia, was unhappy that he would not be there when the President was briefed on a subject of such paramount importance.

The next day, October 11, Johnston made the presentation to Bush at the White House. In the Situation Room, Johnston laid out the same plan. The meeting took nearly two hours. Bush was interrupted several times. He and Scowcroft had many questions on various subjects, such as minefields and weapon systems. When Johnston said Schwarzkopf would need a full corps of three additional heavy divisions to have the capability to attack on the ground, he was asked how long it would take to move that many divisions.

Two to three months to get them in place, Johnston said.

He hoped his briefing proved that the existing forces were inadequate for an offense.

Bush's reaction was similar to Cheney's, particularly on the Phase Four ground plan. The military was not ready for an offensive operation; they didn't have enough strength.

What would be enough? Bush asked.

Cheney promised the President a detailed answer soon.

. . .

Bush had asked Powell to appear and speak for him at the anniversary celebration of President Eisenhower's 100th birthday, to be held in Abilene, Kansas, that Sunday, October 14. Over the years, Powell had become a minor student of Ike. He had discovered that the great combat leader of World War II was also very much a believer in limits and restraint. Deeply suspicious of power and the military, as President he had pursued a policy of containment instead of war.

Powell worked hard on the Kansas address. He sensed a kinship with Eisenhower and aspired to be like him. This speech was from the heart. Powell said:

"General Eisenhower was no proponent of war. He was a proponent of peace. At the foot of the great statue here at the library we see the words, 'Champion of Peace.' And so he was."

. . .

On Wednesday night, October 17, Bush was scheduled to attend the second game of the World Series, but he canceled to have a veal and pasta dinner alone with Scowcroft to review the Gulf crisis.

That week Cheney was on a trip to Europe and the Soviet Union to confer with allies and supporters of the U.N. resolutions against Iraq. Powell made lots of public appearances while Cheney was away—remarks to the American Stock Exchange, a short briefing on counternarcotics programs, a memorial service, a military artwork presentation, a meeting with the military aide to the president of France, a few interviews and receptions.

When a story appeared in the newspapers about Air Force Secretary Rice using an Air Force jet to attend the Air Force–Notre Dame football game at a cost of over $5,000, Powell called in one of his aides.

"What the fuck is the Air Force doing now?" he asked. Air Force officers were quoted by name contradicting each other, leaving the impression that someone had willingly spent the taxpayers' money for a football weekend and that others were trying to cover up. "Don't they know how to answer questions like that up there?" After raging at the Air Force some more, he finally calmed down. "I just wanted to get that off my chest."

Powell's Plans and Policy staff, J-5, sent him an option paper for the Gulf. J-5 was headed by Lieutenant General George Lee Butler, who was slated to be promoted to four stars and take over the Strategic Air Command. Butler outlined four possibilities: (1) maintain the status quo to deter and defend; (2) prepare for long-term containment, ratcheting up the sanctions that would have to be in place for six months to one year to be effective; (3) go to war; (4) up the ante by adding sufficient forces for a credible offensive threat.

Butler favored option two: long-term containment, with increased pressure through the sanctions. According to Butler's analysis, a war would be very messy.

Powell listened to the summary but didn't indicate his preference—not by so much as a lifted eyebrow, Butler noted.

Powell still wasn't positive which way the President might go, but he had a pretty good idea. This was a political choice, it was going to be made in the White House. He felt he had to mask his conclusions on this question even from his most senior staff.

After the Johnston briefing, Cheney leaned hard on the system. He wanted the planners to move away from throwing all the forces straight through the Iraqis' front-line barriers. He asked Powell to think about making a ground assault into Iraq somewhere far west along the Saudi-Iraq border, 300–400 miles from Kuwait, out toward the Jordanian border. Such an unexpected attack on the western approaches to Baghdad would put a ground force in a location where there would be no Iraqi fortifications or resistance, would cut the lines of communication between Baghdad and Jordan, and would allow a direct ground attack on the fixed SCUD missile sites in western Iraq that threatened Israel.

Powell quickly came back with an answer: No, it was way too far to take U.S. forces.

· · ·

On Sunday, October 21, Powell left Washington for Saudi Arabia. He arrived in Riyadh late the next day and went right to Schwarzkopf.

Powell immediately saw that everyone in the command, including Schwarzkopf, was pretty raggedy. They had been deterring and defending for nearly three months. The uncertainties, risks and discomforts had been building on each other.

Schwarzkopf was still angered about the short-notice order to send Johnston to Washington with an offensive war plan that was not ready.

Orders were orders, both soldiers knew.

Powell reported that he did not have a decision from the President about the next stage—whether they would be directed to continue the current mission or prepare the offensive option.

Whatever the case, Powell said, they now had to come up with a fully scrubbed offensive plan. More important, Schwarzkopf had to state what additional forces he would need for that mission. Powell remembered that in the first days of the crisis, Schwarzkopf had told President Bush at Camp David on August 4 that it would take 8 to 12 months to build up U.S. forces to a level sufficient to push Iraq out of Kuwait. Saddam had had 100,000 troops in Kuwait then. He now had 430,000.

Powell said he needed Schwarzkopf's wish list. He pledged to back him up.

Schwarzkopf had said in a recent *Life* magazine article that he was no fan of war: "In a lot of ways I am a pacifist—though that might be too strong a word. But I know what war is. I am certainly anti-war. But I also believe there are things worth fighting for."

Frankly, he told Powell now, he was not sold on an offensive operation as the solution. Pushing Saddam out of Kuwait at this point would be dirty and bloody. "Do they know that back in Washington?"

"They know," Powell replied.

Schwarzkopf estimated that it would take about twice the force level he had. Double the Air Force presence; double the Navy carriers from three to six; double the Marine and Army ground forces. "I want the VII Corps," he said finally.

The VII Corps was the centerpiece of the U.S. ground defense in Europe—three of the best-trained, best-equipped divisions—two heavy tank and one mechanized. It was a stunning request, inconceivable even a year ago, before the virtual disappearance of the Warsaw Pact threat in Europe. But Gorbachev and the collapse of the Warsaw Pact made it feasible. If the President was serious about offense, Schwarzkopf said, he was going to have to send the VII Corps.

Powell said he would back the requests. He wanted to go even further. He was determined to make the buildup as massive as possible. There was an Army division based in the United States that had trained with the VII Corps. The Big Red One, the 1st Mechanized Infantry Division, would fit in nicely, Powell suggested. Schwarzkopf agreed.

Schwarzkopf's main staff officers were summoned. Powell wanted to question them personally. He was aware of Schwarzkopf's tendency to shoot messengers bringing bad news. Powell wanted to sit and listen patiently to see if any hidden facts bubbled to the surface, as often happened when subordinates were given a chance to talk at length. The next morning Powell met for another five hours with Schwarzkopf and his staff. The only major problem was that the mail was not being delivered to the troops as fast as it should.

Powell indicated that President Bush still had not decided; they had to prepare for possible offense and for continuing the defense.

If the mission remained only defensive, Powell and Schwarzkopf agreed, some kind of rotation policy would be needed, allowing the units that had served for months to be relieved. Schwarzkopf recommended that the troops be rotated out of Saudi Arabia after serving six to eight months. Overall, he felt the buildup was working and evidence was mounting that the sanctions were beginning to bite. He counseled patience.

Powell visited some of the troops briefly. He told them: "I know you want to know the answer to two questions: What are we going to be doing here? And when are we going to go home? Because I can't give you answers to those questions, we are giving our political leaders time to work this out. Not answering those questions gives them that time."

Powell felt that the troops understood this point. But he was not sure how long their patience would last. Troops would fight for each other and for certain core values: national survival, the lives of American citizens. They would fight for their leaders—presidents, even generals, if the reasoning was presented clearly and honestly. Powell felt they would also fight for American interests but that could get very fuzzy. It was problematical whether they would fight for another country, such as Kuwait, or to ensure that a Saddam was not rewarded for aggression.

.   .   .

On Wednesday, October 24, Cheney was summoned to the White House. The administration had finally reached a budget compromise with the Democrats after a bruising and politically damaging six months, particularly the last two. Now Bush had time to focus on some of the answers to the question he had left with Cheney—how much additional force? The President said he was leaning toward adding the forces necessary to carry out offensive operations to expel Iraqi troops from Kuwait. Nothing could be announced for two weeks, until after the November 6 elections, because any move would be assumed to be an attempt to influence the elections. Cheney said that he was waiting for Powell's report from Saudi Arabia, and they should wait.

It was apparent to Cheney that Bush would be happy with some public hint. Cheney was already scheduled the next day to go on the early morning shows of the three major networks and CNN. He felt that the White House's inept handling of its budget talks with Congress had cast a pall over the entire administration, and raised fundamental questions about whether Bush and the cabinet knew what they were doing. It had affected Bush's standing in the polls and the way people looked at Washington and government, even eroding confidence in the Gulf operation. Cheney also felt that it was best to prepare the public for the likely decision. He had consistently stated that there was no upper ceiling on the troop deployment and had repeatedly warned that the United States was in for the long haul.

Later that day Cheney joined Baker in giving a classified briefing to legislators in the secure room, S-407, in the Capitol. Neither dropped a hint that a reinforcement was being considered.

But in the television interviews the next morning, October 25, Cheney intentionally laid the seed. "We are not at the point yet where we want to stop adding forces," he said on ABC. On CBS he was asked if the Pentagon was getting ready to send another 100,000 troops. Cheney replied, "It's conceivable that we'll end up with that big of an increase."

He repeated this point on NBC, but added that this would not affect the relief of troops already there after six to eight months. "There clearly will be a rotation policy. . . . I would guess we'll end up around six months."

The big news of Cheney's statements reached Powell, who was on a stopover in Europe. "What is going on?" he asked an aide. When it sank in, he told one person, "Goddammit, I'll never travel again. I haven't seen the President on this." There had been discussions but no decision as far as he knew. But there it was in clear language from Cheney, a man who chose his words carefully.

Bush, Scowcroft and Sununu were making decisions again without a full airing of views. Powell was tired of learning of major administration decisions after the fact. Sununu had been advising and urging the President to speak out strongly and to back up his words with a military threat. He or someone else apparently had won.

One thing that could be said for Bush: he had stated consistently that the Kuwait invasion would not stand. Powell, however, felt that the economic sanctions still loomed as the large unknown. When might they work? When would they be deemed to have failed? He was eager to get back to Washington.

In Saudi Arabia, Schwarzkopf also heard Cheney's remarks.

Before his own surprise and distress could fully register, the Saudis were on the phone pounding him with questions: What is this? What's going on? Where were the consultations before making such a decision or announcement? Schwarzkopf tried to stumble through with some answers. He was fuming. Not only did he have to learn about something this important from the media, but he had to explain it to the Saudis without any guidance from Washington.

Schwarzkopf gave a long interview to *The Atlanta Journal and Constitution* that week. "Now we are starting to see evidence that the sanctions are pinching," Schwarzkopf said. "So why should we say, 'Okay, gave 'em two months, didn't work. Let's get on with it and kill a whole bunch of people?' That's crazy. That's crazy." He recounted how in Vietnam the United States, unopposed in the air, would pound the villages with bombs and then go in and find the North Vietnamese coming right out of their holes fighting like devils. Schwarzkopf also said, "War is a profanity because, let's face it, you've got two opposing sides trying to settle their differences by killing as many of each other as they can."

Wolfowitz, who visited the Central Commander around this time, felt that Schwarzkopf was making these statements partly for the benefit of his troops, to make it absolutely clear that if there was a war, it would be the civilians who would be taking them there.

Schwarzkopf told Wolfowitz that he had had some discussions with Middle East experts who had convinced him that while war would be damaging to the United States in the region, a failure to go to war would be far more damaging. Schwarzkopf said he felt that a prolonged stalemate would be a victory for Saddam.

Powell arrived back in Washington, but Cheney was going off the next day to do some fishing in Wyoming with Baker. A White House meeting with the President was planned for early the following week to discuss the Gulf options.

· · ·

The new Air Force Chief, General Merrill "Tony" McPeak, told Powell that if they were going to launch an offensive operation, the sooner the better for the Air Force. A 6-foot-2, rail-thin fighter pilot, McPeak, 54, said the airpower combat advantage would be at its maximum from about right now up to November 1. It would deteriorate steadily after that, he said, because Iraqi defensive preparations were reducing the U.S. combat advantage. The Iraqis were digging in deeper in the desert and organizing themselves. They had acquired some U.S. ground-to-air HAWK missiles in Kuwait that they might be able to use against U.S. planes. In addition, the weather was never going to be better.

Powell countered that the other services needed more time to increase their advantages. There was no requirement to take any unnecessary risk in this operation, Powell said. The prudent course was to double the force. The military and the President would be in serious trouble if an offense didn't succeed.

Come on, Jesus, McPeak said, somewhat overstating his point, this is a Third World country, a little one-city country for Christ's sake. We're making it look like World War III. We're going to get no style points at the end of this thing. We ought to be trying to make it look easy, instead of making it look hard. My worry is that we wait too long.

I understand, Powell said. But if we go later, you'll still have a combat advantage, and we need the time to do some other things —principally, get the Army ready to go. Get them in there. Get them on shore and unloaded. I don't care about style points. Too much is at stake. "We go, we win," Powell said, summarizing his belief that he wanted to be certain.

McPeak didn't make his arguments to Cheney or the President. He saw he was a minority of one. The other chiefs agreed with Powell.

There was unanimity on one matter, however, McPeak could see. None of the chiefs was itching for a fight. They did not want an offensive operation if there was any other honorable way out for the United States.

. . .

Over the weekend Powell was watching NBC's Saturday *Nightly News* broadcast with Mary Alice Williams. She introduced a report on troop morale from Saudi Arabia.

"Relief is what they're waiting for," Williams said, "or a call to action." Then reporter Arthur Kent came on, saying that "nerves are being severely strained in Saudi Arabia. . . . U.S. troops here spend most of their energy just killing time . . . many Marines told us they're fed up with inactivity." He said that the troops longed for home. "But home is a mirage. The days drag on. . . . There are still no clear military objectives to go after."

"How deep does the bad morale go?" Williams asked him.

"Pretty deep," Kent said. "Perhaps half of the troops we spoke to said they were very unhappy with the way things are going."

What the hell are they talking about? Powell asked himself. The report had offered nothing hard. It was foolish, but it reminded him that if war came, it would be on television instantly, bringing home the action, death, consequences and emotions even more graphically than during Vietnam. The reporters and the cameras would be there to record each step, vastly complicating all military tasks. Powell was sure of one thing: a prolonged war on television could become impossible, unsupportable at home.

. . .

Several times in October, Robert Teeter, Bush's chief pollster, talked with the President about the Gulf policy. Teeter said he thought the administration had too many messages flying around. There was a lack of focus. He suggested that Bush return to the fundamentals that he had stated in August. The two with the strongest appeal were fighting aggression and protecting the lives of Americans, including the more than 900 Americans being held hostage in Iraq and Kuwait. About 100 had been moved to Iraqi military and industrial installations to serve as "human shields" to deter an American attack.

Bush acknowledged the points, but nonetheless seemed confident. The President said that he felt he knew more than anyone about the region, and also about the diplomacy, the military, the economics and the oil. I have been dealing with these issues for 25 years, Bush said. One night he told Teeter it was important that he had served as United Nations ambassador, U.S. envoy to China, CIA director and Vice President. Those experiences allowed him to see all the pieces. Now he could put them together.

Bush described how, since taking office as President, he had been laying the groundwork, building relations with other heads of state. He'd had no specific purpose in mind, just a strategic sense that it was a good idea. Now his good working relationships with the Thatchers, Mubaraks, Fahds and Gorbachevs of the world could be put to use. There might be some rough times, some down times, Bush conceded, but he felt good. "This will be successful," he assured Teeter.

. . .

For months Scowcroft had been concerned that Baker was not a supporter of the Gulf policy. In the inner-circle discussions he seemed to oppose the large deployment of troops, favoring a diplomatic solution almost to the exclusion of the military pressure. But Baker was coming around. Cheney was fishing with him over the weekend and they would have time to talk.

Baker felt the foundation for the Gulf policy was not solid enough. The plight of the emir of Kuwait, his people, aggression and oil were not selling to the American people. The polls showed that the greatest concern was over the American hostages in Iraq and Kuwait. Baker had argued that the focus of the Gulf policy should be shifted to the hostage issue. It was the one issue that would unite Americans and the international community because most nations, including the Soviets, had hostages held in Iraq. It was the one issue that might justify a war.

Scowcroft thought a new emphasis on the hostages would be changing horses in the middle of the stream, but he saw that public opinion polls were showing increasing doubts about the military deployment. Baker wanted to play the hostage card himself in a strong speech. Scowcroft was willing to go along. The national security adviser also realized that Baker saw the handwriting on the wall. The Bush presidency was likely to rise or fall on the outcome of the Gulf policy. Baker, Bush's friend of 35 years, his campaign manager and the senior cabinet officer, had no other choice than to become an aggressive supporter of the policy.

On Monday, October 29, Baker addressed the Los Angeles World Affairs Council. The more than 100 American human shields, he said, "are forced to sleep on vermin-ridden concrete floors. They are kept in the dark during the day and moved only at night. They have had their meals cut to two a day. And many are becoming sick as they endure a terrible ordeal. The very idea of Americans being used as human shields is simply unconscionable."

The Secretary of State added: "We will not rule out a possible use of force if Iraq continues to occupy Kuwait."

. . .

Bush had 15 congressional leaders from both houses and both parties to the White House the next day, October 30. He opened the meeting with a status report, noting that Iraq had released the French hostages, but more reports of maltreatment of American and British hostages were being received. He said that he was reading Martin Gilbert's *The Second World War: A Complete History,* which described the appeasement of a dictator and the sequence of events leading up to the conflict.

Visibly riled up, Bush said that he was just not going to let that happen again. The treatment of the hostages was horrible and barbarous, the President said. He described a report of one foreign hostage family that had been taken to a hospital, where the Iraqis had shot the children in front of the parents and then shot the parents.

Baker then made some supporting points about the treatment of the hostages.

House Speaker Thomas S. Foley said, Mr. President, we're with you to this point. He hoped there would be more such meetings and consultations in advance of any military action in the Gulf.

Barring some event that required quick action, Bush said, he would continue consulting.

Has there been more maltreatment of the hostages? Senate Majority Leader George Mitchell asked. The Congress didn't know about that. It was not documented.

Isn't deprivation of liberty maltreatment? Baker asked indignantly.

It certainly is, Mitchell responded, but the question is whether there has been an escalation of the maltreatment as the President suggested.

Senator William Cohen, the vice chairman of the Senate Intelligence Committee, raised his hand. He said that the CIA and DIA had testified in the committee last week that there was no new evidence of more maltreatment.

Baker, unused to being challenged, lit up and turned several shades of red. He asked what the group considered maltreatment. Was not kidnapping and murder sufficient?

Yes, Cohen and Mitchell agreed. But the hostage taking was nearly three months old. Is this new? Is this considered a provocation by Saddam?

The questioning zeroed in. Several Democrats suggested pointedly that this new focus on the American hostages had a bad aroma. Was it going to be used as justification for military action now? It would not withstand outside scrutiny, they suggested.

Cohen said the administration might be so concerned for the hostages that it might wind up eliminating their maltreatment permanently by getting them killed. He had never seen emotions —including his own—quite so high in a White House meeting.

Bush shifted the discussion to the situation of the U.S. Embassy in Kuwait City where a few U.S. diplomats remained. The Iraqis were denying them food and water. He had no way to use the military effectively to protect them without a full-scale invasion, he said. And what would it mean if the American flag were lowered and the U.S. diplomats also made "guests," Saddam's term for the hostages? I will not sit still for it, the President said, tension showing in the muscles of his neck.

Representative Les Aspin estimated that it would take some ten months for the sanctions to work.

Representative John P. Murtha, a hawkish Democrat from Pennsylvania, said he supported the President strongly, adding that there might be no choice but to go in militarily, and as far as he was concerned the sooner the better.

Afterwards, Cohen went up to Cheney, who had said nothing during the meeting. "You managed to duck this one," Cohen said lightly. "We'll be coming back to you on what options are being considered."

Cheney smiled and left.

. . .

At 3:30 that afternoon, Bush met with Baker, Cheney, Scowcroft and Powell in the Situation Room.

"We are at a 'Y' in the road," Scowcroft began. The policy could continue to be deter-and-defend, or it could switch to developing the offensive option.

Powell was struck once again by the informality of the rolling discussion among these five men who had been friends for years. There was no real organization to the proceedings as they weighed the options. Ideas bounced back and forth as one thought or another occurred to one of them. Bush and Scowcroft seemed primed to go ahead with the development of the offensive option. Baker, less anxious and more cautious, was measured, inquiring about the attitudes in Congress and in the public, but he was no longer reluctant.

Listening, Cheney saw no willingness on Bush's part to accept anything less than the fulfillment of his stated objective, the liberation of Kuwait. The Secretary of Defense was not going to recommend any military action unless they were sure of success. He said that he had a growing conviction that they had to develop the offensive option. The international coalition was too fragile to hold out indefinitely—to outsiders it might look different, but they knew, from the inside, that the arrangements were delicate. Cheney felt it was quite likely that some outside event could absolutely shatter the coalition.

Powell saw that patience was not the order of the day. As in the past, he did not advocate containment. Powell had found the others previously tolerated his broad political advice, but now he sensed that he had less permission to speak up, having already made the case for containment to the President. Now no one was soliciting Powell's overall political advice on this subject.

The meeting had been billed in advance as a chance for the Chairman to report on his discussions with Schwarzkopf.

"Okay, okay, okay," the President finally said, "let's hear what he has to say."

"Mr. President," Powell began, "we have accomplished the mission assigned." The defense of Saudi Arabia had been achieved earlier than expected. He described how Schwarzkopf had moved some of his forces around to accomplish this in light of the continuing Iraqi buildup.

"Now, if you, Mr. President, decide to build up—go for an offensive option—this is what we need." He then unveiled the Schwarzkopf request to double the force. A central feature was the VII Corps so Schwarzkopf would have the high-speed tanks to conduct flanking attacks on the Iraqis. In this way, they could avoid a frontal assault into Iraqi strength.

Scowcroft was amazed that Schwarzkopf wanted so much more. The request for three aircraft carriers in addition to the three he already had especially surprised Scowcroft. Several oohs and ahs were heard around the table, but not from Bush.

Powell said he supported Schwarzkopf's recommendations, if the President wanted an offensive option. He turned to the President. "If you give me more time, say three months, I'll move more troops. It's that important. You can take me to the Savings and Loan bailout account, and we'll all go broke together." Powell's message: it was going to be expensive.

As far as Powell was concerned, the only constraint was going to be the capacity of the transportation system.

Cheney said he supported Schwarzkopf and Powell without conditions. He went even further. It was not a question *if* the President wanted the offensive option; the President should want it and should go ahead and order it, Cheney said. He explained that this would guarantee success if they had to fight. He did not want to be in the position of making another request for more forces come January or February. Saddam was fully capable of responding with more of his own forces. Cheney did not want to be back here in the Situation Room saying then, "Mr. President, I know what we told you back in October, and we put the additional force over there, but we still can't do it."

Finally, Bush said, "If that's what you need, we'll do it."

The President gave the final approval the next day.

. . .

Paul Wolfowitz, who as undersecretary for policy was one of few Pentagon civilians granted oversight of war plans, was worried that the administration had transitioned into the decision on the offensive option without a lot of clear thought. There was little or no process where alternatives and implications were written down so they could be systematically weighed and argued. Wolfowitz, a scholarly senior career government official and former ambassador, thought it would have been possible to decide to send additional troops and not say specifically whether they were replacements or an offensive reinforcement. The decision as to their ultimate purpose could be made later. But Wolfowitz didn't have time to get the idea considered.

The deputies committee, the second-tier interagency group that included Wolfowitz, had not met on the subject.

Wolfowitz felt that the inner circle of Bush, Baker, Cheney, Scowcroft and Powell was perhaps a little too close knit. Their meetings, given their frequency and privacy, ought to have been the forum for discussing and debating alternatives and fundamentals. But Wolfowitz did not get that sense. There was no feedback from Cheney, and if there was any kind of organized debate within the inner circle, it was done without benefit of staff. At times Wolfowitz felt he was out in the deep darkness on vital questions.

Wolfowitz was also worried that the announcement of this very big decision would be flubbed. The whole administration, Bush in particular, disliked explaining itself in an organized, coherent way. Bush just didn't like to give speeches and the White House speechwriters didn't write very good ones.

Baker for his part was worried about the allies. What did they think about whether to use force—or when or how? What was their resolve? Did they fully understand President Bush's determination to roll back the invasion? It was agreed that Baker would visit Saudi Arabia, Egypt, Turkey, London, Paris and Moscow so all the soundings could be made before the announcement on doubling the force was made.

. . .

Saturday, November 3, the day Baker was leaving, Powell picked up his *New York Times*. Under the headline, "Baker Seen as a Balance to Bush on Crisis in Gulf," Powell read that unnamed senior administration officials were saying that Baker "has been a brake on any immediate impulse to use military force. . . . When the issue was how much time was needed to give the sanctions an opportunity to work, Mr. Baker advised more time rather than less."

Though hedged and qualified, the story at least put the issue of a policy debate out in the open. Powell thought to himself: Hey, look at this, I'm off the hook.

But the story's substance—a brake on the President, containment, more time for economic sanctions—had no second bounce. There was no serious discussion or comment on it. The only comment Powell heard was that Baker and his aides had put out another self-serving story to distance the Secretary of State carefully from a possible disaster.

Scowcroft saw the story as a classic piece of State Department spin. But it was about a week late. Baker was now on board.

22

On THURSDAY, NOVEMBER 8, Cheney called the major congressional chairmen to inform them that Bush was going to make an announcement that afternoon about a troop reinforcement. He reached Les Aspin in Kenosha, Wisconsin. The Chairman of the House Armed Services Committee had just been elected without opposition to his 11th term.

Aspin had pretty much given up on trying to communicate with Dick Cheney, and had taken to calling him "the Sphinx." Instead, Aspin's channel into the administration was Scowcroft.

After telling Aspin about the reinforcement package, Cheney listed some of the units, including the Army's VII Corps of heavy tank divisions from Europe, but didn't provide an overall number of troops.

"That's a lot bigger than I expected," Aspin said. He did the arithmetic in his head and realized it meant another 200,000 men.

Cheney tracked down Sam Nunn in a restaurant. The senator was unhappy that he was being informed rather than consulted. Why the hurry, he asked. Were they sure the economic sanctions would not work?

Cheney sensed a real change in Nunn and attributed much of it to politics. Ever the political calculator, Cheney had concluded that Nunn was planning a long-shot run for the Democratic presidential nomination in 1992 and wanted to get in the good graces of his party by taking on President Bush.

The decision, Cheney said, was to nail down with certainty a viable offensive military option for the President.

Baker was meeting with Gorbachev in the Soviet Union when he received word that Bush was going ahead with an announcement on the troop increase. He questioned the timing and wondered about the hurry. This was not something to drop out of the sky without carefully laying the foundations. There ought to have been a round of Washington consultations and hand-holding sessions, particularly in Congress. Once again, he felt the White House was not handling an announcement properly; but there was nothing he could do from Russia.

. . .

Cheney was monitoring the public debate. The administration still had not found a successful formula for speaking to the various publics out there. It was trying to keep the American people behind the policy, and explain to the troops what was being done and why, while attending to the Congress, the United Nations and the Arabs. It was also trying to manage the Israeli problem. Saddam was attempting to link resolution of the Kuwait question with resolution of the Palestinians' grievances against Israel.

It was difficult to come up with one single message to speak with equal credibility and force to all those groups. And the message the administration wanted to convey now—its rationale for deploying an offensive capability—was different from the one it had wanted to convey in August when the mission was defensive. Cheney did not feel that the communications effort to date was a triumph. Now they were entering a new, critical phase of trying to keep all the constituencies happy.

. . .

Bush and Cheney appeared at a 4 p.m. news briefing. Powell, who had been included in the major Desert Shield announcements so far, was not there.

"I have today directed the Secretary of Defense to increase the size of the U.S. forces committed to Desert Shield," Bush said, "to ensure that the coalition has an adequate offensive military option should that be necessary to achieve our common goals." He mentioned no numbers.

Asked why he wanted to put an offensive force in Saudi Arabia, Bush said he was acting "upon the advice of our able Secretary of Defense and others."

The President left to spend the long Veterans Day weekend at Camp David.

The next afternoon, Friday, November 9, Prince Bandar stopped by the Pentagon to see Powell. It seemed to him that Powell and Baker were the members of the Bush inner circle least inclined to go to war against Saddam.

"If we don't have to fight, it will be better," Powell told the prince. "If we have to, I'll do it but we're going to do it with everything we have." Powell said that the President had ordered that this not turn into another Vietnam. The guiding principle was going to be a maximization of firepower and troops.

Later, Cheney told Bandar, "The military is finished in this society, if we screw this up."

. . .

The White House had made no arrangements for administration officials to appear on that Sunday's television talk shows or the morning shows on Monday. These shows are a primary arena for Washington players to slug it out and make headlines. The Democrats were out in force. Democratic Senator Daniel Patrick Moynihan of New York said sharply, "It's as if the great armed force which was created to fight the Cold War is at the President's own disposal for any diversion he may wish, no matter what it costs. He will wreck our military. He will wreck his administration, and he'll spoil a chance to get a collective security system working. It breaks your heart."

The weekend newspapers were filled with stories about discord among the coalition members and the difficulties Bush would have in selling a war, and the problems of fighting a distant war on the ground.

Scowcroft and his staff began referring to the three-day weekend as the Veterans Day Massacre. Scowcroft felt the administration was facing not so much a military problem as a public relations problem. He was not sure what could be done. A poll published in *USA Today* was headlined "Bush Support Slim." It said 51 percent approved of Bush's handling of the Gulf crisis, down from 82 percent approval three months before.

Powell found the stories exaggerated, alarmist and speculative. But those stories—not the administration—were defining the issues and debate.

· · ·

The political uproar continued over the next several days. On Tuesday, November 13, Cheney and Powell had an 8:15 breakfast with Senators Sam Nunn and John Warner. Nunn said he thought the administration's Gulf policy would play into Saddam's hands. He was going to open public hearings later in the month. Hearings were his strongest weapon to force the issues of goals and potential costs out in the open.

Cheney met later in the day with a hundred of his former House colleagues. The main issue was the offensive option. It was a chaotic discussion; everyone present seemed to have a different idea about the new policy.

After an hour, Cheney said, "I assume all of you guys want to vote up or down on the proposition."

The room erupted. There were shouts of no and yes. It only confirmed Cheney's view that Congress was not equipped to deal with the issue. He found himself thinking of August 1941, just four months before Pearl Harbor, when the House was able to muster only a one-vote margin for continuing the Selective Service system.

· · ·

Bush and Scowcroft were astounded at the speed with which the support for the Gulf operation seemed to be unraveling. Bush recalled that when he was a congressman during the Vietnam War his fellow Texan, President Lyndon Johnson, had made a mistake by not formally and officially getting Congress to vote on the war, beyond the controversial Gulf of Tonkin resolution.

Scowcroft was not confident the votes were there. It would be a disaster to go to Congress and lose.

Some of the top Republicans, including Senate Minority Leader

Robert J. Dole of Kansas and Senator Richard G. Lugar of Indiana, were calling for a special session of Congress to debate the Gulf. They argued that Bush would win and congressional backing would strengthen his hand with Saddam. Privately, Lugar was telling Bush it would be better to find out now whether he lacked the congressional support, rather than later.

On November 14, Bush met with the congressional leaders of both parties and made a plea for unity. He insisted that he had not yet decided on war. "I have not crossed any Rubicon," he said.

He pulled out a report of Iraqi news coverage and read aloud some of the headlines showing that Saddam was being presented with a picture of disunity in the United States. The President's implication was obvious: this was the precise message that would make Saddam think he could stay in Kuwait. Bush also pulled out a pocket-sized copy of the U.S. Constitution and read from Article II, section 2, "The President shall be Commander in Chief. . . ."

Bush said he wanted the leaders to call a session, but only if he was going to receive a substantial vote in his favor.

The Democratic leaders said at this time they would not call an emergency session of Congress to debate Bush's Gulf buildup. Instead, they would hold hearings.

• • •

"You can't make someone else's choices. You shouldn't let some one else make yours." Powell's rule number 7.

Now that the President had made his decision to create the offensive option, Powell had his own crucial choices to make about the war plan. He had directed General Tom Kelly to drop out of regular activities as the operations director and set up a special planning cell of half a dozen of his best officers. Working in a special-access room within the Joint Staff, they were coordinating every step with Schwarzkopf's planners. Powell wanted an absolute sense of urgency. He had ordered the planners to address all needs—from supplies and ammunition to the medical teams, rules of engagement and procedures for dealing with potential prisoners of war.

The first commandment for a U.S. military leader is "Take care of your men." Though the overall offensive mission would be to expel the Iraqi Army from Kuwait, the best way to take care of the men was to destroy the Iraqi military. As in Panama, where the Panamanian Defense Forces had to be taken down completely, the Iraqi military capability would also have to be eliminated or disabled—a monumental task compared to Panama.

But the United States had some very secret advantages.

At the beginning of November, after the decision had been made to deploy for the offensive option, Cheney and Powell had made several visits to perhaps the most secret part of the Pentagon —2C865, the Special Technical Operations Center (STOC). Just down the corridor from General Kelly's office in the Joint Staff, the STOC was a Pentagon-within-the-Pentagon, with its own tight rules of access. Here a group of about 30 men ran the only unit in the building where everyone had to take regular lie-detector tests to ensure they were not security risks.

The center was often called the Starship Enterprise because of the high-tech displays, the computers and the communications to clone centers at the key intelligence agencies and the unified commands, including the Central Command in Saudi Arabia.

The STOC was the command and communications center for operations involving the sensitive "black" programs known only to those cleared to the special-access "compartments." Included were special operations units, intelligence-gathering capabilities, and advanced weapons systems and equipment—everything from the Navy SEAL teams to the Stealth jet fighters to special spy satellites. The Navy captain who had headed the STOC from 1982 to 1989 had to be cleared out of 235 special-access compartmented programs when he retired.

Most of the super-secret black weapons had been developed primarily with one scenario in mind: war with the Soviet Union. But since Iraq had been a Soviet client state, purchasing many of its key weapons from the Soviets, the U.S. weapons were tailor-made to fight the new adversary.

The United States would be able to capitalize on decades of work. Under a top-secret program code-named EYRE, the CIA and Pentagon over a number of years had acquired specifications and test data on key Soviet electronics, radar, planes and missiles. Many of these systems were used by the Iraqis. In other intelligence operations, the Pentagon had obtained actual Soviet weapons, and then designed U.S. weapons to defeat the Soviet models.

In another top-secret program, code-named PARCAE, and related signals-intercept operations, the Pentagon could listen to and read some Soviet-made communications systems.

Satellites had been placed over the Middle East that sent down real-time pictures of Kuwait, flashing them to television consoles. Commanders with battlefield consoles could closely monitor the activities of the Iraqi occupiers.

The Iraqis behaved as if they thought much of their communications were secure. But the National Security Agency, the largest of the U.S. intelligence agencies, could intercept some of it. The Iraqis' equipment all came from the Soviets, the United States or Europe, so NSA knew the frequencies and characteristics.

Yet another black program held out the possibility of covertly destroying all the main electrical power grids in Iraq without leaving any tracks back to U.S. forces. The success of a possible offensive military option depended in part on disabling Iraqi radar, air defenses and communications, all dependent on electricity. It was a military planner's dream, promising a complete, baffling surprise blow.

Powell was skeptical of such miraculous whiz-bang solutions. He wasn't thrilled with the STOC's cost of approximately $100 million. The center reminded him of Room 208, the high-tech command center in the Old Executive Office Building next to the White House that Ollie North had used for some of his far-flung, ill-fated operations during the Reagan administration.

One of the STOC briefings Cheney and Powell received in November was on the special operations capabilities that might be used against Iraq. In the offensive war plan, eight special operations Apache helicopters would start the war by crossing the border to take out key air defense installations inside Iraq.

Like the Chairman, Cheney was taking all the high-tech with a grain of salt. He expected the people who ran the black programs to be enthusiastic advocates, but he also knew that systems often didn't perform as advertised. He wouldn't soon forget the flawed combat debut of the Air Force's F-117A Stealth fighter bomber in Panama, where the plane's precision bombs had missed their targets by 50 yards or more.

Cheney had learned the value of questioning everything. During his 18 months as Secretary, he had spent many hours delving into the top-secret Single Integrated Operation Plan (SIOP) for nuclear war with the Soviet Union and Warsaw Pact nations, the most important war plan by far. He discovered that the military had worked rather hard to keep Pentagon civilians out of the process. The SIOP had been running on automatic pilot for years. An incredible system cranked away, applying rules, models, formulas and concepts without adequate thinking or questioning. He had brought the generals and admirals into his office for repeated grillings, taken them to the White House for special briefings, ordered a dozen studies and insisted on answers. The military responded when asked, and Cheney didn't attribute bad motives to anyone. But he had uncovered a rat's nest hidden away from civilian oversight.

It was one of the great secrets: the U.S. military had thousands more nuclear weapons than necessary and the SIOP called for them to be used in a way that would have done far more nuclear violence to the Soviet Union than necessary to achieve the military objectives in a war. Cheney had also discovered that some of the flexibility that all presidents wanted in the plan, and had ordered in a series of presidential directives, was missing. For example, the ability to demonstrate restraint to the Soviets by limiting or controlling the size of a nuclear attack was not there. These issues went right to the heart of presidential and civilian control over the military. Cheney was gradually reforming the SIOP system. Some day when the Gulf crisis was over, he and the President would be able to go public with an outline of sweeping reforms.

In the same way, he was not taking anything on faith in the Gulf operation. Just as he was determined to understand the SIOP as well as his military commanders did, he was going to understand the Gulf war plan.

He knew the military was confident about what its weapons and men could deliver. But the line between desirable confidence and dangerous overconfidence was hard to draw. Cheney had adopted what he felt was an appropriately skeptical view of what any single piece of the war plan might be able to accomplish. He took three steps.

First, he had been very careful not to paint too rosy a picture to the President, the public or the Congress. He had worked to lower expectations, so as to avoid being like the candidate for office who is expected to receive 70 percent of the vote, winds up with 60 percent, and is thought to have failed.

Second, he had insisted on redundancy in the war plan. He

wanted to make sure there was the capability to go to particular key targets several times.

Third, he personally was digging into the war plan, and the concepts behind it. Drawing on outside experts, briefings he'd received, stories in the press, and background reading he had done on the Iran-Iraq War, he had compiled as many questions as he could, and was using them to pulse the system for information.

Cheney told Wolfowitz that he didn't want to micromanage the planners, although he was going to watch closely and ask questions. He had no intention of trying to redo the war plan. "But I intend to own it when it's finished," the Secretary said.

Most mornings Cheney was given an operations and intelligence briefing by the Joint Staff. It was pretty boring, describing the locations of Iraqi and coalition forces, accidents that had occurred on the coalition side, and routine problems. Fidgety, Cheney wanted to know more. He requested that the Joint Staff give him some highly classified presentations on offensive war planning. Beginning November 26, he was given a series of nuts-and-bolts tutorials on such subjects as Building an Air Attack Plan; Target Categories for an Air Campaign; Breaching Iraqi Forward Defenses; Logistics Sustainment; Command, Control and Communications; Deconfliction of Coalition Forces in an Air Campaign; Army Anti-Armor Capabilities; Amphibious Operations; and other sensitive topics like special operations and intelligence.

Cheney listened in dead earnest. He peppered the Joint Staff experts with questions, and drew them out about uncertainties and reservations. In less than a month, he received 15 briefings. At the last of them, Tom Kelly presented him with a framed diploma stating that Dick Cheney had completed a course in war planning and was now designated a "Joint Planner."

"This will be my most treasured possession," Cheney said with evident sarcasm.

• • •

One of Powell's primary tasks in planning for an offensive war was developing the lists of key strategic targets in Iraq for the three air phases. The targets were divided into categories and then priorities were set within each category.

Initial target categories were:

• Command, control and communications systems.

- Air defense systems and radar.
- Airfields used by Saddam's 800 combat planes.
- The 30 main SCUD missile-launching sites.
- Iraq's nuclear reactor.
- Production and storage facilities for chemical and biological weapons.
- The eight Republican Guard divisions—the backbone of Iraq's army.
- The supply network—storage depots, ammunition dumps, transportation hubs, roads, bridges and railroads.
- The 12 major petrochemical facilities, including the three refineries.
- The electrical power system.
- Other industrial war-supporting facilities.
- The 400,000 Iraqi troops occupying Kuwait.

Schwarzkopf's planners were working with a series of matrixes and computer models to match the targets with the available weapons over a timeline of 20 to 30 days of bombing. It was a giant puzzle. The pieces had to be put together in such a way as to inflict the most damage while ensuring that the U.S. and allied forces were given maximum protection from Iraq's offensive forces.

The Phase Four ground campaign would hinge on the levels of damage done in the air war, and finding some way to engage the Iraqi Army on terms favorable to the allies.

. . .

On November 28, former JCS Chairman Admiral Crowe testified before Nunn's committee. It was the day before that he'd told Powell, over lunch at the Pentagon, that he thought it was time for patience in the Gulf crisis.*

Crowe told the senators: "Our dislike for Hussein seems to have crowded out many other considerations. . . . I would argue that we should give sanctions a fair chance before we discard them. I personally believe they will bring him to his knees, ultimately, but I would be the first to admit, that is a speculative judgment. If, in fact, the sanctions will work in 12 to 18 months instead of six months, the trade-off of avoiding war with its attendant sacrifices

* As described in the Prologue, pp. 35–39.

and uncertainties, would, in my estimation be more than worth it."

Without directly criticizing Bush, Crowe hinted at his fear that the President was leaning toward war. "In my judgment, we are selling our country short by jumping to the conclusion that we can't stare down our opponent. . . . It is curious that just as our patience in Western Europe has paid off and furnished us the most graphic example in our history of how staunchness is sometimes the better course in dealing with thorny international problems, a few armchair strategists are counseling a near-term attack on Iraq. It is worth remembering that in the 1950s and '60s, individuals were similarly advising an attack on the USSR. Wouldn't that have been great?"

The testimony of Crowe and another retired former JCS Chairman, General David C. Jones, both calling for a continuation of the sanctions instead of war, was the main news event that night on television and in the next day's newspapers.

Surprised that Crowe had come down so hard for sanctions, Powell vowed that when he left office, he would not publicly second-guess his successors and would not appear voluntarily before Congress. They would have to subpoena him.

Scowcroft was irked at Crowe. The national security adviser felt that someone who had been in such a senior role in the administration should try to find common ground, not undercut the policy. And Bush told Scowcroft that he was personally disappointed in Crowe.

Crowe heard about Bush's distress and wrestled with a letter to the President. But he was too angry, and too convinced that Bush was making a terrible mistake. Going to war—and to Crowe it looked inevitable now—was a failure of policy. He wondered why he should make peace with a president who had failed the country when it needed him most. The letter went unfinished.

Crowe did, however, compose a letter to his son, Marine Captain Blake Crowe, who was stationed in Saudi Arabia. He told his son not to be guided by his father or his father's testimony. "You have a strong sense of duty and I know you'll perform it. When it comes time to fight, you fight. The American people are behind you, you can count on that no matter what they or I say about the policy or the administration. You kids in the desert they are behind."

Crowe's son phoned and told his parents that the bravado, the talk of kicking ass, was gone. It now looked serious and his men and the other Americans there just wanted to be used properly by their leaders.

Later Crowe received a holiday card from Bush. The President had written a personal note: "May God bless your son."

. . .

The next day, November 29, the United Nations Security Council met to vote on an authorization to use force to expel Iraqi forces from Kuwait. If it passed, the resolution would be the broadest authority for war it had granted since Korea in 1950.

Baker had touched down in various world capitals to bring key heads of state on board and iron out the language of the resolution. He had spent ten weeks traveling 100,000 miles and had held more than 200 meetings with foreign ministers and heads of state.

His strategy had been to obtain ironclad assurances of support from the key U.N. countries before publicly acknowledging that the administration was even seeking a resolution on the use of force. He had hedged, saying repeatedly that he was taking soundings and that such a resolution was merely under consideration.

Any one of the five permanent members of the Security Council —the United States, China, Great Britain, France or the Soviet Union—could veto the resolution. The Chinese turned out not to be much of a problem; early on, they agreed not to veto. Britain's Prime Minister Thatcher was ready and willing to use force. The French were a problem and required a major effort, but Bush and Baker had succeeded in bringing them on board.

The Soviets were the big question mark. From the beginning of the crisis, Gorbachev had opposed the possibility of military force, but he had finally come around. Bush administration lawyers had said it would be best for the resolution language to be a model of clarity, spelling out directly the authority for use of force.

In a series of conversations and meetings in the weeks and days leading up to the U.N. vote, Baker and Soviet Foreign Minister Shevardnadze had hashed it out.

Baker presented Shevardnadze with a draft that included the phrase "use of force."

"Can you live with this?" Baker asked.

"After our Afghanistan experience, that won't fly with the Soviet people," Shevardnadze said. There had to be some other way, an indirect way of saying it, a euphemism. The Soviets could support the idea of force but the resolution itself had to be vague.

Baker said that would be hard. Force was force, after all, and they could not run the risk of not saying exactly what they meant. Scribbling on a piece of paper, Baker tried out some ideas—lawyerly phrases to substitute for "use of force." He tried five different formulations.

In one of their conversations, Shevardnadze said he wanted some language that would allow force but also encompass all other possible measures—diplomacy, sanctions, anything that might work. The broader the better.

How about "all necessary means," Baker proposed. In Russian, the same word could be used for "means" and "measures."

They went back and forth. Soon Shevardnadze was favoring "all necessary means." It was the broadest phrase they had found.

Now Baker backed off his own phrase. It was too indefinite.

"The United States knows what 'all necessary means' is," Shevardnadze said. "Don't embarrass us. Don't push us. Don't be extreme." Shevardnadze said for the Soviets it wasn't a moral problem, it was a practical problem. The Soviet Union could not go to the United Nations and be seen voting for war. At home, war still meant Afghanistan.

Baker said the United States wanted to avoid ambiguity. The Gulf policy was too volatile at home, and the Bush administration did not want a domestic debate on the meaning of a U.N. resolution.

Shevardnadze was immovable. Finally Baker gave in and they settled on "all necessary means." The coalition would be authorized to use "all necessary means" to eject Saddam's forces from Kuwait if he had not pulled them out by the resolution's deadline, January 15, 1991.

Baker said that since he would be the temporary president of the Security Council during the vote, he would speak afterwards and characterize the resolution as an unambiguous authority to use "force." That would be a permanent part of the record, and if no one objected, it would stand as the interpretation of "all necessary means."

Fine, Shevardnadze said.

The Soviet foreign minister had another problem. He wanted the resolution to include language devised by President Gorbachev stating that the six weeks before the January 15 deadline was "a pause of goodwill." Gorbachev was proud of that language. He wanted the 45-day delay to be a real opportunity for diplomacy to work. The Soviet leader intended to exploit the Soviet-Iraqi bilateral relationship and seek a peaceful solution. He considered the phrase nonnegotiable, a diplomatic sine qua non. Without it, the Soviets could not support the resolution.

Baker agreed.

Before the vote, Shevardnadze said to Baker, "Mr. Secretary, you know you can't back off once you start down the road. You will have to implement the resolution" if January 15 passes without an Iraqi withdrawal.

"I'm afraid you're right," Baker said.

The resolution passed 12 to 2. Yemen and Cuba were the two countries voting against it. China abstained.

In his address to the Security Council, Baker said: "Today's resolution is very clear. The words authorize the use of force, but the purpose, I believe, and again as many have already said, is to bring about a peaceful resolution of this problem."

. . .

Prince Bandar, delighted by the U.N. resolution, received word that night that the Iraqi ambassador to the United Nations wanted to see him. It was an emergency. At last, Bandar thought, Saddam was scared. The resolution was already having an impact. Bandar agreed to set up a meeting for the next day.

At 10:30 the following morning Bandar received a call at home from the White House, saying that President Bush wanted to arrange a phone call with King Fahd for noon.

About what? Bandar inquired.

Nothing special, just to check in with His Majesty.

Bandar soon received word that President Bush was going to be on television at 11 a.m. He sat down in front of a television.

Bush appeared and went through a 20-paragraph statement about his Gulf policy, listing all the steps he had taken. "However, to go the extra mile for peace," he said, he would receive Iraqi Foreign Minister Tariq Aziz in Washington. "In addition, I'm asking Secretary Jim Baker to go to Baghdad to see Saddam Hussein . . . at a mutually convenient time between December 15th and January 15th of next year."

Bandar nearly shot out of his chair in disbelief and surprise. How stupid, he thought. Americans would never understand Arabs. A peace offering 24 hours after the United States and the coalition had scored the United Nations victory would send precisely the wrong message to Saddam: a message of weakness. Bandar complained to the White House.

Why did you not consult with us? he asked Scowcroft. The timing could not have been worse. The offer to meet right up to the deadline of January 15 would be an invitation for Saddam to stall. Bandar predicted that Saddam would offer to receive Baker on January 14. To you, Bandar said, sending Baker is goodwill; to Saddam, it suggests you're chicken.

Scowcroft replied that he was not crazy about the timing, not enough thought had been given to it. It had been a last-minute decision—but a needed step to prove to Congress and the American public that the President was willing to exhaust all diplomatic alternatives before war. Baker's offer to visit Baghdad demonstrated that the "pause of goodwill" was being taken seriously.

Maybe it was the right domestic message, Bandar conceded, but it was the wrong telegram to Saddam. King Fahd was extremely displeased at the failure to consult with him. What is going to happen if there is a war? Bandar asked. Are we going to get a call saying, "Oh by the way, we just started"?

Bandar also spoke with the Iraqi mission at the United Nations, inquiring about the emergency meeting Saddam's ambassador had requested the night before. The staff said the Iraqi ambassador just wanted to chat, he hadn't seen Bandar for a long time. There was no reason in particular to meet, and certainly there was no emergency.

Bandar concluded that Bush and Baker had given Saddam great comfort at what should have been the Iraqi leader's moment of greatest distress.

· · ·

Baker had recommended the Baghdad mission to Bush. He had been thinking of it for weeks. He had never been to Iraq and never met Saddam. By every account available to Baker, Saddam was pathological. He literally shot people who brought him bad news. And he was totally isolated. The Soviets had told Baker that the only way to get a message to this guy was to sit before him and state it.

The domestic political considerations were as important to Baker as the diplomatic possibilities. Public support for the administration policy was dropping, Sam Nunn was challenging Bush, former Joint Chiefs chairmen were testifying against the policy. Now that the United Nations had authorized force, people were scared. The President had to stop the political bleeding, Baker had argued.

Cheney thought there was no harm in trying the Baker mission. He dismissed suggestions by some of his staff that Baker would make a deal at any cost and get taken to the cleaners by Saddam. Cheney knew the President's mind and he knew that Baker knew the President's mind.

When *The Washington Post* published a poll showing that 90 percent of Americans approved of the Baker-to-Baghdad offer, Bandar received three separate calls directing his attention to the wide support. The calls were from Scowcroft, Baker and Cheney.

. . .

Later on November 30 Bush met with the congressional leadership in the Cabinet Room. The announcement of the Baker mission had nearly all the two dozen men in a jocular, even boisterous mood. The atmosphere was like a men's clubhouse, with much backslapping and joking. It only calmed down when Bush took his seat. Quayle, Baker, Scowcroft, Cheney and Sununu also sat down.

"The Secretary of State has been engaged in a marathon to get the United Nations on board," Bush said. "He knows of the difficulty concerning the issue of force. It's a combination of [our increased] deployment and the United Nations resolution which gives us the best chance to get a peaceful resolution of the issue." The President added, "I know there are differences around the table, and with former chiefs. But I want to show you I have no second thoughts at all." The Iraqi nuclear weapons potential is a real danger, he said. "And I'm going to err on the side of caution."

Bush mentioned his concern about oil and the effects of increased energy costs worldwide.

"There is brutality in Kuwait," he said. "We really ought to care." He became very emotional. "If the United States can't care about this, then I don't know. I'm not sure that up to yesterday, maybe even today, that Saddam Hussein thinks that the United States is serious."

Baker is going to Baghdad and Aziz is coming to Washington, Bush continued. He said these would not be sessions to find common ground, to let Saddam save face. "He doesn't deserve it."

The President said he hoped Saddam got the message, that the purpose was not to find a compromise. A compromise would guarantee that the coalition would vanish.

"If the Congress wants to come back and endorse the U.N. resolution, let's go. But let's not have a hung jury. If you can't support, frankly, I'd be wary. So I'd welcome your support."

Then Bush turned the meeting over to Baker. "In this 45-day period, let us use the threat of force to solve this peacefully," the Secretary of State urged. "It's the only hope we have, unless you want us to buy off on a compromise. The threat of force is not the same as the use of force." In a beseeching tone, he added, "You've got to give us the threat as a diplomatic tool."

Speaker Tom Foley praised the administration for being open and forthcoming. He said that Bush should consult the new Congress in January, adding that he thought the allies would support economic sanctions for a year.

Bush shook his head at this.

"If after January 15th you decide to go to war, you'll have to come to Congress," Foley added.

Senator Mitchell was emphatic on the same point: a vote was necessary and constitutionally required. As the Senate Majority Leader spoke, Bush stared coldly in the other direction.

Bush said: "Don't underestimate the strength of the signal it would send if Congress would endorse the U.N. resolution. It would be the most powerful guarantee of getting his [Saddam's] attention. . . . There's an enormous price to pay if we try to help him save face."

Sam Nunn said there was common ground. "Iraq has to get out of Kuwait. The question is: with or without war? There's a difference between the U.N. voting and our people going to die. Secondly, time is on our side. . . . The strategy's working. It's working. We're winning."

Baker, looking for consensus, asked whether Congress might approve offensive operations limited to the use of superior allied airpower. "If we are unified on the use of air, could you give us that?"

"No," Mitchell said.

Senator Cohen cited Mark Twain's observation that a man would fight to defend his home, but that he might have a different view toward a boardinghouse. "Right now, the American people are not persuaded that Kuwait is in fact our home, or Saudi Arabia's our home, but rather the equivalent of the boardinghouse. . . . Why are we willing to die for the Kuwaitis at this moment?"

Cohen told Bush that he had to answer that satisfactorily. "The second question is, what kind of a war is it going to be? The notion that we're somehow going to use our land forces to go in and dig the Iraqis out of Kuwait only generates images of young men and women being stacked up like cordwood."

Senator Alan Simpson of Wyoming, the Republican Whip, interjected that the U.N. resolution was for peace, not war. A hung jury would be a disaster. Cohen and some of the others were dropping a bag on old George Bush, talking about bodies as cordwood.

"I've never said anything publicly," Cohen replied. "I'm telling you what's in their minds."

Senator Lugar told the group that he had counted seven times in the meeting when the President had appealed for the support of the Congress, yet the congressional leaders were saying they weren't going to give it. "It just seems inconceivable that we are going to leave it at this," Lugar said. There is no more important issue facing the country, he said, and the Congress has to stand up to its responsibility. "It's imperative to find a way out of this dilemma that we face."

Cheney pointed out that it was a massive undertaking to move the 200,000 additional troops to the Gulf. Some 600 trains were being used just to transport the forces out of Europe.

"We don't need another Vietnam War," Bush said. The logistics would be different. "World unity is there. No hands are going to be tied behind backs. This is not a Vietnam. . . . I know whose backside's at stake and rightfully so. It will not be a long, drawn-out mess. As Mubarak says, we trained the Iraqi pilots. They stink."

The room filled with laughter again.

23

O N SATURDAY, DECEMBER 1, the chiefs went to Camp David to meet with the President. They had done some private grousing about not having seen the President in the middle of the largest military deployment since Vietnam.

Admiral Kelso and General Gray gave straightforward descriptions of the forces from their services that were in the theater or on their way.

General Vuono said that the size and power of the U.S. force would convince Saddam that he could only lose. "Is this son-of-a-bitch really dumb enough to fight us?" the Army chief asked.

General McPeak, the newest chief, expanded his presentation into a forecast. If the offense is launched, he said, the air operation ought to last about 30 days before a ground operation begins. Mr. President, you will lose about four to five airplanes a day or about a total of 150 airplanes down over the 30 days.

Bush did not show any emotion.

About half the pilots would be rescued, McPeak estimated. A quarter would be killed. The other quarter would be made prisoners of war and paraded on television through downtown Baghdad. There would be accidents, mistakes, he said. The precision

missiles and bombs would not all perform perfectly. Damage to
military targets would spill over to civilian areas. McPeak estimated that the bombing would kill 2,000 Iraqi civilians—people
the President was not angry at. McPeak said he thought that overall the 30-day bombing campaign would destroy 50 percent of the
main Iraqi military equipment on the ground—tanks, artillery and
armored personnel carriers.

Privately, McPeak thought it would be greater than 50 percent,
but he knew that over the years airpower advocates had discredited themselves with wild predictions.

.   .   .

Cheney thought the United Nations resolution on the use of force
was a watershed for the President. Bush now had many of his
international friends, most of the major heads of state—Gorbachev, Thatcher, Mubarak and Fahd—in an unusual coalition.
If Saddam did not withdraw during this 45-day pause, Cheney did
not doubt that Bush would use the military to drive Iraq out.

The Secretary had been asked to be the first witness to testify at
Nunn's committee hearings on the Gulf operation, but he had
declined. The White House, less confident it would have its way
in Congress than in the United Nations, did not want anyone from
the administration testifying while the U.N. resolution was being
debated. Instead, Crowe and several others critical of Bush's push
for an offensive option had opened the hearings.

Cheney agreed to appear in the second week of the hearings.
He and Powell would testify together.

Make the opening statement long, Cheney had instructed his
staff, make it very long. Not only did he want to lay out all his
reasoning; he wanted the senators to be exhausted by the question
period so he would have an easier time.

At the December 3 hearing, Cheney read aloud a lengthy statement reviewing the entire history of the Gulf operation. He said
that since Saddam would probably be able to ride out sanctions,
force was the only way to guarantee that Iraq got out of Kuwait.

Powell was the only other witness. He had spent the day before,
Sunday, rewriting his testimony. His staff had not quite captured
his thinking and he wanted to explain it exactly. Nunn's hearings
were very important, Powell felt, providing the major public
forum for the debate on Bush's Gulf policy.

Powell took the opportunity to criticize those who believed that airpower alone could drive Saddam from Kuwait. "Many experts, amateurs and others in this town, believe that this can be accomplished by such things as surgical air strikes or perhaps a sustained air strike. And there are a variety of other nice, tidy, alleged low-cost, incremental, may-work options that are floated around with great regularity all over this town." He said an air-only strategy could not guarantee success because it would leave the initiative to Saddam. Basic Army doctrine stressed taking and holding the initiative, fighting on terms favorable to the United States. Powell was a believer. "One can hunker down, one can dig in, one can disperse to try to ride out such a single-dimension attack. . . . Such strategies are designed to hope to win, they are not designed to win."

He did not come down on either side of the key question before the committee, how long they should wait to see if economic sanctions would work. "In the final analysis, how long to wait is a political, not a military, judgment."

At the conclusion of Powell's statement, Nunn asked him about a recent interview given by General Schwarzkopf. He had said that time was on the side of the United States and the coalition, as long as the sanctions remained in place. Nunn quoted Schwarzkopf saying, "If the alternative to dying is sitting out in the sun for another summer, that's not a bad alternative." What do you think? Nunn asked Powell.

"I wouldn't criticize General Schwarzkopf," Powell said, "or in any way disagree with him. What I would say is that we don't know if the sanctions will work. . . ."

"If we have a war," Nunn said sharply, "we're never going to know whether they would have worked, are we?"

"Well—" Powell began.

"That's the major point here," Nunn interrupted. "I mean, the way you find out whether sanctions work or not is to—is to give them enough time to work."

Later in the hearing, Senator Cohen quoted former Secretary of State Henry Kissinger: "High military officers have an innate awe of their commander-in-chief and it tempts them to find a military reason for what they consider to be barely tolerable. And contrary to some of the public mythology, they rarely challenge the commander-in-chief. They seek excuses for support, not to oppose him." What did Powell think of this? Cohen asked. "Do you stand in awe of the commander-in-chief?"

Powell replied, "I am not reluctant or afraid to give either the Secretary of Defense, the President or any other members of the National Security Council my best, most honest, most candid advice, whether they like it or not. And on—on some occasions, they do not like it." Turning to Cheney, who was by his side, Powell asked, "Isn't that right?"

"I will confirm that," Cheney answered.

There was laughter.

"Which part, sir?" Powell asked.

"All of it, Colin," Cheney replied.

. . .

On Sunday, December 16, Bush left Camp David for the White House where he had to do a taping of a public television interview with David Frost, to be broadcast January 2. He had a copy of a new Amnesty International report on human rights violations carried out by the Iraqis in Kuwait since the August invasion. In the helicopter on the way down to Washington, he opened the 79-page report. It said that the torture and murder were "entirely consistent with abuses known to have been committed in Iraq over many years." It was standard language for an Amnesty International report, even for those on some of the key U.S. allies, but Bush was horrified by the graphic accounts included.

"Oh, David," he told Frost several hours later, "it was so terrible, it's hard to describe." Bush explained how Barbara had read two pages and said she could not read any more. "The torturing of a handicapped child. The shooting of young boys in front of their parents. The rape of women dragged out of their homes and repeatedly raped and then brought into the hospital as kind of basket cases. The tying of those that are being tortured to ceiling fans so they turn and turn. The killing of a—of a Kuwaiti and leaving him hanging—this is a picture of this one—leaving him hanging from a crane and so others will see him. Electric shots to the private—shocks to the private parts of men and women. Broken glass inserted in—jabbed into people. I mean, it—it is primeval. And I—I'm afraid I'd get very emotional if I described more of it." But Bush went on, describing how a 15-year-old boy had been beaten on the bottom of his feet, and how the Iraqis pulled out the fingernails of their victims.

The President said that a more peaceful world was possible if the United States and the coalition stood up to Saddam. "It won't happen if we compromise. When you have such a clear case of good and—good versus evil. We have such a clear moral case. . . . It's that big. It's that important. Nothing like this since World War II. Nothing of this moral importance since World War II."

"What will you do after the 15th?" Frost asked. "What is your inclination?"

"Well," Bush said, "I haven't made a determination."

.   .   .

Powell was determined not to be crushed or even nagged by ambivalence. He felt that Bush did not want to go to war if the objective still could be achieved by other means. He remained convinced that Saddam did not want a war with the United States, and he wanted to keep giving Saddam reasons to feel that way.

But if there was a war, the United States had to win it. It was a David and Goliath match-up, with the United States as Goliath. If the U.S. military did not succeed in a pretty clear-cut way, it could be devastating. A spectacular victory was required. At stake was not only the nation's foreign policy, but also the reputation and morale of the military for years, even decades, to come.

On December 17, President Bush spoke twice to reporters. At the first session, he was asked what he was going to do after expiration of the deadline on January 15.

"You just wait and see," Bush said.

At the second session that afternoon, a reporter asked why he was avoiding a specific threat of military force, why he had not come right out and said he would attack.

"Because I'm not in a threatening mode," Bush answered. "I don't think any of us are. We are in a determined mode."

That day, Powell and Wolfowitz discussed Bush's method of getting his message out. Powell was in real agony. Although he didn't intend to, the President was sending mixed signals. In that single day he had blown hot, then cold. Explaining the policy and managing the message was very close to the single most important thing the President did, and Powell hated to see it botched.

Powell and Wolfowitz went so far as to wonder whether they might be able to find a way to suggest a new communications manager for the White House.

This period before the January 15 deadline was particularly critical. It was a war of nerves, and the President's words were very important. First, Saddam had to be intimidated. Second, the

Congress had to be kept on board. And third, if force had to be used, reasonably strong public support had to be maintained.

Powell did not want to be forced into a war because of a monumental lapse in communication.

. . .

That week of December 17, Les Aspin went to the White House for a session with Scowcroft. Aspin's House Armed Services Committee had just completed its own hearings on the Gulf policy. To Aspin, the problem was all about oil, nuclear weapons and aggression, and he had concluded he could support a war. If the United States didn't use its military in a case like this, when might it be used?

It was obvious to Aspin that Scowcroft had lost his patience with diplomacy. Saddam had said that he could only receive Baker in Baghdad on January 12, three days before the deadline. Bush had rejected this. Saddam was jerking everyone around. There was no reason to deal with him, Scowcroft said. The four months of diplomacy and economic sanctions had failed. War would take less time than the exhausting and frustrating four-month dance they just had been through, Scowcroft said. He was now convinced that war would be a two- to three-week solution.

Prince Bandar also stopped by to see Scowcroft that week. The Saudi ambassador knew that Scowcroft was a nearly perfect mirror of Bush. If Scowcroft was hot or cold on something, it meant Bush was the same.

"Basically the President has made up his mind," Scowcroft confided. Referring to the diplomatic efforts, he told Bandar, "These are all exercises."

. . .

On December 19, Cheney, Powell and Wolfowitz arrived in Saudi Arabia for a detailed examination of Schwarzkopf's war plan. The plan was complicated, with lots of military jargon, but Powell and the Joint Staff had tutored Cheney. Cheney admitted he was no war planner, but he said he wanted to make sure they could explain every detail to him. If there were things he didn't agree with, they were going to have to convince him.

Eight reporters traveling with Cheney and Powell had a 30-minute interview with Schwarzkopf's deputy, Army Lieutenant General Calvin A. H. Waller. Powell had placed Waller, a temperate man, at the Central Command to act as a calming influence on Schwarzkopf. Waller told the reporters candidly that the Army would not be ready for an offensive operation until early or middle February, and he couldn't imagine that President Bush would order an attack before then.

Asked what he would say if Bush asked him if he'd be prepared to attack on January 15, Waller replied, "I'd tell him, 'No, I'm not ready to do the job.'"

Waller's statements were the major headlines the next day. Powell was furious. Every time the iron fist was shown to Saddam, something or someone came along to pull it back.

Cheney felt that Waller, who had little experience dealing with the media, had been thrown to the wolves in the press. The interview should not have been arranged. Nonetheless, the remarks and the ensuing uproar served Cheney's purposes, conveying the impression that it was not likely the United States would go to war until February. It would be just right if Saddam thought he could not be attacked until then.

As far as Cheney was concerned, if Saddam was not out of Kuwait, they were going to have to begin the air war right after January 15, and the Air Force and Navy air would be ready then.

During this trip, Powell, Cheney and Wolfowitz had time to talk in a more relaxed atmosphere. Powell said that, looking at the whole situation, he thought Saddam would pull his forces out of Kuwait at the last minute. When Saddam saw that he was facing some of the best forces the United States had created to fight the Soviet Union, he would back down. Saddam was a ruthless survivor who would do anything to hold power. They had seen it time and time again—most recently when he gave up all the territory he had taken from Iran during the eight-year war. Or two weeks earlier, when he had suddenly and unexpectedly released the 2,000 American and Western hostages.

Cheney didn't buy any of this. Look at the evidence, he told Powell and Wolfowitz. Saddam was still moving reinforcements into Kuwait, not taking troops out. There was not one concrete piece of evidence to support this optimism. It could become dangerous. Let this attitude of "gee-he'll-withdraw" linger too long, Cheney said, and the decision makers would be infected with wishful thinking. It was the wrong basis for policy. That was why he wanted to make sure that Schwarzkopf was ready for war and had made the plan sufficiently bold and imaginative.

The three men spent a day and a half with Schwarzkopf. The

first morning's briefings were on intelligence, the readiness of the forces and logistics. Cheney fired away with questions. He didn't want anyone making optimistic assumptions; he wanted to make sure the command was stocking up supplies for a long conflict. He wanted more bombs and munitions for the air war on hand.

At the afternoon session, Schwarzkopf laid out the war plan. It was not a series of options from which Cheney and the President could select. Rather, it was one overall plan, based on the guidance he had received to use the maximum military force available and necessary to do the job. Like the earlier plan, it included three air phases followed by a fourth phase, the ground campaign. If any phase went better than expected, it was possible to move to the next target group sooner, speeding up the war.

The first phase of the air campaign was directed at the Iraqi air defenses, airfields, 800-plane air force and Saddam's command, control and communications network. One intelligence analysis had concluded that 80 to 85 percent of Iraqi airpower could be eliminated in the initial days, providing the United States attacked first and achieved "tactical surprise."

Wolfowitz wanted to make sure all the alternatives were addressed and considered. He knew that military officers often interpreted questions from civilians as a challenge to their authority, but he tried to draw Schwarzkopf out on the air campaign.

Schwarzkopf said he feared that the political apparatus—the President, the Secretary or the Congress—would call a halt before he could achieve his objectives in either the air or ground phases.

Wolfowitz tried to reassure the general, pointing out that the President and Cheney had said it would be politically acceptable for Schwarzkopf to take all the time the field commanders needed.

The President has said he does not want another Vietnam, Cheney reminded Schwarzkopf. The administration was committed. The military commanders would not have their hands tied. The President, Cheney and Powell had to sign off on the plan, but once it was approved, it would for the most part be in Schwarzkopf's hands. The President would make the final decisions, such as when to launch the Phase Four ground campaign.

Key portions of the ground campaign had been developed by half a dozen junior officers in their second year at the Army Command and General Staff College at Fort Leavenworth. These majors and lieutenant colonels, nicknamed the "Jedi Knights," had

been sent to Saudi Arabia to apply the elements of advanced maneuver warfare—probing, flanking, surprise, initiative, audacity
—to the war plan.

Working in a small top-secret corner of Schwarzkopf's headquarters, they had applied the principles of the Army's unclassified
200-page operations manual. Chapters 6 and 7 on offensive operations were built around concepts established in General Grant's
1863 Civil War campaign at Vicksburg. Instead of attacking directly into enemy fortifications, Grant sent his troops in a wide
maneuver around the Confederate front line, and then attacked
from the side and rear. This indirect approach was deemed the
best way to beat Saddam.

The initial terrain analysis had concluded that the ground in the
Iraqi desert was too soft. But reconnaissance proved this wrong.
The desert was in fact adequate to support a tank attack. A ma-
neuver plan would work.

Since Saddam had most of his forces in southern Kuwait and
along the Gulf coast to the east, the ground plan called for moving
the VII Corps several hundred miles in a wide arc to the west, and
attacking through Iraq to hit the Republican Guard. It would
amount to a gigantic left hook. Massive, swift, crushing tank attacks were central to the plan.

Meanwhile, in a helicopter air assault, other U.S. forces would
be dropped behind the Iraqi lines, where they would be unopposed.

The idea was to force Saddam to move his hundreds of thousands of troops from dug-in positions so they could be picked off
with superior U.S. air and ground fire.

Marines would carry out a frontal ground attack at the Saudi-
Kuwait border, attempting to breach and get behind the Iraqi lines
there. Other Marine forces offshore would also do everything they
could to make it appear as if they were going to launch a major
amphibious landing on the Kuwaiti Gulf coast, where the Iraqis
had built extensive defenses. But it would be a feint, designed to
keep the Iraqis pinned down. The Marines would never land.

"Here come my warlords," Schwarzkopf said in introducing the
Army and Marine ground commanders who gave the rundown on
their units' plans. The most confident were the tank commanders.
The commanders of the light forces appeared most worried.

Cheney had many questions about the ground plan. With so

many variables, chief among them how Saddam might move his forces around, it was going to be much trickier than the air war. The plan was dependent on achieving and holding air superiority, and on ensuring that Saddam did not have intelligence on the large-force movement to the west. There was also a huge logistical challenge: at least 100,000 men, as well as their equipment and supplies, would have to be moved several hundred miles in several days to the west—an almost impossible task. If Saddam did learn of the plan, he would not believe it could be done.

There was much discussion of chemical weapons. It was a virtual certainty that Saddam would use them. When? How? No one knew exactly what supplies he had, but certainly they were vast. The military and psychological impact of a chemical attack was hard to measure.

The Army had some new technologies. A radar "fire finder" allowed the United States to locate Iraqi artillery emplacements by establishing the trajectory of an artillery shot while it was still in the air. A computer solved the mathematical problem, instantly determining the point of origin. Before the enemy round landed, the U.S. forces would have a return barrage fired on that point, hopefully knocking out both the weapon and the Iraqis operating it. "We will teach them if you shoot your artillery, you die," one of the officers explained.

Since many of the targets, like communications centers and airfields, were fixed, the updated and revised air plan was much neater and more predictable than the ground plan. The planners had worked hard matching weapons to targets, Cheney could see.

Cheney and Powell told Schwarzkopf to expect execution of the air phases soon after January 15.

The Secretary and the Chairman received a highly classified medical briefing on anticipated casualties. The senior medical officer said they were planning on 20,000, including about 7,000 killed in action.

The room fell silent.

Then Schwarzkopf spoke up. "That's a worst case planning model," he said. "It isn't a prediction. I don't make predictions."

The Pentagon leaders also had a chance to visit troops in forward positions. Powell was treated like a Pope returning to the village where he had been the parish priest. Mobbed for autographs, he scribbled his name on anything available—magazines,

Saudi currency, a skateboard. He helped one soldier lift a sandbag, wished Merry Christmas all around, and posed for photographs. He visited the 2nd Brigade of the 101st Airborne Division, a special air assault unit. Fourteen years earlier, Powell had commanded the 2,000-man brigade. Now he told the men he knew and understood the uncertainty of their assignment—the waiting, the long nights, the churning in the stomach.

To all those who made inquiries about their future, and to many who did not, Powell repeated four words: "Be ready for war."

.   .   .

On Friday, December 21, Bush invited the ambassadors from each of the countries in the 28-member coalition to the White House. After the meeting, he took the group for a tour of the White House Christmas decorations.

Prince Bandar was the last to leave.

"Are you in a hurry?" Bush asked.

"No."

"Come say hello to Barbara."

Bandar wished the First Lady a Merry Christmas, then went with Bush to the Oval Office, where the two men stepped outdoors to talk.

"Is he crazy?" Bush asked about Saddam.

The two men had discussed the same question before. In their regular conversations over the months, Bandar had told Bush about Saddam's paranoid obsession with his own personal security, and Bush had heard many other such stories. Bandar was still convinced that if Saddam had to choose between his own neck and leaving Kuwait, he would act to save his neck. Saddam did not want to die. He was not a martyr.

Bush also asked, "Does he know what he is up against?"

For several months, Bandar had privately been saying to Bush and others that the quality of the Iraqi military was greatly exaggerated. He still felt that Saddam could be defeated in two weeks.

Bandar noticed that Bush was stiff. He sensed a massing of determination in the body language. None of the loose, flappy awkwardness. There was no smile. Though Bush's eyes were cool and calm, he seemed to be carrying some inner weight. When Bandar looked more carefully and deeper, the eyes looked scary. In the Middle East, there was a saying that a quiet man should not be made angry because he will be hard to handle. For months, Bandar had seen both the public and private anger building, resulting in an eerie accumulation of willfulness.

"If he does not comply," Bush said of Saddam, "we'll just have to implement the resolutions."

Bandar nodded, thinking to himself: this is serious, he's going to do it.

. . .

Meanwhile, CIA Director Webster was assembling a pre-Christmas Special National Intelligence Estimate designed to provide the best forecast of whether Saddam would pull out of Kuwait before the January 15 deadline. In discussions among the various intelligence agencies, Webster, the CIA and the State Department's intelligence branch had concluded that once Saddam realized the size of the force arrayed against him and the determination of the United States and the allies, he would withdraw.

At DIA, Pat Lang registered a strong objection. In his view, it was a repeat of the classic mistake made prior to the Iraqi invasion of Kuwait. Again the intelligence officers were mirror-imaging, looking at the world through their own limited Western perspective, pretending if they were Saddam they would recognize the overwhelming military might poised against Iraq and the determination of the international coalition. Since it was logical for Saddam to come to this conclusion, he would see the light and withdraw.

Lang suspected the opposite. He was pretty sure that Saddam was focused mainly on the size of his own force, and on his own determination. DIA Chief Soyster and the heads of the four separate military intelligence services agreed with Lang. They insisted on inserting a written dissent in several footnotes in the intelligence estimate. It was published and sent to President Bush.

In an interview with *Time* magazine shortly before Christmas, Bush was asked if there would be a war.

"Oh, God," he said, pausing and then reflecting the majority view in the intelligence estimate. "My gut says he will get out of there."

. . .

Cheney and Powell returned from the Gulf and flew up to Camp David to brief the President on Christmas Eve. Scowcroft and Gates were also there.

It was true that the ground forces would not be ready until February, Cheney reported. In fact, he was not yet fully satisfied with the Phase Four ground plan. But the air campaign was ready, and he was pleased with the details.

Both Cheney and Powell said that it was entirely possible to start and sustain the air campaign before the ground forces were in place. Schwarzkopf had been aiming at the diplomatic deadline of January 15.

By then Schwarzkopf and the troops would have gone through Thanksgiving, Christmas and New Year's in the desert. They would have lived with the 45-day "pause for peace" with no results. Some would have been in the desert five months. January 15, an implied date certain, had been a real morale booster.

Bush said they should think seriously about starting the air campaign at the best and soonest point after January 15, if Saddam had not withdrawn.

It was agreed that Powell would talk with Schwarzkopf and obtain his recommended execution date and time, based on the moon and the weather forecasts.

Powell already had the draft of a top-secret warning order to send to General Schwarzkopf. According to JCS publications, a warning order is "a preliminary notice of an order or action which is to follow." Once sent, it would direct Schwarzkopf to be fully prepared to carry out the war plan.

Operating on the secure telephone, Powell asked Schwarzkopf for his recommended date and time, after the January 15 United Nations deadline. Schwarzkopf said 3 a.m. Saudi time on January 17. That would be 7 p.m. Washington time on January 16, just 19 hours after the U.N. deadline. It would be a moonless night, a crucial factor for the F-117A Stealth fighter bombers. Since these planes would be virtually invisible to Iraqi radar, there was no point in allowing the Iraqis to see them or any other planes in the moonlight. Indications were that the weather would be clear.

Stormin' Norman said that when the offensive had begun, he would change the name of the operation from Desert Shield to Desert Storm.

Powell had the two-page warning order refined, specifying that

Schwarzkopf be fully prepared to begin Desert Storm on January 17 at 3 a.m. It was hand-carried to several Pentagon officials for review, and a final version was readied to be sent out when the President gave his final authorization.

. . .

By December 29, Powell had received his authorization to send the warning order to Schwarzkopf. To maximize secrecy, he had a copy faxed to Schwarzkopf on a special top-secret fax circuit. It was designated "Eyes Only" for Schwarzkopf. That way only one copy would appear at Schwarzkopf's headquarters. Powell did not want multiple copies spewing out in the Central Command communications center.

The warning order went out on Saturday morning, December 29, with the communications date-time-group designator 29/1612 December 1990, meaning it was sent December 29 at the universal time of 1612, which is 11:12 a.m. Washington time.

. . .

In the afternoon of New Year's Day, Tuesday, January 1, Bush returned from his Camp David holiday. That evening he met in the White House residence with Quayle, Baker, Cheney, Powell and Sununu.

Bush directed that the NSC staff begin drafting a formal presidential order called a National Security Directive that would lay out the policy reasoning for going to war. Since this would be a historic document, he wanted it given the attention it deserved.

Baker still wanted to make sure the President exhausted all the diplomatic possibilities. He proposed that Bush make one more offer to Saddam for a meeting.

Cheney worried about a last-minute trick. He felt strongly that the coalition was shaky. As he understood it, the coalition partners—particularly those in the Middle East, such as Saudi Arabia, Egypt and Syria and the smaller Gulf states—feared that the United States would find a reason not to act.

Cheney didn't think the decision to go to war had occurred in a definite moment or sequence of moments. There was no single discussion or meeting where it had been made. As best he could piece it together, however, by Christmas Eve it was close; by

December 29, when the warning order was sent, it was solidified; and at this New Year's Day meeting it was finally ratified.

Since Baker's Baghdad meeting had never come off—Saddam had said he could only see Baker three days before the deadline—Bush decided to propose publicly that Baker meet the Iraqi foreign minister in Switzerland during the period January 7 to 9, when Baker would be in Europe anyway. But there would be no negotiations, no compromises.

. . .

The next day, Wednesday, January 2, Scowcroft was somber. He began telling his trusted staff members that he was feeling fatalistic. It is going to be war, he said.

Gates convened a deputies' committee meeting. He said they had two tasks. First, Bush was going to offer a last Baker-Aziz meeting in Switzerland; they were to begin finalizing a draft letter from Bush to Saddam, which Baker would present to Aziz as a final declaration and ultimatum. Second, they were to begin drafting the National Security Directive, the presidential directive on war.

Wolfowitz thought that the letter to Saddam might still make a difference. He found one draft done by the NSC staff rather mild. He and Admiral Jeremiah, Powell's Vice Chairman, were eager to make it tougher. They proposed changes that the others on the deputies committee accepted. In its final form, the eight-paragraph letter said: "We stand today at the brink of war between Iraq and the world." It stated that the future of Iraq was at stake and the failure to withdraw would mean "calamity," "tragedy" and "further violence" for Iraq. The final sentence read: "I hope you weigh your choice carefully and choose wisely, for much will depend upon it."

At 8:45 the next morning, Thursday, January 3, Bush met again with the congressional leaders. He announced that he was making one last diplomatic effort: the Baker-Aziz meeting the following week. The President also made two strong references to the Amnesty International report he had read before the holidays, and he urged the congressmen to read it.

The leaders told Bush that he still could not be assured of a majority vote in Congress authorizing the use of force after January 15.

As they discussed the possible war, Bush said, "There is no Vietnam parallel."

Cheney reported that there were 325,000 troops in the Middle East now and another 12,000 were moving into Saudi Arabia each day.

Privately, Cheney felt that the diplomatic window was still open a crack, and the President had to keep it open. If Saddam suddenly pulled out of Kuwait, the United States could declare a great victory. The administration could say: hurrah, the United States displayed determination, led the world, created the coalition, deployed the forces and drove the son-of-a-bitch out of Kuwait.

But in Cheney's view, now more than ever, it was not going to happen that way.

· · ·

Bush convened his inner circle in the residential quarters again on Sunday night, January 6. Baker was already in Europe. Saddam had agreed to a Baker-Aziz meeting in Switzerland on Wednesday.

The President said he wanted to get the Congress to authorize the use of force if possible. It was the one final box that had not been checked, the one piece missing from his overall strategy.

Cheney was dubious. Absent Saddam's withdrawal, it is very important that force be used after January 15, Cheney said. Mr. President, you have pretty well made that decision. Congress was never a sure thing. A no vote by "my former colleagues," as he referred to them with mild sarcasm, would undermine everything. Cheney was deeply suspicious of the Democrats, who controlled Congress. He thought they would love to slam the door on the administration's efforts.

The administration, the coalition, the troops in the field could not afford a negative vote, Cheney said. He said he felt strongly that if the use of force turned out to be successful, if the objectives were achieved at the lowest possible cost and casualty levels, it wouldn't matter what kind of debate or vote there had been in Congress. On the other hand, he said, if the military campaign came a cropper or the costs were extraordinarily high, it wouldn't matter what Congress had approved in advance, they would be all over the President's case anyway. He saw no gain and lots of risk.

No one else said he shared Cheney's deep reservations. The meeting was adjourned with the issue unresolved.

The next day, January 7, Speaker Foley announced that the House would begin debate later in the week on a resolution authorizing the use of force. He personally opposed the use of force until economic sanctions were given more time, but he said that he believed the authorization would pass by a narrow margin. Senate Majority Leader Mitchell said the Senate would probably also begin debate on a resolution.

Bush began calling Senate and House Republicans that night to obtain a head count. He personally typed out the draft of a letter he could send to the Congress requesting that both houses endorse the "all necessary means" language of the United Nations resolution. He then directed that his senior advisers and cabinet officers, and their top lawyers and legislative affairs directors, meet with him the next morning at the White House.

Powell felt that it would be important to get congressional authorization. He was fearful of sending the troops to war without the explicit backing of Congress. He didn't want the troops left dangling out there, knowing they were in a war even though the politicians called it something else. It had been a "police action" in Korea, a "conflict" in Vietnam. Both were unsatisfactory. A nation at war had to say it was at war and had to speak with one voice.

Knowing Cheney's view, Powell didn't want to attend a large White House meeting where he would differ with the Secretary. So Powell called in his legal counsel, Army Colonel Fred K. Green, and told him to attend the meeting and report back.

At 11 a.m. on January 8, Bush went to the Cabinet Room. Present were Cheney, Scowcroft and Sununu. Eagleburger was sitting in for Baker. Boyden Gray and the senior lawyers from the departments, including Fred Green of the JCS, were also there.

Bush had a copy of his draft letter. He said that he was inclined to send it. The question was whether to remain passive or attempt to control the outcome with a specific administration proposal. Would he win, he asked the legislative directors for the White House, NSC, State and Defense.

The consensus view was that he would. But it was not 100 percent sure. Head counts were being taken.

Bush asked for another evaluation of his legal authority.

William P. Barr, the Deputy Attorney General, said that in his opinion and that of the senior department lawyers, the President had full authority to conduct military operations as the com-

mander-in-chief, regardless of whether Congress voted a resolution of support. The Constitution gives you the power to employ
the forces, he said. The congressional role is to provide the forces
and the laws under which they operate. The Congress has done
that. If they do not like the way you are employing the forces, they
can take away the money for them to operate. Barr said that he
nonetheless thought the President should be active in seeking the
most explicit declaration of support from the Congress.

"Is your advice solely political?" one of Bush's advisers asked.

No, Barr said. War is in the gray zone. The war power is a
shared power with Congress; the Constitution intends it to be
shared. Congress has the power to declare war, but it usually has
voted after the war has started. As with any shared power, your
hand is strongest when the executive branch and Congress agree,
he said. You would be in the least advantageous position if Congress does something inconsistent. An inconsistent resolution
would not take away your power. Congress can only take away
the money or disband the forces. Congress can put you in a difficult political position, so it's worth being active to affect what
they might do, the Deputy Attorney General added.

Bush then asked each of the government lawyers present to
speak. He wanted to be reassured about this constitutional authority. What were the alternative outcomes if members of Congress voted down a resolution, or talked themselves into a
stalemate? Could the courts somehow become involved now or
down the road?

Though not immune from legal challenge, the lawyers said, the
President was on solid constitutional ground. They basically af-
firmed Barr's outline.

Barr said that presidents from the beginning had acted unilaterally to employ the forces. In all there had been more than 200
occasions when presidents had done so, and only five declarations
of war. The situation most closely resembling the current crisis
was the Korean War, when Truman acted without Congress under
a United Nations resolution somewhat similar to the current one.

Scowcroft spoke in favor of going to Congress, and of submit-
ting a proposed resolution. Even if he had constitutional authority, the President's political authority would be vastly enhanced
with congressional backing, Scowcroft said. The President would
not want to start a war with a country divided.

Cheney cautioned about sending the letter. The simple act of requesting the resolution would carry immense implications. No matter how the President's letter was phrased, it would be interpreted to mean that the President thought he needed a vote. From ten years of experience, Cheney knew that Congress was not equipped to deal with such a large question in a short time. To go with the letter and lose would be devastating.·

Bush said he had to try. After sending the letter, they would mount a full-scale lobbying campaign. He said that he just could not believe that the Congress would leave the troops in the Gulf hanging.

"We've got to," Sununu said. "We've got to try to shape it."

The lawyers reworked the letter, and within the hour it was on its way to the Hill.

. . .

In the early afternoon, Bush settled into his large white high-backed armchair before the fireplace in the Oval Office. Cheney took the other armchair by the fireplace because, with Baker still in Europe, he was the most senior cabinet officer present.

Powell, Webster, Sununu, Scowcroft and Gates sat on the two couches.

Richard Haass, the chief of the Middle East division of the NSC staff, had called in four of the government's senior Arab experts to address the situation for the President.

Haass first introduced Ambassador April Glaspie, who had never returned to her post in Baghdad but had continued to work in the State Department.

Saddam had a hammer-lock on his troops, Glaspie said. The reason they didn't surrender or rebel was fear that he would harm their families. "There will not be a revolt because Saddam Hussein controls the military. He will not withdraw from Kuwait, in my opinion. He knows we are going to go to war with him if he does not withdraw." The steady buildup of troops showed he was bracing for an attack.

Are you saying that Saddam has understood right along that we're going to come get him? Sununu asked.

Yes, Glaspie said.

"How can you tell that?" Sununu inquired.

"By what he's saying and to whom he's saying it," she replied. The day before, Saddam had addressed his troops on the 70th anniversary of the Iraqi Army. The speech was also broadcast on the state-controlled television and radio. "We don't believe the sacrifices will be small," he had said, promising "the mother of battles." Glaspie interpreted the speech as an internal message to the Iraqi Army to prepare for a war that would not be short.

She also said that although in the West Saddam was not generally recognized as a legitimate leader, a great many Iraqis supported him. They may not like him, but they like his program. "It is an illusion to think he is not supported."

Haass then introduced William Rugh, a longtime foreign service officer and former ambassador to Yemen.

Rugh said if there was a full-scale war, the longer it lasted, the worse it would be because many Arabs would rally to Saddam as the man standing up to the West. He would grow into a hero. Winning is very important to Arabs, Rugh said, and even losing to the superpower could be winning. Saddam had some potent issues to exploit—the Palestinian question, deep suspicion about neocolonialism, and the divisions between rich and poor Arabs.

A CIA analyst spoke about the likely strong reaction in Israel if there was a war. It would be hard to restrain the Israeli leadership if they were attacked by Saddam.

Pat Lang of the DIA spoke last. He presumed he had been asked to the meeting because he had predicted the invasion of Kuwait. He imagined this meeting was similar to the war councils Lincoln and his cabinet held in the days before the Civil War started.

We have a perennial inability to comprehend alien cultures, even marginally alien cultures, Lang began. We don't understand the Iraqis. Two flawed assumptions are often made. First, that the Iraqis are cowards. This is untrue, Lang said, stating that he had studied them for five years, been to Iraq many times, seen their troops on the ground, studied the Iran-Iraq War, studied Arabs, studied warfare. "My conclusion, after taking all these things into consideration, is as follows," he said. "They won't back away. They will fight skillfully and hard. They are tough. . . . They won't surrender." A war to expel them from Kuwait would eventually require a prolonged ground campaign to dig them out, he added.

Powell did not say anything, but he nodded several times at these assessments.

Lang stated that he was a specialist on the eight elite Republican Guard divisions that had been used in the Kuwait invasion. These units of some 110,000 were positioned as a reserve force for Saddam's front line of 400,000-plus troops. The Guard was very well trained, equipped and led, he said, equivalent to the U.S. Army in these respects.

"If you break the Republican Guard," Scowcroft asked, "will the rest of them surrender?"

"No," Lang replied.

The second flawed assumption, Lang said, is that because Saddam is a criminal, brutal and inhumane, he is not a legitimate leader. This too is not true, Lang stressed. He agreed with Ambassador Glaspie. Saddam has either the support of the people or such tight control over them that he is legitimate in their eyes. Don't be deluded about that, Lang said. A war with this small country, with its overdeveloped military and entrenched leadership, would be difficult and long.

"Other people say differently," Bush said. "Nobody else is telling me that. Shamir, Mubarak, [Syrian President] Assad and Bandar all tell me it will be a pushover."

Lang had decided he wasn't here to scratch Bush's back, so he replied, "Sir, if I may say, that sounds to me like a collection of the uninformed and self-serving."

"Okay," Bush said.

"Are they going to spring anything—surprises on Baker tomorrow over there?" Bush finally asked.

The four experts said probably not.

24

IN GENEVA THE NEXT DAY, January 9, Baker held a six-and-a-half-hour meeting with Tariq Aziz at the Intercontinental Hotel. The Secretary of State presented Bush's eight-paragraph "brink-of-war" letter. Aziz read it and left it on the table. He declined to accept it or to carry it to Saddam.

Baker appeared afterward at a press conference, his face drawn and solemn. "I heard nothing that suggested to me any Iraqi flexibility whatsoever," he said. Watching on television back at the White House, Scowcroft knew that negotiations were now really over.

The Secretary of State flew on to Saudi Arabia to meet with King Fahd. Under the secret agreement with the United States, Fahd had to give his permission for any offensive military operation that might be staged from his country. Baker now asked for that permission. Fahd quickly gave his approval, asking only that he receive advance notification prior to war.

Baker promised that he would personally pass the word to Prince Bandar in Washington before any attack.

They agreed that very careful communications arrangements

between Bandar in Washington and Fahd in Saudi Arabia had to be worked out to prevent a leak. So they would not have to worry about transmitting messages or finding secure phones, Fahd and Bandar arranged to use a codeword, "Suleiman," the name of an employee of the royal family when Bandar was a child. If Bandar mentioned Suleiman in a phone call to the king, that would mean war.

Though Cheney had cautioned against seeking a resolution of support from the Congress, he lobbied hard for its approval. He was sent to the Hill to lobby his own constituency, the Republicans; the White House did not send him to talk with wavering Democrats. He spoke to a closed-door caucus of all House Republicans and then a similar session with all Senate Republicans. He did not tip off anyone that a war was imminent. But he did say that they should have no illusions: don't vote for this resolution if you are reading it as another diplomatic lever.

Bush and the White House leaned hard, however, on the argument that the resolution was the last, best chance to persuade Saddam to withdraw.

On Saturday, January 12, after three days of sober debate, the Congress granted Bush the authority to go to war. The resolution it passed included the "all necessary means" language of the United Nations resolution, but also specifically authorized "use of military force."

The vote was close in the Senate—52 to 47. The House approved it 250 to 183.

Cheney decided he had to eat a little crow. He called the President and congratulated him. Cheney acknowledged that he had been wrong, the President had read the Congress better.

Bush told reporters: "This clear expression of the Congress represents the last, best chance for peace." Asked if this made war inevitable, Bush said no.

"Have you made the decision in your mind?" one reporter asked.

"I have not because I still hope that there will be a peaceful solution." He added that "an instant commencement of a large-scale removal of troops with no condition, no concession, and just heading out could well be the best and only way to avert war, even though it would be, at this date, I would say almost impossible [for Saddam] to comply fully with the United Nations resolutions."

Eagleburger and Wolfowitz had been dispatched to Israel that weekend. Israel was still the wild card. The previous month, Prime Minister Yitzhak Shamir had made an extraordinary pledge directly to Bush. Despite Iraq's obvious preparations to attack Israel, and the Iraqis' public assurances that they would, Shamir said Israel would not launch a preemptive attack on Iraq. This would be a departure from the traditional Israeli emphasis on surprise attacks, which had obvious military advantages. Israel would not start the war.

Among other things, Shamir did not want to discourage immigration, which would fall off if Israel became directly involved in the war and began looking like a dangerous place.

But no one on the U.S. side was sure what Israel would do when it was attacked by Saddam, as was now certain to happen. Wolfowitz and Eagleburger tried to sound out the Israeli leadership. Shamir said that he naturally could not make promises about what Israel would do. No state could make such a pledge, particularly not Israel, with its long tradition of answering any and every terrorist incident. But he agreed to consult with the United States before acting, and promised it would not be just a perfunctory notification after the cabinet had decided to respond. It would be a genuine consultation. Shamir said he saw the advantages of staying out of a war, but the tried and tested principles of state survival might dictate unilateral action.

Eagleburger and Wolfowitz offered to improve Israel's defenses through an expansion of a deployment of U.S. Patriot missiles that was already under way. These ground-to-air anti-missile missiles could be used against Iraqi SCUDs. It was not a proven system, but it was the best system available. The Israelis were skeptical, but they agreed to accept the offer, which would eventually include U.S. operation and maintenance crews.

Bush had also authorized a special top-secret, secure, voice communications link between the Pentagon operations center and the Israeli Defense Force headquarters in Tel Aviv. U.S. personnel in Israel would monitor and operate the cryptographic equipment that was part of the system. Cheney would be able to plug into this secure line, given the codename HAMMER RICK, from his office. President Bush promised that Cheney would give the Israelis advance notice before any offensive operation was commenced. HAMMER RICK would also be used to pass the very latest and best intelligence to the Israelis about any possible attacks on Israel.

The system became operational on Sunday, January 13.

That night, Bush met with Cheney, Scowcroft and Powell at the White House residence. Baker was still traveling. Having made the crucial decisions, the group now just had to keep the operation on track. Schwarzkopf's preferred date and time for the attack, an H-Hour of 3 a.m. Saudi time on January 17, was still good. The question was when and how to make the necessary notifications to the allies and the Congress. Soon enough but not too soon, they agreed. An hour or two before the operation in most cases.

Cheney also reviewed the target list with the President, to make sure Bush was aware of potential points of controversy. He wanted Bush to be happy with all of it.

The President was concerned about one set of targets and asked that it be dropped. It included statues of Saddam and triumphal arches thought to be of great psychological value to the Iraqi people as national symbols.

.   .   .

On Monday morning, January 14, Cheney and Powell spent an hour in the STOC going over the targets for the air campaign one final time. Special task forces made up of hundreds of intelligence officers and planners had coordinated all the information—satellite photos, intercepted communications and anything else available—to make sure that a crippling blow would be dealt to Saddam's communications and air defenses in the first 24 hours. Thereafter, the air campaign would be a systematic juggernaut that would reduce the Iraqi war machine more each day.

Bush invited Air Force chief of staff McPeak, Cheney and Scowcroft for lunch that day in the White House residence. McPeak had just returned from 10 days in the Gulf visiting Air Force units, and Bush, a Navy pilot in World War II, wanted a firsthand account.

McPeak still felt that the operation could be done with much less force. He believed in air power as much as the departed General Dugan, and felt the other services had gone way overboard in their deployments. The Marines were too willing to build another Iwo Jima Memorial for their dead comrades. The Navy didn't need six aircraft carriers for the operation, and the Army certainly didn't need the VII Corps. Ground forces would be needed so someone could walk into Saddam's office with a bayonet and make him sign the surrender papers, but not for much more. But McPeak was keeping his mouth shut. He had quickly grasped Powell's doctrine of maximum force and was not arguing.

The Air Force chief told Bush that in order to satisfy himself about his own service's readiness, he had visited 16 of the air bases in the Gulf and gone out with the air crews in elaborate rehearsals over the Saudi desert. Routes had been created to duplicate the distances and conditions the air crews would encounter inside Iraq.

"These guys are ready to go," McPeak told Bush. "I've been out there. I've been flying with these guys. They are very good. They're peaked up." He said that if the President decided to launch the offense, his recommendation was to do it as soon after the January 15 deadline as possible. In the first weeks of the deployment in August, McPeak said, there had been lots of fighter pilot talk: "We're going to rip his head off" and so forth. Now there was no bravado. The pilots were calm and cool. It reminded him of the experienced gunfighters in the movie *Shane*, knowing there would be a shootout but not eager for it.

Bush wanted details.

I went out with a flight of four F-15s, McPeak explained. I flew in position number two, which is where they always put the weak guy. Carrying live 2,000-pound bombs, I flew six sorties. Combat conditions were duplicated. Radio silence. We flew in an armada with electronic jamming aircraft and tankers to refuel. It looked like the movie *Star Wars*.

The pilots could not withstand much more delay, he told Bush. Any substantial delay past tomorrow would really let the air out of their balloons psychologically, he said. It would be ruinous.

Congressional leaders were summoned later in the day to an urgent meeting at the White House. Asked when the United States would attack, Bush replied, "Sooner rather than later."

Late in the afternoon, Baker and Bob Kimmitt went to the Pentagon and spent an hour in the STOC reviewing the targets. Cheney wanted Baker to apply his political eye to the air campaign, to see if he spotted any unforeseen consequence. No other changes were made in the target lists.

. . .

Bush spoke with Baker by phone at 6:30 a.m. on Tuesday, January 15, then went for a solitary walk around the White House south lawn.

The President called two clergymen that morning. One was the head of Bush's own church, Bishop Edmond Browning, the presiding bishop of the Episcopal Church. Browning had led a peace vigil the night before outside the White House.

Bush also phoned the Senate chaplain, the Reverend Richard C. Halverson, who joined him in a prayer for the nation.

At 10:30 a.m. Bush met in the Oval Office with his inner council: Quayle, Baker, Cheney, Scowcroft, Powell, Sununu and Gates. Bush had the two-page draft of the top-secret National Security Directive (NSD) before him.

It had been modified to include two conditions. It now authorized the execution of Operation Desert Storm, provided that: (1) there was no last-minute diplomatic breakthrough, and (2) Congress had been properly notified. The document basically laid out the administration's case for launching the offensive soon after the deadline. It stated that it was the policy of the United States to get Iraq to leave Kuwait; all peaceful means, including diplomacy, economic sanctions and a dozen U.N. resolutions, had failed to persuade Iraq to withdraw; waiting would be potentially damaging to U.S. interests because Iraq was continuing to move additional forces into the Kuwaiti theater of operations, and was improving its fortifications in occupied Kuwait; Iraq continued to pillage Kuwait and brutalize its people; Iraq's military had to be attacked in order to defend U.S. and allied forces. It also directed that civilian casualties and damage to Iraq should be minimized consistent with protecting friendly forces, and that Islamic holy places should be protected.

The President signed it. The NSD was intentionally not dated. The date and time would be added when and if the two conditions were met.

Bush authorized Cheney to sign a formal execute order and send it to Schwarzkopf that day.

Cheney went to have lunch with the Senate Republicans. At a separate meeting with Democratic senators, he was asked, "When the deadline expires, are you going to wait or will you move fairly rapidly?"

Operational security was foremost in Cheney's mind, but he did not want to mislead them. "Sooner rather than later," he replied, using the phrase Bush had used the day before in speaking to congressional leaders.

By 5 p.m., Cheney was back in his office. Powell arrived with a top-secret folder containing the execute order. The Chairman had written it out himself. He went over it with Cheney. An orange cover sheet explained that the order was authorizing Schwarzkopf to execute Desert Storm pursuant to the warning order of December 29.

If it had been a normal execute order, Cheney would have just initialed a block on the front to indicate he had approved it. Powell would then formally release it, under his authority to transmit communications between the Secretary and the CINC.

But both men knew this was a historic document. They signed their full names.

Powell had a copy faxed "Eyes Only" to Schwarzkopf on the top-secret fax circuit. In about 26 hours, Operation Desert Shield was to become Desert Storm.

Until now, Powell had kept the decision secret from his staff. Now he called Tom Kelly in. The war begins tomorrow night, Powell said. Kelly, the former journalism major, would be the daily briefing officer for the press at the Pentagon, as he had been for the Panama operation. There was no telling how many daily briefings might be required. Answer questions but don't make any news, Powell instructed him.

Yes, sir, Kelly said. Though Kelly had not known for sure, he had become convinced over the last several weeks that there would be a war. The intelligence showed that Saddam was preparing. He was still extending his fortifications, digging in, sending in more troops. There was more oil in the Iraqi trenches for burning American tanks, more barbed wire, more mines, more bunkers. Kelly was amazed by Saddam's apparent expectations. He seemed to think that the United States planned to let this become another Iran-Iraq War, with two ignorant armies throwing themselves directly into each other's defenses for eight years. Imagine, Kelly thought, what Saddam and his generals would think if they glanced at the unclassified U.S. Army operations manual, with its emphasis on maneuver warfare.

Kelly was astonished at the calm in the Pentagon. The Panama operation had seemed more chaotic to him. There was one similarity to Panama, however. Even with the months of preparation and the uncountable advantages of the U.S. and coalition forces, he was still not sure there wouldn't be a screw-up. The old fear of failure had taken hold.

Prince Bandar came to visit Cheney that afternoon.

"Any word?" Bandar asked. "Are we days or weeks away?"

Cheney smiled obliquely. It looks like a good week, he said.

Bandar took this to mean soon, but as he later went over the conversation he could not be sure.

. . .

After many meetings and consultations with the news media, Pete Williams that day released the ground rules for reporters in the event of hostilities in the Persian Gulf. The 12 rules, listed on a single page, banned publication or broadcast of specific information the department wanted kept secret, including numbers of troops, aircraft, weapons, equipment and supplies; future plans and operations; locations of forces; and tactics. All combat reporting would be done by groups of reporters in pools, whose work would be subject to security review before it was released. No reporters would be allowed to rove freely in combat zones as they had in Vietnam.

Kelly marveled at how Powell had controlled his piece of Desert Shield, the military planning and decision making. Much of the real business not done at White House meetings was conducted on "the magic telephone," the latest generation of secure telephone. It linked only the President, the Vice President, Scowcroft, Sununu, Baker, Cheney, Powell and the CINCs, including Schwarzkopf. Powell's big white console hooking him into this loop sat prominently on his office credenza. He made extensive use of it, ensuring that he was the military's point man in Washington with the civilians. Using his own "magic" extension, Schwarzkopf played the same role in Saudi Arabia.

To avoid a repeat of the military's Vietnam nightmare—President Lyndon Johnson leaning over maps in the White House, circling specific targets—Powell had kept as much air-targeting information as possible out of Washington. The most up-to-date target list for the first day's air strike was not even available to Kelly or his staff. Kelly had been told he would receive it the day after, with reports on what had happened. And the daily air-tasking orders, laying out all the planned air strikes, were not going to come to Washington in advance.

Powell had used the service chiefs quite effectively, Kelly thought. He kept them informed so they did not feel out of it, but in fact they played almost no role in the decision making. Their influence hovered somewhere around zero, Kelly thought.

General Vuono had helped in one sense, making sure that Schwarzkopf had the latest equipment. Sometimes it had to be forced on him. Vuono had insisted that more than 1,000 of the latest modernized tank, the M-1A1, be sent to the Army units that had already been deployed without this state-of-the-art model. Schwarzkopf had at first resisted because he wanted to avoid the disruption of switching to new equipment that the troops would have to learn to use. But the new tanks improved combat effectiveness and the confidence of the soldiers. The effective range of the M-1A1 was about double that of the best Iraqi T-72 tank. It would make the United States like a boxer with a six-foot arm. Schwarzkopf agreed to take the tanks.

The Army chief had also pushed Schwarzkopf to accept a surveillance system called J-STARS (Joint Surveillance Target Attack Radar System). Brand new and untested in battle, J-STARS detected the movements of tanks and other ground vehicles, covering the ground the way AWACS planes covered the air. The two J-STARS units sent to Schwarzkopf provided a full ground radar picture of the terrain 100 miles into Kuwait and Iraq, virtually guaranteeing that the U.S. forces could not be surprised or outmaneuvered at the front by the Iraqis.

·   ·   ·

The next morning, January 16, before going into the Pentagon, Cheney packed a suitcase. He expected to spend several nights in his office. So as not to tip off his driver and security people, he decided to leave the packed bag at home. He could dispatch his driver for it as H-Hour approached.

By the time Cheney arrived at the office, B-52 bombers had been launched from Barksdale Air Force Base in Louisiana, flying to the Gulf. They were to be refueled in flight during the 18 hours it would take them to reach their targets. These planes could be recalled. The decision had not yet reached the point of no return.

Cheney had cleared his schedule, pushing budget and other matters to his deputy, Don Atwood. He picked up the hand-held remote-control unit for the television in his office and clicked it to CNN. He thought the first leak or hint that the air operation was under way would most likely come from the 24-hour news service.

The Secretary wondered how well the U.S. forces would perform. At what cost? At what casualty level? He had received the estimates produced by various computer models, but he had concluded they were no more than guesses. There was no knot in his stomach. It was out of his hands.

.   .   .

That morning Baker summoned Bandar to the State Department to say it was a go that night: 7 p.m. here, 3 a.m. in Saudi Arabia.

Bandar called King Fahd. After they'd chatted for a few moments, Bandar, trying to make it sound like an afterthought, said, "Our old friend Suleiman is coming at 3 a.m. He's sick and I'll ship him out, and he'll get there at 3 a.m."

Bandar was amazed that it looked like the U.S. and the coalition forces were going to be able to achieve surprise. The reason, he concluded, was probably that the message to Saddam had been so mixed and confused over the months. George Bush apparently had been unreadable to Saddam. The ironic truth, Bandar felt, was that the war had been sealed by cultural misunderstanding.

At 4:50 p.m., the first F-15 Eagles were taking off for their targets. They too could be recalled. Air-refueling tankers were up. More and more of the air war was moving toward the brink. Cheney saw that no one in the press was picking up on it. The news reporters were so bottled up by the rules, and there had been so much air activity over the previous months, that it all looked routine.

The White House had assigned Cheney the responsibility of keeping the Israelis plugged in, but not so plugged in as to make them de facto members of the coalition. It was a delicate assignment. Saddam had promised to attack Israel in some way if the coalition attacked him, and the Israelis were entitled to a warning. But any Israeli participation in the war would have negative reverberations in the Arab world, and might weaken the coalition. At around 5 p.m., Cheney picked up the HAMMER RICK line, to call Israeli Defense Minister Moshe Arens with the first notification that the offensive was being launched.

. . .

At precisely 5:30 the U.S.S. *Bunker Hill*, an Aegis-class cruiser in the Persian Gulf, fired a Tomahawk missile to its designated target inside Iraq. This unmanned cruise missile could not be recalled. There was no turning back now.

About 20 Tomahawks were preprogrammed to hit Saddam's presidential palace, the main telephone exchange and Baghdad's electrical power-generating stations at H-Hour. Nine U.S. Navy ships were assigned to fire 106 Tomahawks in the first 24 hours of the war. Since the missile had never been used in combat, there were Air Force bombers assigned as back-ups for all the Tomahawk targets. The air campaign would involve more than 1,000 sorties in the first 24 hours, and expand after that.

At 5:31 the U.S.S. *Wisconsin* launched its first Tomahawk.

An intelligence unit embarked on the *Wisconsin* dispatched a report of the firing on the military's CRITIC emergency alert system, designed to send out a flash message whenever there were "strong indications of the imminent outbreak of hostilities of any type." CRITIC was created to make sure all U.S. forces worldwide would receive the earliest alert of possible hostilities, especially an attack by the Soviet Union. The message overrode all other message traffic, automatically ringing bells on teletype machines at thousands of commands worldwide.

"Why did those dumb bastards do that?" Kelly said. "The Navy did it again." He notified Powell at once.

My God, Powell thought, we are going to blow operational security on ourselves.

The *Wisconsin* was ordered to cancel the message. The cancelation message went out with equal speed. Military men and women throughout the world know that the first report on any incident is frequently wrong, so no one had jumped to conclusions. Operational security held.

Cheney and Powell ordered that the CRITIC system be temporarily disconnected. Powell tried to find out who had been stupid enough to activate it, so he could disconnect them.

Cheney continued to watch CNN. Anchorman Bernard Shaw was in Baghdad interviewing former CBS anchorman Walter Cronkite in New York about covering wars. Cronkite was reminiscing about his experiences going back to World War II. Shaw explained that he had gone to Baghdad to interview Saddam, but the interview had not worked out and therefore he was leaving on a flight the next afternoon.

There weren't going to be any flights out the next afternoon, Cheney knew. He felt a strange sensation watching this conversation, knowing that hundreds of attack missions were heading for Kuwait and Iraq, unbeknownst to the media and almost all Americans.

As H-Hour approached, the Secretary sent his driver to McLean for his suitcase. Someone in the office was dispatched for Chinese food.

25

P

OWELL DID NOT WANT TO KEEP A DEATHWATCH down in the operations center. He felt that's what they had done during the Panama invasion as Cheney and he had taken up positions of command at the center table. Now Cheney was upstairs in his office. Powell was staying in his office for the hour or so before 7 p.m.

He sat down in his large maroon leather executive chair. He was alone. In his last conversation with Schwarzkopf earlier that day on the secure phone, Powell had said, "Good luck, Norm." The White House seemed satisfied.

As in Panama, Powell felt he had adequately prepared President Bush. Bad things are going to happen, Mr. President, Powell had said. There will be bad news, things will blow up in our faces. You'll be very tempted to get hands-on, to try to fix problems yourself. You'll collect scar tissue and people will be kicking you around on television. This is going to take a while, and the more you can leave us alone to work our way through it as military professionals, the better it will be.

Despite all the firepower, anticipated swiftness and violence,

Powell had worked hard with Schwarzkopf to make sure the offense showed some restraint. Collateral damage had to be minimized. Of the half dozen bridges inside the Baghdad city limits, the air campaign was, at Powell's urging, only going to hit two. Four would be left standing. Powell was convinced that it would not be in the U.S. interest to have a totally defeated Iraq with no capability to defend itself. So some of the Iraqi tanks and military would have to be left intact. Baker had been briefed. Cheney's questions had been answered. Powell's Joint Staff was calm. The chiefs—"the six brothers," as he had come to call them—were all in agreement.

Powell's rule number 8 was "Check small things." There were none left. The minutes ticked by. He found himself mentally reviewing the specifics from the air-war target list. Is that a good target? Is that a bad target? Should we have a Tomahawk or an F-15E on that? Or both? Or none? The targets had been worked and reworked, he knew. He had to stop.

This is the end, he realized. Metaphors of gambling went through his mind. Poker. It was high stakes. They were using all their advantages—technology, superior intelligence, a plan that looked and sounded nearly perfect. All the odds were on his side. Almost a sure thing; but still, as in poker, he knew there was uncertainty.

Craps. The country was at the table and the dice had been thrown. This was the moment of waiting, the dice in midair. Soon they would hit the cloth and arrive at the far end, crash and come abruptly to rest.

Pool. He had written out and tucked underneath the glass on his desk a line from the movie *The Hustler:* "Fast Eddie, let's shoot some pool." It was the moment of confrontation.

"Never let them see you sweat," was another aphorism he had placed under the glass.

In this moment, however, he was sweating. Saddam could still pull a stunt of some kind. In several minutes, the Iraqi leader could flash some message of capitulation and possibly derail the entire operation. Powell remained convinced that Saddam did not, could not, should not want war. Saddam had misread American resolve, and he certainly did not comprehend the magnitude of what was about to hit him.

How could we be maintaining operational security? Powell wondered. They had grown very good at keeping secrets. But how good? Maybe the operation was blown? Unlikely to impossible, but there was no telling for sure.

Powell expected the air campaign to last about three weeks. After that, the coalition would have to seize the initiative from Saddam. The ground war was inevitable. At the thought of a ground war, he found himself worrying about the Marines. They would have the hard job, driving into the front-line fortifications. God, Powell thought, we could lose a lot of Marines. The Army, with its large flanking operation, was going to be safer.

He would have thought this would be the most important day of his life. More than 32 years in the Army and he was the top military man on the eve of a big war. But the day was falling short. The old Robert E. Lee quote went through his head: "It is well that war is so terrible, or we should grow too fond of it." Lee had been watching the slaughter of enemy Union troops at Fredericksburg in 1862. How the military loved the preparation for war. From the Pentagon, war at times looked like a great game. If people were not going to die, it would be great fun, Powell thought. He had to remind himself constantly that this was real, not a game. The public and the world were going to see an incredibly limited and antiseptic version of the war. The media were going to be kept away. Even the videos from the gun cameras in the bombers showing the attacks were going to be distortions when they were made public. The audio would be edited out in most cases so the pilots' nervous yells of "Holy shit!" or whatever would be excised. The distinctive, rapid-fire hyperventilation of the pilots feeling the pressure of their G-suits and the terror of combat would not be heard by the public.

He thought of the troops and pilots as kids, even teenagers. They would be flying in the darkness or dropping down behind the lines to spot targets. It would come down to one American kid dealing with one Iraqi kid. Both would want to live.

Powell felt a foreboding and a chill. The war was in the hands of these kids. And if they screwed up, it would mean that Powell and the generals—the adults—hadn't done their jobs well enough. That was as it should be.

It would be hours before Powell would learn what happened. Schwarzkopf was in charge of the battlefield. Informing Washington was not going to be his top priority.

Powell was still alone. It remained quiet in the Chairman's office. No one knew or had any real idea how many Americans would die in the war, he realized. Some of the senior officers on the Joint Staff had confidentially estimated that the killed in action on the American side would be about 1,000. But there was no hard estimate. Of course it could be more. He knew they would lose some. He was hoping it would not be a lot.

On this most important day of his life, he had one overriding thought. There was no cheering, no thrill, no eagerness, no battle fever. None of the emotions of war raged. He thought only one thing: "How many will not come back?"

Over the border inside Iraq, it was nearly 3 a.m. A U.S. Army Apache helicopter was 12 kilometers from the electrical power-generating station at an Iraqi air defense radar site protecting Baghdad. This was going to be the first target of the war. The pilot could see the building on his Forward-Looking Infrared Sensor, a tiny dancing square on the horizon. His equipment showed that the time of flight for his Hellfire missile to the target was 20 seconds. He launched. "This one's for you, Saddam," he said. The equipment ticked off the seconds and on the screen he could see the Hellfire come in over the building and descend like a rock. The tiny square became an explosion, suddenly and quietly filling his radar screen.

In the White House, Bush, Quayle, Scowcroft and Sununu gathered in the small private study adjacent to the Oval Office to watch television. When the sounds of bombing could be heard behind the voices of the reporters still in their Baghdad hotel rooms, Bush, visibly relieved, said, "Just the way it was scheduled."

The Gulf War lasted 42 days. The three air phases took 38 days. The ground war took four days before Bush declared a cease-fire. The U.S. and coalition forces overran Kuwait and southern Iraq, destroyed Saddam's army, routed the Republican Guard, dictated the terms of peace, and killed tens of thousands of Iraqis. Kuwait was liberated. American casualties were seven missing in action and 137 killed in action.

Acknowledgments

Richard E. Snyder, the chairman of Simon & Schuster Inc., has faithfully backed all my books. This, my sixth, was his idea. In 1987, he suggested a book on the Pentagon and Joint Chiefs of Staff, saying that the American military was probably the institution that was both the most powerful and the least understood in the country. I had always wanted to write about the military and we soon agreed it would be my next book. Over the next four years he gave me all the support he promised. That's unusual in any relationship, and I thank him for that and for his continuing friendship.

Benjamin C. Bradlee and Leonard Downie, Jr., the two top editors at *The Washington Post,* generously gave me the time I needed. This project was repeatedly extended as military operations, deployments and wars overwhelmed me. These two editors, the best in the business, support intense and neutral inquiry. The latitude they granted me allowed me to better understand the military and the Bush administration. Deputy Managing Editor Robert G. Kaiser offered his usual thoughtful, tough reading of the manuscript. Steve Luxenberg, the deputy projects editor and one of the most caring people practicing journalism today, did both my job and his at the *Post*. I owe him much. Lucy Shackelford, master researcher at the *Post*, is owed a thousand thanks. So is the staff of the *Post* library, which is always there to help. The *Post* photo department and the White House photo office helped on many occasions.

David Hume Kennerly, the White House photographer to President Gerald Ford, supplied the best pictures of Dick Cheney and Colin Powell that I've ever seen. Kennerly is an artist.

Though nearly all the information in this book is based on my own reporting, I also used hundreds of newspaper and magazine articles. The Pentagon's daily *Early Bird*, normally 14 to 16 pages of newspaper clippings reprinted each morning, is one of the best, most sophisticated packages of information put out. The *Early Bird* staff has an extraordinary eye for news.

The Washington Post, The New York Times, The Los Angeles Times and *The Wall Street Journal* cover military and foreign policy so well and thoroughly they not only present the news but frame the debate. I have relied on them frequently. Much gratitude to *Post* colleagues Rick Atkinson, David Hoffman, Jim Hoagland, Barton Gellman, Molly Moore, Ann Devroy, Dan Balz, George Wilson, R. Jeffrey Smith, Walter Pincus, Don Oberdorfer, Al Kamen and dozens of others. I give extra appreciation to Michael Getler, David Ignatius and their team of extraordinary foreign correspondents, who have done such spectacular work over the last two years. No one can attempt to write about the Pentagon or military affairs and not acknowledge the exceptional work of Patrick E. Tyler, Michael Gordon, R. W. Apple, Jr., and others of *The New York Times*.

Television news assisted me greatly. Pentagon reporters such as Fred Francis of NBC, David Martin of CBS and Bob Zelnick of ABC often have the story first. Any examination of the news coverage of recent military crises would show how serious and comprehensive their work is. Someday these reporters will receive the credit they deserve. The Public Broadcasting Service's *MacNeil/Lehrer NewsHour* offered the most in-depth forum for discussion of the recent military actions.

At Simon & Schuster, I extend my appreciation to Adelle-Marie Stan, Sophie Sorkin, Marcia Peterson, Eve Metz and Frank Metz. To Ann Adelman, gratitude for her careful, discerning copyediting.

Alice Mayhew, my editor at Simon & Schuster, helped immeasurably with the concepts, tone, language and clarity. She found many pages that needed to be cut or tightened as her variously colored pens marched through the manuscript time and time again. My affection and esteem to her.

Robert B. Barnett, agent and lawyer extraordinaire, was guide and counselor in a manner that would make Ed Williams proud.

Tali, my terrific daughter, is also one of my best friends. She, too, urged that I do a book on the military and provided much encouragement. Thanks to Rosa Castillo, who fed and cared for Bill, Marc and myself.

My greatest thanks go to the hundreds of sources. By the end, some were very unhappy to hear from me with one more request for more information. There are many special people in the Pentagon and elsewhere, high and low in rank, who gave me their time and trust. They know who they are. Most must go unnamed and unidentified. Extra thanks to the many able people in Pentagon public affairs, particularly those in the offices of Pentagon spokesman Pete Williams and JCS spokesman Colonel William Smullen.

My wife, Elsa Walsh, gave daily personal and professional sustenance. A procession of interview notes, chapter drafts and my doubts were delivered to her at the end of her own work day, on weekends, and even vacations. Cheerfully and critically, she examined and helped me revise and understand. She has brought balance to my life.

Index

PHOTO CREDITS

PEACEFUL
WEIGHT LOSS
THROUGH YOGA

by Brandt Bhanu Passalacqua

It would be impossible to thank everyone who helped me with this book. That being said, I would like to acknowledge a few folks.

Donna and Melissa for modeling. Mike and Hope for work on the video. Annie for her proofreading. Mukunda Stiles for letting me use his work, and for his teaching. Integral Yoga Institute for existing. Mom for always being there for me.

And finally, Eva, my editor, graphic designer, illustrator, cooking expert, support system, and wife. Without you this book wouldn't have been possible.

TABLE OF CONTENTS

> Peace is your
> own true
> nature.
>
> Swami Satchidananda

introduction

You are probably reading this because you think you need to lose weight. If you ask most people if they are the "right" weight, they will say *no*.

But how do we know when we are the perfect weight? Can we refer to a chart, or the bathroom scale? You may not like what you see in the mirror. Maybe you think you should be the same weight you were 20 years ago.

The fact is, there is only one reliable source to tell you how much you should weigh. You have an inner voice, an internal system, that will determine your optimal weight – and how to get there. We are all born with this voice. We all still have it, but it gets obscured by the stresses of life.

What causes us to be heavier than we think we should be? Stress, poor diet, lack of exercise, lack of sleep, physical ailments, self-criticism – all these factors contribute. They all interfere with our body's natural internal systems.

How will you know when you are the ideal weight? Your body will tell you. But you need to be able to hear it!

Why yoga for weight loss?

With so many diets and exercise programs in this world, why choose to take up yoga?

Yoga is different from other options because it is NOT a weight loss plan...which is its strength – most weight loss options don't work for most people in the long run.

Yoga addresses our relationship with our body, our mind, and our spiritual selves. It cuts through the fads, diets, exercise plans, and pills, and gets to the core. The same concepts that have led yogis and yoginis towards peace for thousands of years will help you to achieve a weight that is comfortable for you.

Everyone can do yoga.

A yoga practice is a pleasant addition to your life. You don't need natural ability, a lot of flexibility, or a lot of strength to develop a regular yoga practice. Unlike other exercise options, you need very little skill.

Everyone's abilities and needs are different. The full benefits of your yoga practice come from working at your own pace and skill level. At the heart of asana practice is movement and breath. As long as you can breathe, you can do yoga.

What can we learn from regular yoga practice?

Asana practice, (the physical practice of yoga), addresses your physical, mental, and spiritual aspects. By performing asana regularly, our minds and bodies begin to help each other. In this physical practice we use our bodies to practice skills that we will use in day-to-day life.

An easy, comfortable, steady yoga practice will not only bring you to a perfect weight. You will feel lighter in general. Your physicality will become easier, your relationships will become smoother, your day-to-day life will be better. You will be more relaxed, more aware of your actions, stronger-willed, steadier.

Yoga helps eliminate stress.

Breathing, relaxation, and asana practice in yoga all help us eliminate stress. There is a biological link between stress and weight: the hormones produced by stress have been shown to increase appetite and fat deposits. And, for many of us, stress can lead to emotional eating.

Regular yoga practice can reduce not only immediate stress, but your overall stress level. Asana practice is a direct way to get at our other issues. As our body tenses, so does our mind. As our body relaxes, so does our mind. As our body releases tension, our emotional life becomes less intense.

Your body will work with you.

If your goal is to be healthy and happy, yoga is a perfect choice. Yoga encourages our entire body, all our systems – including our minds – to work together, in harmony, to their true potential. As your body becomes more in sync, your metabolism will function better. You will allow your internal systems to regulate your weight.

Many weight loss systems have us eating by their fixed plan, and exercising to burn more than we eat. Yoga helps us eat the right amount of food and burn it efficiently.

Most of us have been taught that if we exercise, we will burn off fat. While vigorous exercise does burn calories, it will not make you healthy, happy, and the perfect weight. *You are what you do.* Going to the gym makes you good at going to the gym. A daily yoga practice makes you a healthy, peaceful human being.

Cultivating awareness

By working with our bodies, we practice being aware. How much of the day do we spend acting unconsciously? How much food did you eat last week that you didn't enjoy every bite? The practice of cultivating awareness of your body will translate to the rest of your life. As you become more aware of your physical self, your internal world will be easier to access. It will be easier to have awareness of your physical and emotional state.

Learning self-discipline

Okay – I admit it. It does take some effort. But again, asana practice is a great arena in which to try out self-discipline. As you learn to be friends with your body, you will find that it becomes harder to do things that are bad for it. Walking by the bakery becomes easier. As you practice keeping steady postures, you'll get used to owning your mind.

Long-term steady practice

Yoga will improve your experience of each and every day. It's an easy addition to your life. Once you find your regular practice, it will be hard to quit.

Unlike short-term diet and exercise plans, yoga will bring long-term results through sensible, gradual change. You will come to understand that you are perfect; and, given the chance, your physical self will find its ideal weight.

Regular yoga practice helps your physical, emotional, and spiritual lives connect to each other. It can be your port in a storm of emotional turmoil, and a beacon to bring joy to your life. For thousands of years, people have been using yoga practice to find the beautiful light within themselves.

my story

At 30, I found myself with a potentially fatal autoimmune disease, overweight, and confused.

At my peak I was 100 pounds heavier than I am now. I had gained the weight slowly over ten years or so. I've always loved food, but I was disconnected from how it made me feel. And, looking back, I had many obsessive food behaviors. I ate when I was happy, depressed, bored...

I'd eat cheese as a snack before going to bed and wondered why I burped so much.
I drank a lot of coffee and twitched in my sleep.
I ate a lot. Some good food, some bad.
I tried to lose weight through exercise – I ran 4 times a week while smoking 3-4 packs of cigarettes a day.
My weight bobbed up and down.
My knees hurt.

My illness landed me in the hospital for a couple of weeks, followed by several months of recovery. My near-death experience highlighted my need for a spiritual life – at the time, I had none. My legs were weak, and I was completely out of shape. I needed to do something. I was grateful for being alive and wanted to continue that condition.

My girlfriend (now my wife) suggested I go to a yoga class with her – so I went. I had no real desire – no expectations for myself. The only thing I had on my mind was that a lot of women did yoga, so I would probably be out of place. I didn't know it at the time, but I was completely unattached to the result. I just did it.

It was fantastic.

I started doing yoga regularly and really felt it was changing me. I started to eat differently. Gained the willpower I had been lacking. As my body became more easeful, the weight fell into place.

My stress level lowered. How stressed had I been, anyway? I think I was in a constant state of stress.

I was not doing a strenuous practice. But I did it every single day. I have to admit – I thought that's what everyone did. Like music lessons: I would go to class, learn some things, then try them at home. I didn't realize this wasn't always the case. Also, I wasn't a "natural." I couldn't sit comfortably. I had no range of motion. Things others did effortlessly, I considered impossible. But I did the yoga anyway.

I put myself on a new eating regimen which progressed all the time. Got addicted to various foods, and unaddicted again. This time there was a difference. I was aware of it. By practicing yoga every day the awareness came. The desire for awareness came, too. I wanted to know more and more about food. How much and what did I really need to eat?

The pounds came off. My diet evolved into this beautiful thing. I got rid of most of my addictive behavior. I enjoyed my practice. I got into my spiritual self through reading and meditation. Just bowing at the end of my practice and thanking the universe for letting me be alive changed me.

Awareness of more subtle aspects of my health and nature continue to reveal themselves to me. A taste of peace can effect your entire self. Developing a regular practice gave me that. That is how I lost the weight.

Now I continue on my path, sharing the little I have discovered with others and trying to continue uncovering myself. I still have my food weaknesses. I still eat too much sometimes. I still stress sometimes – but it feels different from before.

Brandt Bhanu Passalacqua, RYT, is a private food coach and a certified hatha yoga teacher registered with the Yoga Alliance. After struggling with weight, food and substance addiction, and serious illness, he found his way to an easeful restorative yoga practice. He has lost 100 pounds and maintained his health by being kind to his body. He currently has a practice teaching yoga for weight loss and wellness in New York City.

how to use this book

This book is not intended as a diet or exercise plan like others you may have seen. You will not be cutting off foods for six months to lose 20 pounds, or doing hours of heavy exercise to "feel the burn." This book will help you develop new, energy-enhancing, weight-optimizing patterns for your life.

It's best to bring as few preconceived notions to this process as possible. You have information – from previous diets and exercise plans, your parents, infomercials – all these things need to be put to the side for a little while so you can focus on changing your eating and lifestyle patterns in a permanent, healthy way.

You will be finding out what is absolutely right for your body, mind, and spirit. You are a unique individual; "cookie cutter" information won't help you in this process. And be honest, whatever you've done before hasn't worked for you. Be happy that this doesn't feel the same.

This book is divided into
six main sections:

The first three sections contain the concepts that you will be working with.

- **The Four Points** examines the basic ideas you will be working with to transform yourself. Each chapter contains some exercises to help you begin to apply these concepts.

- **Your Daily Yoga Practice** will help you to set up a daily asana practice and integrate it into your life.

- **What and How to Eat** contains the principles that will guide you toward your optimal eating practice.

The next two sections are systems which you may choose to follow to help you apply these principles. Whether or not you choose to follow the systems exactly as written, they contain many tools that you may find useful.

- **Developing Your Daily Yoga Practice** is a week-by-week guide to developing your asana, meditation, and relaxation practice.

- **Developing Your Eating Practice** is a step-by-step guide to food practice, including specific exercises and worksheets.

Finally, this book also contains **A Guide to the Asanas** which provides drawings and written instructions for the asanas, as well as points of focus for each pose.

ONE WAY TO USE THIS BOOK:

I suggest you start by developing your yoga practice. Start by reading "Your Daily Yoga Practice" (page 47) to set yourself up to begin. Then move to "Developing Your Daily Yoga Practice" (page 79). In this system you will be learning the asanas and beginning to apply the four points, which include some preliminary eating exercises.

Now that your regular yoga practice is in place, it will be time to start on food. The system outlined in "Developing Your Daily Yoga Practice" will guide you on the correct time to begin working with your eating practice.

Start to work on your eating practice by reading "What and How to Eat" (page 53). Then you can work through the food system ("Developing Your Eating Practice" page 85), while deepening your asana practice.

Once you have worked through these steps, you will be well on your way to a peaceful relationship with your physical, mental, and spiritual self. You may then refer back to any or all of these steps as tools to stay on your personal path of transformation.

You will be using this book to develop a steady yoga practice that promotes health, energy, and awareness. This includes developing a steady eating practice that brings you vitality and supports your natural, perfect self. Remember, your asana practice and food work will support each other. Developing a yoga practice will help you change your eating patterns. As you eat differently it will support your yoga practice.

A final note before you begin:

Having gone through this process, I know how challenging it can be. Everyone is different; you will find some parts of the process more challenging than others. You will undoubtedly encounter setbacks along the way. Please remember this: these setbacks are part of the process. They are not "wrong," or a sign of failure, in any way. Learn from them and come back to the practice. Your new yoga practice will always be there for you.

> Your body is a tool
> to deepen your
> understanding of yourself.
>
> And deepening these
> premises in your mind will
> affect your body.

an introduction
to the four points

As my personal yoga practice has evolved, several themes or ideas have recurred over and over. As I examined why and how yoga helped me to lose weight, these points came up again.

The steadiness I found in asana practice had moved into my eating patterns. As I gained physical benefits through effort, it strengthened my resolve to eat well. I became aware of my mind's ability to be lazy – to distract me in asana. I then noticed my unconscious eating patterns – my mind misbehaving, distracting me, convincing me I needed to snack. As I learned to let go of physical tension, my anxiety level decreased, and I let go of many unhelpful eating habits.

These chapters contain four points that we can focus on. Working with these concepts will help you to apply the lessons learned in asana to your food and eating patterns.

- Letting go
- Awareness
- Effort
- A steady comfortable pose

So work with these ideas. It's the work that matters more than the result. It is unlikely we will ever master or finish them!

Each point has its roots in classical yoga texts. I've distilled them for our weight-optimizing purposes, but I highly recommend looking more into the philosophy behind them.

I suggest reading the Yoga Sutras of Patanjali. *Written between 200 BC and 300 AD, these terse verses provide guidance along the yogic path. There are many excellent translations and commentaries available. I have found books by Swami Satchidananda, B.K.S. Iyengar, and Mukunda Stiles all useful.*

Visit my website at **peacefulweightloss.com** *for more information, or use the resources list on page 171.*

Yoga Pose is mastered
by relaxation of effort,
lessening the tendency for restless breathing,
and promoting an identification of oneself
as living
within
the infinite breath of life.

sutra 2-47
Translation by Mukunda Stiles

letting go

Let all of your preconceptions go.

By letting go, we begin the process of finding ourselves. We are going to peel away the layers covering our true self. You probably have ideas about the weight you'd like to be, or the body type you'd like to have. Your first step is to release these thoughts from your mind. Other people's ideas of what you should look like are not relevant. Our own distorted ideas of what we should look like have no place here. Your body knows its ideal weight. It's in there. We are going to access it.

Let go of your stress.

Stress is directly related to our eating habits, our weight, and the way we view our bodies. Many of us play out our stress with eating – we eat when we're nervous; when we're under emotional strain.

Stress also makes your body retain fat. When we are stressed, our bodies release hormones which suppress our appetite – then make us incredibly hungry – and then store fat for the next stressful time.

If you become less stressed, your body will not enter these cycles, and you'll have an easier time losing weight.

Stress and Yoga

But what is stress? Is it mental or physical? I believe it's both. We all retain stress in our bodies – our jaw, our shoulders, our stomach – anywhere. During yoga practice, relaxing your tensed jaw or dropping your clenched shoulders will send signals to your mind to relax. **These things are connected.**

Regular yoga practice will help you get used to being more relaxed. You don't have to do a lot of yoga. I noticed changes immediately from short sessions and regular practice. Don't worry about how long, how short, how intense your yoga practice is. Just do something. Think of little. The asana practice will relax your body and mind. All you need to do is show up.

When we go to exercise, we must do so holistically. The first step in this process is to let go of goals and desires – and concentrate on the task at hand. Do the asanas (yoga postures) in the present moment. With a clear calm attitude. The asanas have been used for thousands of years to balance and rejuvenate the energy already present in your body. Trust in the experience of the yogis and yoginis before you and allow yourself to move through the practice supported by them.

In each asana we have a golden opportunity to relax. We may come into a yoga session or individual posture with an idea of how it "should be." The first lesson is to let go. Find the pose and relax into it. That's impossible, you may say. Of course, we don't slump onto the floor in a ball. But we can relax parts of ourselves that have no need to work.

This is an amazing lesson. How much energy do you use in yourself while going about your daily tasks? Are your shoulders hunched while you ride the train? Are you worrying about work while trying to sleep?

Let go of everything.

This applies to eating, dieting, and weight loss in general. Once you have a taste of letting go, try to extend this to all aspects of your life. Take the goals you have about losing a certain amount of weight this week, next week, next month – and let them go.

Do your asanas. Relax as much as possible. Eat well. You only have one goal: to be peaceful and happy.

Letting go around food in your daily life

Think about eating the same way. Am I feeling good while I'm eating? Am I calm and happy while eating? If not, stop and wait until you are. Try breathing to get you there. Try changing your facial expression. Try meditating for one minute (see page 158). Don't ponder all the nutritional aspects of the food you're eating. Focus on your calm state of mind. Your attitude. There is no result from your eating. Just eat – be in the present; let go of desire.

Meal times should be calm and joyful. This will support your body in digesting properly. Make time to eat. Eating, like your yoga practice, should have some ritual around it. Respect it.

A little can do a lot.

Try just this for a little while. Regular asana practice. Eating in calm, relaxing situations. Eating foods that make you feel relaxed and well. Eating until you are full but not stuffed. Have faith – remind yourself every day that a happy mind is a happy body, and vice versa.

Your body has its own rhythms, and relaxing will help you find them. Smile as you do your yoga practice every day. Go nice and easy – you are not in a rush.

SUGGESTIONS FOR LETTING GO

• Do an easy asana practice every day. Follow the hints for letting go. Don't worry about doing it correctly or perfectly. Have fun doing your short practice. Don't work hard! Have fun learning.

• Do yoga nidra every day if you can (see page 155). Give your nervous system a break at least once a day!

• Don't weigh yourself.

• Eat in calm, relaxing situations. If possible, eat alone or with people you like.

• Don't worry about what or how much you are eating. Just try to eat foods that make you feel relaxed and well.

• Before you eat, smile and meditate on your breath for a minute, or take a few three-part breaths (see page 115). Also, pause for a moment before taking second helpings. This recentering will bring you into the present moment and allow you to access your body's wisdom.

• Remember to do things you find relaxing (take in a movie, walk in the park, get a massage). Make time for yourself. Don't overschedule.

• Meditate 2 or 3 minutes a day with a timer (see page 158).

> Awareness,
> like a flame,
> reveals the essence
> of truth.
>
> David Frawley
> *Vedantic Meditation*

awareness

Training yourself to be aware

Are we aware of our actions? How we feel? Most of the time, we're not. Our mind is constantly filtering information. We can be uncomfortable, or in pain – but if we are not aware of it, we don't change the things that cause the pain or discomfort. We need to train our mind to be more aware. The more aware we are, the richer our experience of life will be.

Our body is set up to tell us exactly what to do to be the perfect weight. It is a complex, beautiful system. As humans, we have the ability to override it...to override our awareness. Even to the point where we change those natural biological signals for the worse. The good news is, through awareness training, we can regain the natural weight-optimizing system we were born with.

Being aware in asana

The opportunities to work on awareness are endless. This is such great training. As we all know, being fully aware of our minds and bodies is a challenge. How difficult it can be to completely focus on the task in front of us!

We will be practicing awareness in asana. There is so much to become aware of in each pose. We will train our minds to be aware of our bodies again, and this will translate right into our lives, our food choices, our enjoyment of eating, and the entire metabolic process.

In each asana you have the opportunity to examine yourself...to allow your mind to see clearly again. Through being aware in asana we'll begin to find balance in our bodies and our lives.

Living aware

Try this. For one week, be mindful in all you do. Take an everyday task like walking to work, or washing the dishes, and do it with complete attention. Examine yourself. How do I breathe when I wash the dishes? Where is my mind? Try to be in the present; to just do the task at hand. When you do a difficult asana, where does your mind go? The difficulty of the pose can help your mind to be in the present. Try to bring that kind of focus to the activities you do every day. Train your mind to be aware.

Eating aware

One of the best places to use this awareness is in our relationship to food. As we become more aware, we are able to see the many aspects of our eating patterns, and let them fall in line with our natural rhythms.

So how do you start? In asana you might bring your attention to your shoulders. Are they relaxed, are they doing what you would like them to do? So begin to use this same awareness at eating times. Ask, *am* I hungry? Maybe you are very hungry. Maybe you are eating out of nervousness. Or because it is dinner, and you figure you should eat.

The main point here is to be aware of yourself around food. Be aware of your hunger levels. Your body was designed to give these signals and, although it may take a little while, you can reconnect with your body's natural weight-optimizing hunger signals.

Be aware of the food you eat.

Are you aware of what you eat? You learn something new about your body with asana practice – maybe you can learn something new about the food you eat. Read labels, talk to friends, think about your food. If you don't know what an ingredient is, find out.

What do you eat, anyway? I have a policy. I try not to eat anything if I don't understand the ingredients. Do you have to do this? No. You can certainly achieve your optimal weight without this. But I find it helps me every day. When I'm shopping, so many foods that are bad for me are not options.

I discovered that real, whole foods satiate me more. I eat less when the food I eat is real. Your taste buds were not intended to interpret and respond to artificial ingredients.

Food is delicious. Taste it.

Be aware of food and its beauty. Are you aware of how your food tastes? Of what you truly like? Of which foods make you less sluggish and more energized? Eat in the present moment and enjoy every bite. Pay complete attention to eating when you are doing it. Snack away – but be aware of it.

If a food makes you feel bad when you eat it, avoid it. You are not denying yourself that food. You are engaging in life by not slowing yourself down.

Try engaging with food. Get into cooking; be aware of the ingredients you are using. Use the best you can find. Try organic fruits and vegetables. Really taste the food you are eating.

Be in the present.

You may be fooling your body by concentrating on another activity while eating. When I'm driving, I can eat any amount of food. My mind is so focused on driving that it overrides my ability to be aware of how full I am. What a waste of good food!

Eating, like asana practice, is always in the present moment. Relish it. Achieving your ideal weight will come from building awareness and living fully. Diets are about denial – yoga is about becoming aware of as much as possible. Live life!

Don't diet. Set goals to build awareness.

To be aware, always write down what you eat. The food and the quantity. Then you can learn more about the food you're eating and how it makes you feel. You can't make changes if you don't know what you're changing!

But don't worry about someone else's idea of what you need. Be aware of how your body reacts to what and how much you eat. Different people need different foods and different amounts of them.

Food Journal (example)

Date: Tuesday, August 24

Woke up: 7 AM

Meal	Time	Food
Breakfast	7:30 AM	1 bowl oatmeal with 2T syrup, 1 cup juice, 2 cups coffee
Snack	11 AM	Lowfat muffin
Drinking	Throughout morning	1 bottle Poland Spring
Lunch	2 PM	Hamburger & fries, Diet Coke
Snack	4 PM	Apple
Drinking	Throughout afternoon	1 bottle Poland Spring
Dinner	7:30 PM	Grilled salmon, mashed potatoes with butter, green beans, 1 glass red wine
Snack	10 PM	Handful of Hershey's kisses
Drinking	Evening	1 glass water

To sleep: 11 PM

Notes:

Got really hungry around 1:30.

Felt kind of gross after lunch; drinking water helped.

SUGGESTIONS FOR AWARENESS

- Do the asanas every day, focusing on the awareness principles.

- Take a simple task that you do most days (like washing dishes) and be completely aware of it. Try to focus on it, and not doing anything else.

- Keep a food journal: write down everything you eat and when you eat it. Continue to do this even as you move on through this process. This is one suggested format, but you can use anything that works for you.

- Begin to read the ingredients of your food.

- Take one day and, with awareness, ask yourself these questions each time you eat:
    What is it made of?
    What do I think of those ingredients?
    Does this bite taste better or worse than the last?
    How fast am I eating?
    How delicious is this thing on my spoon/fork/chopstick/hand?
    How did I feel before this meal/snack ?
    How did I feel after this meal/snack?
    Was I hungry? Am I hungry now? Can I tell?
    Am I eating because I'm hungry? If not, then why am I eating?

- Remember to let go! Don't forget the things you focused on last chapter.

Food Journal

Date:										
Woke up:										
Meal	**Time**	**Food**								
To sleep:										

Notes:

The practical means for
attaining higher consciousness
consist of three components
    Self-discipline and purification
    Self study
    And devotion to the lord

sutra 2-1
Translation by Mukunda Stiles

effort

How do we get anywhere without effort? We don't. Discipline and effort are an important part of yoga. (And certainly an important part of weight loss.) We can't get our body and mind to change without trying. The real question, then, is: how do we apply effort? How do we know when we are working hard enough? How far do we go?

Effort. It's obvious in asana. It takes effort to move your body. But what kind of effort and how much? Effort does not have to be exhausting. By using the right amount of effort, we build energy.

This concept may seem new to you. Most people have been trained that pushing ourselves to the limit is the way to success. Instead, we have to find the magic balance between what brings us energy and what tires us.

Finding balance

We can use some effort to achieve our balance. Working towards balance is different from working towards a goal. Balance is a natural state. "I want my weight to steadily decrease until my body is in balance" – this is seeking our body's natural state. Sure, we all get excited when we're working hard on ourselves and we get results like losing weight. The key is to keep your eye on the prize – **balance**.

Effort and self-discipline can be things that are difficult at first, but then help. What does this mean in terms of asana practice? In terms of food?

You have to find the line, not of how much you can stand, but the natural edge for your body. What do you need to eat every day so that you lose weight but don't hurt your body? Go gradually – find your balance.

Should you exercise more? Certainly, you can extend your practice time. But, more important, use effort and self-discipline to do it every day. Let yourself be bored and get through it. You'll often find in the middle of your practice that the boredom is gone.

Giving less than one hundred percent

Explore this in each asana. We want to progress, and correctly so. Use as much effort as it takes to perform the asana to the best of your ability without strain. By doing this we progress. Using 50-75% of your possible effort will allow your body energy to process the change. Effort should not be exhausting. Done correctly, yoga produces energy.

You want to apply effort, but not too much effort:

- Make the effort to do your daily asana practice even when you don't want to.
  Too much effort: Doing your practice when you're sick, or sore, or injured.

- Make the effort to go further in an asana. For example, come up a little higher in bridge pose.
  Too much effort: Pain, heavy breathing, strain in parts of your body that are not supposed to be working.

Training the mind

Take some time and energy to examine your reaction to yoga practice. Does your mind tell you that you can't do it; does it try to distract you? Don't get caught up in these distractions; stay focused and you will find your way to a beautiful rejuvenating practice. If you find yourself getting caught up in your thoughts, bring your attention to your breath. You will find using your breath as an anchor will tend to quiet the mind.

Make the effort to examine the food you eat and your reaction to it. See if you can step back and observe your reactions around food. Do you feel anxious? Nervous? Shut down? Distracted? Try focusing on your breath to quiet your mind a little. You can use effort to focus yourself during eating and stay in the present with it.

Don't use too much effort here, though. Gently remind your mind to focus on the task at hand without causing yourself stress. If this is done firmly, but with compassion for yourself, it will become a little easier every day.

Using effort to find true balance

Your body is so good at this balance thing that it will fight you. It tends towards homeostasis; it likes to assume that whatever weight you are right now is the weight you should continue to be. Lying underneath the superficial and annoying behavior of your body is your true nature, which wishes to be in perfect harmony. So we are going to use a little effort to remind our body of what it truly wants.

Here is the up side to homeostasis – once your body loses weight, once your body feels the joys of released hamstrings, it will ask you to do things to keep them there. Your body will beg for asana practice. Your mind will beg – please stretch me. As you find a new balance, it will take effort to avoid your practice.

Willpower and resolve

It takes effort to deal with craving. Your brain will crave things that are bad for your body and mind. Think of it like a bad child. It doesn't know any better. You need to teach it. Do you deny yourself all cravings? No. You gently remind your mind of what it wants. Does it want to be healthy, to feel good, to sleep easier?

Regular yoga practice will deepen your resolve. By using effort in our body, we strengthen not just our physical selves, but our spiritual core. You develop inner strength and stamina. At first you may sometimes deny yourself the foods you crave, or eat less, or eat them less frequently.

As you get used to applying the right amount of effort in your practice, it becomes easier to remind your brain of what it truly wants. Eventually you may not want that food at all, no effort needed! At first you apply effort to cut down on a craving, and then it goes away.

How much effort to lose weight?

As with your asana practice, you should apply effort – but not too much.

- In eating, your stomach shouldn't be more than 75% full. This leaves room and energy to digest.

- Make the effort to cook more meals.
  Too much effort: Denying yourself all social interaction based on food.

- Make the effort to do meal planning. Shop for food regularly, bring food to work, carry snacks with you.
  Too much effort: Eating as little as possible, unrealistic eating or weight loss goals, being hungry all the time, inflexible plans that can't be maintained.

SUGGESTIONS FOR EFFORT

- Do your asanas every day, with a mind on the effort suggestions. Make sure you are not just going through the motions. While you are practicing, focus on your practice.

- Make the time to cook one meal you absolutely love, but you don't usually take the time to prepare.

- Think about foods that make you feel less than great. Remove one food from your diet that you suspect doesn't work for you.

- Find one thing in your life where you apply too much effort, and back off a little. Examine the results.

- Find one thing in your life where you don't apply enough effort, and apply a little more effort. Examine the results.

- Stay relaxed and aware! Don't forget the things you learned about letting go and awareness.

a steady comfortable pose

What is a yoga asana? The classical yoga definition is "a steady comfortable pose." When we achieve this, we are on our path. We all like regular income and regular sleep. Become steady and comfortable, and your optimal weight will come through.

Give yourself the chance to find and live within your natural rhythms. The more steadiness you have in your life, the more you will have to lean on. We are asking our bodies to work with us, maybe for the first time. Make the process of finding your ideal weight easy by keeping things simple and steady.

Steadiness in asana

In each asana we look for the steady comfortable pose. The right amount of effort and relaxation. Awareness of our body, breath, and mind. This is where we want to be. Find the joy in each pose. Become friends with your body. Watch your whole self work in union in the posture.

Steadiness in practice

Our practice needs to be steady as well. Try to practice at the same time of day if you can. Keep to a schedule – this will make everything easier. But make sure your schedule is realistic. Don't plan to do more than you can.

Let yoga practice be something you enjoy. If it is uncomfortable, you will do the only reasonable thing – stop. Try to do it every day. If you don't skip too many days, you will still remember how good you felt after your practice yesterday – which helps a lot with enjoying today's practice.

This steady practice will create energy in your life. If it doesn't, you may be working too hard. Regular practice will yield more results than working really hard at it irregularly. Steady and easy.

Steadiness in eating

Steady diet is the key to weight loss. Eat too little, and your body believes it is starving and holds onto fat. Eat too much and your body stores the excess for the lean times. Once you've found the right amount to maintain your weight, you must eat a little less.

Eat less food? Not necessarily – it depends on what you are currently eating. You can eat a lot more food if it is the right food for you. Empty calories and artificial ingredients don't do it for your body. It asks for more. Try to remove all unnatural substances from your diet. Try to remove anything processed. Replace those things with high-quality whole foods that you like, and eat until you are satisfied but not stuffed.

A steady comfortable diet

Find eating patterns that work for you. Enjoy eating. Losing weight does not have to be about denial. As you begin to give your body what it truly wants, it will be clearer in asking for what it needs. Find eating patterns that make you feel good and bring you joy. You eat every day – it should be comfortable for you.

Try to have regular meal times. As you get used to your new eating patterns, you will find that you are hungry for about the same amount of food at the same times every day. Plan healthy snacks so that you have food when you're hungry. Try to make sure that you have the food you want available, so that you don't eat things you don't want.

Monitoring your weight

There are many ways to monitor your progress. For some, the easiest and best way is the scale. If this works for you, make a regular time to weigh yourself and do so consistently. Once every two weeks is more than adequate. In this, as in all things, find steadiness. Don't weigh yourself more frequently than you've planned.

Your weight will naturally move up and down based on time of day, time of month, muscle to fat ratio, etc. Remember that the goal is to be healthier in the long term. Don't worry if you don't lose weight or even gain a little at first. This is quite common. Just stick to your practice and the weight will decrease at a reasonable pace for you.

If the scale makes you stressed or obsessive, or brings back bad associations, don't use it! Instead, use another way of monitoring your progress. Such as how your clothes fit. Or how much energy you have.

Whatever your method, keep a journal of your progress. Every two weeks, write down your weight, or how your clothes fit, or how you've been feeling. Do this in a steady way and you will have a clear view of your practice and how it is affecting you.

A final note

Live in the present. Work each day to find peace with food and your body. Notice and reflect on positive changes which occur to you. Did you sleep better, do you smell better, did you feel more energetic, do you have a new love for spinach? Focus on these positive changes.

SUGGESTIONS FOR
A STEADY, COMFORTABLE POSE

- Make a schedule that is realistic for your asana practice.

- Make the same for yoga nidra.

- Do the same for meditation.

- Find the most convenient time to grocery shop in your schedule and leave yourself enough time around it to enjoy it.

- Pick your method of monitoring yourself, and how frequently, and write it down. (Following are some examples of how you can track your progress — but choose something that works for you.)

- Try to eat in the same way, at the same times, each day.

- Don't forget the things you learned in the last three chapters. Letting go, awareness, and effort all contribute to your steady, comfortable practice.

Progress Tracking Worksheet (example 1)

Date	Status
5/4	157 LBS
5/18	158 LBS
6/2	156 LBS
6/16	152 LBS

Progress Tracking Worksheet (example 2)

Date	Status
5/4	JEANS ARE TIGHT AT WAIST
5/18	JEANS ARE COMFORTABLE AT WAIST
6/2	CAN FIT ONE FINGER INSIDE WAISTBAND
6/16	JEANS ARE LOOSE AT WAIST

My Progress Tracking Worksheet

Date	Status

your daily yoga practice

The science of yoga is the science of finding yourself. Is yoga asana exercise? Of course – but it is more than that. The body is a manifestation of the mind. It is linked to the inner workings of your brain. By coming to the mat every day you are engaging in svadhyaya – self-study. Not just of your body, but your whole self.

Finding your perfect weight is not just a matter of changing your body. It is a healing process that involves all aspects of your being. As you develop a regular practice your whole self will begin to heal and re-integrate. Your muscles will strengthen as your resolve gets firmer. You will grow calmer as your breathing deepens.

A regular practice will allow your body and mind to find themselves and to function flawlessly. Each day is full of distractions. A short time out to reconnect with yourself is all that is needed to progress towards the perfect you.

The most important thing is to make space in your life to do your practice regularly. If you're feeling tired or stressed, that's even more reason to do it. You will feel better after your practice. If you're tempted to skip it, don't – just do a shorter practice that day. Even fifteen minutes a day will make a difference. If you just can't bear to do asana practice, do yoga nidra instead (page 155). Once you have established a regular practice, it will only bring you joy.

On pages 113-158 you will find pictures and instructions for the asanas (poses). The companion CD and DVD have instructions for two different sequences (under 30 minutes each), as well as a yoga nidra (about 20 minutes).* The CD and DVD give minimal instruction – they are intended as guides for your daily practice. Use the drawings and written instructions for more detailed help with the asanas.

As with everything else, please feel free to contact me if you need additional help. My contact information is on page 171.

When should you do your daily practice?

You may do your asanas any time of day (although I suggest the morning). But make sure you haven't eaten for at least one hour before practicing.

Where should you do your daily practice?

Find a place to do the asanas in your home. Keep it as calm and free of distractions as you can. Music is okay if it is not too distracting

---

If you purchased a copy of this book which did not include the CD or DVD, you can use the form on page 177 or visit peacefulweightloss.com.

– you want to be able to focus on your breathing. I mainly use music to mask distracting or disturbing sounds (like street noise or other household activity). The instructional tracks on the CD and DVD include music for this reason.

What supplies do you need?

I suggest a sticky mat and possibly a blanket or pillow to prop yourself. But don't let the absence of these tools stop you from doing your daily practice. I've done my short practice without a mat on the floor in many hotel rooms. It's better to do it in an imperfect environment than to skip it.

What if this asana sequence is too challenging?

I recommend the joint freeing series as taught by Mukunda Stiles (page 163) if you are finding the yoga sequences in this book too challenging. Instead of the asana practices, do the joint freeing series and yoga nidra daily for two weeks. Then try slowly working on the asanas. When teaching, I start almost everyone with this series. And remember, it's regular practice that will work. So don't push yourself. Just be consistent and your body will work with you.

How much yoga each day?

You may certainly do all of the asanas daily if you like; however, I have broken them up into shorter sequences which you should be able to finish in under 30 minutes. The CD and DVD contain instruction for you to follow if that is easier for you.

I suggest alternating the two asana sequences. If you do sequence one on Monday, do sequence two on Tuesday. If you need to skip days, just keep alternating the sequences.

I use the joint freeing series as taught by Mukunda Stiles as my warm up before asana practice. If you have the time, I encourage you to do the same. (See page 163.)

But stick to some sort of schedule. If your time is limited, just do deergha swaasam, sun salutation, and a few minutes of relaxation or meditation. Consistent steady practice is the key. By doing these asanas regularly your body will change. This is pretty much what I did – I learned the poses in class, and then did a short practice every day.

What's most important?

Centering yourself at the beginning of your practice and lying still in savasana at the end are the most important parts. Do not skip them.

Relax and meditate.

In addition to asana practice, I suggest doing a separate deep relaxation (yoga nidra) practice, and a separate meditation practice.

These can be done at the end of your asana session, or at a different time of day. Just like the asanas, schedule times you can do these so they are not missed. Many people like to do them in a series: asana, then deep relaxation, then meditation.

Another suggestion is to do a daily asana practice, followed by a 5 minute meditation in the morning. Then, either before dinner or later at night, do a deep relaxation.

If you are truly busy, you could do asana practice five days a week, deep relaxation three days, and five minutes of meditation daily.

Especially if you are a "stressed-out" person, I suggest you find the time for relaxation. Remember that stress=unwanted weight. After you are used to it, you will find the deep relaxation so enjoyable that you'll miss it when you don't do it.

> By the purity of food,
> follows the purification
> of the inner nature.
>
> Swami Sivananda

what and how to eat

What is the perfect diet? It is eating in a way that gives your body exactly what it needs. We must learn to listen to our bodies' biological signals and respond appropriately.

Here is the whole plan:

Eat good wholesome food that you enjoy.
Plan to eat.
Eat in a conscious way.
Food and eating should make you feel good.
Make changes that will last.

It will take all aspects of your asana training to realize this. You will have to **let go** of your mind's desires around food. You will need to maintain an **awareness** of your body and how it feels before, during, and after eating. You will need to apply **effort** to change your eating patterns and curb your reaction to unhealthy cravings. And you will need to maintain this in a **steady comfortable way** until it is simply what you do.

Eat good wholesome food that you enjoy.

What does your body truly want? What nourishes your body? The answer is a little different for everyone. In general, it will be a diet rich in whole foods that contains few empty and harmful artificial elements. This food needs to be of the highest quality possible, and taste great. By filling your diet up with these foods, your weight will optimize and stay that way. You can maintain it because it is what you need. You can maintain it because it will taste good to you.

WHAT IS A WHOLE FOOD?

A whole food, for our purposes, is a food that is easily identifiable in one of the following categories: fresh fruit and vegetables, organic meat, poultry, and fish,* legumes, organic dairy, whole grains and whole grain flour, seeds and nuts. A whole food generally has no other ingredients but itself. It has been minimally processed or not at all.

*although this author is not a fan for ethical/energetic reasons

Eat more whole foods.

Why should you eat whole foods? Have faith in nature. Whole foods are the way nature intended them. They are full of all the wonderful elements we hear about all the time, and low in things we don't need. By eating whole foods, you receive all the nutrients and components you need without having to think about it.

There are a million vitamins and supplements out there – why? Because people are trying to make up for not eating whole nutritious food. By eating more whole foods you will be giving your body the nutrition it needs, so it won't be constantly asking for more food. You will be more easily satiated, and you will naturally cut down your caloric intake.

Rice is an excellent example. Brown rice has many more vitamins and minerals than its milled, processed cousin, white rice (see chart). White rice has been stripped of its fiber, so it is less satisfying – you want to eat more of it. Eating brown rice will not only give you more nutrients, it will satisfy you more.

(1 cup cooked)	Brown Rice	WhiteRice
Calories	232	223
Protein	4.88 g	4.10 g
Carbohydrate	49.7 g	49.6 g
Fat	1.17 g	0.205 g
Dietary Fiber	3.32 g	0.74 g
Thiamin (B1)	0.223 mg	0.176 mg
Riboflavin (B2)	0.039 mg	0.021 mg
Niacin (B3)	2.730 mg	2.050 mg
Vitamin B6	0.294 mg	0.103 mg
Folacin	10 mcg	4.1 mcg
Vitamin E	1.4 mg	0.462 mg
Magnesium	72.2 mg	22.6 mg
Phosphorus	142 mg	57.4 mg
Potassium	137 mg	57.4 mg
Selenium	26 mg	19 mg
Zinc	1.05 mg	0.841 mg

How can you integrate whole foods into your diet?

Shopping regularly will make it so that you have more whole food in the house. When it comes time to cook, have whole foods around.

Read labels and make sure the food you are buying contains whole foods. It's surprising how many seemingly "natural" foods have additives and overprocessed components. Know what you are eating.

Cook for yourself. Other people (especially the ones at most food companies) don't have the same food agenda as you. The best way to know what you are eating is to cook it yourself. Cooking with whole foods doesn't have to be difficult or complex. In a short time, you can build a personal repertoire of foods that are easy to cook and enjoyable to eat.

Bring some food with you when you are on the go. Throw a piece of fruit, some veggies, or some nuts in your bag whenever you are out of the house. If your day doesn't go as planned, you will have whole food with you. You won't have to resort to eating junk.

Actively choose whole foods and you'll have less room for the other stuff.

Use common sense.

We live in a complex world of food choices. When eating, opt for foods that are simple and natural. All the foods won't be "whole foods," per se. Many soy products are not whole foods, but for most people they are a pleasant and healthy addition to their diet. As a general rule, try to eat food that is closer to being whole. Real orange juice is much closer to a whole orange than orange soda. Remember, the more whole food you eat, the less other stuff will work its way into your diet.

So try to eat more natural, "real" food. This is a grey area, but if you think about it, it becomes easy to understand. What did you have for lunch today:

Whole wheat pasta with fresh tomato sauce
A garden salad with balsamic vinegar
water
And an orange

Or

Pasta from white flour with jar tomato sauce made with sugar and preservatives
A white roll with margarine
A Coke®

As you can see, the first pasta-based lunch has many whole or close-to-whole elements, while the second is actually free from whole foods. With just a little awareness, you will be able to shift your diet to something more natural and nourishing.

Eat high quality foods.

Eating high-quality, fresh, delicious food makes you less hungry. It also makes you feel better in general. I say this from personal experience. Try it. You'll be more satisfied and have more energy.

Try to find great organic produce. I'm lucky that I live in a place with a huge inexpensive food co-op. Most supermarkets now carry organic produce, and there are many health food and organic specialty stores. There are delivery services that will bring it to you. Community-supported agriculture is now cropping up in many areas. (Visit *peacefulweightloss.com* for some resources.) If none of these options are available, get the best quality you can at the store. No matter where you buy produce, look at it, smell it – don't just grab it off the shelf.

If you eat meat, try to get hormone-free, antibiotic-free meat and fowl. If possible, eat fresh, not farmed fish. At the very least, buy your meat and fish from the best source available. Look at all the stores, farmers' markets, and specialty shops in your area. Try to find a clean, well-run store you trust.

Just as your body slowly changes in asana practice, it may take your palate a while to adjust. Change slowly, but also give your body a chance to get used to it. Make the distinction between foods you are not used to and foods you don't like. Also, there are many versions of foods. The quality of fish, meat, and produce varies greatly and tastes different. Discriminate and build your awareness. All potatoes are not created equal!

Know what you're eating.

In order for your body to function most efficiently, and to attain its optimal weight, you need to avoid foods that confuse or upset it. You should only be eating foods that support your body's health. Cut down or eliminate foods with ingredients you don't understand. Do you understand FD&C blue #1?

Eat fewer prepared foods. If you do eat them, read the ingredients. Know what you're eating. Don't trust manufacturers' claims on the front of the package. Read the ingredient list and decide for yourself if the food is good and appropriate for you.

What do you like to eat?

Think about the foods you like best. What are you missing? Make a list of every food you love. My clients often find several nutritious whole foods on their list that they rarely eat. Bring these foods back into your life.

Of course, there are also usually some not-so-healthy foods on your list. Here is my suggestion. When you do occasionally eat something not so healthy for you, MAKE SURE YOU LOVE IT. If you are not enjoying it as much as you had hoped, STOP EATING IT. You must love the food you eat. Don't hurt your body and mind by filling up on food that does nothing for you.

Be ready to have some new favorite foods. As you become more aware, your tastes will change. Start sampling different foods. Don't let old opinions stop you from enjoying food today. Just because your aunt served you terrible overcooked brussels sprouts doesn't mean you won't like them now if you buy them fresh and make them yourself. Keep engaging with food and you will be rewarded by an ever-growing list of favorites.

SOME OTHER SUGGESTIONS FOR MAKING HEALTHY FOOD CHOICES:

- Don't eat hydrogenated and partially hydrogenated oils — if you must, eat little. Yes, they appear often — avoid them. Read labels and don't eat in fast food restaurants. These oils have trans fats, which raise LDL cholesterol levels, (the bad cholesterol), while lowering HDL levels, (the good cholesterol), in your body. This raises the risk of heart disease. More importantly, you don't need them, and they do nothing positive for you.

  There are plenty of foods and brands that don't contain hydrogenated oils. If you can't find what you need, try a different supermarket or health food store. Even the most likely suspects like crackers can be made with no hydrogenated oils.

  [More on hydrogenated oil: www.cspinet.org/new/transpr.html]

- Avoid fake sweeteners and other fake ingredients — Splenda®, Sweet 'n Low®, Nutrasweet® etc. — you don't need them! They will not nourish you at all, and are quite possibly harmful. If you need sweetener, opt for a natural sweetener (like honey, maple syrup, fruit juice or dehydrated cane juice). If you use five packets of Equal® in your coffee, maybe it's time to take a few breaths and re-evaluate whether coffee is the beverage for you!

- Try to use olive oil or canola oil. Do not overheat it (it shouldn't smoke). If you can, use organic oil. (Non-organic oils may have a lot of pesticide residue in them.) Use oil, but don't go crazy — i.e., dipping hunks of bread in oil before dinner. It's fat, after all. Respect it as such.

- Avoid fried food, especially when eating out. Many restaurants (especially fast food) fry in partially hydrogenated oil. Old oil and overheated oil breaks down and is not healthy. Food fried at the incorrect temperature allows more oil to absorb into the food. So if you must eat something fried, fry it yourself, and correctly!

- Avoid nutritional powders, shakes, bars, etc. Get your nutrition from the original source — food. Don't add calories with these non-satiating items. If you need easy-to-eat food on the run, carry whole foods such as fruit, raw veggies, or small amounts of nuts and seeds.

For more discussion of foods to avoid
visit peacefulweightloss.com

Change what you eat.
It will change how you feel and function.

It is our job to nourish ourselves. We eat every day. Each mouthful should expand and enhance our life. We need to enjoy our food both for how it feels and tastes in the moment as well as how it supports us throughout our day.

The food choices we make are an active step toward our spiritual goals. Choosing to put positive nutritious whole foods into our body is an act of peace. Your happy, peaceful self will respond by sending happy, peaceful signals to your brain and body. You will be less hungry, less stressed, and a comfortable weight.

Plan to eat.

Create a meal/eating plan.

Make a plan. Have a list of the different breakfasts you eat; the lunches and dinners; what are you allowed to eat as a snack; when, where, and what you eat out. A steady diet is the best.

Taking the time to create a meal plan can save you time, confusion, and anxiety at every meal. Your meal plan should not be a "straitjacket" – it should be a tool to help you at every meal.

Eat regularly! Eat meals of the same size at the same times each day. Respect the schedule you make for eating regularly. But don't force yourself to eat if you're not hungry.

Many people fall into patterns of eating out or ordering in a little too often. This "time-saving" habit puts other people in control of your food intake. Eating out is certainly not bad in itself, but to lose and then maintain a healthy weight, you should be making clear choices of what to eat every day.

Prepared and restaurant food often has excess ingredients we would never use ourselves. By preparing your own food, you will be able to move towards eating in harmony with your body's needs. Most likely your foods will become simple and tasty. Consider making the time to cook a spiritual practice. Respect your food and its preparation, and it will respect you.

Does this mean you can't eat out anymore? NO! Personally, I love to eat out. But excess in anything brings us out of balance.

Eat Snacks

You don't want to be hungry and possibly binge. By eating a regular snack in between your meals you will even out your hunger levels and have a baseline from which to observe yourself. Once you are eating regularly, you can clearly evaluate your body's needs. Pick a few healthy snacks and have them in between meals and, if you like, after dinner. (Suggestions: a piece of fruit, baby carrots, eight almonds, up to 10 cups air popped popcorn, yogurt.)

DRINK WATER

Don't mistake thirst for hunger. When we're thirsty, our brains can sometimes send hunger signals out by mistake. Drink water and plenty of it.

Don't confuse your body with too many other beverages. When we drink water, we give our body exactly what it needs. The calories, sugars, caffeine, and carbonation of other drinks are not necessary for hydration.

Keep other drinks to a minimum and try to drink 40-50% of your body weight in ounces of water every day. Try this for a while and see how you feel. The best way to do this is to HAVE WATER WITH YOU AT ALL TIMES.

Shop Regularly.

Decide where and when you will be obtaining your food. Make this as solid a part of your weekly schedule as working, or walking the dog. Since you've made a list of the types of things you eat, the choices should become clearer at the store.

BUT I DON'T DO THE COOKING OR SHOPPING!?

First, ask yourself, why? It could be for a perfectly good reason — like your spouse shops while you are working. Or your spouse is an amazing cook who loves cooking.

So what do you do?

1. Recruit your family — explain to them what you are doing and ask for help.

2. Be willing to change and cook occasionally — maybe Sunday brunch or dinner once a week?

3. Try to shop with your partner. At least go once and take some notes. Then ask the shopper to get you specific items.

4. Purchase cookbooks that you can work from (see some ideas on page 171). Invite someone over and cook something for them.

Make sure to go with a list so that you definitely buy the correct food for the meals you plan to cook. Always have your house and work stocked with healthy food that you like. The better and more regularly stocked your kitchen is, the less effort you will use on a daily basis.

By bringing steadiness into your diet you are doing yoga. You will be more clear-headed and your cravings will be reduced as you fall into stable eating patterns. The initial effort of planning good nutritious meals will soon become easeful, and you will be rewarded with a healthier, less troubled, body and mind.

Eat in a conscious way.

Be aware of your hunger levels.

Begin to notice your hunger levels before meals. You should be hungry, but not ravenous. Cultivating this awareness helps you understand what your body truly wants, and helps you eat appropriately. I suggest writing down your hunger levels. You will then be able to modify your eating plan so you don't get too hungry and accidentally overeat. In the "systems" section you will find worksheets designed to help you record your hunger and satiation levels.

Be aware of your satiation levels.

Eat until you are satisfied, but not stuffed. Our body needs to be satisfied so that it doesn't panic and decide to store fat. We need to be satisfied so that we can maintain our new eating patterns. But we need to leave room in our stomach for our food to digest properly. Again, chart your satiation levels and begin to adjust your eating to a point that's right for you.

Apply effort to change portion sizes. Eat more vegetables – and make sure your carb and protein portions are not too big for you. It's very common to eat a huge piece of meat or fish as a centerpiece, or multiple servings of rice or mashed potatoes. Try a week of smaller portions with larger vegetable portions. This is different for everyone, so pay attention to how these portions make you feel.

Many people have the habit, left from childhood, of finishing everything on their plate. Especially at dinner. Don't eat more than you want to. You should feel good after a meal, not weighed down.

Be aware of your cravings.

You have attachments to certain foods. We all do. Step back and examine them. Identify foods you eat for the emotional effect they have on you. Simply bringing awareness to your cravings often reduces them. With strong cravings, take a gentle approach. Be sure to take a few breaths when they surface so that you may stay in the present and see them for what they are. And remember that it can take some time to eliminate food cravings, so be kind to yourself.

Be aware of habitual eating.

Many of us have those places in the day we eat out of habit. For many people I've worked with, this often comes at times we are alone. Late at night, driving, etc. See if you can identify these times, and take a few breaths before eating. Begin to skip those snacks you "needed."

For some, it will be easier to change the habits associated with the eating at first, such as watching TV before bed. You could try reading instead. Also, drinking herbal tea may help at first with the craving. Try something gentle and non-caffeinated. Many teas are sweet and can help with your sweet tooth. Be easy on yourself and go slowly on this one. It took time to create these habits; it will take time to change them.

TOOLS FOR DEALING WITH HABITUAL EATING

1. Before eating anything, take a few deergha swaasam breaths (three part breath — see page 115). Then take a few three part breaths after eating.

2. Change your yoga practice to help with habits/cravings.

    Example: If you find yourself eating too much in the late afternoon, begin doing yoga nidra at that time. If this is inconvenient, do three-part breath and naadi suddhi (page 156), or meditate (page 158).

3. If sweets are an issue, replace them with fruit or naturally sweet herbal tea.

4. If alcohol is a problem, replace it with another beverage, such as tea or seltzer.

5. Move yourself from the place you habitually eat.

    Example: If you eat too much in front of the TV in the living room at night, read in the bedroom instead.

Habitual eating can stem from difficult emotional issues we are avoiding. This is a very individual challenge. My suggestion is to let your yoga practice support you as much as possible. My clients and I have had success doing asanas, pranayama (breathing), or meditating through these times.

Make time to eat and enjoy your food

Make time to eat. Eat slowly and enjoy your food. Your meal times should be calm and joyful. Listen to your body and what it needs. Re-examine the way you eat, and try not to rush through your meals.

Pay attention to the eating process itself. Be a kid again. Decide again how many times to chew each piece of food. On which part of your tongue do different kinds of foods taste best? Pay attention to your eating. By doing this you will feel more satiated. You need to let all your senses focus on eating in order to feel the most satisfied.

Bringing awareness to anything changes it. In asana we bring it to our bodies and breath. We now extend this awareness to our eating habits. As we observe ourselves from a distance, we become more able to make changes that are in tune with our deepest, most authentic self.

Food and eating should make you feel good.

Eating habits affect our energy levels. How do you feel after you eat? Sluggish, tired? Really energized? We often ride a roller coaster of energy levels based on our eating habits. Eating regularly will stabilize your energy levels.

Examine what times you eat and what size meals you eat.

If you eat the right amount of food at a meal you should feel satisfied, but not too "weighed down." Of course it's nice to take a little time to digest your food, but you shouldn't be tired from eating.

Many of my clients (and I, also) have had the habit of not eating much during the day, and then eating most of the day's calories at night. See if you can more evenly space your food. You may try having lunch as a main meal since your body can use the day to digest.

Also, examining the type of food you're eating can help. Don't eat heavy foods near bedtime. Eat foods that are more difficult to digest during the day and eat something easier to digest at night.

Don't deny yourself foods you love.

If you have things you absolutely love, build them into your plan and don't eliminate them completely. Don't make it so if you eat a cupcake or have one drink you've "blown it."

If you are going on vacation, or love ice cream in the summer, it's okay. Get small portions and eat things that are high calorie only occasionally. Just make sure this food is all natural and good. If you are at the beach and have a small cup of ice cream, you are fine. A banana split and a side of fries is probably not the best choice for you.

Learn to enjoy the food you are eating and portions won't need to be as big. Trust me on this. At the local ice cream place at my favorite vacation spot, I get a baby cone of frozen yogurt and I'm perfectly happy. A few years ago it was a huge sundae. Listen to your body – not your mind.

Don't deny yourself social enjoyment.

Food and eating are an important part of social life. See what part of your social life around food you enjoy, and what parts you do out of habit. For some, having a beer Friday night after work with friends is the perfect and enjoyable end to a productive week. For others it's a self-destructive activity that hurts your body and psyche. Is Tuesday pizza day? Great, have a slice. Is every day at lunch pizza day? Remove yourself from the situation.

Working with myself and others I haven't come across a social food situation that is an insurmountable problem. Go out, have fun, order out with your family, have a donut. Have a beer after work. None of these things individually will make you too heavy. But don't use the situation as an excuse to sabotage yourself.

ALCOHOL

Alcohol inhibits our awareness. You are working on enhancing your awareness. If drinking is a regular part of your social life, try keeping drinking to a minimum (I suggest no more than two drinks). By limitng or stopping drinking, you will be able to see the effects of alcohol more clearly and make appropriate choices.

Eating is part of your yoga practice. After asana practice you should feel good. Many describe the feeling as a sense of well-being. You have relaxed, steady energy to face the day. Eating should leave you feeling the same way. In the short term, you should feel happy and not weighed down. In the long term, you should have more energy and feel clean inside and out.

Making changes that will last

Do not go on a diet.
Make changes in your eating patterns.

Do not go on a diet.
Make changes in your eating patterns.

Do not go on a diet.
Make changes in your eating patterns.

"Going on a diet" implies the process will end, and you will then go back to eating what you used to. This doesn't work. It's associated with more weight gain. "Yo-yo-ing" your weight is more unhealthy than being overweight in the first place! Once you start eating better food on a regular schedule, you won't want to go back.

If you are used to eating a lot more than you need to, this will be difficult at first. Go slowly; live in the present. Write down what you've eaten, so you don't need to go over things in your head.

You will succeed. You are reconnecting with your body's natural signals. They are there for you. Explore food. Take some time to acquaint yourself with new food options. Don't stay in your current patterns. You've come this far – you're changing your physical patterns slowly with yoga – do the same with food.

Find support.

Does your spouse or roommate cook? Let them help you. Ask them to show you what they do. It's a great compliment to them and you'll have fun. If you have children, spend time cooking with them. Put yourself in supportive environments. They are out there for you if you are willing to seek them.

Go to yoga classes. You are not alone. New yoga studios are opening all over the country every day. Let other people's fondness for the practice infect you.

Visit my online forums at *peacefulweightloss.com* and talk to others about your experience.

Be open to new experiences. Finding groups and classes on food, yoga, and spirituality will be a great help. Of course, not everything is for everyone. But if your old patterns didn't work for you, try something new.

Don't get discouraged.

I know there are times when it seems impossible. I lost a lot of weight and at times it was difficult. I had periods when I thought I'd give up. I had days where I totally screwed up and ate way too much. I lost weight anyway.

Even though it may seem like a daily struggle, journal everything and look at the trends. Always think back to where you started. If you are in a better place now, it is working.

Your yoga practice is the best support.

If you find yourself looking at what you did and criticizing yourself – do your practice. Go to a class if you can. Yoga reminds us to live in the present. Stay calm and continue. We don't panic if we can't do the perfect asana. We shouldn't panic if we don't make perfect food choices. We are all students. Enjoy the learning process.

Often we have a tendency to rush change. We feel that that if we don't change now, the opportunity will be lost. When we do this, we are allowing the process to be driven by fear, instead of the positive self within us. When we relax and allow the change to come naturally, it will stay with us. Why? Because what we see as change is actually the uncaging of something that is already there.

This is a lot of information to process and integrate into your life. We all have inner wisdom – start by taking the steps that resonate with you. If you need guidance, you can look at the system on page 85. I developed it to work with my clients. You can use it as a reference to help you understand your unique experience.

Don't wait for the end of the road to enjoy what's happening now. You will lose weight – you will be peaceful. And, most of all, don't listen to me – listen to yourself! There is an open positive beautiful voice inside you. Sound corny? Before I went through this process I would never have said anything like this. Now I see that voice is part of me. You are reading this – you are ready to walk down the road of peace. You always have been.

Om shanthi.
Om peace.

the systems

Developing your
daily yoga practice

Modifying this suggested schedule is fine. Find your own rhythm. This advice comes from my experience – which will undoubtedly be different from yours. Remember, the process is as important as the result. Getting too excited and involved in short term success will only set you up for being upset at short term setbacks. Enjoy your practice, and keep moving forward. Do this and change will sweep through your life.

You will notice I don't suggest working on the food section until you have been building your asana practice for at least six weeks. While nothing is set in stone, my clients and I have found it most effective to work on our bodies first.

You are introducing a lot of changes into your life. Working gradually will help you to make these changes permanent.

Weeks 1 and 2

Learn the asana sequences, practice them every day (in the morning if possible) with or without the CD or DVD.

If one section is giving you trouble, try using your asana time that day working from the book to understand it better.

Once a day, meditate for 3 minutes.
Once a day do yoga nidra (relaxation) to the CD.

That's it. Do not skip ahead; don't worry about food. One thing at a time. Just start by integrating these fantastic activities into your life.

Week 3

Read the chapter on Letting Go. Try working with the suggestions at the end of the chapter.

Read the letting go points in the asana section and use them during your daily yoga practice. You don't need to focus on all of the asana points every day. For example, on day one, you might read and focus on the letting go focus point for two asanas. Then, on day two, you could do two different ones. Do what you can.

Meditate 5 minutes a day.

Yoga nidra daily.

Week 4

Read the chapter on Awareness. Try working with the suggestions at the end of the chapter.

Read the awareness points in the asana section and focus on them during your daily yoga practice.

Meditate 5 minutes a day.

Yoga nidra daily.

Week 5

Read the chapter on Effort. Try working with the suggestions at the end of the chapter.

Read the effort points in the asana section and focus on them during your daily yoga practice.

Meditate 5 minutes a day.

Yoga nidra daily.

Week 6

Read the chapter on A Steady Comfortable Pose. Try working with the suggestions at the end of the chapter.

Read the steady comfortable pose points in the asana section and focus on them during your daily yoga practice.

Meditate 5 minutes a day.

Yoga nidra daily.

> This is a nice time to begin your food practice. Think of your asana/breathing/meditation practices as your foundation. Don't neglect your work here to "move on" to food. Your practices here are the most important support you have in making changes to your eating habits.

Weeks 7-10

Cycle through the four points again in your asana practice. As you go through these points again, you will get more out of them.

Meditate 8 minutes a day.

Yoga nidra daily.

Weeks 11-14

Cycle through the four points again in your asana practice. As you go through these points again, you will get more out of them.

Meditate 10 minutes a day.

Yoga nidra daily.

Weeks 15 on

Keep doing your daily practice.
Keep thinking about these points of focus.
Add one minute to your daily meditation every week until you reach 20-45 minutes.

Developing your eating practice

The following is a system I developed to work with my clients. It is intended as a reference to help you understand your unique experience. Just as every individual will perform an asana differently, individual paths to dietary peace also vary. With my clients I invariably custom-tailor these points to their individual needs. That being said, I thought it important to have this available to you as a reference.

This system consists of tools for applying the concepts in this book. If you like, you can use these points individually as reference. If you work better with structure, feel free to work though the system step by step. Go slowly, so each step brings a deep, permanent change for you. Keep your mind, heart, and stomach open. Do what feels right and natural to you.

As I wrote in the "How to use this book" section, I suggest that you begin your process with yoga asana and working with the four points. This will give you a foundation on which to build your food practice. I have found this sequence to be most effective.

Resist the urge to rush into dietary change – if you have dieted in the past, you will simply be repeating the same pattern. Put that energy into your asana practice and allow yoga to transform you.

As a general guide, six months is a good time frame to think of in terms of working through these systems. If it takes longer, that's fine – don't rush this process.

If you've worked through the four points, you should already be keeping a food journal and tracking your progress according to the schedule you set (see pages 32-34 and 45-46).

A) What are your favorite foods?
   Eat more of them!

In order to make sustained change you must be enjoying the food you eat.

The first step in your process is to become aware of the foods you like. The worksheet on the next page is divided into different categories so that you don't get stuck on chocolate cake.

Making this list should also help you to identify the foods that are most important to you. As you begin to eat more of them, you will eat less of the foods you are eating with indifference.

> Often we forget to eat foods we love. When I first meet with clients I often hear something like, "Oh yeah, I love green beans, I don't know why I haven't had them in years."

Use the Favorite Foods Worksheet as a tool to make a list of the foods you like, and how often you eat them. Begin to eat more foods you love and fewer foods you feel indifferent about.

Favorite Foods Worksheet

FOOD	When did I eat this last? How often do I eat this? Should I eat it more?
Fruits	
Vegetables	
Meat/Fish	
Legumes (beans, peas, soy foods, etc.)	
Grains & Grain Products (rice, bread, pasta, oatmeal, etc.)	
Nuts and Seeds	
Dairy (cheese, yogurt, milk, etc.)	
Sweets (candy, ice cream, cake – not including fruit)	

B) Cook regularly.

Cooking regularly brings awareness to our eating. It helps us learn what is in the food we are eating. Additionally, it lets us appreciate the labor – others' and our own – that goes into the preparation of food.

This worksheet will help you track times you cook and the times you eat out. It also helps you see the amount of prepared food in your diet. The more you begin to cook real foods for yourself the better.

> Refer back to the list of
> favorite foods you made –
> these are the foods you should be
> cooking and eating.

If cooking is new to you, pick a couple times a week to cook at first, and then slowly add more times you prepare your own food. If someone else in your household usually does the cooking, take over a meal or two. If you cook all the time, begin to spend a little more time preparing meals or use more real foods.

Cooking Worksheet

	Cooked from mostly real food	Cooked from mostly prepared food	Take Out	Ate Out
Day 1: MONDAY (example)				
Breakfast **Lunch** **Dinner**	X	X	X	
Day 1:				
Breakfast **Lunch** **Dinner**				
Day 2:				
Breakfast **Lunch** **Dinner**				
Day 3:				
Breakfast **Lunch** **Dinner**				
Day 4:				
Breakfast **Lunch** **Dinner**				
Day 5:				
Breakfast **Lunch** **Dinner**				
Day 6:				
Breakfast **Lunch** **Dinner**				
Day 7:				
Breakfast **Lunch** **Dinner**				
TOTALS:	Breakfast___ Lunch___ Dinner___ Total___	Breakfast___ Lunch___ Dinner___ Total___	Breakfast___ Lunch___ Dinner___ Total___	Breakfast___ Lunch___ Dinner___ Total___

C)   Add Snacks.

Don't let yourself be hungry. Eating regularly evens out your hunger levels. At this stage, I recommend eating snacks between meals. Bring them with you. Carry your snacks in serving-size portions.

Great snacks are:
- fruit
- 1/4 cup of nuts and/or seeds (raw or toast them yourself)
- air-popped popcorn

> Be careful here:
> you don't want to snack so much
> that meals are not appealing.

D)   Add water.

We can often mistake thirst for hunger. Make sure you're drinking enough! I suggest you have water around as much of the day as possible. Try to drink 40-50% of your body weight in ounces as a starting point. So if you weigh 190 pounds, you should be drinking 76-95 ounces of water, or 10-12 eight-ounce glasses. If this is difficult, begin by keeping a bottle of water with you always and see if that increases your water consumption.

E) Examine your hunger, satiation and energy levels

Now we will expand your food journal to include tracking your hunger and energy levels. It is also a great idea to keep track of your yoga practice in the same place so that you can start to make connections about how this all comes together.

In your journal, be sure to make note of times you are hungry or full even when you're not eating. You don't have to fill everything out, just what's applicable. If this format doesn't suit you, feel free to keep a notebook instead.

Your journal is your most important tool. You will continue this journal throughout the rest of this process. Often our memories can play tricks on us. Looking back and evaluating your journal will be a clear way to decide what changes need to be made to progress towards your optimum eating patterns.

Your Journal (example)

Date: Monday Aug 23

Time	Notes on Activity, Food and Drinks	Before/During Hunger/Satiation — Not hungry	Moderately hungry	Very hungry	Satisfied	Stuffed	Before/During Energy — Low	Fine	Fantastic	After Hunger/Satiation — Not hungry	Moderately hungry	Very hungry	Satisfied	Stuffed	After Energy — Low	Fine	Fantastic
7 AM	Woke up		X				X										
7:45 AM	Oatmeal (1 c) Juice (1 c) 2 cups coffee			X			X						X			X	
10 AM	1 bottle Poland Spring			X			X					X			X		
11 AM	Yoga (45 min)			X			X				X					X	

Notes on today's yoga practice:

I WAS VERY HUNGRY AND LOW ENERGY ALL MORNING.

Conclusions:

MAYBE I SHOULD TRY EATING A MORE SUBSTANTIAL BREAKFAST.

COFFEE ISN'T DOING IT FOR ME ANYMORE.

Date:															
Time	Notes on Activity, Food and Drinks	Before/During									After				
		Hunger/Satiation					Energy			Hunger/Satiation					Energy		
		Not hungry	Moderately hungry	Very hungry	Satisfied	Stuffed	Low	Fine	Fantastic	Not hungry	Moderately hungry	Very hungry	Satisfied	Stuffed	Low	Fine	Fantastic

Notes on today's yoga practice:

Conclusions:

F)   Make a plan to eat six times each day.

I've found that by making a firm plan and sticking to it, I am able to become more aware of my hunger/energy/satiation levels. Make times to eat six times per day: three meals and three snacks (two in between meals and an after-dinner snack). Since you've been cooking and adding snacks, you may already be doing this. Try to eat your meals at about the same time every day.

> Breakfast,
> snack,
> lunch,
> snack,
> dinner,
> snack.
>
> This is your
> eating plan
> for now.

For many of my clients, the tendency has been to not fully participate in this step. It seems easy, or not enough like "dieting." Take the time to really make this step concrete. It will make the coming steps more valuable if you establish a steady pattern of regular eating. Just stay here for a while and use your journal to examine how regular eating affects you.

MY SCHEDULE TO EAT
SIX TIMES A DAY:

BREAKFAST: 7 AM
SNACK: 10 AM
LUNCH: 1 PM
SNACK: 4 PM
DINNER: 7 PM
SNACK: 9 PM
BED: 11 PM
REPEAT DAILY!

EXAMINE YOUR HUNGER, SATIATION AND ENERGY LEVELS.

Each week that you are working on this step, review your journal and see how eating steadily has affected you. Compare this week with weeks when you were not eating so consistently. Make any adjustments that seem reasonable to you.

G)   Create a meal plan and add whole foods.

Now that you are eating very regularly, it's time to make some changes in what you're eating. Start by adding whole foods to your diet (see page 54 for more on whole foods).

You will have to do a little planning. I suggest planning out a few meals you would like to have (that are all whole foods) and shopping for them. Fill your cart up with excess amounts of whole foods you like, or have never had, and keep these foods in the house.

This is a good time in your process to spend a little more than usual at the store – better to have too many whole foods around than to run out. Eat as many whole foods as you can.

You should use a planning method that works for you. Included here is a worksheet that will help you list the general foods you plan to eat and where you will shop for them.

For some, making a very specific shopping list works even better. To keep it simple, I often start clients with this format and then expand from there.

If this step seems overwhelming, begin slowly. Pick a few breakfast, lunch, and dinner options – write them down and purchase what you need to make them. Take as much time as you need to make this step work with your life.

For tips on choosing a store,
refer back to page 58.

For information about whole
foods, refer back to page 54.

Remember, it's not an all or nothing proposition. You are simply trying to bring more whole foods into your diet than there were before.

**EXAMINE YOUR HUNGER,
SATIATION AND ENERGY LEVELS.**

After you have added some whole foods, review your journal and see how you've been feeling. Have your dietary changes been a positive change? See if there are places you need to adjust to feel even better.

Meal Planning and Shopping Worksheet (example)

MEALS	SHOPPING	WHERE TO
Breakfasts I eat:	**Foods I need to buy:**	**BUY THIS**
Oatmeal	Whole Oats	Organic Food Store
Yogurt	Yogurt (lowfat organic)	Organic Food Store
Fruit	Pears, plums, strawberries	Farmer's Market
Lunches I eat:	**Foods I need to buy:**	
Greek Salad	Lettuce, Tomato, onion	Farmer's Market
	Feta Cheese, olives	Organic Food Store
Fritatta	Eggs	Organic Food Store
	Chard, potatoes, garlic	Farmer's Market
Snacks I eat:	**Foods I need to buy:**	
Toasted Almonds	Almonds	Organic Food Store
Fruit	Apples, Pears, Grapes	Farmer's Market
Yogurt	Small yogurts (lowfat organic)	Organic Food Store
Dinners I eat:	**Foods I need to buy:**	
Spaghetti	Whole Wheat Pasta	Organic Food Store
	Canned Crushed Tomatoes	Organic Food Store
	Fresh Parmesan Cheese	Organic Food Store
Special meals I plan to cook:	**Foods I need to buy:**	
Stirfry	Brown Basmati Rice	Organic Food Store
	Tofu	Organic Food Store
	Broccoli, Carrots, Ginger	Farmer's Market
	Soy Sauce, Rice Vinegar	Organic Food Store
SHOPPING TRIPS:		
Time	**Place**	
Thursday Evening	Organic Food Store	
Saturday Morning	Farmer's Market	

Meal Planning and Shopping Worksheet

MEALS	SHOPPING	WHERE TO BUY THIS
Breakfasts I eat:	Foods I need to buy:	
Lunches I eat:	Foods I need to buy:	
Snacks I eat:	Foods I need to buy:	
Dinners I eat:	Foods I need to buy:	
Special meals I plan to cook:	Foods I need to buy:	
SHOPPING TRIPS:		
Time	Place	

H) Create a new meal plan with fewer non-whole and excess foods

At this point you are eating quite a bit of whole foods. But most likely there are things in your diet that shouldn't be there. They may have made sense in your former diet, but now they are just excess. These foods don't serve you anymore, so it is time to be rid of them.

Look through your journal and identify the non-whole foods in your diet so that you can minimize your consumption of them. The best way to do this is to make a clear meal plan and stick to it. Be more specific in this step on what you will be eating. By making specific plans to eat real foods, there will be fewer opportunities for foods that don't serve you.

EXAMINE YOUR HUNGER, SATIATION AND ENERGY LEVELS.

Feel free to repeat this step — keep planning meals and adding more whole foods — until you are ready to move on.

You should be consistently using your journal and meal planning tools to optimize your diet.

Unwanted cravings are going to surface. Remember, you've learned to use effort in your asana practice. Take your confidence in that and try to apply effort to reduce those cravings. (See page 68 for more.)

If you end up eating a few things you think you shouldn't, don't worry. The point here is to be on your way to a whole-food-based diet you can live with.

1) Reduce Habitual Eating

The work you have done up to this point has probably made you aware of some eating habits you have. Ask yourself the following questions:

- Are your habits affecting how you create your meal plan?

- Are you unable to keep to your plan because of habits?

- Are you eating more than your plan because of habits?

Use the following worksheets to cultivate awareness about your habits.

Habitual Eating Awareness Worksheet

Time of Habitual Eating	Place	Activity	Food
Monday before bed	Couch	Watching TV	M;Ms

Conclusions:

Based on what you have become aware of, work to reduce habitual eating situations and foods. Go slowly with this. It may bring up emotional issues. Refer back to the tools on pages 68-70 for help. You can also use the habitual eating awareness and effort worksheets to track your progress.

EXAMINE YOUR HUNGER, SATIATION AND ENERGY LEVELS.

Create your shopping/meal plan with care. Be sure to buy all the food you need. While trying to change habitual eating patterns, it is important that your meals are nourishing and satiating. Keep your journal up to date and clear.

Habitual Eating Effort Worksheet

Action	Result	Conclusion
Tried popcorn instead of M&Ms	Ate too much popcorn	
Stopped watching TV	Ate just a few M&Ms	Better
Read and did breathing when hungry	Didn't eat	Will try again

J)   Re-examine portion sizes and adjust.

If your meals are too large, you will be stuffed. Remember, you need a quarter of your stomach free in order to digest properly. If you feel like you can't eat another bite, you've already gone past your limit.

Another sign that your meals are oversized can be low energy. Digestion takes energy. If your meal size is out of balance, you will be spending too much energy on digestion, making you lethargic.

Check back in your journal.
Is your energy low after meals?
Are you often stuffed?

At this point, you may want to examine the portion size of not just the entire meal, but of its components. Often I find people are eating the right amount of food – but not the right portions. Begin to notice the signals your body sends you as you are eating. The slower you eat, the easier it is to notice these signals.

> Don't forget –
> keep adding
> whole foods
> and reducing
> non-whole foods.

K)   Adjust frequency of eating.

By now you have charted your energy levels for many weeks. For some, eating very often is perfect. For others, their system needs more time to digest food. If you find yourself with low energy levels, or full too often, experiment with eliminating some of your snacks.

Be sure to keep your journal clear and see if not eating a snack for a week or two affects your energy positively.

L) Examine your social scene
and make adjustments.

If you have arrived at this step, you have probably noticed that your friends, family, and co-workers are not necessarily on the same page as you are.

Many of our social activities revolve around eating and drinking. It is useful to become aware of what social activities that involve food and drink are important to you and how you can participate in them without harming yourself.

It is also nice to begin to change your habits with your friends and family so that they work for you. For example, if you usually go out to eat at a not-so-healthy restaurant with friends on the weekend, try having a dinner party and see if it catches on.

A combination of changing social habits, using self-control during ones you can't change, and skipping detrimental experiences, all together will allow you to find a new social groove that works for you.

Use this worksheet as a tool to track your social eating experiences so that you can see how you might want to adjust them.

Social Eating Worksheet

Day & Time	Place	With whom	What did I eat/drink?	How did it make me feel?	Would I feel better if I skipped this?	If I enjoy it, how can I adjust and still enjoy it?
MONDAY 4 PM	JENNY'S OFFICE	CO-WORKERS	4 COOKIES	NOT GREAT, DIDN'T REALLY LIKE THE COOKIES	NO, I DON'T WANT TO MISS TAKING A BREAK WITH MY FRIENDS	JUST HAVE ONE COOKIE
TUESDAY 6 PM	BLARNEY STONE	LISA & JACK	TWO WHITE RUSSIANS	HORRIBLE	YES	SKIP IT
THURSDAY 8 AM	MORNINGSIDE DINER	BOB	EGGS, HOMEFRIES, TOAST, BACON, COFFEE	NOT GREAT. TOO GREASY	NO, I LOVE MEETING BOB FOR BREAKFAST	INVITE BOB TO HAVE BREAKFAST AT NATURAL GARDEN INSTEAD
FRIDAY 8 PM	CITY BISTRO	BOB & IN-LAWS	BROILED SALMON DINNER, BITE OF DESSERT	FINE	NO	NO NEED.

Once you have moved through these stages, you have done quite a bit of work. Hopefully you have more awareness of your relationship with food, and have found new ways to eat that work for you.

We eat every day. While our bodies are alive, the practice of eating never ends. Just like your flowering asana practice, your ways of interacting with food will continue to evolve. You may need to cycle through these steps over and over, or simply revisit a point now and again to keep yourself present with your eating practice.

While we want to have a steady comfortable food practice, don't let what you have learned become static. As you change, so will your food needs. I recommend continuing your journal as a way to observe yourself clearly.

Be open to what your body has to say and it will reward you with clear information. As you become more and more comfortable with your new self, eating will become more easeful, and be a help, not a hindrance, on your road to peace.

the asanas

A guide to the asanas

The following pages contain drawings and directions for the asanas. You can use these drawings along with the CD or DVD as a guide for your daily practice. With each asana, four points of focus (letting go, awareness, effort, steady comfortable pose) are listed to help you focus and learn from your daily practice.

Deergha Swaasam

THREE-PART BREATH

1. Sit comfortably with your spine erect.

2. Inhale – first into your abdomen, then expand your ribs, then your upper chest.

3. Exhale – upper chest, then ribs, then abdomen.

4. Gently blend the three parts together so it's a smooth continuous breath.

5. Don't hold your breath – keep your body relaxed.

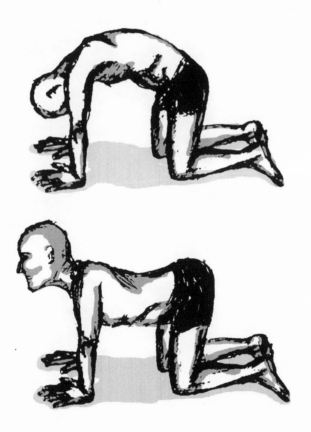

1. Be on your hands and knees. Your hands should be positioned under or just in front of your shoulders and your knees under your hips.

2. On an exhale, roll your tailbone down, arching your back upward; your head comes down (like a scared cat).

3. On an inhale, raise the tailbone up, abdomen relaxing downward, chest forward, head up.

4. Repeat with the breath.

letting go

Notice how your breath affects your spine.
Feel how easy it is to curl as you exhale.

awareness

Keep your focus on your spine — creating space
between each vertebra.
Try to feel as if you are moving one vertebra at a time.

effort

As you exhale, press gentry into the floor, feeling the
extra stretch between the scapula (shoulder blades).
Engage your abdomen to help with the curl.

steady comfortable pose

Following your breath, curling as you inhale, arching
on the exhale. Nice, even breath.

Tadaasana

MOUNTAIN POSE

1. Stand with your feet hip width apart.

2. Your hips should be directly over your ankles. The outside edges of your feet should be about parallel.

3. Your knees should be straight but not locked.

4. Lengthen your spine up from your hips.

5. Relax your hands and arms.

6. Relax your shoulders down your back.

7. Your chin should be parallel to the floor.

8. Feel as if you are exerting no effort to maintain this pose.

Downward-facing Dog

1. Raise your buttocks toward the ceiling.

2. Your back is lengthened.

3. Your head is relaxed down.

4. Your heels coming towards the floor.

5. Draw your hips away from your hands.

6. Place equal weight on your hands and feet.

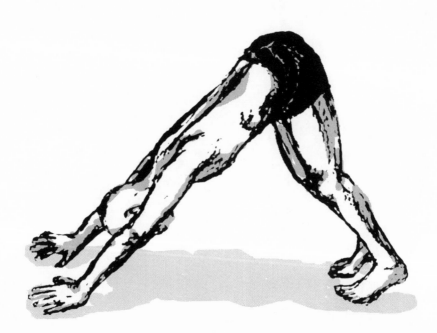

Surya Namaskaaram

SUN SALUTATION

1. Stand in tadaasana.

   Bring your palms together
   in front of your chest.

2. With your palms facing each
   other, reach out in front of you,

   reach up until your arms are
   alongside your ears,

   and then bend gently back.

3. Bend your knees slightly.

   With a straight back, bend forward
   until your hands reach the floor.

   (Forward Bend)

4. Step your left foot back.

   Bring your left knee to the floor.

   With your fingers in line with your front foot, look up.

   Your front knee should be directly over your ankle.

   (Lunge)

5. Step your right foot back to meet the left.

   (Downward-facing Dog, or Down Dog – see page 119 for detailed instructions.)

6. Bring your knees, then your chest, then your chin to the floor.

   Your pelvis should be slightly raised.

SUN SALUTATION (CONTINUED)

7. Lower your pelvis to the floor.

   (Baby or Easy Cobra – see page 134 for detailed instructions on Cobra.)

8. Press into your hands back into Down Dog.

9. Step your left foot forward into Lunge.

   If you can't reach your foot the whole way, use your hand to bring it forward between your hands.

10. Bring your right foot forward to meet your left.

    (Forward Bend)

SUN SALUTATION (CONTINUED)

11. With your arms alongside your ears, come up with a flat back.

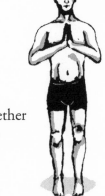

12. Bring your palms together in front of your chest.

letting go

Keep your body relaxed.
This is a warm up — make it as easy as possible.

awareness

Focus on your breath — make sure you are breathing easily and steadily. If not, slow down or relax a little more into each posture.

effort

Each round, pick a different step to focus on and go a little deeper. For example, do the best down dog you can in Round 1. In Round 2, focus on the lunge.

steady comfortable pose

Put on a gentle smile. Try to have a smooth easy motion from one position into another.

Surya Namaskaaram

SUN SALUTATION (AT-A-GLANCE)

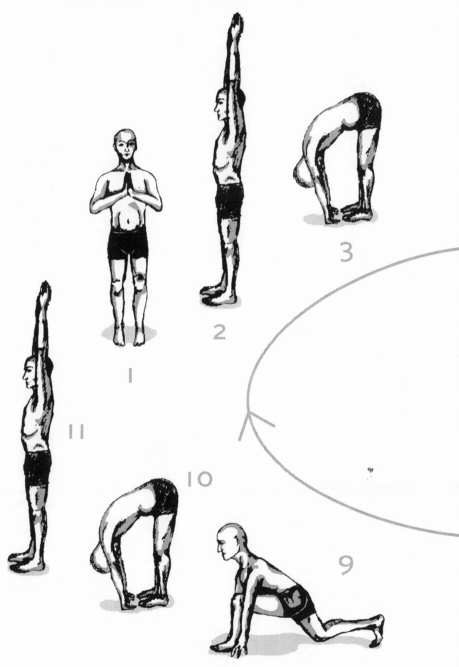

SUN SALUTATION (AT-A-GLANCE)

Surya Namaskaaram

SUN SALUTATION MODIFICATIONS

Here are some common variations on Sun Salutation I use with students. If you are having trouble with any part of Sun Salutation, ask a teacher for modifications. Everyone has different physical issues. Remember – if you can breathe, you can do yoga!

1. Stand in tadaasana.

   Bring your palms together in front of your chest.

2. With your palms facing each other, reach out, reach up until your arms are alongside your ears, and then reach gently back.

3. Bend your knees slightly.

   Stretch your arms out to the sides in a "T."

   With a straight back, bend forward and have your hands reach for the floor.

   (Forward Bend)

4. Step your left foot back.

   Bring your left knee to the floor.

   With your fingers in line with your front foot, look up.

   Your front knee should be directly over your front ankle.

   (Lunge)

4a. Bring your right leg back, knees on the ground.

5. Press into your hands and straighten your legs, raising your buttocks.

   (Downward-facing Dog, or Down Dog – see page 119 for detailed instructions)

6. Bring your knees to the floor.

Surya Namaskaaram

SUN SALUTATION MODIFICATIONS

6a. Slide your palms forward,

Bring your elbows to the floor,

then lower your abdomen, chest, and chin to the floor.

7. Raise your head, neck and chest.

(Baby Cobra – see page 134 for detailed instructions on Cobra)

7a. Press into your hands and come onto your knees.

8. Press into your hands back into Down Dog.

8a. Lower your knees to the ground.

9. Step your left foot forward into lunge.

If you can't reach your foot the whole way, use your hand to bring it forward between your hands.

10. Bring your right foot forward to meet your left.

(Forward Bend)

11. With your arms stretched out to the sides in a "T", come up with a flat back.

When you are fully upright, reach straight up and slightly back.

12. Bring your palms together in front of your chest.

Virabhadraasana II

WARRIOR II

letting go

Relax your shoulders, jaw, eyes —
anything that doesn't need to work.

awareness

Bring your focus to your strong, grounded feet,
your lengthened spine — breathe easily.

Virabhadraasana II

WARRIOR II

1. Separate your feet wide apart – 3-4 feet, or about under your wrists. The distance is different for each person. You can adjust once you come into the pose.

2. Turn your right foot out 90 degrees and left foot in slightly.

3. Your hips should be facing forward.

4. Inhale – reach your arms up alongside your ears.

5. Exhale – bring your arms parallel to the floor, palms down.

6. Bend your right knee over the right ankle (not further).

7. Your torso is erect, your weight evenly distributed on both feet.

8. Look over your right fingertips.

9. Hold for four breaths (about 20 seconds).

10. Inhale – straighten the right leg, bring your arms down, walk your feet in.

11. Repeat on the other side.

effort

Engage both quadriceps muscles (front of the thigh) – feel this action ground you.

steady comfortable pose

Even weight in your feet will increase energy flow.
You are steady and strong.
Feel the air beneath your arms maintain their weight.

Vrikshaasana

TREE POSE

1. Find a point to focus your eyes.

2. Stand in tadaasana and transfer your weight to your right leg.

3. Lift your left foot and place it on the inside of your right thigh, calf, or ankle, opening the left hip.

4. If it's comfortable, bring your hands together in front of your chest and hold for about 30 seconds.

5. To release, gently bring your raised leg to the floor.

6. Release your hands.

7. Stand in tadaasana.

8. Repeat with the other leg.

Vrikshaasana

TREE POSE

letting go

Relax your shoulders and neck.
Mentally release any preconceptions you have
for this pose. Every day is different — see how
your balance is today and accept it.

awareness

Bring your awareness to the breath. How does
focusing on the breath affect it? Breathe easily.
Once you find the pose, scan your body and find
what's working — enhancing what is needed,
releasing what is not.

effort

Feel as if you are rooted into the ground through
your extended leg.

steady comfortable pose

Finding your breath, relaxing,
allowing yourself to find stillness.

Advaasana

RELAXATION ON THE ABDOMEN

1. Lie with your abdomen on the floor.

2. Cheek turned to one side.

3. Bring your arms alongside the body, palms up.

   Advaasana is a relaxation pose. Let your whole body release into the floor.

Advaasana

RELAXATION ON THE ABDOMEN

letting go

Expend no effort here.

awareness

Scan your body for areas of tension and relax/adjust for it. Send a mental message to any areas of tension to relax them.

effort

Keep your mind on your releasing body and breath. If it strays, gently bring it back.

steady comfortable pose

This pose should feel great. If it doesn't, adjust until it does.

Bhujangaasana

COBRA

1. Lie on your stomach in advaasana.

2. Bring your legs together, palms on the floor beneath the shoulders and a little toward the hips, forehead on the floor.

3. Stretch out your chin along the floor and, without pressing on your hands, lift your head, neck and chest.

4. Keep your shoulders down and use only the muscles of the upper back. Gently squeeze your shoulder blades together and down your back.

5. To come out, roll down slowly, extending your spine.

6. Lower your chin to the floor.

7. Turn your head to the side - relax in advaasana.

Bhujangaasana

COBRA

letting go

Come up easy — not too high; feel as if you are hardly
working.

awareness

Scan your back. Identify the muscles that are working.
(If it's your lower back, come down lower).

effort

Squeeze your shoulder blades together — come up a
little higher, still using mostly your upper back muscles.

steady comfortable pose

With a nice steady even breath, find the height you
can stay at comfortably and hold here.

Arddha Salabaasana

HALF LOCUST

1. Lie on your stomach in advaasana.

2. Bring your chin to the floor, arms along the sides of your body, palms down. Legs together.

3. Extend your right leg along the floor towards the wall behind you.

4. Keep extending as you raise the leg slowly up.

5. Hold for ten seconds.

6. Gently lower the leg.

7. Repeat with the other leg.

Arddha Salabaasana

HALF LOCUST

letting go

Just extend and raise your leg. Try to keep your body fairly relaxed. It doesn't have to be hard.

awareness

Become aware of your engaged buttocks. Use just the lower back muscles. Leave both hips on the floor.

effort

Stretch the leg as far back as possible, then lift as high as you comfortably can.

steady comfortable pose

Find the height at which you are working but not straining. Breathe easy.

Dandaasana

STAFF POSE

1. Sit on the floor, sitting up on your sitz bones, legs together and stretched out in front of you.

2. Place your palms on the floor alongside your hips.

3. Extend out your heels, feet parallel, toes facing up.

4. Press your palms into the floor. Lengthen and lift your back and sides; bring your shoulders back and down.

5. To come out, gently release the hands, maintaining the lengthened spine.

Vajraasana

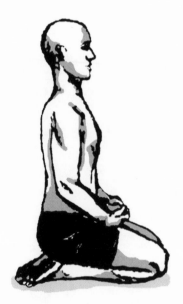

1. Kneel with toes together and heels apart.

2. Lower your buttocks between your heels.

3. Sit with a long spine, hands on your thighs.

    If this is too intense, sit on your heels.

    If that is too much, place a blanket or pillow between heels and buttocks.

Child's Pose

1. Kneel on the floor in vajraasana (see page 139).

2. With knees wide, press your buttocks back toward your heels.

3. Bring your arms either alongside your body or extend them in front of you.

4. Lower your forehead to the floor.

    Child's pose is a relaxation pose.

Child's Pose

letting go

Expend no effort here.

awareness

Scan your body for areas of tension and
relax/adjust for it.

effort

Breathe deeply into your lower back to relax the
lumbar spine.

steady comfortable pose

This pose should feel great —
if it doesn't, adjust until it does.

Janusirshaasana

HEAD TO KNEE

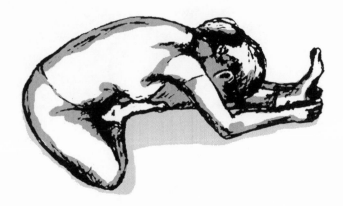

1. Sit in staff pose (see page 138).

2. Bend your right leg and place the sole of your right foot along the inside of the left leg. Keep your hips even; readjust if necessary.

3. Inhale – extend your arms alongside your ears.

4. Exhale – hinge forward from the hips. Keep the spine long.

5. Gently place your hands on your leg or foot.

6. Relax the head and shoulders completely.

7. To come up, reach your arms alongside your ears and hinge up from the hips with a long spine.

8. Repeat on the other side.

Janusirshaasana

HEAD TO KNEE

letting go

Resist the urge to go further in the pose.
Let your head and shoulders relax.
Let this pose happen to you.

awareness

Where is the stretch happening? Breathe deeply into it.

effort

At first, find a gentle stretch along the back side of
your body.
Then relax all effort once you're in the posture.

steady comfortable pose

Find your pose and bring attention to your breath. As
your mind wanders, gently bring your attention back.
There should be no strain in your body.

Paschimotanaasana

FULL FORWARD BEND

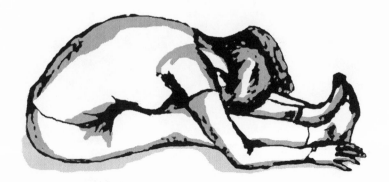

1. Sit in staff pose (see page 138).

2. Remove flesh from under your sitz bones.

3. Your toes should be facing up.

4. Inhale – bring arms alongside your ears.

5. Exhale - hinge forward from the hips with a long spine.

6. Place your hands on the legs, ankles, or feet.

7. Relax your neck and shoulders.

8. Hold for about one minute – breathing easily.

9. To come up, reach your arms alongside your ears and hinge up with a long spine.

Paschimotanaasana

FULL FORWARD BEND

letting go

Once in the pose, relax your shoulders, head and neck.

awareness

Focus on your breath. Feel how each breath naturally creates space in the body. Keep your mind focused on the breath — be aware of its wandering.

effort

Focus on hinging from your hip crease and keeping the spine long.

steady comfortable pose

Let everything go and enjoy this pose.
You don't need to do any work once you're in it.
Patience.

Sethu Bandhaasana

BRIDGE POSE

1. Lie on your back.

2. Bend your knees – place your feet on the floor close to the buttocks.

3. Bring your ankles directly under your knees, feet parallel.

4. Gently lift the hips as high as is comfortable.

5. If it's comfortable, walk your shoulder blades together behind your back, externally rotating your shoulders.

6. Keep your knees over your ankles, chest coming towards the chin. Start by holding this for 15 seconds; then try holding it longer.

7. Come out gently – lower your spine down slowly, vertebra by vertebra, tailbone coming down last.

Sethu Bandhaasana

BRIDGE POSE

letting go

Don't go higher than is comfortable. Find a place you can easily hold the pose. Your breath is steady and easy.

awareness

Check your breath — it should be steady. Examine which muscles are working in the pose. Then identify where you feel muscles are stretching.

effort

Press into your feet, chest comes toward your chin. See how high you can elevate your hips while keeping your knees in line with your ankles.

steady comfortable pose

Count how many breaths you take while holding this pose. Hold as long as comfortable, then release before fatigue makes you lose alignment of knees or shoulders.

Legs Up Wall

1. Sit with your side against a cleared wall.

2. Position yourself so that your legs are up the wall with your buttocks as close to the wall as possible.

3. This position should be comfortable. Stay here for at least two minutes.

    Legs up wall is a relaxation pose.

letting go

Expend no effort here.

awareness

Scan your body for areas of tension and relax/adjust for it.

effort

Focus your mind on the sensations in your body.
As your mind wanders, bring it back.

steady comfortable pose

This pose should feel great —
if it doesn't, adjust until it does.

Matsyaasana

FISH POSE

1. Lie on your back, legs together, arms along sides of the body.

2. Take hold of the sides of your thighs.

3. Sit up halfway, weight on your elbows, looking at your feet.

4. Tilt your pelvis forward, arch your spine, and place the top of your head on the floor.

5. Open your chest.

6. With your weight on your buttocks, elbows, and some on your head, hold for 30 seconds.

7. To come out, place your weight on your elbows, sit up half way, and roll your spine gently back down to the floor.

Matsyaasana

FISH POSE

letting go

Relax your lower body a little.

awareness

Bring awareness to your spine.
Feel as if there is space between each vertebra.

effort

Breathe as deeply as you can into your open chest.

steady comfortable pose

There should be a gentle smile on your face
in this pose.

Jathara Parivartanaasana

LYING TWIST

1. Lie on your back, legs together.

2. Extend your arms out along the floor at shoulder level, palms down.

3. Bend both knees and bring them toward your chest.

4. Bring both legs to the right toward the floor.

5. Look over your left shoulder.

6. Relax here for about 30 seconds.

7. Repeat on opposite side.

Jathara Parivartanaasana

LYING TWIST

letting go

This pose is a tension reliever — let it relieve tension!

awareness

Breathe into the side of the body that is opened up by the twist. Examine how this changes the feeling of the pose.

effort

Keep both shoulders on the floor as you twist as far as is comfortable.

steady comfortable pose

Breathe deeply and steadily. Allow your breath to expand to any areas of tension so that they may release.

Savaasana

CORPSE POSE

1. Lie on your back with your feet about shoulder width apart and your arms slightly away from your body.

2. Scan your body for any tension.

3. If you find any, send a mental message to relax.

4. Feel yourself completely relaxed.

   Savaasana is a relaxation pose.

letting go

Expend no effort here.

awareness

Scan your body for areas of tension and relax/adjust for it.

effort

Send a mental message to any areas of tension to relax them.

steady comfortable pose

This pose should feel great —
if it doesn't, adjust until it does.
Allow your pulse and breath to be slow and steady.
No movement is required.

Yoga Nidra

YOGIC SLEEP

Yoga Nidra is deep relaxation, or yogic sleep. The mind is awake but the body is fully relaxed. This is an incredibly powerful stress fighter. If you can, you should use the CD to guide you through this.

The general idea is this:

1. Lie in savaasana.

2. Tense and relax different parts of your body to release tension.

3. Scan the body for any remaining tension and relax the body mentally.

4. Remain completely still and relaxed.
   Let your nervous system rest.

5. Observe the body, then breath, then thoughts –
   then find stillness as you let thoughts go.

6. Rise slowly and gradually.

Naadi Suddhi

1. Sit in a comfortable position with a long spine.

2. Make a gentle fist with the right hand.
    Release the thumb and last two fingers.

3. Inhale gently.

4. Close your right nostril with the thumb.

5. Exhale through the left nostril.

6. Inhale through the left nostril.

7. Close your left nostril with the last two fingers.

8. Exhale slowly through the right nostril.

9. Inhale through the right, close, and exhale through the left.

10. Continue this pattern – exhale, inhale, change.

11. The breath should be gentle and the exhalation should be at
    least as long as the inhalation.

Naadi Suddhi

ALTERNATE NOSTRIL BREATHING

letting go

Breathe easily.

awareness

Bring awareness to your lengthened spine and relaxed shoulders.

effort

Make the exhale a little longer than the inhale.

steady comfortable pose

This should be a subtle, gentle, easy, meditative breath.

Meditation

Meditation is a large and deep subject which this book can't begin to cover. It is included here because meditation is an extremely powerful tool which can help you in the process of finding your ideal weight.

As your body goes through large changes, it gets shaken up. Meditating just a little every day will help you stay focused and calm. Although I now enjoy longer meditations, during my weight loss I often meditated 5-10 minutes a day. I found it helped me greatly. I encourage you to do the same.

The first stage of meditation is concentration. That's what we will be doing here.

Sit in a comfortable position on the floor or in a chair.

Keep the spine long and the body relaxed.

Close your eyes and observe your breath.

The important thing is to watch your breath – not control it.

As you breathe in, count "in one" and exhaling count "out one."

Continue until you reach ten – then repeat.

Keep focusing on counting your breath.

As thoughts or feelings come up, gently guide your focus back to the breath.

If you lose count, simply begin again.

As you progress, you may stop counting and simply focus on the breath, saying "I'm breathing in ... I'm breathing out."

Set a timer. Begin with 3-5 minutes and gradually increase the time you meditate.

Visit peacefulweightloss.com for more meditation resources.

afterword

You probably bought this book with weight loss as your final goal. In my process, the most surprising development was the realization that weight loss was the beginning of my path of transformation.

By carving out time to do asana practice, we insure a space in our lives to allow our physically and spiritually happy selves to arise. By interacting with food in a positive way, we can change it from something that constricts or binds us to a tool for freedom.

Losing weight allowed me to see a glimmer of my internal potential. Unveiling that light is the reason we live. I hope this book in some way helps you find the light within yourself.

Om shanthi.
Om peace.

appendices

Joint Freeing Series
AS TAUGHT BY MUKUNDA STILES

Mukunda Stiles was kind enough to allow me to print this in my book. Details of this series can be found in Mukunda's book *Structural Yoga Therapy*. I use this as a beginning with all my private students. I use the joint freeing series as a warm-up to my own daily asana practice.

The aim is, as the name implies, to free your joints. Do each exercise three to six times with that in mind. These motions will take your joints through their range of motion, freeing energy and promoting health. I can't recommend this series enough, especially to those who find yoga asanas too difficult for them. I have seen this series alone completely change my clients physically.

I have demonstrated this series on the companion DVD. You may also buy Mukunda Stiles' video at his web site, *yogatherapycenter.org*. Feel free to contact me on my forums at *peacefulweightloss.com* for help.

Joint Freeing Series
©2002 Mukunda Stiles

1. Stick pose   **EXHALE**   **INHALE**
   (Dandaasana)   feet toward head,   point foot,
                       toes spread   curling the toes

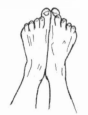 

2. INHALE soles face out   EXHALE soles face in
   keep feet upright   keep feet upright

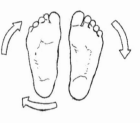

3. INHALE circling out
   EXHALE circling in

4. INHALE with a mild   EXHALE hold lower shin
   arm effort, straighten knee   as you pull heel to thigh

5. INHALE turn leg out
   & swing it wide open

EXHALE turn leg in
& swing it back

6. INHALE head up
   spine down

EXHALE back up
abdomen in

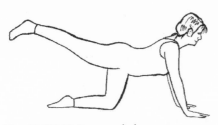

7. INHALE stretch leg
   back and up, spine level

EXHALE bring knee
toward chest, spine lifted

8. INHALE center pose
   squeeze thighs

EXHALE hips to side
feet opposite, toes forward

9. INHALE hands
   down fingers curled
   toward forearms

EXHALE hands
up fingers toward
head & spread

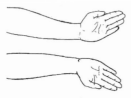 

10. INHALE palms
    flat & out

EXHALE palms
flat & in

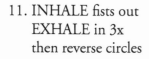

11. INHALE fists out
    EXHALE in 3x
    then reverse circles

12. INHALE arms
    straight, palms up

EXHALE knuckles
to shoulders

13. INHALE elbows
    wide apart

EXHALE elbows
together

14. INHALE arms up
    palms facing forward

EXHALE arms down
palms face backward

15. INHALE arms up
    with palms facing in

EXHALE arms
behind back

16. INHALE arch
    back, squeeze blades

EXHALE round back
open shoulder blades

17. INHALE erect
    EXHALE side

18. INHALE sit erect
    EXHALE spinal twist

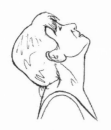 

19. INHALE head up   EXHALE head down

20. INHALE sit erect
    EXHALE head to side

21. INHALE center head
    EXHALE rotate head

more information and support

Please don't hesitate to contact me if you need any help. You can visit my web site, *peacefulweightloss.com*, for updates and additional information. You can also use the forums there to ask questions, or email me directly at *bhanu@peacefulweightloss.com*.

Following are some books and web sites that I have found particularly helpful. Additional resources can be found at *peacefulweightloss.com*.

Structural Yoga Therapy – *yogatherapycenter.org*

Integral Yoga Institute – *yogaville.org*

Vegetarian Cooking for Everyone
by Deborah Madison
©1997 Deborah Madison
Broadway Books, New York

Indian Light Cooking
by Ruth Law
©1994 Ruth Law
Donald I. Fine, Inc., New York

Yoga Sutras of Patanjali
as interpreted by Mukunda Stiles
©2002 Mukunda Stiles
Red Wheel/Weiser, LLC, Boston, MA

The Yoga Sutras of Patanjali
Translation and commentary by Sri Swami Satchidananda
©1990 Integral Yoga® Publications
Buckingham, VA

Structural Yoga Therapy™
by Mukunda Stiles
©2000 Mukunda Stiles
Weiser Books, Boston, MA/York Beach, ME

Vedantic Meditation
by David Frawley
©2000 David Frawley
North Atlantic Books, Berkeley, CA

what's on the cd

track one: asana series one

Sit and Breathe – Deergha Swaasam Breath
Cat / Cow
Downward-Facing Dog
Forward Bend
Tadaasana / Mountain Pose
Surya Namaskaaram / Sun Salutation
Vrikshaasana / Tree
Advaasana / Relaxation on Abdomen
Bhujangaasana / Cobra
Child's Pose
Vajraasana
Dandaasana / Staff Pose
Janusirshaasana / Head to Knee
Savaasana / Corpse Pose
Sethu Bandhaasana / Bridge
Jathara Parivartanaasana / Lying Twist
Savaasana / Corpse Pose

track two: asana series two

Sit and Breathe – Deergha Swaasam Breath
Cat / Cow
Downward-Facing Dog
Forward Bend
Tadaasana / Mountain Pose
Surya Namaskaaram / Sun Salutation
Virabhadraasana II / Warrior II
Advaasana / Relaxation on Abdomen
Arddha Salabaasana / Half Locust
Child's Pose
Vajraasana
Dandaasana / Staff Pose
Paschimotanaasana / Full Forward Bend
Savaasana / Corpse Pose
Legs Up Wall
Matsyaasana / Fish
Savaasana / Corpse Pose

track three: yoga nidra

173

what's on the dvd

asana series one
   (see page 173 for contents)

asana series two
   (see page 173 for contents)

yoga nidra

joint freeing series
   (written instructions and illustrations on pages 163-169)

alternate sun salutation
   (written instructions on page 126-127)

naadi suddhi
   (written instructions and illustrations on pages 156-157)

Use this form to mail order additional materials (money orders only, please). To order using credit card or electronic check, visit *peacefulweightloss.com*.

Name: _____

Address: _____

City/State/Zip: _____

. Phone: _____

Email: _____

	Quantity	Price	S/H	Total
Book only		$19.95	$4.95	
Book plus instructional DVD and CD		29.95	4.95	
DVD/CD set		12.00	2.50	
NY residents add 8.75% sales tax:				
TOTAL				

For mail orders, please allow three weeks for shipping.
Send this form and your money order (payable to EVQ) to:

EVQ
245 Eighth Avenue, #233
New York, NY 10011

For questions regarding wholesale orders or customer service, contact *bhanu@peacefulweightloss.com*.